To my parents, Albert and Jean Holston,
for facilitating my 50s and 60s moviegoing experiences with
Tommy Aaron, Reggie Shaw, Eddie O'Brien, and Frankie Armstrong
at the Warner, Congress, State, Boyd, Lyric and Mac theaters

The English-Speaking Cinema

An Illustrated History,
1927–1993

by Kim Holston

McFarland & Company, Inc., Publishers
Jefferson, North Carolina, and London

Acknowledgments: I want to thank Keith Smith for two decades' worth of correspondence, Tom Winchester for analyses of science fiction and film music, Robert Castle for insight into the filmmaking of Stanley Kubrick and Sam Peckinpah, Steve Griffin for opinions of movie posters, and my wife, Nancy, for pinpointing the attraction — or lack of — of Jack Nicholson and Jon Voight. Also deserving mention are Terry Moore, Warner Theater projectionist Bill Davis, Elena Watson, Howard Eck, James Tanner, Jim Murray of the Movie Poster Place, Movie Star News, the British Film Institute Stills Department, Stephen Sally, Gayla Rauh and Film Favorites, Collectors Bookstore, Leonardo's (Cinema Classics), San Francisco's Cinema Shop, Kathy and Arthur Spicciati, Carmela Carroll, Nancy Panati, Warren Hope, Daryl Hall, Michael Betz, James Robert Parish, Nancy Spellman, Judy Pisarek, and Anne Swigart. The Interlibrary Loan Department of the Wilmington Library found everything for which I asked. The open periodical stacks at West Chester University's Francis Harvey Green Library and the University of Delaware's Morris Library were, as usual, a godsend.

British Library Cataloguing-in-Publication data are available

Library of Congress Cataloguing-in-Publication Data

Holston, Kim R., 1948–
    The English-speaking cinema : an illustrated history, 1927–1993 / by Kim Holston.
        p. cm.
    Includes bibliographical references and index.
    ISBN 0-89950-858-8 (lib. bdg. : 50# alk. paper) ∞
    1. Motion pictures — United States — History. I. Title.
PN1993.5.U6H596   1994
791.43'0973 — dc20   92-56652
                                                            CIP

Manufactured in the United States of America

McFarland & Company, Inc., Publishers
  Box 611, Jefferson, North Carolina 28640

Contents

The, ah, stuff that dreams are made of.
—Humphrey Bogart, in *The Maltese Falcon*, 1941

Only rarely does a movie-goer have the experience of seeing real
human beings living in a complicated world.
—Hortense Powdermaker, *Hollywood, the Dream Factory*, 1950

The fact is I am quite happy in a movie, even a bad movie.
—Walker Percy, *The Moviegoer*, 1961

Film should be poetic, integrating all the components of art.
And it should show the inner truth, not merely the "realistic" truth,
in a stylized manner. It must also have rhythm.
—Rouben Mamoulian, in Charles Higham and Joel Greenberg's,
The Celluloid Muse, 1971

I have no preferences about movies. Discrimination, in fact, is contrary
to a true movie buff's nature. Enthusiasm, however, is a major requirement.
Enthusiasm—and avarice. The more movies the better.
—Joe Baltake, *Philadelphia Daily News*, April 20, 1973

The strength of the movies is that people must believe in them.
—Ethan Mordden, *The Hollywood Studios*, 1988

I can accept just about any premise, no matter how dumb,
as long as there is one,
and some consistency is maintained.
—Elena Watson, May 16, 1990

Preface

There are many cinema histories: single volume and multivolume encyclopedias, analyses of film as art, glossy photo survey coffee table books. Like most of those, this book was written in the hopes of entertaining and informing veteran filmgoers who have watched a high proportion of their films in a theater. Nevertheless, it is especially aimed at cinemagoers born in the 50s and later. This audience came of age when television was no longer a novelty but a fact of life. They probably did not attend double feature science fiction matinees, buy tickets in advance for reserved seat "roadshows" presented in grandiose motion picture palaces, or pay attention to *Shock Theatre, Schaefer Award Theatre,* or *The Late Show* when these programs telecast films of the 30s and 40s on television for the first time. They probably have little or no recollection of the 1961 premiere of *Saturday Night at the Movies,* which filled gaps for a teenage audience desirous of seeing movies they had only heard about. As a moviegoer who did experience these events, I hope to explain and pass on some of my generation's enthusiasm for theatrical films.

For the most part, this is a history of narrative cinema whose "images cry out for meaningful interpretation, though their removal from reality can, as has frequently been noted, afford them a quality closer to dreams than to life."[1] Narrative cinema *can* be art. And art is hardly authentic. Director Josef Von Sternberg told *Evening Standard* critic Alexander Walker,

> When I made *Underworld* I was not a gangster, nor did I know anything about gangsters. I knew nothing about China when I made *Shanghai Express.* These are not authentic. I do not value the fetish for authenticity. I have no regard for it. On the contrary, the illusion of reality is what I look for, not reality itself. There is nothing authentic about my pictures. Nothing at all. There isn't a single authentic thing.[2]

For those who have seen the films herein discussed, this is a refresher. For others, it is a survey of trends, important events, major and minor players, and technicians, as well as a preview of the pleasure that revival theaters and videocassettes can provide.

The chronology references significant silents, serials, animation, documentaries, international films, and underground cinema. The text deals exclusively with theatrical films. If a movie was not released in a theater, it will not be discussed in this book. Rigid, perhaps. Or merely literal. Included is a glossary of basic film terms.

For decades, English-language films have dominated the world. International audiences have always appreciated their pace. This popularity has been the result of an ability to cover a wealth of genres. Money, population, and geography have permitted American moviemakers to make adventure, comedy, crime, drama, horror and fantasy, musicals, mystery and suspense, science fiction, and westerns. A far-flung, centuries-old British Empire has provided exotic locales for many a United Kingdom film. Sadly, some genres have disappeared or been modified into almost unrecognizable forms — for example, the westerns subsumed by space opera.

Omissions in the following work are regretted, but only in the abstract. The only fair tribute to movies and their makers would be thousands of pages long. There are always more movies to see, there is always more to learn. "A lot of movie history must be written with one's eyes on the films themselves."[3] For now, it is possible to research the history of filmmaking, review movies in theaters and on videocassette, and *remember* the moviegoing experience during its infant century. As the 21st century dawns, it will be impossible to write a firsthand account of the moviegoing adventure.

A Chronology

1877	Emile Reynaud invents Praxinoscope
Dec. 15, 1877	Thomas Edison receives U.S. patent for his Tinfoil Phonograph, or Speaking Machine
1877–79	Eadweard Muybridge takes still photographs of racing horses (1877), publishes results (1878), invents zoopraxiscope to reconstruct motion from photographs (1879)
1882	Etienne-Jules Marey invents a hand-held motion picture camera
1884	George Eastman, Henry Reichenbach, and Hannibal Goodwin introduce transparent, flexible film (patented Dec. 10, 1889)
1887	C. J. Hohenstein puts sound on film
1888	William Kennedy Laurie Dickson invents Kinetoscope in Thomas Edison's laboratory
1889	William Friese-Greene patents a motion picture camera that uses perforated film
1890	Motion picture camera projector inventor Louis Aimé Augustin Le Prince disappears
1894	Mrs. H. Henderson Wilcox names her and her husband's ranch "Hollywood"
Nov. 11, 1895	Filoteo Alberini patents Kinetograph for making, printing, and projecting films
Dec. 28, 1895	Louis and Auguste Lumière use Edison's inventions to develop Cinématographe, a camera-projector-printer
1898	Gaumont Company organized
1902	Georges Méliès' *A Trip to the Moon*
1903	Edwin S. Porter's *The Great Train Robbery*
1906	*The Hand of the Artist*, first U.K. animated film
1906	American Biograph and Mutoscope Company studio locates in Los Angeles
Dec. 26, 1906	Charles Tait's *The Story of the Kelly Gang* (Australia) may be first feature film
Jan. 15, 1907	Lee De Forest patents Audion Three-Electrode Amplifier Tube to pick up weak sounds received by radio or telephone cable, thus increasing sound in an auditorium
1907	Francis Boggs' *The Power of the Sultan*, first dramatic film lensed in Hollywood
1907	Camille Saint-Saëns writes score (Opus 128) for *L'Assassinat du Duc de Guise*
1908	Ten-year patents war ends with nine film companies merging into the Motion Picture Patents Company

1

1909	National Board of Censorship formed (becomes National Board of Review in 1916)
1910	Carl Laemmle launches star system with Florence Lawrence
1911	Sigmund Lubin provides restaurant on premises of his Philadelphia film company plant
1911	West Coast branch of Centaur Company becomes first Hollywood studio
1911	Britain's *The Durbar at Delhi,* first major two-color film
1912	*Oliver Twist,* Britain's first feature
1912	Bell and Howell introduces perforator, standardizing the shape and number of film sprocket holes
1912	Board of Film Censors (U.K.) sets U (Universal) and A (Adult) ratings
July 12, 1912	*Queen Elizabeth,* with Sarah Bernhardt, premieres at New York's Lyceum Theater
1912	Universal formed by Carl Laemmle
1912	*What Happened to Mary,* with Mary Fuller, first serial
1912	Mack Sennett founds Keystone Company
1912	*Photoplay* begins publication
1913	*The Adventures of Kathlyn,* serial with Kathlyn Williams
1914	*The Squaw Man,* first feature shot in Hollywood
1914	*The Perils of Pauline* serial, with Pearl White
1914	Hal Roach founds comedy company
1914	Paramount Pictures Corporation organized by W. W. Hodkinson
1915	Triangle Film Corporation organized
1915	D. W. Griffith's *The Birth of a Nation*
1916	Goldwyn formed by Samuel Goldfish, Arthur Hopkins, Margaret Mayo, Edgar and Arch Selwyn
1917	*Boy Scouts Be Prepared,* first British serial
1917	Motion Picture Patents Company's power curtailed by courts
1917	First National Exhibitors' Circuit organized
1918	Charlie Chaplin and Mary Pickford sign $1 million-plus contracts
1919	Robert Wiene's *The Cabinet of Doctor Caligari*
1919	United Artists formed by D. W. Griffith, Douglas Fairbanks, Mary Pickford, and Charles Chaplin
1920	*Photoplay's* first Gold Medal Award to *Humoresque*
1921	Charlie Chaplin's *The Kid*
1921	Death of young actress Virginia Rappe ruins Fatty Arbuckle's career
1921	Rudolf Valentino stars as *The Sheik*
1922	Motion Picture Producers and Distributors of America formed under leadership of Will H. Hays (became Motion Picture Association of America)
1922	Western Associated Motion Picture Advertisers (WAMPAS) elects its first "baby stars": Colleen Moore, Mary Philbin, Patsy Ruth Miller, Jacqueline Logan, Lila Lee, Bessie Love
1922	F. W. Murnau's *Nosferatu*
1922	*The Film Daily* initiates Ten Best of the Year
1922	Robert Flaherty's documentary, *Nanook of the North*
1922	First National becomes production company
1922	Technicolor demonstrates its new process
1922	Erich Von Stroheim's *Foolish Wives*
1922	Hal Roach introduces *Our Gang* series (Spanky McFarland joins in 1932)

1923	Cecil B. DeMille's *The Ten Commandments*
1923	Warner Bros. is incorporated
1923	*Safety Last,* with Harold Lloyd
1923	James Cruze's *The Covered Wagon*
1923	*Where the North Begins,* first Rin-Tin-Tin film
1923	Erich Von Stroheim's *Greed*
1924	Panchromatic film in general use
1924	F. W. Murnau's *The Last Laugh*
1924	Columbia Pictures Corporation renamed by Cohn-Brandt-Cohn
1924	Metro-Goldwyn (later Metro-Goldwyn-Mayer) organized
1924	John Ford's *The Iron Horse*
1925	Sergei Eisenstein's *The Battleship Potemkin*
1925	King Vidor's *The Big Parade*
1925	Charlie Chaplin's *The Gold Rush*
1925	Lon Chaney stars in *The Phantom of the Opera*
1925	Warner Bros. buys Vitagraph
1925	Ronald Colman's first teaming with Vilma Banky, *The Dark Angel*
1926	Lotte Reiniger's *The Adventures of Prince Achmed,* first full-length animated feature
Aug. 6, 1926	Vitaphone exhibited in Broadway's Warner Theater via a Will Hays prologue, musical shorts, and the feature film with music and sound effects, *Don Juan*
1926	Columbia Pictures acquires its own studio
1926	Fred Niblo's *Ben-Hur*
1926	Buster Keaton's *The General*
1927	F. W. Murnau's *Sunrise*
1927	William Fox presents first Movietone shorts
1927	Loretta Young debuts at age 14 in *Naughty but Nice*
1927	Fritz Lang's *Metropolis*
1927	Cecil B. DeMille's *King of Kings*
1927	Academy of Motion Picture Arts and Sciences founded
Oct. 6, 1927	Al Jolson stars in first "talkie," *The Jazz Singer*
1927	Cinematograph Act of 1927 begins quota system in Britain
1927	Abel Gance's *Napoleon*
1927/28	Silent *Wings* wins first Best Picture Academy Award
1928	George Bernard Shaw makes Movietone short
Sept. 1928	Warner Bros. acquires First National
Nov. 18, 1928	Mickey (Mortimer) Mouse introduced by Walt Disney in *Steamboat Willie*
1928	*Lights of New York,* first all-talkie
1928	RKO (Radio-Keith-Orpheum Corporation) created when RCA acquires Keith Orpheum theater chains
1928	King Vidor's *The Crowd*
1929	University of Southern California initiates Appreciation of the Photoplay course
1929	*Hell's Heroes,* first Universal outdoor talkie
1929	Alfred Hitchcock's *Blackmail,* first British sound feature
1929	King Vidor's *Hallelujah!*
1929	*The Clue of the New Pin,* first all-talking (sound on disc) British feature

1929	Raoul Walsh uses sound equipment on location in Utah for *In Old Arizona*
1929	Warner Bros.' *On with the Show,* first all–Technicolor talkie
1929	Fox's *Hearts in Dixie,* first all-black talkie
1929	Louise Brooks stars in G. W. Pabst's *Pandora's Box*
1929	Marx Brothers debut in *The Cocoanuts*
1930	Selected theaters show MGM's *Billy the Kid* in 70mm
1930	*Anna Christie,* Greta Garbo's first sound film
1930	National Board of Review's 10 best American films initiated
1931	Tod Browning's *Dracula*
1931	Fritz Lang's *M*
1931	Charlie Chaplin's *City Lights*
1931	Ealing Studios open
1931	James Whale's *Frankenstein*
1931	London Films organized
1932	Walt Disney's first color cartoon, Silly Symphony *Flowers and Trees*
1932	John, Ethel, and Lionel Barrymore costar in *Rasputin and the Empress*
1932	Tod Browning's *Freaks*
1932	*Tarzan the Ape Man,* first Johnny Weissmuller–Maureen O'Sullivan jungle adventure
1932	*Sight and Sound* first published
1932	Gaumont-British opens
1932	Radio City Music Hall opens
1933	Toby Wing plays the *Young and Healthy* girl in *42nd Street*
1933	Screen Actors Guild founded
1933	British Film Institute founded
1933	*Flying Down to Rio,* first Fred Astaire–Ginger Rogers teaming
1933	Merian C. Cooper and Ernest B. Schoedsack's *King Kong*
1933	*Popeye the Sailor* created by Max Fleischer
June 6, 1933	First drive-in in Camden, New Jersey—featuring *Wife Beware*
1934	Frank Capra's *It Happened One Night*
1934	Production Code implemented
1934	Gene Autry's first film, *In Old Santa Fe*
1934	Louis de Rochemont and Roy E. Larsen create *March of Time* newsreel
1934	Three Stooges begin their two-reel comedies
April 11, 1934	Legion of Decency announced by the Catholic Church
July 22, 1934	John Dillinger killed by FBI when he emerges from Chicago's Biograph Theatre (showing *Manhattan Melodrama*)
Nov. 1934	Hammer Productions, Ltd., registered
1934	Donald Duck introduced in *The Wise Little Hen*
1935	Roy Rogers' first film, *The Old Homestead*
1935	Leni Riefenstahl's *Triumph of the Will*
1935	*Naughty Marietta,* first teaming of Jeanette MacDonald and Nelson Eddy
1935	*Becky Sharp,* first three-color Technicolor film
1935	*Captain Blood,* first Errol Flynn–Olivia De Havilland pairing
1935	New York Film Critics initiated and give best motion picture award to *The Informer*
1935	Republic Pictures formed by Herbert J. Yates and Consolidated Film Industries
1935	James Whale's *The Bride of Frankenstein*

1935	First of four straight years Shirley Temple is top boxoffice draw
1935	20th Century–Fox formed by merger of William Fox's company with 20th Century Players of Darryl F. Zanuck and Joseph Schenck
Sept. 14, 1936	Irving Thalberg dies at 37
1936	Buster Crabbe stars in Universal's *Flash Gordon* serial
1936	Pinewood Studios opens
1936	Denham Studios opens
1936	2,000 foot film-reel standard adopted
1936	*The Trail of the Lonesome Pine*, first outdoor Technicolor feature
1936	Walter Brennan wins first of three supporting actor Academy Awards, this one for *Come and Get It*
1937	90 million average weekly theater attendance
1937	Jean Renoir's *Grand Illusion*
1937	Walt Disney's *Snow White and the Seven Dwarfs*, first color and sound animated feature
1937	*I, Claudius* abandoned
1938	Erich Wolfgang Korngold wins best original score Academy Award for *The Adventures of Robin Hood*
1938	Ernst Lubitsch's *Bluebeard's Eighth Wife* coscripted by Billy Wilder and Charles Brackett
1938	Sergei Eisenstein's *Alexander Nevsky*
1938	Bugs Bunny introduced in *Porky's Hare Hunt*
1939	John Ford's *Stagecoach*
1939	Gregg Toland wins black and white cinematography Academy Award for *Wuthering Heights*
1939	Tom and Jerry introduced by Hanna-Barbera in *Puss Gets the Boot*
1939	Basil Rathbone plays Sherlock Holmes for first time in *The Hound of the Baskervilles*
1939	Jean Renoir's *The Rules of the Game*
1939	Frank Capra's *Mr. Smith Goes to Washington*
1939	National Film Board of Canada founded
1939	Producers Releasing Corporation (PRC) presents first film, *Hitler — Beast of Berlin*
1939	David O. Selznick's *Gone with the Wind*
1939	Zoltan Korda's *The Four Feathers*
1940	*Down Argentine Way*, Carmen Miranda's English-language film debut
1940	Woody Woodpecker introduced by Walter Lantz in *Knock Knock*
1940	John Huston's *The Maltese Falcon*
1940	Bud Abbott and Lou Costello debut in *One Night in the Tropics*
1940	Ludwig Berger's *The Thief of Bagdad*
1941	Tom Tyler stars in Republic's *The Adventures of Captain Marvel* serial
1941	*Two-Faced Woman*, last Greta Garbo film
1941	Orson Welles' *Citizen Kane*
Jan. 16, 1942	Carole Lombard killed in plane crash
1942	Kane Richmond stars in Republic's *Spy Smasher* serial
1942	Simone Simon stars in Jacques Tourneur's *Cat People*, produced by Val Lewton
1942	Elizabeth Taylor debuts in *There's One Born Every Minute*
1942	*Woman of the Year*, first Spencer Tracy–Katharine Hepburn film
1943	Carmen Miranda sings "The Lady in the Tutti Frutti Hat" in *The Gang's All Here*

1943	Ida Lupino receives New York Film Critics nod for best feminine performance in *The Hard Way*
June 3, 1943	Leslie Howard killed in plane shot down by Nazis
1943	Michael Curtiz' *Casablanca*
1944	*Mouse Trouble* with Tom and Jerry wins Academy Award for cartoon short subjects
1944	Preston Sturges' *The Miracle of Morgan's Creek*
1944	Marcel Carne's *Children of Paradise*
1944	Academy Award nominees reduced to maximum of five per category
Feb. 1945	California State Supreme Court upholds Olivia De Havilland's contention that Warner Bros. violates state's antipeonage laws by tacking suspension time onto the end of her contract
1945	Carol Reed and Garson Kanin direct wartime documentary *The True Glory*
1945	Roberto Rossellini's *Open City* begins neorealist school
1945	Ealing Studios' *Dead of Night*
Dec. 17, 1945	Paulette Goddard as *Kitty* on *Life* cover
1946	Cannes Film Festival begins
1946	Frank Capra's *It's a Wonderful Life*
1946	William Wyler's *The Best Years of Our Lives*
1946	David Lean's *Great Expectations*
1946	"Big 8" studios (Fox, MGM, Paramount, Warner Bros., Columbia, Universal, United Artists, RKO) have record combined profits of $122 million
1946	*A Matter of Life and Death,* first Royal Film Performance
Nov. 1946	Universal and International Pictures merge
1947	Jacques Tourneur's *Out of the Past*
1947	*Song of the Thin Man,* last Thin Man film
1947	Vittorio De Sica's *Shoeshine* wins special Academy Award
1947	"Big 8" studios' combined profits fall to $89 million
Spring 1947	Director John Huston protests House Un-American Activities Committee investigation of Hollywood writers
Oct. 20, 1947	House Committee on Un-American Activities (HUAC) begins hearings on Communist subversion in Hollywood
1948	"Hollywood Ten" director, producer and screenwriters refuse to testify on communist affiliations and are jailed for contempt of Congress
May 1948	Supreme Court's "Paramount decree" divorces exhibition from production and distribution
July 5, 1948	Carole Landis dies at age 29
July 23, 1948	D. W. Griffith dies at age 74
1948	RKO sold to Howard Hughes
1948	National Film Finance Corporation formed by Britain's Labour Government
1948	Howard Hawks' *Red River*
Feb. 1949	Hammer Film Productions, Ltd., registered
1949	*Criss Cross* features Esy Morales and His Rhumba Band
1949	Carol Reed's *The Third Man*
1949	Eastman Kodak's safety-base film begins replacing flammable nitrate stock
1949	*Jigsaw* features unbilled Henry Fonda in his last film until 1955
1949	Dean Martin and Jerry Lewis debut in *My Friend Irma*

1949	Vittorio De Sica's *The Bicycle Thief*
1949	Joseph L. Mankiewicz wins direction and screenplay Academy Awards for *A Letter to Three Wives*
1950	Joseph L. Mankiewicz wins direction and screenplay Academy Awards for *All About Eve*
1950	Jackie Robinson plays himself in *The Jackie Robinson Story*
Feb. 1950	Ingrid Bergman creates furor by bearing Roberto Rossellini's son out of wedlock
1950	Billy Wilder's *Sunset Boulevard*
1950	Luís Buñuel's *The Young and the Damned*
May 1, 1950	Ruth Roman on cover of *Life*
1950	George Pal wins first of five special effects Academy Awards for *Destination Moon*
1951	First Place PATSY (Picture Animal Top Star of the Year) to *Francis*, the talking mule
1951	Akira Kurosawa's *Rashomon* wins top prize at Venice Film Festival
1951	First nationwide television telecast
1951	Decca Records buys Universal
1951	*Cahiers du Cinéma* begins publication
1951	X certificate introduced in Britain
1951	*Showboat*, first Howard Keel–Kathryn Grayson MGM musical
1952	*Burstyn v. Wilson* ruling covers *The Miracle* segment of *Ways of Love* under First and Fourteenth amendments
1952	Elizabeth Threatt plays Teal Eye in *The Big Sky*
May 20, 1952	John Garfield dies at age 39
1952	Gene Kelly's and Stanley Donen's *Singin' in the Rain*
1952	*This Is Cinerama*
1952	MGM's *The Wild North* in Anscocolor
1952	Warner Color (aka Eastmancolor) introduced in *Carson City*
1952	*Bwana Devil*, first 3-D commercial feature
1952	Akira Kurosawa's *Ikiru*
March 9, 1953	Vanessa Brown on cover of *Life*
March 19, 1953	Academy Award ceremony telecast for first time
March 23, 1953	Elaine Stewart on cover of *Life*
Sept. 17, 1953	*The Robe*, first CinemaScope feature
1953	Otto Preminger's *The Moon Is Blue* released minus Production Code seal
1953	*House of Wax*, first 3-D feature with stereophonic sound
1953	Victor Jory plays romantic lead in *Cat-Women of the Moon*
1953	Henri-Georges Clouzot's *The Wages of Fear*
1953	Yasujiro Ozu's *Tokyo Story*
1953	Teinosuke Kinugasa's *Gate of Hell*
1953	Kenji Mizoguchi's *Ugetsu Monogatari*
1953	George Stevens' *Shane*
1954	*White Christmas*, first feature in VistaVision
1954	*Godzilla*
1954	Disney forms Buena Vista after terminating deal with RKO
1954	Britain's first full-length animated feature is *Animal Farm*
1954	Saul Bass designs credits for *Carmen Jones*
1954	*Vera Cruz* in SuperScope
1954	Federico Fellini's *La Strada* wins best foreign film Academy Award

1955	Todd Duncan sings Alex North's "Unchained Melody" in *Unchained*
1955	Liberace stars in *Sincerely Yours*
July 1955	RKO sold by Howard Hughes
1955	Akira Kurosawa's *The Seven Samurai*
1955	Henry Fonda returns to screen after five year absence to recreate stage role of *Mister Roberts*
Sept. 30, 1955	James Dean killed in Porsche Spyder crash, Paso Robles, California
1955	Nicholas Ray's *Rebel Without a Cause*
1955	Robert Aldrich's *Kiss Me Deadly*
1956	American Releasing Corporation becomes American International Pictures under aegis of James H. Nicholson and Samuel Z. Arkoff
1956	*Love Me Tender* features Elvis Presley in film debut
1956	*Carousel* and *The King and I* in CinemaScope 55
1956	*High Society*, Grace Kelly's last film
1956	*Around the World in 80 Days*, first film in Todd-AO
1956	John Ford's *The Searchers*
1956	Satyajit Ray's *Pather Panchali*
1957	Ingmar Bergman's *The Seventh Seal*
1957	RKO and Republic go out of business
1957	Otto Preminger introduces Iowan Jean Seberg as *Saint Joan*
1957	*Photoplay*'s Gold Medal Award to *An Affair to Remember*
1957	*The Bridge on the River Kwai* popularizes the "Colonel Bogey March"
1957	Billy Wilder and I. A. L. Diamond, first collaboration, on script, *Love in the Afternoon*
1957	*Raintree County*, first film in Camera 65 (later known as Ultra-Panavision)
1957	Hammer inaugurates modern color horror film cycle with *The Curse of Frankenstein*
1958	Legion of Decency condemns *And God Created Woman*, with Brigitte Bardot
1958	Alfred Hitchcock's *Vertigo*
Nov. 21, 1958	Cesar Romero gives eulogy at Tyrone Power's funeral
1958	Steve Reeves is *Hercules*
1959	Academy Award telecast reaches record audience. Winners: *Gigi*, David Niven, Susan Hayward
1959	Alain Resnais' *Hiroshima Mon Amour*
1959	Raphael Portillo's *The Robot vs. the Aztec Mummy*
1959	Ingmar Bergman's *The Virgin Spring*
Aug. 1959	*The Siege of Pinchgut*, last Ealing film
1959	Ed Wood's *Plan 9 from Outer Space*
1959	William Wyler's *Ben-Hur* wins record 11 Academy Awards
1959	Russ Meyer's *The Immoral Mr. Teas*
Jan. 15, 1960	Screenwriters on strike, directors follow suit
April 1960	*Picturegoer* ceases publication
July 1960	*Picture Show* ceases publication
1960	Alexander Ptushko's *The Sword and the Dragon*
1960	*Scent of Mystery* in Smellovision
1960	Mario Bava's *Black Sunday*
1960	Jean-Luc Godard's *Breathless* inaugurates *Nouvelle Vague* movement
April 17, 1961	James Stewart announces honorary Academy Award for gravely ill Gary Cooper

May 13, 1961	Gary Cooper dies at age 60
June 17, 1961	Jeff Chandler dies at 42, following spinal surgery
1961	*The Misfits,* final film of both Clark Gable and Marilyn Monroe
1961	In-flight movies begin
Sept. 23, 1961	*Saturday Night at the Movies* premieres on NBC
1961	*West Side Story* wins 10 Academy Awards
Sept. 21, 1962	Bette Davis advertises for job in Hollywood trade papers
Nov. 1962	Bette Davis and Joan Crawford costar in *Whatever Happened to Baby Jane?*
1962	Gene Pitney sings *The Man Who Shot Liberty Valance*
1962	*Dr. No,* first James Bond film
1963	Universal drops International from name
1963	Sidney Poitier receives best actor Academy Award for *Lilies of the Field*
March 15, 1964	Elizabeth Taylor and Richard Burton wed
1964	Sergio Leone's "spaghetti western" *A Fistful of Dollars,* with Clint Eastwood (U.S. release, 1967)
1964	Shirley Bassey sings "Goldfinger"
1964	London Pavilion premiere for Beatles in *A Hard Day's Night*
1964	Four out of five best actor Academy Award nominees are British: Rex Harrison (*My Fair Lady*), Richard Burton and Peter O'Toole (*Becket*), Peter Sellers (*Dr. Strangelove*). Anthony Quinn (*Zorba the Greek*) is the only American
1965	Citadel Press publishes Clifford McCarty's *Bogey: The Films of Humphrey Bogart*
1965	Stunt pilot Paul Mantz killed making *The Flight of the Phoenix*
March 12, 1965	Julie Andrews on cover of *Life*
1965	Gulf and Western Oil acquires Paramount
1965	*The Sound of Music* released, displaces *Gone with the Wind* as all-time top grosser
Dec. 1965	Hollywood: Finland's Tuula Mattila, 21, wins Doris Day lookalike contest
Jan. 7, 1966	Sean Connery in *Thunderball,* on cover of *Life*
June 1966	Elke Sommer sends lifesize cutout to Company B, 1st Battalion, 28th Infantry, Vietnam
1966	Sisters Lynn (*Georgy Girl*) and Vanessa Redgrave (*Morgan!*) get Academy Award nominations as best actress
Dec. 15, 1966	Walt Disney dies at age 65
June 1967	Warner Bros.–Seven Arts, Ltd. created when Jack Warner sells his shares in WB
1967	Mike Nichols' *The Graduate*
1967	Arthur Penn's *Bonnie and Clyde*
1967	Philippe De Broca's *King of Hearts*
1967	American Film Institute founded
1967	Stanton Theatre, Philadelphia: "Special Midnight Swingers Premiere" of *Tony Rome*
1967	Transamerica Corporation acquires United Artists
1968	Sergei Bondarchuk's *War and Peace*
1968	Hammer Studios receives Queens Award to Industry
1968	Stanley Kubrick's *2001: A Space Odyssey*
1968	Voluntary rating system (Rating Code becomes G, PG [previously M, then GP], R, and X) supplants Production Code

1968	AVCO takes over Joseph E. Levine's Embassy Films
Oct. 2, 1968	ABC's *Cat Ballou* telecast achieves highest Nielsen rating of any films that year (28.5, a 49 percent share)
Oct. 18, 1968	Paul Newman and Joanne Woodward on cover of *Life*
1969	John Schlesinger's *Midnight Cowboy*
May 1969	20th Century–Fox plans 800 car drive-in in Natal Province, South Africa
June 22, 1969	Judy Garland dies at age 47
1969	Roger Corman retrospective (1957–64) at Trieste Festival of Science Fiction Films
1969	Hammer Films moves from Bray Studios
1969	*Easy Rider* is best film by a new director (Dennis Hopper) at Cannes
Sept. 1969	*I Am Curious (Yellow)* makes $1,087,942 in New York City
Sept. 23, 1969	American Film Institute Opens Center for Advanced Film Study in Beverly Hills
1969	Jerry Lewis and Network Cinema Corporation franchise theaters open
1970	Bekim Fehmiu is Dax in *The Adventurers*
1970	U.K.'s Board of Film Censors revises rating: U, A, AA, X
1970	Chico State College holds First Annual Strother Martin Film Festival
May 1970	At MGM auction, Judy Garland's shoes from *The Wizard of Oz* sell for $10,000, Gina Lollobrigida's panties net $50
1971	*Wings* (1927) revived and on tour with John Thomas on organ
May 1971	Darryl F. Zanuck relinquishes control of Fox
1972	Francis Ford Coppola's *The Godfather*
1972	*Raintree County* (1957) soundtrack worth $150
April 1972	Burt Reynolds poses "nude" for *Cosmopolitan*
1972	Luís Buñuel's *The Discreet Charm of the Bourgeoisie*
1972	*Deep Throat*
1973	*The Devil in Miss Jones*
July 20, 1973	Bruce Lee dies of brain edema at age 32
Aug. 31, 1973	John Ford dies at age 78
June 1974	U.S. Supreme Court rules *Carnal Knowledge* not obscene
1974	Robert Bresson's *Lancelot of the Lake*
1974	*EarthQuake* in Sensurround
1975	Australian Film Commission reconstituted from Australian Film Development Corporation
1975	Dolby System noise reduction–high fidelity introduced in feature films
June 1975	Army and Air Force Exchange Service acquires Army and Air Force Motion Picture Service
July 29, 1975	Coconuts given away when *Monty Python and the Holy Grail* opens, Buffalo, New York
1975	Rene Bond is Veronica in *Beach Blanket Bango*
Sept. 1975	New York–Montreal Psychic Film Festival
1976	*To the Devil . . . a Daughter,* last Hammer film
April 24, 1976	Joan Collins awarded lifetime honorary membership in Count Dracula Society for her performance in *The Devil Within Her*
Jan. 12, 1977	Cinémathèque Française film library founder-director Henri Langlois dies at age 62 in Paris
1977	George Lucas' *Star Wars*
June 24, 1977	Adult Film Association holds First Annual Erotica Awards Ceremony
Aug. 16, 1977	Elvis Presley dies at age 42

1977	Lina Wertmuller first woman nominated for directing Academy Award, for *Seven Beauties*
1978	Woody Allen's *Annie Hall*
Feb. 12, 1979	Jean Renoir dies at age 84
June 11, 1979	John Wayne dies at age 72
Dec. 22, 1979	Darryl F. Zanuck dies at age 77
1979	Candice Bergen sings "Better Than Ever" in Neil Simon's *Starting Over*
1982	Steven Spielberg's *E.T. — The Extraterrestrial*
Sept. 1982	Critics Gene Siskel and Roger Ebert leave PBS' *Sneak Previews* for syndicated *At the Movies*
Oct. 1982	Linda Blair does nude spread in *Oui* magazine
Dec. 1985	Colorized version of *Miracle on 34th Street* telecast
1986	Ted Turner acquires 3,650 films from MGM, RKO and Warner Bros.
1987	Bernardo Bertolucci's *The Last Emperor*
1988	National Film Preservation Act of 1988
July 1989	Mel Blanc dies at age 81
1989	Giuseppe Tornatore's *Cinema Paradiso*
1989	Disney Studios' *The Little Mermaid* sets record initial gross for animated film
April 15, 1990	Greta Garbo dies at age 84
Oct. 1990	Boris Karloff and Vincent Price inducted into Horror Hall of Fame
1990	MPAA substitutes NC-17 (No Children Under 17 Admitted) for X rating
May 1991	*Citizen Kane* theatrical rerelease
May 1991	Restored *Spartacus* shown in selected theaters
Nov. 1991	Disney Studios' *Beauty and the Beast*
Oct. 6, 1992	Denholm Elliott dies at age 70
Jan. 20, 1993	Audrey Hepburn dies at age 63
Feb. 5, 1993	Joseph L. Mankiewicz dies at age 83
Feb. 27, 1993	Lillian Gish dies at age 99

Chapter 1

The Silent Era

Like the airplane and the automobile, motion pictures as they are known today were invented and developed on both sides of the Atlantic in the last quarter of the 19th century.[1] As with other inventions, a web must be untangled to determine firsts. For instance, was the hand-held camera invented by Etienne Jules or Jules Etienne Marey? Presumably authoritative books give different versions. One calls him Morey. It appears that William Kennedy Laurie Dickson, working in Edison's lab, was more responsible than his famous employer for contributions to the development of cinema. And what of Eadweard Muybridge? According to one of the earliest silent film historians, Muybridge merely took advantage of his situation.

In 1877 Muybridge used a battery of cameras to prove that while Leland Stanford's racehorse was running, all four of his feet were off the ground simultaneously. Technical problems bedeviled Muybridge, however, and Stanford asked railroad engineer Arthur Brown for advice. Engineering staff member John D. Isaacs, an 1875 graduate of the University of Virginia, perfected the system by using electrical contacts. And Paul Seiler constructed the mechanism that eventually tripped the cameras.[2] Nevertheless, Muybridge traveled, lectured, and has received overall credit.[3] Information about a great deal of material — films and documentation and people like Louis Aimé Augustin Le Prince — remains lost or shrouded in mystery.

During the final quarter of the 19th century, equipment and filmmaking proceeded at an increasingly fast pace. The first "movies" were shorts or peep shows (trains, prizefights, scenes from stage shows, natural disasters, dancing girls) viewed in kinetoscopes in streetfront shops or arcades converted for the purpose into what were called nickelodeons.

At the turn of the century companies were formed to produce films for a domestic audience swelled by an influx of nine million immigrants between 1901 and 1910. A large number of the newcomers needed no English to appreciate the movies, but the title cards doubtless helped them learn the language. And the movies were cheap.

> Immigration was at its peak in 1902–1903, and the movies gave the newcomers, particularly, a respect for American law and order, an understanding of civic organizations, pride in citizenship and in the American commonwealth. Movies acquainted them with current happenings at home and

13

abroad. Because the uncritical movie-goers were deeply impressed by what they saw in the photographs and accepted it as the real thing, the movies were powerful and persuasive. More vividly than any other single agency they revealed the social topography of America to the immigrant, to the poor, and to the country folk. Thus from the outset movies were, besides a commodity and developing craft, a social agency.[4]

As the foregoing suggests, there was also a rural audience. In fact, the U.S. population was mostly agrarian. Tents, amusement parks, YMCAs, and library basements served as theaters for this audience.[5]

Films with plots developed. Edwin S. Porter's 11-minute western, *The Great Train Robbery,* was filmed in 1903 "on location" in New Jersey. Features came later, and it was not until after World War I that theaters were built with films primarily in mind.[6]

> The first moving-picture "theater" in Galveston was called the Globe and its owner-manager was named Claude Brick. Claude operated a music store on Market Street but he had quite a struggle making a go of it. When motion pictures came along, Claude pushed all of his pianos, drums, and fiddles to the front of the store and built a thin wall across the center. In this partition he constructed a box-office window and two openings, one marked "Entrance," and the other "Exit." By this simple process, Claude Brick became Galveston's first motion-picture exhibitor.[7]

When theaters were designed specifically for movies—in the 1920s and well into the Depression—audiences were as attracted by their magnificent architecture as by the films shown.[8] Theaters, with their lobbies and refreshment counters, became community gathering places.

The men who became studio moguls and supplied films for the theaters had backgrounds in commerce, not art. "As employers of artists rather than artists themselves, their artistic sensibilities are as untrustworthy as their financial judgment."[9] But after all, this, like some musical compositions and quilt making, was a collaborative art. Hungarian-born furrier Adolph Zukor (Paramount) and Hungarian-born cloth-sponger William Fox saw the possibilities and made small fortunes from nickelodeons. Universal's Carl Laemmle had been a bookkeeper and department store manager. Harry Cohn was a vaudevillian, song plugger, and trolley conductor before heading Columbia. Louis B. Mayer, scrap-metal dealer, became mogul number one at Metro-Goldwyn-Mayer. Samuel "You can include me out" Goldwyn was once the glovemaker Goldfish. These men and others not only realized that feature-length films would be successful, they also figured out that the company which produced the films could also distribute them, lucratively, if it owned the theater chains. Thus developed vertical integration—producing studio, distributor, exhibitor.

HOLLYWOOD'S BEGINNINGS

At first movies were made everywhere. In the United States, there were studios in Fort Lee, New Jersey. Biograph was in New York City. Astoria is still in use in Queens. But Southern California became the mecca for several reasons: light (no need for electricity), space, variety of scenery, and cheap labor. Lacking these advantages, Britain, for instance, could hardly overcome its other problem developing a film industry.

> In England, where Victorian puritanism found its most fertile soil, work was only dignified if the work itself had dignity. This was a period when leisure for many was spent in eating, sleeping, and traveling to work. A period when the thought of making money from entertainment—from ill-spent leisure—was considered immoral. The entertainment world was regarded with a lofty indifference; visits to the theater or music hall were accompanied by feelings of guilty indulgence. Hampered by such moral opposition, the silent-film industry in England never flourished.[10]

Another advantage for filmmakers on the American West Coast was the three thousand miles separating them from suits by the Motion Picture Patents Company (1908) as well as from their own New York executives' interference. The Motion Picture Patents Company was a trust aimed at controlling the making and use of cameras and projectors. They made an exclusive contract with George Eastman, thus forcing independents to buy his film. For distribution, MPPC formed the General Film Company of 57 exchanges.[11]

Some residents of the sleepy, backwater Los Angeles community were not thrilled with the newcomers, but budding screenwriter Francis Marion found them a tonic.

> How could anyone resent the lively fun they had brought into this dull environment? You encountered their gypsy-like caravans wherever you went. Indians in full war paint rode hell-bent for leather across the dusty riverbeds. Mack Sennett's cops leapt aboard the cable car that climbed a midget hill known as Angel's Flight. Even the little parks became outdoor stages. During the noon hour you were apt to see Bluebeard and all his wives cozily eating ham sandwiches and hard-boiled eggs, while the Apostle John sat under a pepper tree with his arm around a bathing beauty. These flocks of young people, dotting the lawns like giant butterflies, their faces shining with youth and the gay, improvident air that comes with unexpected prosperity, added color to the sunburnt grass. Some of the boys looked half-baked, and the girls as if they had cleared the "wrong side of the railroad tracks" in one broad jump. But who doesn't secretly envy youth on the threshold of a new experience?[12]

The moviemakers were a breed apart.

> It is no wonder that Hollywood cut itself off from the rest of the world, becoming a sort of Graustark, a dream factory, which was a bit dreamlike itself. The defenses it erected were not so much to repel outsiders as to conceal its true feelings. Hollywood was out of balance with the rest of the world and was acutely aware of the fact.
>
> To allay the guilt which furtively gnawed at certain souls, technicians and players often endured the most incredibly rigorous conditions "for the sake of the picture."[13]

THE FIRST ERA OF THE DIRECTOR

In France Georges Méliès made *A Trip to the Moon* in 1902, and the American Edwin S. Porter made *The Great Train Robbery* in 1903. When the French film *Queen Elizabeth,* starring the great stage diva Sarah Bernhardt, premiered on July 12, 1912, it was a "cultural event, not an aesthetic one," but it proved that "feature films were economically viable."[14] Directors came to the fore with feature films.

Directors originally exercised plenty of control over their films, in many instances owning their own studios. Such was the case with D. W. Griffith, Thomas Ince, Mack Sennett, Marshall Neilan, and Charlie Chaplin. Cameramen and directors were one and the same. But of art there was little.

> It is a fact, and a disturbing one in many ways, that every basic device of cinematic storytelling had been established by 1912. The close-up, the tracking shot, the high angle, the flashback, the insert, effect lighting, masking, fades, dissolves—the whole gamut was there. But it was as though the components of a steam train had been assembled, and no one knew how to light the boiler. For while all the components of the narrative film had been devised, no one was fully exploiting them.[15]

D. W. Griffith, whose name is synonymous with the silent cinema, was a former actor, a romantic Kentuckian of southern chivalric leanings who "saw life through Victorian opera glasses."[16] Before Griffith, the camera had been immobile. He and cameraman G. W. "Billy" Bitzer changed things. "Then David Wark Griffith decided to push the camera up close enough to see what was going on in the actors' eyes, and his mind, and thus the camera, started on its rambunctious march."[17] Griffith's main contribution may lie in his integration of the close-up, better editing, and the tracking shot. The film most associated with him is *The Birth of a Nation* (1915). Artistically important, it has posed problems via its content, a part of which features the Ku Klux Klan in a positive light. The NAACP and others objected.

> The National Association for the Advancement of Colored People is conducting a campaign against the feature picture, *The Birth of a Nation,* based on Thomas Dixon's novel, *The Clansman,* at the Liberty Theatre.
>
> It was explained at the offices of the association, 70 Fifth Avenue, yesterday, that many protests had been received because of the characterization of the negro in the story. The association has the opinion of a number of prominent men who have condemned it, and today the Rev. Dr. Perry Stickney Grant and Rabbi Stephen S. Wise will preach against it, it is said.
>
> So far the association has found no way to interfere with the film, which has been viewed by crowded houses at every projection.[18]

Protests then as now failed to deter the audience. There were two shows daily for one or two dollars. A symphony orchestra of forty supplied the soundtrack.

An alternate analysis is a recent one:

> The twelve reels of *The Birth of a Nation* represented, first of all, an American answer to the Italians; secondly, a celebration of the fiftieth anniversary of the end of the American Civil War; thirdly, the belief of a Kentucky-born director that the United States had not truly become a nation until the overthrow of Reconstruction in the South; and lastly, the dream of a cinematic messiah that by dramatizing the horrors of the battlefield he could inspire a world convulsed by war to lay down its arms.[19]

Broken Blossoms (1919) and the roadshow *Way Down East* (1920) were other early triumphs.[20] His masterpiece, *Intolerance* (1916), was not recognized as such at the time of its release.

As ads demonstrated, Cecil B. DeMille, like Griffith, was a behind-the-scenes name that could sell a film: "Cecil B. DeMille's Production, *The Squaw Man*" or "*The Ten Commandments, Cecil B. DeMille's Masterpiece.*" In silent days DeMille made intimate dramas as well as epics. Bath scenes were a specialty in both forms.

Directors lost much of their control as the studio system solidified.

> Under Mayer, MGM was the authoritarian studio, a place of moguls. Thus the new corporation, officially founded in mid–1924, instituted an important break with the movies' oldest tradition: that of the independent director serving as source and overseer of the art, Griffith-style. At MGM, filmmaking was an assembly line of departments, each answerable to a producer, each producer answerable to the head of production, and the head answerable to Mayer. MGM's stars, moreover, would be nothing like the merry players of the old days, culling their favorite directors, idea men, and supporting players into mini-studios, choosing their properties, cutting their films. MGM would choose, cull, cut. The directors would direct, the writers write, the actors act—all separate, all supervised.[21]

Women came in on the ground floor of the cinema, both in front of and behind the camera. Mary Pickford was not only a superstar[22] — "America's Sweetheart" — but, along with actor husband Douglas Fairbanks, Charlie Chaplin, and D. W. Griffith, the founder of United Artists, which was formed to combat trusts and maintain performer salaries. Behind the scenes were many women who directed, edited, and wrote. Frances Marion wrote *Stella Maris* (1918) and *The Love Light* (1921), both starring Pickford, and *Stella Dallas* (1925). Dorothy Arzner was a director. June Mathis scripted the 1921 epic *The Four Horsemen of the Apocalypse*. Anita Loos was a screenwriter, adapter, and dialogue provider for silent and sound films, and the author of *Gentlemen Prefer Blondes*. Bess Meredyth scripted the 1926 *Ben-Hur* and 1926 *The Sea Beast*.

Writers were in demand. A notable recruit was reporter Ben Hecht. Herman Mankiewicz wrote him in the spring of 1925 about the big bucks to be had writing for the screen. "Millions are to be grabbed out here and your only competition is idiots."[23]

STARS

Mary Pickford starred in many silent films including *The Mender of Nets* (1912) and *Sparrows* (1926). Douglas Fairbanks, Pickford's husband from 1920 to 1936, was the swashbuckler of *The Mark of Zorro* (1921), *Robin Hood* (1922), and *Thief of Bagdad* (1924). Other idols of the silent film audiences were Italian-born Rudolph Valentino of *The Sheik* (1922) and *The Four Horsemen of the Apocalypse,* "It" Girl Clara Bow of *Daughters of Pleasure* (1924) and *It* (1927), screen lovers John Gilbert and Greta Garbo, Lon Chaney, the "Man of a Thousand Faces," westerner William S. Hart of *Hell's Hinges* (1916), Rin Tin Tin of *The Night Cry* (1925), Emil Jannings of *The Last Command* (1927), Richard Barthelmess of *Broken Blossoms* (1919), John Barrymore of *Dr. Jekyll and Mr. Hyde* (1920), Mae Marsh of *The White Rose* (1923), and Lillian Gish of *Way Down East* (1920).

Above: Douglas Fairbanks was the original swashbuckler, thrilling audiences in such epics as *The Mark of Zorro* (1921), *Robin Hood* (1922) and *The Thief of Bagdad* (1924). *Opposite:* One of director D. W. Griffith's financially unsuccessful epics was *America* (United Artists, 1924). Perhaps its failure contributed to the belief that films about 18th century America were boxoffice poison.

COMEDY

Even in the 1990s silent comedy has an unparalleled reputation. "Good twenties silent comedies never made the comic hero into a joke; what was funny about him was his gravity in the midst of comically chaotic circumstances."[24] The clown princes of silent comedy were Harold Lloyd (*Safety Last,* 1923), Charlie Chaplin (*The Kid,* 1921, *The Gold Rush,* 1925), Buster Keaton (*Sherlock, Jr.,* 1924, *The General,* 1927), and Harry Langdon (*Tramp, Tramp, Tramp,* 1926).

Stan Laurel and Oliver Hardy's silent shorts are often considered their best work. "The comedy teams went after 'character' instead of 'story line,' psychic insight instead of moral lesson."[25]

Most famous and influential of all silent comedians was British-born Charlie Chaplin: "Of all comedians he worked most deeply and most shrewdly within a realization of what a human being is, and is up against.... The minute he began to work he set standards—and continually forced them higher."[26]

On- and Off-Location

On-location shooting was frequently done during this stage of film history. The need for sunlight had necessitated outdoor shooting from the beginning. Now locations to fit the story were sought. For instance, *The Winning of Barbara Worth* (1926) was filmed in Black Rock Desert, Nevada, to which the water had to be carted from two hundred miles away.[27] *The White Sister* (1923) and *Romola* (1924) were made in Europe. Much of *Ben-Hur* was lensed in Italy. King Vidor made *Wild Oranges* (1924) in Florida.

Developments in film began facilitating indoor shoots at the same time. In 1924,

> panchromatic film came into general use, beginning the era of a personal style in cinematography. The crude film stocks of the early days had lacked sensitivity, responding only to harsh blue-white light, which resulted in exterior shooting, a shallow depth of focus (caused by wide-open apertures) and heavy make-up to define features as black on a white ground. Orthochromatic film, common after the First World War, had recorded blue and green, but red registered as black, and pink, light blue and yellow as white.[28]

Theaters

By the 20s, theater design for the movie palace absorbed elements of any past style that symbolized opulence. Architects mixed features from classical French to 16th-century Spanish, from Venetian to Moorish. For their top houses Balaban and Katz favored the "French" style, even copying the monumental staircase of the Paris Opera House and the grand, column-lined lobby of the Hall of Mirrors at Versailles. King Tut's tomb was discovered and opened by Howard Carter in 1922 and became the inspiration behind "Egyptian" theaters.[29] "These wonder-theaters were not haphazardly thrown together but formulated in assembly-line fashion by specialized architectural firms headed by John Eberson, Thomas Lamb, and the brothers Rapp."[30] Suitably impressed, 20s audiences, "supervised by scores of ushers, behaved far better than their grandchildren, who declared film an art."[31] Of great importance in the success of these palaces was the introduction of air-conditioning.[32]

Chapter 2

The Coming of Sound,
1927–1929

Wait a minute, wait a minute. You ain't heard nothin' yet. Wait
a minute, I tell ya. You ain't heard nothin'.
— Al Jolson, *The Jazz Singer*

Two requirements for "talking" motion pictures were synchronization and amplification. Development of the phonograph paralleled the development of the motion picture, and sound on disc was a method for providing talking pictures. Nevertheless, discs could not be a long-term answer because they could not hold enough sound to accompany a reel of film. Eventually sound would have to be placed on the film itself. Permitting a large crowd to hear the voices and music was dependent on the perfection of Lee De Forest's audion tube, introduced in 1907.[1]

THE JAZZ SINGER

Sound did not come to theaters unheralded in 1927. Sound effects machines, organists, orchestras, singers, and lecturers had accompanied silent images.[2] But it took Western Electric to develop a viable system for sound on film, which they described to the Warner brothers. The financially strapped Sam, Jack, Albert, and Harry Warner knew that if sound films were successful, their studio could rival Paramount and MGM. And small exhibitors who could not afford orchestras would go for it. In that scenario, the studios could strengthen their hold over exhibitors if they helped them install sound equipment.[3]

Based on their success on August 6, 1926, with *Don Juan,* which had music and sound effects and was preceded by musical shorts and a spoken introduction by the president of the Motion Picture Producers and Distributors of America, Will Hays,[4] the Warners produced *The Jazz Singer.* Because he was perceived as an assimilated Jew, Al Jolson got the lead over George Jessel.[5] The story concerns young New Yorker Jakie Rabinowitz (Al Jolson), who yearns to sing ragtime and jazz rather than accompany his father (Warner Oland) as a cantor in the synagogue. He leaves home and returns as the adult Jack Robin,

21

"It talks like Jakie, but it looks like his shadow"

Filial love or Broadway's call...the jazz singer must decide

The Cantor is sick, will Jakie sing in his stead?

WARNER BROS. present

AL JOLSON

in

"THE JAZZ SINGER"

with

May McAvoy Cantor Rosenblatt
Warner Oland   Eugene Besserer

OTTO LEDERER   RICHARD TUCKER
BOBBY GORDON

Scenario by Al Cohn
Directed by ALAN CROSLAND

A WARNER BROS. EXTENDED RUN PRODUCTION

Jack is signed for a new show and starts rehearsals

Mary pleads that Jack put his career before everything

signed for a musical revue. Attempting to mend fences, he is spurned by his father, but his dad becomes ill and, in dying, causes a major dilemma for Jack: sing the Kol Nidre before the Day of Atonement or appear that night on Broadway.

The film opened in New York's Warner Theatre and was received enthusiastically.

> Mr. Jolson's persuasive vocal efforts were received with rousing applause. In fact, not since the first presentation of Vitaphone features, more than a year ago at the same playhouse, has anything like the ovation been heard in a motion-picture theatre. And when the film came to an end Mr. Jolson himself expressed his sincere appreciation of the Vitaphoned film, declaring that he was so happy that he could not stop the tears.
>
> The Vitaphoned songs and some dialogue have been introduced most adroitly. This in itself is an ambitious move, for in the expression of song the Vitaphone vitalizes the production enormously. The dialogue is not so effective, for it does not always catch the nuances of speech or inflections of the voice so that one is not aware of the mechanical features.
>
> The Warner Brothers astutely realized that a film conception of *The Jazz Singer* was one of the few subjects that would lend itself to the use of the Vitaphone. It was also a happy idea to persuade Mr. Jolson to play the leading role, for few men could have approached the task of singing and acting so well as he does in this photoplay.[6]

The Jazz Singer was still playing there in January 1928. Matinees cost 50 cents. The public didn't care that most of the film was silent. Title cards were much used ("In every living soul, a spirit cries for expression—perhaps this plaintive, wailing song of Jazz is, after all, the misunderstood utterance of a prayer.... Leave my house! I never want to see you again—you jazz singer!"). The songs included "Dirty Hands, Dirty Face," "Toot Toot Tootsie," "Blue Skies," and "Mammy."

It is certainly interesting as a sociological, historical document. The Warner brothers may have used Jolson because he seemed a perfectly Americanized Jew. Yet there is much Jewishness to the film. Mention was made of Jack's duty to his race. The mother (Eugenie Besserer) seems fearful that her son may be in love with a shiksa—a non–Jew. The importance of tradition and Jewish holy days is stressed.

BEGINNINGS OF THE ACADEMY AWARDS

The silent epic *Wings* (1927) was the first Academy of Motion Picture Arts and Sciences best picture winner. Janet Gaynor, age 22, won best actress for three films: *Seventh Heaven, Street Angel,* and *Sunrise.* Emil Jannings won best actor for *The Last Command* and *The Way of All Flesh.*

COMPLAINTS AND PROBLEMS

The motion picture industry was transformed. Warner Bros. became a major studio and its competitors strove to catch up. The public wanted more

Opposite: The Jazz Singer (Warner Bros., 1927).

"talkies." There were, of course, some problems that *The Jazz Singer* made evident. Technically, "there are also times when one would expect the Vita-phoned portions to be either more subdued or stopped as the camera swings to other scenes. The voice is usually just the same whether the image of the singer is close to the camera or quite far away."[7]

Soundstages of wood and cloth were replaced with concrete hangarlike structures. Cameras were encased in soundproof covers ("barneys" or "blimps") to prevent the sound of cranking from blemishing the soundtrack. True stasis was created by weak microphones hidden at the center of the action.

> Until it was put on a mobile boom, and could thus discreetly follow the players, everyone in the shot had to *stand* by it or around it. It was the real cause of the tableau-esque effects which soon made the old silent films seem absolutely bubbling over with *elan* and vitality.[8]

Theater critics objected to talkies because they knew Broadway would lose talent. Movie theater musicians lost their jobs. Stock companies felt the competition.[9] The deaf had no titles to read.[10] Audiences complained about inaudible sound — or sound too loud — and outside traffic noises.

Might not silents coexist with sound films? Perhaps amateurs could make silent movies.[11]

Some had valid points. Aesthetically, "the addition of dialogue did not simply add a dimension to the experience: it replaced an attitude towards it. It shattered the emotional communion between the silent movie and its audience."[12] And, it was said, "The film which in a universal language seldom said anything of importance, gives up its claim to universality the moment it begins to talk in a single tongue."[13]

1928: SOUND HERE TO STAY

Nevertheless, there was no going back — there were too many advantages. Finally there could be offscreen dialogue. There was no need for the title card or the insert of a letter, clock, or calendar to inform the audience of time passing. Composers rushed west for big bucks. So did elocution coaches. What did they find?

> The entire motion picture industry at this time represented an investment of two thousand five hundred million dollars; by far the greater bulk of it comprised the theatre chains owned by the major producer-distributors. . . . In all of the United States in 1928 there were about twenty thousand places showing pictures, producing a gross annual revenue of three hundred and sixty million dollars, although many of these were small or dilapidated theatres, not much advanced from their nickelodeon beginnings in back streets, amusement arcades and fairgrounds.[14]

Lights of New York: In 1928 appeared this first "all-talking" film, a tale of urban youth that makes good despite proximity to cabarets and bootleggers. Of the cast, only Eugene Pallette became a Hollywood mainstay, a gravel-voiced, rotund character actor of many major 30s films.

> It is interesting in an experimental way — showing that it is possible to use vitaphone in a full-length picture, more or less in the manner of the stage.

In *Lights of New York* (Warner Bros., 1928), the first "all-talking" feature, Cullen Davis and Helene Costello stay close so the primitive microphone can pick up their voices.

> It can be classed only as experimental, however, for an audience attempting to take it by any other category of merits would only laugh it away. . . . The picture trundles haltingly along for about a third of its length, and, then, when music and dancing enter, it zooms upward. . . . More care has been lavished on the sound than on the camera's ordinary sphere of activity, for none of the players will better their records by the performances in *Lights of New York*. They all overact at times, underact at others, and do not seem able to forget even momentarily that not only their faces but their voices as well are being taken for posterity. . . . The only evidence of careful direction to be found is in a cabaret scene when a door opens and the music sounds louder. Then, when it closes again, the music grows dim.[15]

EARLY TRIUMPHS

Hallelujah! (1929) was an "all black film" directed by King Vidor on location in Tennessee and Arkansas. After making the film silent, Vidor added the sounds.

> To a motion-picture studio in 1929 this was a fresh and unexplored adventure. We found ourselves making big puddles of water and mud, tramping through them with a microphone while a sound truck recorded the effect. Rotting branches and fallen trees were crawled over; strange birds flew up from the morass. Never one to treat a dramatic effect literally, the thought

struck me—why not free the imagination and record this sequence impressionistically?

When someone stepped on a broken branch, we made it sound as if bones were breaking. As the pursued victim withdrew his foot from the stickiness of the mud, we made the vacuum sound strong enough to pull him down into hell. When a bird called, we made it sound like a hiss or a threat of impending doom, rather than a bird call.[16]

It was "a most impressive audible film with a negro cast. . . . Although it is a talking venture, Mr. Vidor has not permitted sound to interfere with chances for telling photography, and several of the sequences are set forth with flashes of uplifted hands and magnified shadows. The dying gasp of Chick, the wayward wench, is accomplished by realistic horror."[17]

The Great Gabbo (1929) featured "Color Sequences by Multicolor." Erich von Stroheim played a ventriloquist.

Broadway Melody (1929), the first sound best picture Academy Award winner, showed how far sound had come. This was a tale of a midwestern sister act trying their luck on Broadway in a Zanfield (read Ziegfeld) review. The music by Nacio Herb Brown, with lyrics by Arthur Freed, was written specifically for it and included the title tune, "You Were Meant for Me," and "The Wedding of the Painted Doll." The picture opened with aerial shots of New York City minus the not yet completed Empire State Building. Lots of noise was generated at the Gleason Music Publishing Company, where Eddie (Charles King) tries his new tune ("The Broadway Melody") out on the firm's owner, Jimmy Gleason (played by James Gleason, who would survive the rest of the cast as a character actor of innumerable sound films). Dramatic tension was created by the desire of Queenie (Anita Page) to have her own life while her sister Hank (Bessie Love) runs shotgun for her. As the less naive of the pair ("Calories, what are they?" asks Queenie. "Oh-h-h, acrobats, ya big sap!" responds her sister), Hank feels she must protect her sister. Unbeknownst to Hank, her fiancé Eddie falls for Queenie, who tries to resist a reciprocal attraction by dating a wealthy playboy. Some of the chorine tap-dancing routines are a foretaste of what Busby Berkeley would perfect at Warner Bros. in the 30s. Apparently moviemakers were not yet confident with transitional scenes, for title cards were occasionally used. Certainly superfluous was one that indicated a time change to Queenie's party that night. Did the filmmakers believe the moviegoers would think the party someone else's?

BANKERS AND THE DEPRESSION

By 1929, although the West Coast studios were consolidating their positions (traffic noise in New York helped the western site) and East Coast retrenchment was being aborted, eastern bankers were taking control of the commercial film industry. Their loans had been vital to the talkie revolution. By 1929, forty-plus banking and electrical company presidents were on the boards of the ten largest film companies.[18]

The stock market crash on October 29, 1929, preceded by a depression in

Broadway Melody (Metro-Goldwyn-Mayer, 1929) starred Bessie Love and Charles King. It was the second film and the first talkie to win the best picture Academy Award.

agriculture, coal mining, railroads, and textiles, did not start in time to hinder loans to studios. If it had, it might have stalled talkies and led to television instead.[19] Wide-screen movies might have come then, but exhibitors could not afford to install more new equipment and screens.[20]

DIRECTORS RESURGENT

The power that directors lost to studios with the coming of sound was regained to some extent by strong-willed, visionary directors like John Ford, Raoul Walsh, King Vidor, William Wyler, Frank Capra, and Victor Fleming. "These men were confident iconoclasts. They were natural story-tellers. They were action-conscious. They were self-dramatising."[21]

STARS

Some silent stars hit the skids because of poor voices. John Gilbert is the most famous example. Yet Gilbert projected well in the 1933 *Queen Christina*. Although lousy films and personal reasons contributed to his decline,[22] his demise was the result of the novelty of the audience's hearing intimate love talk for the first time: the performers made public exhibitions of themselves to a modest public.[23] These views were supported by King Vidor: "Admittedly Jack's speaking voice on the sound track was a problem, but I don't think it was a question of tone or quality. The literal content of his scenes, which in silent films had been imagined, was too intense to put into spoken words."[24]

Swiss-born Emil Jannings' German accent prevented him from moving to English-language sound films. He returned to Europe, achieving success in *The Blue Angel*. Perhaps Louise Brooks' decline was due to her voice. It was dubbed in 1929 for *The Canary Murder Case*.[25] Gloria Swanson's career came to a standstill because her sound films failed financially.[26] Lon Chaney, the "Man of a Thousand Faces," who had been a master of makeup and pantomime in many films such as *The Hunchback of Notre Dame* (1923) and *The Phantom of the Opera* (1925), died on August 6, 1930, of throat cancer.

On a more successful note, Broadway star Jeanne Eagles (*Rain*) came to Hollywood for *The Letter* (1929). Broadway's Ruth Chatterton (*Daddy Long Legs*) made two 1929 films, *Sins of the Fathers* and *Madame X*.

Even more fortunate were the Marx Brothers (Groucho, Harpo, Chico, and Zeppo), who made their screen debut in 1929 in *The Cocoanuts*, which featured the infamous "Why a duck?" (viaduct) routine. Chico was also described as an "idle roomer." He had come from Italy, says he — on the Atlantic Auction. An operatic parody features the cast singing "I Want My Shirt" to the overture to *Carmen*. An overhead shot of dancing girls prefigured Busby Berkeley's Warner Bros. 30s extravaganzas.

George Arliss lent status and prestige to biographies like the 1929 *Disraeli*. From a small role, in 1927, in *Wings,* Gary Cooper moved well to sound. In 1929 he played Owen Wister's hero *The Virginian* and uttered the famous line to Walter Huston's Trampas, "If you wanna call me that, smile."

BRITAIN'S CONTRIBUTION: ALFRED HITCHCOCK

Blackmail was about a flirtation turned tragic when the man (Cyril Ritchard, later Captain Hook to Mary Martin's Peter Pan) attempted date rape and was killed by the object of his desire (Anny Ondra). A lowlife (Donald Calthrop) found her out and tried to gain financially but was thwarted by the girl's steady boyfriend, a policeman. *Blackmail* was originally shot as a silent until it was realized it would suffer at the boxoffice. Some of it was reshot with the camera in a soundproof booth. For several minutes into the film there is no dialogue, just the sounds of music, breaking glass, truck horns, and other street noises. Anny Ondra was a German whose English was so poor that Joan Barry dubbed her lines simultaneously by staying out of reach of the camera.[27] A striking scene shows an immense ancient statue in the British Museum, past which the blackmailer descends on a rope during his desperate escape attempt. Heights as well as a staircase figure prominently, as they would in later Hitchcock films like *Notorious* and *Psycho*. Note that Hitchcock appears in the film, as would become his wont, this time on a train, where he takes abuse from a boy in the next seat. An American review was mostly complimentary.

> The diction of the players is very English but none the less pleasing and suitable to the chronicle. Its continuity is smooth, the narrative being told without any extravagant flourishes, and the performances of the players reveal

that two or three of them could do even better work.... The photography is seldom up to American standards, for the director, Alfred Hitchcock, frequently fails to see that his scenes are adequately lighted and more often than not the images do not stand out as distinctly as they might if more attention had been paid to the shading of the interior walls.[28]

Chapter 3

The Golden Age,
1930–1939

So night after night the Faithful would gather, bearing sacks of Butterfinger bars and salami sandwiches, to huddle together in the
darkness, cradled in Mr. Doppler's gum-encrusted seats, staring
with eyes wide with longing and lit with the pure light of total
belief at the flicking image of Ginger Rogers, dressed in a long,
flowing, sequin-covered gown, swirling endlessly atop a piano with
wasp-waisted Fred Astaire, flicking an ivory cane carelessly and spin-
ning his tall silk hat as he sang, in a high, squeaky voice, "The
Carioca." In the darkness the sound of girdles creaking in desire and
the cracking of Wrigley's Spearmint in excitement provided a soft
but subtle counterpoint to Sam Goldwyn's hissing sound track.
    —Jean Shepherd, *In God We Trust, All Others Pay Cash*

The first decade of an artistic movement usually contains its most original
and pleasing elements. So it was with the sound cinema. "Film needed the
stimulus of a disordered and slightly hysterical period to discover its true
potential, as its first great advances had been made under the complex social
pressures of Germany after the First World War."[1] For variety, dynamism, star
power, and behind-the-scenes expertise, the 30s truly deserve the oft-used title
the Golden Age. Would it have been even more lustrous had not the Production Code been implemented in 1934? Or did the Code energize filmmakers
who, through subtlety and ploy, circumvented censors? Conveniently, the
decade is bounded by the outbreak of World War II. The greatest year in film
history is widely identified as 1939.

HOLLYWOOD COMES OF AGE

Even though the country and world were undergoing a depression,
Hollywood did not feel its effects for several years. When theater attendance
dropped, entrepreneurs instituted various schemes to raise it, including giving
out gifts of dinnerware or radios and holding amateur nights on stage. Most
successful was "bank night," when patrons would sign a book in the lobby and

collect cash if their number was drawn. It was so popular that its Colorado founder copyrighted the technique and sold franchises.[2]

Although sound had supplanted its progenitor with one fell swoop, complaints continued about the destruction of the art of silent films and the uninspired, theatrical way in which Hollywood used the new techniques. Not long before, in Alfred Hitchcock's 1930 film *Enter Sir John*, Herbert Marshall listened to a radio while shaving. The music was provided by a hidden 30-piece orchestra.[3] As late as 1932, "By many of the supposed champions of cinematic art dialogue is still held to be an abomination. . . . No representation of life in a talking picture can ever be convincing so long as it carries the hall-mark of the stage battle of words."[4]

But techniques were improving, thanks to studio resources. Under the aegis of production heads like Irving Thalberg and David O. Selznick, studios became all important, turning out product in an almost assembly-line manner. The breaking of the Motion Picture Patents Company monopoly and the increase in studio power lessened the influence of the independent producer-director for the second time. Thus United Artists, founded in 1919 by Pickford, Fairbanks, Chaplin, and Griffith, remained a viable alternative for creative artists.

Because Europe was a major market for American films, some of the Europeans who came to the United States helped dub Hollywood films for overseas. German dramatist Walter Hasenclever arrived in the United States in June 1930 to provide German dialogue for *Anna Christie, The Trial of Mary Dugan,* and *The Big House.*[5]

The lure of money and — by mid-decade — the fear of Hitler prompted a number of Central European directors to flee fascism. As with the atomic scientists, Continental Europe's artists left behind a void. Hungary alone was the birthplace of several executives already in the United States, like Adolph Zukor and William Fox, producer Joe Pasternak, and director Michael Curtiz, who were joined by actor Peter Lorre and character actor S. Z. "Cuddles" Sakall. Emeric Pressburger set up shop in Britain as Michael Powell's collaborator. Composer Miklos Rozsa left Hungary and scored major British 30s films like *Knight without Armor* and *The Four Feathers* before he settled in the United States in the 1940s.

Fritz Lang, director of the silent German classics *Metropolis* and *M*, came over in the 30s. He talked about the difference between European and Hollywood filmmaking, describing 20th Century–Fox's excellent facilities.

> That was the great difference between Europe and America: Hollywood's mechanical superiority. In Europe, for example, we didn't know what a crane was. We had quite different lights. I remember that on *M* I wanted to have a camera follow someone down a staircase, but we had no way of doing it. So we took a chassis — four wheels with ball-bearings — and in front of it we put a very long two-by-four, and at the end of the two-by-four we put the camera, and that was our crane.[6]

From Rumania came artist Jean Negulesco. Paramount director Frank Tuttle, who was pleased with Negulesco's sketches for the opening of *Tonight We Sing,* gave him his break.

> He took me to meet Benjamin Glazer, the producer. I was engaged on the spot. Seventy-five dollars a week! (Every week? Oh, yes, every week.) I was part of a project in a big studio. Every morning I was early on the set, stumbling over electric cables, asking questions which made no sense. But I was on the floor with *stars* and writers, director, cameraman, and operators, the sound man, the boom man, the prop man, the grips, the extras. I went to lunch with them. I listened to their wonderful talk. *I was one of them.*[7]

Negulesco rose to second unit director on *A Farewell to Arms* (1934) and *Captain Blood* (1935).

> The director is working with the stars, getting the desired dramatic or comic performance out of them. But when the setting of their action has to be, say, the sinking of a ship, the burning of a building, a great crowd running or fighting, or a vast cattle drive, the second unit takes on the job. And its director has to use all kinds of ingenuity and artistic and managerial skill to produce the desired effect, as in *Ben-Hur, Titanic,* and *Red River.* So often the whole distinction of a picture may be in the hands of that little group of real movie professionals, the second unit.[8]

BRITISH "INTERNATIONAL" FILMS

While the 1932 *Cavalcade* was a Fox film made in the United States, its theme was British. Clive Brook starred with Diana Wynyard in a panoramic picture of English life that won a best picture Academy Award.

> Never for an instant is the story, which takes one through three decades of life in England, lost sight of, notwithstanding the inclusion of remarkable scenes of throngs in war and peace, and it is a relief to observe that the obvious is left to the spectator.... Miss Wynyard is excellent as Jane Marryot. She portrays her role with such sympathy and feeling that one scarcely thinks of her as an actress.[9]

The Private Life of Henry VIII (1933) won Charles Laughton an Academy Award. It was "the first truly international British picture, and the foundation of this country's best years in the cinema."[10] In 1953 Laughton would again play Henry in *Young Bess. Rembrandt* (1936) was a personal but not commercial success for Laughton.

The science fiction epic of world war and space travel, *Things to Come* (1936), was based on H. G. Wells' novel. "And now for the rule of the airmen and a new life for mankind," said John Cabal (Raymond Massey). "The best of life, Passworthy, lies closest to the edge of death," said Oswald Cabal (also Massey).

Alfred Hitchcock had his biggest successes to date. *The 39 Steps* (1935) was based on the novel by John Buchan, whose hero, Richard Hannay, also appeared in the books *Greenmantle* and *The Three Hostages.* Robert Donat played the Canadian Hannay, innocent bystander (like many Hitchcock protagonists) who gives assistance in London to a frightened woman, only to find her dead in the morning. Both police and criminals pursue him — another common Hitchcock touch. In Scotland Hannay finds himself handcuffed to blond and beautiful Pamela (Madeleine Carroll), but convinces her of his innocence and his goal of unmasking a spy. Back at a London music hall, he realizes that entertainer Mr. Memory (Wylie Watson) is the key to the plane engine design sought by Britain's enemies.

The Lady Vanishes (1938) tells the story of Miss Froy (Dame May Whitty), an unlikely British spy who disappears on a Continental train leaving Central Europe. Only Iris Henderson (Margaret Lockwood) knows she is on board. Music aficionado Gilbert (Michael Redgrave) helps her locate the lady and foil pseudo–Nazi villain Dr. Hartz (Paul Lukas). Cricket fanciers Naunton Wayne and Basil Radford provide comic relief and British common sense. Early in the film Michael Redgrave hums what we have come to know as the "Colonel Bogey March."

> That the elements of a Hitchcock melodrama provoke an excitement utterly lacking when the same elements are combined by less skillful directors is due to Director Hitchcock's unique talent for cinematic story construction and his unparalleled diligence in employing it. Before a Hitchcock picture goes before the cameras, it has been written four times; by Hitchcock himself, by Hitchcock and a scenario writer, by Hitchcock and a dialogue writer, and finally by Hitchcock and his wife, Alma Reville. . . . More popular in England than in the U.S., Hitchcock pictures like *The 39 Steps, Secret Agent* are often too intricately built and written to appeal to mass audiences. To connoisseurs of spy melodrama, they rate as classics, and play steady revival engagements in Manhatten and London.[11]

Margaret Lockwood, Wayne, and Radford would get the opportunity to make a similar film in 1940, *Night Train to Munich.* This time Nazis were called Nazis. Paul von Hernreid was the bad guy. Contrast his character with the freedom fighter he would play in the 1942 *Casablanca,* after he had changed his stage name to Paul Henreid.

Pygmalion (1938) was a rather perfect film version of George Bernard Shaw's play, well known now as the musical *My Fair Lady.* Shaw himself contributed to the script and won an Academy Award. Leslie Howard played Professor Higgins, Wendy Hiller, the cockney guttersnipe Eliza Doolittle.

CENSORSHIP: PRODUCTION CODE AND LEGION OF DECENCY

Mae West's saucy films were some of the straws that broke the camel's back. She took to adding scenes she knew would be cut so others would remain.[12] In the 1933 *She Done Him Wrong* she played Lucky Lou, a bejeweled singer in a Bowery emporium of the gay 90s. Double entendres were rife: "One of the finest women ever walked the streets," "There was a time I didn't know where my next husband was coming from," "When women go wrong, men go right after them," "Ya know I, I always did like a man in a uniform and that one fits you grand. Why don't you come up sometime and see me. I'm home every evening," "Come up, I'll tell your fortune. Ah, you can be had," and "Oh I don't know. Hands ain't everything."

President Harding's Postmaster General Will Hays had been appointed head of the Motion Picture Producers and Distributors of America, Inc., in 1922. The MPPDA had been established in response to movieland scandals like the Fatty Arbuckle rape-murder case and Wallace Reid's drug addiction and death.

A simplistic analogy casts Will Hays as Al Capone, Joe Breen as enforcer Frank Nitti, and the acquiescors the studio moguls. On the positive side, it was a successful attempt to forestall federal intervention and placate state censor boards and force many writers and directors to be more creative. On the negative side, it kept citizens in the dark about how the real world worked. "In practice, what the Code calls 'pure love' is pure because it is passionless; in day-to-day operations, the Code authority eliminates scenes of passion, and human nature and its normal reactions are not honestly acknowledged. Perhaps the most degrading effect of the Code is the mean and mawkish concept of marriage it has forced upon the movies."[13]

The Production Code's foreword:

> Motion picture producers recognize the high trust and confidence that have been placed in them by the people of the world and that have made motion pictures a universal form of entertainment.
>
> They recognize their responsibility to the public because of this trust and because entertainment and art are important influences in the life of a nation.
>
> Hence, though regarding motion pictures primarily as entertainment without any explicit purposes of teaching or propaganda, they know that the motion picture within its own field of entertainment may be directly responsible for spiritual or moral progress, for higher types of social life, and for much correct thinking.
>
> On their part, they ask from the public and from public leaders a sympathetic understanding of the problems inherent in motion picture production and a spirit of cooperation that will allow the opportunity necessary to bring the motion picture to a still higher level of wholesome entertainment for all concerned.[14]

Not only were filthy movies to be eliminated, but "compensating moral values" had to remain in the films.[15]

> "Joe Breen and his merry men," as [Val] Lewton called them, found something morally objectionable in virtually every SIP [Selznick International Pictures] project. Heavy lobbying had been necessary on A Star Is Born, for instance, to convince Breen that the ill-fated hero's alcoholism and philandering were essential to his characterization. Zenda caused problems due to an illegitimate birth that occurred several generations before the story takes place—a seemingly innocuous plot point but a necessary one, since it explains the physical similarities between the vacationing Brit and the Ruritanian monarch. Breen was concerned, however, that there was no indication in the story that the long-dead fornicators had suffered "moral retribution" for their sin.[16]

The Legion of Decency was formed by the Catholic Church in 1934. The original pledge of those who abided by its ratings began,

> I wish to join the Legion of Decency, which condemns vile and unwholesome moving pictures. I unite with all who protest against them as a grave menace to youth, to home life, to country and to religion.

Pygmalion (General Film Distributors, 1938) was an impeccable screen version of Bernard Shaw's play which became the musical *My Fair Lady*. From left: Esme Percy, Leslie Howard, Scott Sunderland, Wendy Hiller, Irene Browne.

> I condemn absolutely those salacious motion pictures which, with other degrading agencies, are corrupting public morals and promoting a sex mania in our land.[17]

That same year the pledge was revised from six to three paragraphs. "Crime and criminals" were stressed, "sex mania" removed. In 1965 the pledge was shortened to one paragraph:

> I promise to promote by word and deed what is morally and artistically good in motion picture entertainment. I promise to discourage by my good example and always in a responsible and civic-minded manner.

The Legion of Decency ratings in 1936 were A-1, Morally Unobjectionable for General Patronage; A-2, Morally Unobjectionable for Adults; B, Morally Objectionable in Part for All; C, Condemned. A separate classification explained certain films to the uninformed.[18]

In Britain the president of the Board of Film Censors was paid the equivalent of $10,000 a year by the film industry. His and the secretary's purpose was deemed by some "to keep people from thinking about what might upset them." The Board praised respect and frowned upon depiction of mental disorders, impending childbirth, drunken women, animal cruelty, miscegenation, nice criminals, police brutality, and the Royal Family.[19]

GENRES

Filming in genres—subject areas—was an easy way for studios to predict returns, a simple means to market to the audience. Comedy, though, surfaced in a variety of formats: screwball, sophisticated, and madcap-irreverent-anarchic.

Screwball comedy was exemplified by such films as *The Awful Truth* (Columbia, 1937), with Cary Grant and Irene Dunne as Jerry and Lucy Warriner. In *Bringing Up Baby* (RKO, 1938), Grant was paleontologist David Huxley, Katharine Hepburn the rich Susan. Baby was a leopard. "Again and again, after no matter how many viewings, the spectator is delighted by small touches of comic business often beyond the critic's reach, since they defy verbal description: matters of gesture, expression, intonation."[20]

> The titles are familiar: *It Happened One Night, Mr. Deeds Goes to Town, My Man Godfrey, You Can't Take It with You, Easy Living, Nothing Sacred,* and *The Awful Truth* have endured the years with grace and verve. And for good reason. They were (and remain) very funny, perfectly paced, and alive with good humor and terrific people.... But the overwhelming attractiveness of the screwball comedies involved more than the wonderful personnel. It had to do with the effort they made at reconciling the irreconcilable. They created an American of perfect unity: all classes as one, the rural-urban divide breached, love and decency and neighborliness ascendant.[21]

> Unlike the backstage musical, the western, or the monster horror, screwball comedy isn't immediately self-defining by setting or characters. It is allotropic, made of so many parts that there is no absolute screwballer as *42nd Street* is the absolute backstager, *She Wore a Yellow Ribbon* the absolute cavalry-post western, or *Frankenstein* the absolute monster picture. Screwball is usually a contemporary courtship tale with a witty script that favors the fashionable classes and instructs us to enjoy life in our own way rather than observe rules on love and work laid down by others.... Elements of screwball informed literally hundreds of Hollywood comedies, from about 1932 to 1943, so the form stayed elastic and vital.[22]

Columbia and RKO excelled at screwball. In 1934 director Frank Capra hit the big time with *It Happened One Night*. The film was the successful attempt of the director and Columbia Studios' chieftain Harry Cohn to break into the inner circle, which they did by winning Academy Awards.

> Working at a Poverty Row studio proscribed him [Capra] from being considered for an Oscar, yet getting an Oscar was the fastest, perhaps the only, way of elevating the studio's status—and his own. In an industry where evaluating quality was always a slippery thing, the Oscars were avidly pursued because they were about the only certification of value one had, and they had escalated from a casual dinner dance where winners were announced at the end of the evening to a fierce competition, where studios bullied their employees to vote in blocks for the company's nominees. The spoils were prestige, which, among the Hollywood Jews, was nearly everything.[23]

Ironically, the script had been rejected until the main characters were changed. Clark Gable had to be loaned from MGM. Claudette Colbert

It Happened One Night (Columbia, 1934).

doubted the studio would meet her salary demands, but they did. What resulted were Academy Awards for best picture, best actor, best actress, best screenplay, and best director.[24]

Colbert typified the Capra female, Gable the Capra man. "The Capraesque women stood for a Depression mentality, fearful but resolute; the Capraesque man was America before the Depression, heedless, boisterous, headed toward catastrophe. The task of the two characters was to come to understand and love each other by the end."[25]

Nothing Sacred (1937) was a nonauteur comedy. William Wellman directed from a script devised by producer David O. Selznick and writers George Oppenheimer, Budd Schulberg, Ring Lardner, *and* Ben Hecht.[26] A reporter (Fredric March) is sent to a small town to make hay out of the case of the presumably dying young lady (Carole Lombard). Lombard was but one of many talented women who served screwball grandly.

Irene Dunne was a major screwball star of *My Favorite Wife, Theodora*

Goes Wild, and *The Awful Truth,* but she was much more — witness her singing role as Magnolia in 1936, in *Show Boat.* "Irene Dunne is a lady — right to the tip of her patrician nose. Maybe that's why we always liked her when she was pretending to be unladylike — as a repressed Theodora going wild ... a lively divorcee impersonating a dese-dem-and-dose chorine in *The Awful Truth* ... a worldly-wise girl in *Love Affair.*"[27]

Jean Arthur found her forte in such films. She evinced an "insouciance, easy wit, or working-girl grace that made Jean Arthur the most accomplished and affecting comic actress of the thirties and early forties."[28] She was strong. "How alone can you be if Jean Arthur's on your side?"[29] She was comfortable. "Jean Arthur ... had the most wonderful speaking voice anyone had ever heard: she was the one movie star men could actually visualize marrying."[30]

Myrna Loy could be the second female lead in the 1932 *Love Me Tonight* and *The Mask of Fu Manchu,* but her star rose in 1934 when she paired with William Powell in *The Thin Man.* "Myrna Loy was hip twenty-five years before 'hip' became an adjective. She was the original cool cat.... (Yes, you could be warm and cool all at once — at least, Myrna Loy could.)"[31]

In addition to *It Happened One Night,* Claudette Colbert added her charm to *The Gilded Lily* (1935) and the 1942 *The Palm Beach Story.*

Certain directors were particularly adept at screwball and attuned to the strengths of the leading ladies.

> The romantic-comedy directors, on the other hand [as opposed to erotic melodrama directors like Sternberg and Brown], brought a style of male-female collaboration into the movies that hadn't yet been seen (except, perhaps, on the earliest movie sets where D. W. Griffith and his young actresses invented the whole art of screen acting). Capra and company treated their leading ladies not as icons of femininity but as companions. This choice wasn't so much a question of methodology as of psychology: these were men who didn't shrink from imagining what it might feel like to be a woman. Their portraits of romance, therefore, turned out wittier and fairer than Brown's or Sternberg's, and just as lyrical.[32]

Sophisticated comedy was defined by director Ernst Lubitsch. The Lubitsch Touch described the wit and sophistication manifest definitively in Paramount's 1932 production *Trouble in Paradise,* in which Continental jewel thieves Herbert Marshall and Miriam Hopkins try to outwit widowed perfume heiress Kay Francis.

Frantic-irreverent-anarchic comedy had several gifted representatives: a middle-aged man, an incongruous duo, a weird team, and a self-sufficient woman. W. C. Fields was the vaudevillian still known as the man who disliked dogs and children. His first feature was 1925's *Sally of the Sawdust,* directed by D. W. Griffith. *It's a Gift* (1934) was possibly his finest sound feature.

British-born Stan Laurel and Georgian Oliver Hardy continued their successful collaboration, concentrating on features rather than the two-reelers for which they were famous. *Sons of the Desert* (1933) was perhaps their best sound film. There seems little doubt that Laurel and Hardy remain the best loved comedy team of all time.

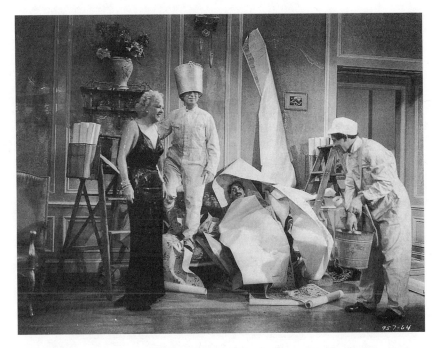

After bashing convention at Paramount, the Marx brothers transferred their mayhem to Metro-Goldwyn-Mayer where one of their classics was the 1937 *A Day at the Races.* Harpo is under the bucket, Groucho is beneath the wallpaper, while Chico and Esther Muir look on.

The Marx brothers had begun at Paramount with the adaptation of their stage success *The Cocoanuts* (1929). The classics *Animal Crackers* (1930), *Monkey Business* (1931), *Horse Feathers* (1932), and *Duck Soup* (1933) followed. The Marxes moved to MGM for *A Night at the Opera* (1935) and *A Day at the Races* (1937)—classic themselves, but films that suffered because "their helter-skelter is mapped, centered, reproved; their films have been turned into musicals with love plots; and, worst of all, the anarchical nature of their comix has been turned around so that now the Marx Brothers are salubrious and even sentimental."[33] An alternate view contends that at MGM the brothers benefited from, in particular, Sam Wood's direction and attention to supporting players and musical interludes. In short, the films were better for being smoother.[34]

Mae West, the bawdy stage star, made her Hollywood debut at age forty in 1932 in *Night after Night. She Done Him Wrong* and *I'm No Angel* followed in 1933 and irked the censors.

> Her relentless search for good times was straightforward and nonexperimental: she took her men unmarried, one at a time. She did not take sex for granted, or take her audience beyond the very familiar. Sex was laughed at and brought in the open: continental sophistication had nothing to do with

The hated mirror perturbs Bela Lugosi in *Dracula* (Universal, 1931). His nemesis is Edward Van Sloan, who was also a foe of Frankenstein's monster and the mummy.

her success. The "strong, confident woman, always in command," emerged from her films, not from Lubitsch's brilliant directorial exercises.[35]

Horror: The Great Depression made the 30s a time of horror on the screen as well as in real life. In *The Bride of Frankenstein* (1935), when Dr. Pretorius (Ernest Thesiger) toasted "To a new world, of gods and monsters!" he spoke for a decade of supernatural monstrosities. German and Gothic influences predominated, and the sets were influenced by silent German expressionist films such as *The Cabinet of Caligari* and *Metropolis*. Universal became *the* studio for the supernatural. (Dr. Frankenstein's experiments *are* science fiction in a sense, but extraterrestrial science fiction after Méliès is two decades away.) *Dracula* kicked off the cycle in 1931, followed the same year by *Frankenstein*, *The Mummy* (1932), *The Invisible Man* (1933), and *Werewolf of London* (1935). The most famous lycanthrope film, in which the gypsy woman Maria Ouspenskaya, pentagrams, silver bullets, and all the paraphernalia come into play, does not occur until 1941 in *The Wolf Man*. ("Even a man who is pure at heart and says his prayers by night may become a wolf when the wolfbane blooms and the autumn moon is bright," warned Evelyn Ankers *and* Claude Rains.)

Bela Lugosi, who had played Bram Stoker's famous vampire count on stage, got the role on film. *Dracula* is at its best in the early going. The

The unholy creation (Boris Karloff, left) attempts to take revenge on his maker (Colin Clive) in *Frankenstein* (Universal, 1932), based on Mary Shelley's novel of 1818.

Transylvanian whistle-stop's innkeeper warnings to Renfield (Dwight Frye) are suitably ominous. The castle is superb. Once the action moves to London, however, the film slows and becomes stagey. Nonetheless, Bela became Dracula for several generations of filmgoers. "I never drink—wine." To this day, Stoker's character—his appearance and abilities—have never really been 'fully exploited.

    Frankenstein was Colin Clive, desirous of creating life from pieces of corpses stitched together and infused with the life force: lightning. Careless, he employed a hunchback (Dwight Frye) as his assistant, who, stealing but breaking a jar with the good brain, settles for a criminal brain. "It's alive!" screams Frankenstein as the bandaged figure raises its arm. Later, unbound, the hulking figure sits beneath the skylight as its creator opens the portal and sunlight streams in. The creature reaches pathetically for the light. Taunted by the hunchback brandishing a flaming torch, the monster kills for the first time. Dr. Waldman (Edward Van Sloan) and Frankenstein subdue it, but Waldman is killed attempting to surgically dismantle it. Escaping, the monster meets a little girl and plays with her flowers. The infamous scene of the monster tossing her into the water when the flowers are gone was excised from original prints and only recently restored. Cornered in a windmill by his maker, the monster tosses his creator off the top onto the revolving blades, and the villagers set fire to the mill. Boris Karloff, billed only as the Monster, became a star who would portray the creature twice more.

In *The Bride of Frankenstein* (1935) the action picked up at the windmill. The monster is not dead but burned and scarred from a fall into the water beneath the mill. When the villagers leave he ascends, wanders off, and meets a blind hermit (O. P. Heggie). In a justly famous scene, the monster partakes of food, wine, and, somewhat reluctantly, a cigar ("Food good, food good!"). Hunters come upon the cabin, the monster runs off, is captured again but escapes and meets Dr. Pretorius (Ernest Thesiger), another "scientist." With the monster as his enforcer, Pretorius blackmails the recovered Dr. Frankenstein into creating a bride for the monster. The female is duly made but evidences little interest in its male counterpart. Whether viewed as a black comedy or a straight horror film, *The Bride of Frankenstein* has enough visual and aural elements to satisfy any taste: the vicious killing of a man and his wife in the windmill ruins, the pathos of monster and blind man, the peasant horde, the castle lab, the electrified hairdo of Elsa Lanchester. Franz Waxman, from Upper Silesia in Central Europe, wrote his first American film score for *The Bride of Frankenstein*. It was so good, Universal extracted large chunks for other films and serials.

Valerie Hobson was the real bride of Dr. Frankenstein. Just 17 when she came over from England, she also played Henry Hull's wife in the same year in *Werewolf of London*. (Warner Oland, who would play Charlie Chan, was Dr. Yogami and created the cliché "But remember this, Dr. Glendon. The werewolf instinctively seeks to kill the thing it loves best.")

Boris Karloff and Bela Lugosi teamed several times. In *The Black Cat* (1934) Karloff was the villain, married to Bela's daughter and custodian of Bela's dead wife. Eventually Bela (Dr. Vitus Verdegast) has enough of the devil worshiper.

> Do you know what I'm going to do to you now? No? Did you ever see an animal skinned, Hjalmar? That's what I'm going to do to you now. Tear the skin from your body. Slowly, bit by bit.

The film was additionally notable for its modernistic architecture.

In *The Raven* (1935) Bela was crushed in a room of moving walls by erstwhile minion Boris. Boris got back in 1936 in *The Invisible Ray* when he touched Bela with his radium-infected self. Bela performed great screams and groans.

Lugosi had turned down the role of the monster in *Frankenstein* because it had no dialogue. He did play the monster in one of the many sequels, *Frankenstein Meets the Wolf Man* (1943). In *Son of Frankenstein* (1939) Bela had one of his best roles as the broken-necked Ygor, who brought the dormant body of the monster to the attention of Dr. Frankenstein's scion, Wolf, played by Basil Rathbone.

Warner Bros. dabbled successfully in the supernatural and pseudo-preternatural with sterling entries like *Doctor X* (1932) and *The Mystery of the Wax Museum* (1933). In the former, Doctor Xavier (Lionel Atwill) helps the police determine which of his researchers at the Academy of Surgical Research is responsible for the viscous murders. Applying a viscous substance — synthetic flesh — to his body, Dr. Wells (Preston Foster) murders and mutilates, hoping to use his knowledge to help the world's cripples! A reporter (Lee Tracy) helps rescue Xavier's daughter — Fay Wray. In *Wax Museum,* Wray was menaced by mad sculptor Henry Jarrod (Lionel Atwill!).

King Kong (1933) was the audacious brainchild of Merian C. Cooper and Ernest Schoedsack. Fay Wray was Ann Darrow; Robert Armstrong, Carl Denham; Bruce Cabot, John Driscoll; Frank Reicher, Captain Engelhorn; and Noble Johnson, the native chief. Willis O'Brien was the special effects man who had begun in silent days with such as *The Lost World.* "What's he really think she's gonna see?" asks Driscoll as filmmaker Denham makes test shots on the ship that is sailing for a previously uncharted isle. The island's native tribe's ancestors had built an immense wall to hold back giant ape Kong and the prehistoric creatures for whom time had stood still. Capturing Ann, the natives sacrifice her to Kong. Smitten with the blond beauty, he carries her off to his mountain lair. A stegosaurus, brontosaurus (apatosaurus), and other creatures hinder their way. Only Denham and Driscoll, with Ann in tow, return. Using gas bombs, they capture Kong and display him in New York — not securely, however; the beast breaks free when it thinks Ann is being hurt by reporters' flashbulbs. After wrecking an elevated train and finding Ann, he ascends the Empire State Building (which had been completed in 1931) and meets his doom. Max Steiner produced a seminal music score. The stop-motion special effects and matte paintings — which created the battle between Kong and the tyrannosaurus and the view from Kong's precipice of the island, the wall, and moored ship — were never equaled.

United Artists gave us Bela Lugosi in 1932 in *White Zombie,* which for years was a "lost" film. Clarence Muse, singer, radio and vaudeville performer as well as attorney, played a coach driver who gave the best description:

> Yes, monsieur. Zombies. The living dead. Corpses taken from their graves or made to work in the sugar mill or fields at night. Look! Here they come!

History and Adventure: Historical and adventure films were popular, allowing much license for those wishing to exploit sex and violence, especially in movies about ancient times. Cecil B. DeMille changed course and for the rest of his career devoted his filmmaking talents to epic stories that usually explored pagan and biblical themes. *The Sign of the Cross* (1932) was, according to one advertisement, "a picture which will proudly lead all the entertainments the world has ever seen. Cecil B. DeMille's Superb Road-Show Dramatic Spectacle." When it premiered the *New York Times* advertisement said, "Cecil B. DeMille's *The Sign of the Cross* is a Paramount Picture. Paramount in Spectacle! Paramount in Appeal! Paramount in its Swift Action! Paramount in Technical Skill! with FOUR STARS. Fredric March, Elissa Landi, Claudette Colbert, Charles Laughton. Assisted by 7500 Others." It played two shows a day at the Rialto, where from Monday to Friday the orchestra seats cost $1.00.

Fay Wray and Bruce Cabot are hauled up by *King Kong* (RKO, 1933). The most famous movie "monster" of all time was for the most part a miniature made real via Willis O'Brien's stop-motion photography.

On Saturdays, Sundays and holidays they cost $1.50, balcony seats were $1.00. A reviewer remarked:

> No DeMille picture would be complete without some suggestion of a bathtub, and here this director goes himself one better by having a small swimming pool filled with the milk from asses. It is the wont of Nero's wife, Poppaea, to revel in this pool and, as another touch from the master of

Madame Satan (Metro-Goldwyn-Mayer, 1930) was director Cecil B. DeMille's second sound film. Singer and stage star Lillian Roth, who would be played by Susan Hayward in 1955's *I'll Cry Tomorrow,* co-starred in a love triangle story climaxed by a dirigible explosion.

Hollywood, one beholds first one cat and then another beside the pool lapping the milk. . . .

This picture is staged impressively and finely photographed. There is an abundance of imagination throughout its scenes and the story is well told. One feels, however, that the players must have been relieved when the production was finished, for all work hard and thoroughly, even to those who merely figure for an instant or so in a death scene in the arena or the more fortunate who are spatting about their seats. . . . Miss Colbert is capital as the seductive Empress who is enamored of the handsome Marcus.[36]

Colbert was also at home as *Cleopatra* (1934), with Warren William as Caesar and another DeMille regular, Henry Wilcoxon, as Antony ("There's no room in Rome for Octavian and me!"). DeMille moved ahead in time for *The Crusades* (1935), again with Wilcoxon, this time as Richard the Lionheart battling Saladin for control of the Holy Land during the Third Crusade. Ernest Schoedsack's *The Last Days of Pompeii* (1935) starred Preston Foster as a blacksmith turned gladiator. The highlight, of course, was the eruption of Vesuvius.

British Empire: The empire on which the sun never set received comprehensive treatment in the 30s. The Elizabethan age was granted exceptional space.

> If there is one historic era from which Hollywood emerged with flying colours, to say nothing of blaring trumpets and thundering cannon, it was the Elizabethan Age. . . . They did Elizabeth proud; no historic figure has been represented more honestly in the cinema, or better served by her players; so far as we can know that remarkable woman, arguably the best ruler England ever had, her images on film seem to be faithful to the original. Secondly, the best of the Elizabethan movies caught the spirit of the age, when English adventurers began to look to the horizon with piratical exuberance, challenged the Spanish Goliath, and created a legend that still shines down the centuries.[37]

Flora Robson portrayed Queen Elizabeth I in *Fire over England* (1937) and *The Sea Hawk* (1940). Bette Davis was Bess in *The Private Lives of Elizabeth and Essex* (1939) and in *The Virgin Queen* (1955).

Clive of India (1935) had arresting camera angles and cutting. Ronald Colman played Robert Clive, who asserted British interests in 18th century India and won the Battle of Plassy in June 1757. *Lives of a Bengal Lancer* (1935) was a pageant of 19th century that starred Gary Cooper, Franchot Tone, and crusty commandant C. Aubrey Smith. Even at this stage of sound film development, there was an added attraction at New York's Paramount Times Square theater: "Extra . . . In Person, RUBINOFF with His Violin and His Own Orchestra."

Captain Blood (1935) starred the Tasmanian-born Errol Flynn, a smash in his first major film. Flynn was Captain Peter Blood, consigned to slavery on a Caribbean isle for applying his medical knowledge to a political refugee. He escapes and wreaks havoc on the British ships till the love of Arabella Bishop (Olivia De Havilland) and a change of government at home ("You mean they've roused themselves at home and kicked out that pimple James?") reforms him. Austrian-born Erich Wolfgang Korngold provided the music score. He had arrived from Vienna, where he had been a child prodigy and a composer of operas and concert items, the previous year. He composed the score for *A Midsummer Night's Dream* the same year he wrote *Blood*.

The Charge of the Light Brigade (1936) was directed by Michael Curtiz, who urged his assistants to "bring on the empty horses." Beginning in India, Captain Geoffrey Vickers (Flynn) romances Elsa Campbell (De Havilland) and rescues her after a battle and surrender that becomes a massacre, thanks to Surat Khan (C. Henry Gordon). Vickers' motivation to lead the charge against Russian field artillery at Balaclava in 1854 during the Crimean War is to get at Surat Khan.

> Men of the 27th! Surat Khan is on the field with the opposing Russian forces, the same Surat Khan who massacred the women and children at Chukoti. Our chance has come! Show no mercy. Let no power on earth stop you. Prove to the world that no man can kill women and children and live to boast of it. Men of the 27th. Our objective is Surat Khan!

The film charge was also lethal to horses, tripped during full gallop.

The Adventures of Robin Hood (1938), made when "Technicolor was like rich velvet,"[38] was the ultimate tribute to the bandit of Sherwood Forest. As Robin of Locksley, Errol Flynn was at the peak of his form. Olivia De Havilland

Almost villainous in appearance, Warren William was an ingratiating leading man in such 30s films as *Golddiggers of 1933*, *Imitation of Life* and as Julius Caesar in *Cleopatra*.

was Maid Marian;[39] Alan Hale, Little John; Eugene Pallette, Friar Tuck; Una O'Connor, Lady Marian's maid; Montague Love the Bishop of Black Canon. Claude Rains was deliciously foppish as Prince John. Basil Rathbone was almost totally evil as Sir Guy Gisbourne. Who can forget the monk who throws off his togs to reveal — King Richard (Ian Hunter). Again, Erich Wolfgang Korngold supplied one of the silver screen's best music scores.

Hal Wallis, the producer, had been quite concerned about director Michael Curtiz's expensive methods and sent Henry Blanke a memo.

> I dropped in on him [Curtiz] last night, and he was shooting a closeup of one of the knights who was answering Prince John, and the knight had one line to speak which probably took ten seconds and which will probably run about six feet on the screen. Instead of shooting a closeup of this man, as he should have done with a couple of squires in back of him or perhaps a piece of wild wall, he shot it at an angle, with the man in the foreground and shooting across the entire room, so that the entire room had to be lighted and approximately one hundred people were in the scene backing up this knight for his one line. These, of course, are the things that cost fortunes, and by the same token these are the same things where, if a little judgment was used, we could save fortunes.[40]

Tarzan: There had been silent Tarzans—notably Elmo Lincoln—but Olympic swimmer Johnny Weissmuller, who had won the gold medal in the hundred-meter freestyle races in 1924 and 1928, was to the loincloth born for a couple generations of cinemagoers. *Tarzan the Ape Man* (1932) was his first. Maureen O'Sullivan was Jane, accompanying her father (C. Aubrey Smith) during his quest for the ivory-rich elephant's burial ground somewhere on the Motira Escarpment. Upon the plateau they encounter the white ape, Tarzan. Unlike the hero of the Edgar Rice Burroughs novels on which these films were based, this is not the infant Lord Greystoke, raised by apes and teaching himself proper human speech. Weissmuller's ape man is more inarticulate and needs Jane's help to become semicivilized. Pygmies capture the party, who have found the elephant's burial ground. Sacrificed to a giant ape in a pit, Jane is rescued by Tarzan and his elephant horde. Tarzan battles the monstrous ape, putting a knife through its eye into its brain. Before implementation of the Production Code in 1934, filmmakers could and did get away with such scenes. Once Jane's dress has been torn off, she dons a makeshift two-piece outfit. Apparently she and Tarzan enjoy a common-law marriage. How would the Code enforcers have modified this illicit relationship? When the Code was enforced, the loincloths became veritable bodysuits.

Tarzan and His Mate (1934) was the rare sequel—better than its progenitor. Tarzan swims fast, battles humongous crocodiles, and rides a rhino. The savage tribe is indeed savage, stringing up captives to be split by flexible saplings or throwing them to lions. All of the Weissmuller-O'Sullivan Tarzan films are of good quality, save perhaps *Tarzan's Secret Treasure* (1941). *Tarzan Escapes* (1936), *Tarzan Finds a Son* (1939), *Tarzan's New York Adventure* (1942)—these are good films, possibly because they hardly varied the premise: evil white hunters seeking booty enter the pristine environment of Tarzan and make life difficult. In *Tarzan Escapes,* John Buckler as Captain Fray sends word to the bad natives: "Tell chief bwana take away ju-ju. Take away great white ape. Tell chief bwana send one white man, two white women for ju-ju. Well, get along there. Pacy, quinda!" The mysterious wonder word *ju-ju* served many purposes in these films.

After O'Sullivan left, the series decreased in quality, featuring serviceable Janes like Brenda Joyce, Joyce Mackenzie, or no Jane at all. Tarzan contributed to the war effort by foiling Nazis in *Tarzan's Desert Mystery* (1943), which was made at RKO rather than at MGM. This led to another reason for the decline: RKO did not lavish as much care on the series.

Buster Crabbe (in a 1933 serial, *Tarzan the Fearless*) and Herman Brix also played the Tarzan role, concurrently with Weissmuller. Brix, who later, as Bruce Bennett, enjoyed a successful film career, was an Olympic shotputter whose Tarzan entries were filmed in Guatemala and presented spectacular stunts. *The New Adventures of Tarzan* and *Tarzan and the Green Goddess* were presented as parts of a serial.

Gangster Films: Prohibition of alcohol, instituted on a national level by the 18th Amendment to the Constitution in January 1919, spawned mob

Tarzan and His Mate (Metro-Goldwyn-Mayer, 1934) remains for many the finest Tarzan
film. Johnny Weissmuller and Maureen O'Sullivan sported attire that would soon
become taboo.

activity and speakeasies. Tailor made for film treatment, the fictionalized
stories of 20th century outlaws, their gun molls and individual initiative
became a film genre.

The history of the gangster film is the history of where the frontier is, both
in the moral and physical senses of the word. For what is the mob movie but

the saga of an enterprising pioneer seeing how far he (yes, it's almost invariably a he) goes before getting caught? From the Snapper Kid to Michael Corleone, the evolution of the movie gangster is the evolution of America, a nation riddled with bullets and contradictions.[41]

The seminal gangster films were *Little Caesar* (1930), *The Public Enemy* (1931), and *Scarface* (1932). Edward G. Robinson made his mark in the first as Caesar Enrico Bandello, who rises to the top of hood-dom, as does James Cagney's Tom Powers in *The Public Enemy*. His brother worked on a trolley—"In 1931, one did not go to movies to see trolley conductors working their way through night school."[42] Cagney's mobster was the more appealing but he too failed to survive, his mummy-bandaged corpse delivered to his mother's door at fade-out. In *Scarface,* Paul Muni played Tony Camonte, an Al Capone–like character with a sister (Ann Dvorak) fixation. (Note Boris Karloff in an important victim role.) Camonte extolled the virtues of his machine gun:

> There's only one thing that gets orders and gives orders and this is it! That's how I got the South Side for ya and that's how I'm gonna get the North Side for ya. Some little typewriter, huh? I'm gonna write my name all over this town with it in big letters! Get outta my way, Johnny, I'm gonna spit! C'mon, fellas!

There was a public outcry against gangster glorification. The studios responded. James Cagney went straight in *G-Men* (1935) and acted yellow on the way to the gas chamber in *Angels with Dirty Faces* (1938) in order to save his admirers, the Dead End Kids, from emulating him. Pat O'Brien, his childhood pal who became Father Jerry Connelly, advised the Kids: "All right, fellas, let's go and say a prayer for a boy who couldn't run as fast as I could." In *Dead End* (1937), home environment was posed as a cause of hoodlumism. Violence was demonstrated vividly in *Show Them No Mercy* (1935), when Bruce Cabot became a sieve at the hands of revenge-minded Rochelle Hudson.

War Films: Cinematic depictions of World War I included *The Eagle and the Hawk* (1933), *The Road to Glory* (1936), and *The Dawn Patrol* (1938), but the best and most famous was the 1930 *All Quiet on the Western Front*. It was directed by Lewis Milestone on a plateau in California. For sound effects they recorded live ammunition shot off in the hills at night, then cut off the first explosion and used the reverberation.[43] The scream and thud of incoming shells, the first trench battle, where Lew Ayres watches a shot French poilu fall onto the barbed wire then disintegrate from an explosion that leaves only his hands gripping the wire, and the butterfly in no-man's-land still pack a punch in this Academy Award–winning film. The irony of the French attack in which they are mowed down by German machine guns, followed by the German counterattack to recapture their first trench—when *they* are mowed down—may make this the best antiwar film ever.

Westerns: Like the gangster story, the western was typically American. Based on Edna Ferber's novel of nation building, *Cimarron* (1931) was the first epic western of the decade. Richard Dix played Yancy Cravat, Irene Dunne, Sabra, his wife and helpmate. The land rush by horse, wagon, and bicycle into Oklahoma's Cherokee Strip was massive in scope and appeared in many other films.

The Plainsman (1936) was a Cecil B. DeMille production about Wild Bill Hickok (Gary Cooper), Calamity Jane (Jean Arthur), and Buffalo Bill (James Ellison). Anthony Quinn plays a Northern Cheyenne warrior fresh from the victory over Custer. In the 1942 *They Died with Their Boots On* he played Crazy Horse opposite Errol Flynn's Custer.

Union Pacific (1939) was yet another Cecil B. DeMille extravaganza, this one about the building of the transcontinental railroad. Joel McCrea was the railroad troubleshooter entrusted with foiling Brian Donlevy's plans to disrupt construction with gambling and gals. Why? So the Central Pacific would get to Utah first and a particular politico could cash in his stock. (Yes, this was an age of simplistic—but not entirely false—reasoning by filmmakers.) Barbara Stanwyck was an Irishwoman, Robert Preston a former Civil War compatriot of McCrea who worked for the bad guys. Preston often essayed this type: the hero's happy-go-lucky pal gone bad.

John Ford began using Monument Valley, that starkly beautiful landscape of pinnacles and assorted rock formations that runs from northeastern Arizona into southern Utah. It was Navajo land, and Native Americans were featured in many films. *Stagecoach* (1939) was probably the first full-length feature to be filmed there. It became the seminal western of the decade and has ranked ever since as one of the half dozen greatest westerns. A disparate group must traverse Indian territory in a stagecoach: the revenge-minded Ringo Kid (John Wayne), the dance-hall hostess Dallas (Claire Trevor), tough but fair sheriff Curly Wilcox (George Bancroft), prim Lucy Mallory (Louis Platt), the jovial driver Buck (Andy Devine), gambler Hatfield (John Carradine), drunken doctor Josiah Boone (Thomas Mitchell), whiskey drummer Samuel Peacock (Donald Meek), banker Gatewood (Berton Churchill).

In this era Warner Bros. ventured west with mixed results. "You don't realize how essentially urban Warners is till you see Cagney and Bogart riding horses and wearing ten-gallon hats."[44] As they had in their gangster films, James Cagney and Humphrey Bogart shot it out in 1939 in *The Oklahoma Kid*. *Dodge City* (1939) was an improvement, but in *Virginia City* (1940), Bogart was a Mexican bandit!

Dramas: Westerns were shot on location, if only inland California, but the studio provided the appropriate backdrop for most dramas.

> He [Michael Curtiz] had a particular eye for locations, many of which had to be painstakingly re-created on the Warner Brothers shooting stages since location filming was comparatively rare in the Thirties. More often the director, or a second unit, would be sent to a location to film stock material, and then the director would rely on the skill of his studio's special effects department to simulate accurately whatever exteriors were needed involving scenes with the principal players. This was the case with a gentle family drama, *Daughters Courageous* (1939), saved from sentimental banality by the adroit direction, holding together the pace and a number of excellent performances against an accurate small town background, superbly lit in soft focus by James Wong Howe.[45]

Erich Maria Remarque's novel *All Quiet on the Western Front* was turned into an Academy Award–winning film for Universal in 1930. Lewis (Lew) Ayres played the German soldier, Raymond Griffith his unlucky enemy.

The Great Depression's effects were treated by such studio executives as Darryl F. Zanuck. "A corn-fed Midwestern daredevil who broke in as a writer during the Third Era and rose to claim power just short of that of a birthright Warner brother, Zanuck believed in plugging the movies into the social currents of the day."[46]

I Am a Fugitive from a Chain Gang (1932), from Warner Bros., was the grimmest of this type. The film was directed by Mervyn LeRoy. Paul Muni plays James Allen, who is consigned to a Southern chain gang when he is forced into helping his unemployed friend Pete (Preston Foster) rob a diner. Escaping, he begins a new life, finds love with Helen (Helen Vinson, who actually utters the line, "There are no 'musts' in my life. I'm free, white, and twenty-one"). Hiding his past and becoming a successful businessman, Allen is nevertheless eventually found out and returned to the chain gang, ostensibly for a brief spell. But his parole is held up and he breaks out again. At the end he pays Helen a brief visit before he fades into the dark, answering her pleading questions about how he will live with the famous "I steal."

Muni was also the star of *Black Fury* (1935), playing the leader of a coal mine strike. "By the time *Black Fury* was made, social reality was being bypassed in favor of a confrontation between Shysters and the New Deal as ritualized as Kabuki drama.[47] (Not until 1940 did a major British film deal with strikes: *The Stars Look Down,* with Michael Redgrave and Margaret Lockwood.)

In *Our Daily Bread* (1934) urban dwellers John and wife (Tom Keene, Karen Morley) trade a small, cheap violin for a scrawny chicken to serve the wife's uncle. Uncle offers them a chance to rally by letting them take over a farm. Swede (who else but John Qualen?) and family happen by on their way to California and are invited to stay and help the novices work it. Swede wonders if John's "yoking." Burma Shave–style road signs attract a passel of job seekers. "There's nothing for people to worry about. Not when they've got the earth. It's, it's like a, a mother. It's wonderful," says John as he and his wife examine new shoots. The set piece is the desperate but disciplined creation of an irrigation channel, described by director King Vidor.

> I had evolved a sequence that would make full use of my interest in silent music and I decided to pull no punches as far as the techniques of this method were concerned. We dispense with all sound-recording equipment and used instead a metronome and a bass drum. The picks came down on the counts of one and three, the shovels scooped dirt on count two and tossed it on four. Each scene was enacted in strict 4/4 time with the metronome's speed gradually increasing on each cut.[48]

Soaps and Weepies: *Back Street* (1932) starred Irene Dunne as Ray Schmidt, vivacious gal of pre–Prohibition, pre–World War I, almost pre-automobile Cincinnati. Attention to detail was great. Ray falls for Walter Saxel (John Boles), but he marries another, keeping Ray in a flat on the side.

In *Imitation of Life* (1934), widowed Beatrice Pullman (Claudette Colbert) toughs it out, achieving fame and fortune when she realizes that the pancake mix of her nanny Delilah (Louise Beavers in an Aunt Jemima–like role) will sell like hotcakes on the Atlantic City boardwalk. The second plot involves Delilah's light-skinned daughter caught between two worlds.

Barbara Stanwyck was *Stella Dallas* (1937), a slightly vulgar but self-sacrificing woman from a blue collar mill town who marries well. Her husband, Stephen (John Boles again), is really in love with another woman, whom he meets again when she is a widower. Divorced, Stella decides that her daughter Laurel (Anne Shirley) will have a better life living with her father and his new wife. At the end, Laurel is marrying while her mother watches from the grill fence outside. Also noble is the new wife (Barbara O'Neil), who makes sure the drapes are open.

Biographies: George Arliss continued lending an aura of prestige to such films as *Alexander Hamilton* (1931), *Voltaire* (1933), and *House of Rothschild* (1934). After Arliss, Paul Muni was the master actor in biopics. He played the famous French scientist in *The Story of Louis Pasteur* (1935) and the Mexican liberator in *Juarez* (1939). In between he starred in *The Life of Emile Zola* (1937). Concerned with prestige, producer Hal Wallis told Jack Warner not to show a cartoon at the premiere.[49]

The Adventures of Marco Polo (1938) featured Gary Cooper as the traveler

Some main dames on *42nd Street* (Warner Bros., 1933): Una Merkel, Ruby Keeler, and Ginger Rogers. The definitive backstage musical had songs by Al Dubin and Harry Warren and choreography by Busby Berkeley.

to Cathay. In 1939 Henry Fonda played *Young Mr. Lincoln.* Don Ameche and Henry Fonda collaborated that same year in *The Story of Alexander Graham Bell.*

Musicals: Choreographer Busby Berkeley, the "Méliès of the Musical,"[50] flowered at Warner Bros. with incredibly camp conglomerations of dancing girls, violin-playing girls, swimming girls, piano-playing girls. He codirected *42nd Street* (1933, with Lloyd Bacon), *Gold Diggers of 1933* (with Mervyn LeRoy), and *Footlight Parade* (1933, with Lloyd Bacon), and *Dames* (1934, with Ray Enright). Joan Blondell, Ginger Rogers, Ruby Keeler, Dick Powell, and Roscoe Karns were some of the familiar faces in these films.

Audiences had tired of "all-singing, all-talking, all-dancing," until *42nd Street* was responsible for a resurgence of the musical. Critics and the public loved it. "The liveliest and one of the most tuneful screen musical comedies that has come out of Hollywood was presented last night by the Warner Brothers at the Strand . . . invariably entertaining."[51] As understudy Sawyer for the musical comedy *Pretty Lady,* Ruby Keeler replaces star Dorothy Brock (Bebe Daniels), who breaks her ankle prior to opening night. Brock has her own spiel: "You look adorable. Now go out there and be so *swell* that you'll make me hate you." After giving her a crash course, director Julian Marsh (Warner Baxter) takes Sawyer's arms and delivers the pep talk to end pep talks:

> Sawyer, you listen to me and you listen hard. Two hundred people. Two hundred jobs. Two hundred thousand dollars. Five weeks of grind and blood and sweat depend upon you. It's the lives of all these people who've worked with you. You've got to go on and you've got to give and give, and give. They've got to like you, got to. D'you understand? You can't fall down, you can't. Because your future's in it, my future, and everything all of us have is staked on you. All right now. I'm through. But you keep your feet on the ground and your head on those shoulders of yours. And Sawyer, you're going out a youngster, but you've got to come back a star.

"Shuffle Off to Buffalo," "Young and Healthy," "You're Getting to Be a Habit with Me," and the title tune were among the fabulous songs.

Love Me Tonight was a musical comedy directed by Lubitsch's stylistic equal, Rouben Mamoulian, in 1932. It was before the institution in 1934 of the Production Code, and the more risqué could still be achieved. "Isn't It Romantic" and "Mimi" were hit tunes sung by Maurice Chevalier.

Flying Down to Rio (1933) introduced Fred Astaire and Ginger Rogers, although Dolores Del Rio and Gene Raymond had the starring roles. But RKO knew that chemistry had been achieved and paired Astaire and Rogers for years to come. Great songs from top popular composers graced these films. Irving Berlin's "Cheek to Cheek" and "Isn't This a Lovely Day" accompanied *Top Hat* (1935). *Follow the Fleet* (1936) included Berlin's "Let's Face the Music and Dance." *Swing Time* (1936) featured Jerome Kern–Dorothy Fields numbers. George and Ira Gershwin provided *Shall We Dance* (1937) with "Let's Call the Whole Thing Off" and "They Can't Take That Away from Me."

Top Hat was reckoned the best of the duo's films in 60s film books. More recently *Swing Time* has come in for plaudits, and a re-viewing makes it clear that this is a masterpiece. Besides the three hummable songs — "Pick Yourself Up," "The Way You Look Tonight," and "A Fine Romance" — there are the "Waltz in Swing Time" and "Bojangles" dance numbers, plus the finale, "Never Gonna Dance," in which Lucky John Garnett (Astaire) and Penny Carrol (Rogers) begin slowly on the main level of the Silver Sandal Café, then ascend opposite stairways to the second level. Up till then, Ginger's spaghetti strap, low-cut white gown has shielded her legs. Upstairs, as she spins to a conclusion, her legs are shown. This must have been planned, and is just one of many instances of genius that make this a classic. Hermes Pan was the choreographer, and a master director, George Stevens, helmed the production. His perfect touch is evident in the "Way You Look Tonight" number. Penny, her hair shampooed, walks up to the piano-playing Lucky. When he finishes his song and turns, he is surprised at the sight but not aghast — surprise is the key, not shock and pratfall. (An important aside: Astaire ordered that the camera include his entire body in the dance numbers.)

Plots were thin, but no matter. "The deep current of romantic tension in these movies came from Rogers's expectations about Astaire and Astaire's callousness, off the dance floor, about those expectations."

The dance artistry of Fred Astaire and Ginger Rogers reached an apogee in *Swing Time* (RKO, 1936). Here they perform in the justly famous "Never Gonna Dance."

One of the great disappointments of the decade was that Astaire and Britain's darling, Jessie Matthews, did not team. *Evergreen* (1934) was her biggest hit. It was

> the most pleasurable musical comedy yet offered us by the ambitious British screen industry . . . a considerable joy . . . fortunate in the presence of Jessie

Jessie Matthews, "The Dancing Divinity," was Britain's supreme musical star of the 30s. In *Evergreen* (Gaumont-British, 1934) she played Harriet Green, and posed as her own mother. Also pictured is Betty Shale as Hawkie.

> Matthews, a nimble and winning dryad of song and dance, who deserves to be better known to American film audiences. A joyous and captivating nymph, she is the feminine counterpart of Fred Astaire. If Hollywood has the welfare of its customers at heart, it will immediately team her with Mr. Astaire in what should certainly be the perfect partnership.[53]

It was said that Matthews could outdance Eleanor Powell. "The chemistry of Astaire & Matthews together would have been very choice. They both had class."[54]

The best Fox musical of the 30s was 1938's *Alexander's Ragtime Band.* Tyrone Power played San Franciscan Roger Grant, who, despite his classical violin training, longs to conduct a ragtime ensemble and does so as "Alexander," with the help of Charlie Dwyer (Don Ameche) and singer Stella Kirby (Alice Faye). A romantic triangle develops. Kirby gets a job in New York, the band falls apart temporarily, World War I sees them in the army. Finding out that the navy has put on a Broadway show, Alexander convinces his colonel to let him develop a similar play for the army. Stella, a big success on the Great White Way, is in the audience and tries to see Alexander during intermission. He refuses.

Heeding the call to board ship in the middle of the production, Alexander strikes up the band, and the cast marches up the aisle and out of

Lost Horizon (Columbia, 1937) was Frank Capra's smash film version of James Hilton's novel of Shangri-La. As Robert Conway, Ronald Colman had another thoughtful hero part. *Opposite:* Tyrone Power leads the doughboys from the stage to the troop ships in a tremendously moving episode from *Alexander's Ragtime Band* (20th Century–Fox, 1938).

the theater. Corny? Yes, but a truly great movie moment: a shocked mother in the audience stands up, realizing her son is off to war; Stella unsuccessfully tries to reach Alexander through the crush. Although she marries Charlie, he finally realizes that she's in love with Alexander—and although it takes time for Alexander to learn this and more time to locate Stella, who is on a admittedly glossy skid singing in cabarets and saloons—everyone lives happily ever after in a Carnegie Hall ending. Irving Berlin songs dominated: the title tune, as well as "Now It Can Be Told" (Faye), "Oh, How I Hate to Get Up in the Morning" (Jack Haley), "Blue Skies" (Ethel Merman), and many more. Merman's rendition of "Heat Wave" was reprised in the 1954 Fox musical *There's No Business Like Show Business*. Although Merman starred, Marilyn Monroe rendered the tune that time.

Literary Adaptations: *A Tale of Two Cities* (1935) had atmosphere in spades. Ronald Colman was Sydney Carton, who would sacrifice himself to the guillotine to save the life of the man loved by the woman he adored. "It looks and sounds and *feels* like Dickens, and is authentic in a way no modern production could hope to be, even those adaptations of Dickens' work which are the cream of television drama today. Why this should be, I don't know—is it black and white photography, or the fact that Selznick could transmit his Dickens mania, or that the cast understood better what I can only call the Dickensian state of mind?"[55]

Based on Victor Hugo's novel, *Les Misérables* (1935) was also full of atmosphere. Fredric March played Jean Valjean, starving thief who makes good only to have his tormenter, Javert (Charles Laughton), pursue and ruin his life. That same year saw Greta Garbo as Leo Tolstoy's heroine *Anna Karenina*.

BEHIND THE SCENES

The Academy of Motion Picture Arts and Sciences Awards, which had been organized in 1927, continued to grow and command respect. In keeping with the large number of films being made at that time, there were more nominees per category than there would be in future. At the same time, Hollywood technicians increased their expertise, until "around 1937, Hollywood production assuredly reached a high point of perfection and, above all, equilibrium—in short, classicism."[56]

Victor Fleming directed big productions for MGM. "His versatility confounds the auteurists—he does adventures, weepies, comedies, musicals. *A Guy Named Joe* and *The Wizard of Oz*. Had he no themes? He had one: to stay employed."[58]

Josef von Sternberg, Vienna born, added the "von" after he came to Hollywood. He made Marlene Dietrich a star in such sumptuous vehicles as *Morocco* (1930), *Dishonored* (1931), *Shanghai Express* (1932), *Blonde Venus* (1932), *The Scarlet Empress* (1934), and *The Devil Is a Woman* (1935). Van Nest Polglase, art director and production designer, gave an exquisite sense of design to *Flying Down to Rio* (1933), *Alice Adams* (1935), *The Last Days of Pompeii* (1935), and *The Hunchback of Notre Dame* (1939).

Dorothy Arzner directed films from 1929 to 1943, including *Merrily We Go to Hell* (1932), *Craig's Wife* (1936), and *Dance Girl Dance* (1940). Frances Marion had scripted many silent films before she wrote *The Big House* (1930) and *The Champ* (1931), and won Academy Awards for both. She also scripted Garbo's *Camille* (1936).

But how much respect was accorded the screenwriter?

> People talk now about a "writers' cinema" of the 1930s, but I never observed the position of a writer in Hollywood as being anything possessed of the slightest dignity, or given any particular importance. Once in a great while . . . when Damon Runyon had a string of successful films, they perhaps found that identifying the picture as a Damon Runyon story helped the publicity. Or a Somerset Maugham story, maybe. . . . Otherwise, I can't remember a writer being given any kind of billing that you could see from the road, without walking through the mud, through the ditch, with a magnifying

glass up to the billboard to find the writer's credit. And then it was the same size type, or a little smaller, as the firm that had printed the sign.[58]

STAR SYSTEM

Although agents and casting houses would not acquire real power for some decades, David O. Selznick's brother Myron started the ball rolling. With over three hundred clients — actors and directors — his agency had grossed $15 million by 1937.[59] Some stars, like Barbara Stanwyck, moved between studios. Most were under seven-year contracts to particular studios, which could loan them out — and did, either trading them for someone more suitable for a part or punishing them for refusing a role at their home studio. Suspensions were common, too.

To canvas studios briefly, United Artists featured Marlene Dietrich, Joel McCrea, Ronald Colman, and Charles Boyer. Universal had Karloff, Lugosi, songstress Deanna Durbin, Marlene Dietrich, and Irene Dunne. Fox had Tyrone Power, Shirley Temple, Henry Fonda, Loretta Young, Alice Faye ("Always appear as if you were about to win at the Oscar banquet").[60] Warner Bros. had James Cagney, Edward G. Robinson, Bette Davis, Errol Flynn, Olivia De Havilland, George Raft, Paul Muni, Dick Powell, Ruby Keeler, Ginger Rogers (until she went to RKO), and Humphrey Bogart, who would not become a big star till 1941. Paramount had Gary Cooper and Paulette Goddard, Kay Francis, Randolph Scott, Ray Milland, Claudette Colbert, Bing Crosby, and Bob Hope. MGM had "more stars than there are in Heaven," including Spencer Tracy, James Stewart, Mickey Rooney, Robert Taylor, Greta Garbo, Greer Garson, Judy Garland, Jean Harlow, Wallace Beery, James Stewart. RKO had Astaire and Rogers, Irene Dunne, later Robert Ryan and Robert Mitchum, Jane Russell, Katharine Hepburn, and Cary Grant. Columbia had Ronald Colman, Jean Arthur, and two others who moved from studio to studio, James Stewart and Cary Grant. Later came Glenn Ford, William Holden, and Rita Hayworth.

Charlie Chaplin sounded an independent note and continued making silent films (some with music and sound effects). His output was not great, however: *City Lights* (1931), *Modern Times* (1936), and the sound films *The Great Dictator* (1940), *Monsieur Verdoux* (1947), *A King in New York* (1957), *Limelight* (1952), and *A Countess from Hong Kong* (1967).

Luise Rainer won Academy Awards for *The Great Ziegfeld* (1936) and *The Good Earth* (1937). Then she rather rapidly disappeared from the screen.

Sweden's Greta Garbo had come to the United States with director Mauritz Stiller during the silent era. Her accent did not adversely affect her, and she made the transition to sound famously in 1930 in *Anna Christie*, based on Eugene O'Neill's play about a prostitute. Frances Marion scripted. Director Clarence Brown was also instrumental in Garbo's American success.

> In her first talking picture . . . the immensely popular Greta Garbo is even more interesting through being heard than she was in her mute portrayals. She reveals no nervousness before the microphone and her careful interpreta-

Anna Christie **(Metro-Goldwyn-Mayer, 1930).**

tion of Anna can scarcely be disputed. She is of the same nationality as Anna is supposed to be and she brings Anna to life all the more impressively through her foreign accent being natural, because it is something for which she does not have to strive.[61]

Garbo's first talking lines were: "Gimme a whiskey. Ginger ale on the side. And don't be stingy, baby." The plot: "Woman hungry" Swedes on a farm in Minnesota were responsible for Anna's life of sin. "Men, all the time. Oh how I hate them. Every mother's son of them! Don't you?" she asked new-found compatriot (Marie Dressler). She hoped to reform with her barge-captain father (George Marion) on New York City's East River and out on the Atlantic. Rescuing survivors of a shipwreck in the fog, she fell for a brawny Irishman (Charles Bickford). When she revealed her background, he left, and her father was distraught. "I am my own boss, so put that in your pipe and smoke it." Both men signed on to a ship sailing for Capetown. But Anna convinced her man that she never loved another.

In the 1931 *Susan Lenox, Her Fall and Rise,* she suffered again. "Garbo goes to the tropics and accepts employment in the Paradise Cafe, where floozies entertain sailors and men in panama hats."[62] In *Grand Hotel* (1932), the first big all-star film, Garbo played ballerina Grusinskaya, who complained of love:

> What is love? Little kisses in the dark, hot breath on the face, a heart that beats with terrible strong blows. Love is just a beast that you feel all through

the night. And when the morning comes, love dies. Well, what do you think of me? I'm so hard, huh?

As the 17th century Swedish monarch in *Queen Christina* (1933), she lost her Spanish ambassador and lover (John Gilbert) in a duel and accompanied his body home. Garbo's stoic presence on the ship's prow may be the cinema's most famous close-up, the film the ultimate star vehicle.

Another *Grand Hotel* star, John Barrymore, "The Great Profile," brother of Ethel Barrymore and Lionel Barrymore, lived the high life. He would die on May 29, 1942, after imbibing too much.

Katharine Hepburn debuted in 1932 in *A Bill of Divorcement*. It was an "intelligent, restrained and often stirring picture.... Miss Hepburn's portrayal is exceptionally fine.... Miss Hepburn's characterization is one of the finest seen on the screen and the producers have been wise in not minimizing the importance of her part because Mr. Barrymore is the star of the film."[63]

In Britain supremely cute Jessie Matthews was *the* queen of the song and dance in such films as *The Good Companions* (1933) and *Evergreen* (1934). Besides her smoothness, she had as beautiful a pair of legs as any cinematic dancer, including Eleanor Powell, Betty Grable, Cyd Charisse, and Juliet Prowse. More popular in Britain than elsewhere was Anna Neagle, who starred in *Victoria the Great* (1937) and *Nurse Edith Cavell* (1939), the latter actually a U.S. production.

Before Marilyn Monroe there was Jean Harlow, the original platinum "blond bombshell," who starred in *Platinum Blonde* (1931) and *Bombshell* (1933). She was Clark Gable's costar in *Red Dust* (1932) and *China Seas* (1935). She died of cerebral edema at age 26 in 1937.

Sonja Henie, Norwegian Olympic figure skating champ of 1928, 1932, and 1936, made a tremendously successful transition to film in Fox musicals like *One in a Million* (1936), *Thin Ice* (1937), and *Happy Landing* (1938).

African American Paul Robeson of Princeton, New Jersey, a graduate of Rutgers University, achieved more fame overseas than at home, moving between England and the United States. He sang "Ol' Man River" in the 1936 *Show Boat*. In Britain his best film was *The Proud Valley* (1940).

Claudette Colbert could essay any role, from ancient temptress to contemporary urban short-order cook or heiress. She could be good, evil, or in between. In 1934 alone she starred in *Imitation of Life* for Universal, *Cleopatra* and *Four Frightened People* for Paramount, and *It Happened One Night* for Columbia.

Many of the stars of this era acquired the status of legend or icon. Why?

> Well, they were people before they were stars. You can have someone new, with a few tricks and a new face and the people will go along with him for a while and then they see through. To last you need to be real. Integrity as a person. And you have to work.[64]

The big three at MGM were Garbo, Norma Shearer, and Joan Crawford, all of whom had survived silents and prospered in the talkies. Shearer married MGM's production head and wunderkind, Irving Thalberg. Her prime 30s

Cesar Romero and Shirley Temple, the most popular child star of all, starred in *Wee Willie Winkie* (20th Century-Fox, 1937). They co-starred again in 1939's *The Little Princess*. Romero played an Indian in both.

films included *The Barretts of Wimpole Street* (1934), *Romeo and Juliet* (1936), *Marie Antoinette* (1938), and *The Women* (1939). Crawford's 30s MGM films included *Possessed* (1931), *Dancing Lady* (1933), and *The Women* (1939).

The era's incredibly popular kids included Shirley Temple, who debuted in 1932 in *The Red-Haired Alibi*. Jackie Cooper, an Our Gang member, played opposite Wallace Beery in *The Champ* (1931), and again with Beery in *Treasure Island* (1934). Mickey Rooney, a vaudevillian with his parents, first appeared in 1932 in *My Pal the King*. Rooney's Hardy family series started in 1937 with *A Family Affair,* in which Lionel Barrymore and Spring Byington played his parents. From the 1938 *You're Only Young Once,* Lewis Stone and Fay Holden would hold the reins. "The Hardys of Carvel, Idaho, are dreary white Protestants who make one feel good to be single, Jewish, or an axe murderer."[65] Lewis Stone had been in silents and talkies of a singular importance — *Treasure Island, Queen Christina, Grand Hotel.* From England, Freddie Bartholomew played with Mickey Rooney in *Captains Courageous* (1937), and on his own as *David Copperfield* (1935) and *Little Lord Fauntleroy* (1936).

A host of talented men and women performers made up Hollywood's character actor and supporting cast. Some, like London-born Claude Rains, were both. His debut in 1933 in *The Invisible Man* kept him faceless till the end. During the 30s and 40s his roles must be counted among the most enjoyable ever seen: the district attorney in *They Won't Forget* (1937), the foppish Prince John in *The Adventures of Robin Hood,* the runaway father in *Four Daughters* (1938), the corrupt Senator Paine in *Mr. Smith Goes to Washington.* An exemplary overview was provided in Shipman's *The Great Stars: The Golden Years:*

> Claude Rains must be reckoned among the finest actors who ever played in films; he managed to get himself into a score or so of the most enjoyable movies of the 30s and 40s, and they, and weaker efforts, all benefited from his presence. He had a fine speaking voice, like honey with some gravel in it, and that neatly typed him as the most suave and sarcastic of villains, very neat and polished, with a scornful right eyebrow. He encompassed almost every sort of worldly wickedness, though he tended to the artistic rather than executive; and he could go the sympathetic line with ease and authority.[66]

Walter Brennan must be reckoned of equal importance. He won three supporting actor Oscars, for *Come and Get It* (1936), *Kentucky* (1938), and *The Westerner* (1940). As decades passed, Brennan became more of a character actor.

Wonderful character performers of this decade included Ned Sparks in *Imitation of Life* (1934), C. Aubrey Smith in *Tarzan the Ape Man* and *Lives of a Bengal Lancer,* Eugene Pallette in *The Kennel Murder Case* (1933) and *The Adventures of Robin Hood,* Ruth Donnelly in *Cain and Mabel* (1936), Edna May Oliver in *A Tale of Two Cities* (1935) and *Drums Along the Mohawk* (1939), Allen Jenkins in *Dead End* (1937), Joe Sawyer in *The Petrified Forest* (1936), Eric Blore, a regular in Astaire-Rogers musicals *The Gay Divorcee* (1934), *Top Hat* (1935), and *Shall We Dance?* (1937), and Alan Hale in *The Adventures of Robin Hood.*

B MOVIES

B or (low budget) movies were begun during the Depression to attract viewers and made up the second half of a double bill. Director William Beaudine was heard to say: "You mean somebody out there is actually waiting to see this?"[67] Mr. Wong (Boris Karloff) and the Cisco Kid came from Monogram. Republic, Grand National, and Producers Releasing Corporation stayed viable through these products. Take the Mr. Moto series:

> I suppose one should not be too sentimental about a string of second features made to a rigid and parsimonious studio pattern, but the fact is that in most

Bette Davis played Gabrielle Maple, Leslie Howard played Alan Squier and Humphrey Bogart (right) was Duke Mantee in *The Petrified Forest* (Warner Bros., 1936), an adaptation of the Robert Sherwood play.

> cities around the world the eight films in which Peter Lorre played John P. Marquand's Japanese detective Mr. Moto were thought good enough to top the bill, and forty-five years later when revived on television they have enabled many people to recapture the simple charm of filmgoing at the end of the thirties.... The skill is unobtrusive, but even the layman may occasionally note how remarkable it is that the camera is always in exactly the right place, and the eye is never allowed to be bored.[68]

Peter Lorre's comments about wrestling in *Mr. Moto in Danger Island* (Fox, 1939) still apply: "You see, the art of professional wrestling consists of three parts groan, two parts acting, and but one little part of skill."

Charlie Chan Carries On (1931) starred Swedish-born Warner Oland as the Asian master detective. By 1938 Sidney Toler was playing the title character in *Charlie Chan in Honolulu*. Boris Karloff was *Mysterious Mr. Wong* (1935), *Mr. Wong, Detective* (1938), and *Mr. Wong in Chinatown* (1939). In the last he explained one of his deductions: "Must I tell you that I exhumed the body of the dwarf from the pet cemetery? One does not bury the body of a vicious dog in a pet cemetery under an expensive headstone." Several series were initiated in 1938. *Young Dr. Kildare* (1938) starred Lew Ayres. *Blondie* starred Penny Singleton and Arthur Lake as the comic strip characters come to life. *Nancy Drew, Detective,* was Bonita Granville. In 1939 came Warren William in *The Lone Wolf Spy Hunt*.

England's Vivien Leigh did not win the role of Scarlett O'Hara in *Gone with the Wind* (Metro-Goldwyn-Mayer, 1939) until the film was in production and the Atlanta set in flames.

THE GOLDEN YEAR: 1939

Gone with the Wind, Margaret Mitchell's mammoth novel of Civil War and Reconstruction, was published in 1936 and won a Pulitzer Prize. Several directors worked on it, including George Cukor and Sam Wood, but Victor Fleming received onscreen credit. *GWTW* was a producer's picture. David O. Selznick let Cukor go, to the dismay of actresses Vivien Leigh and Olivia De Havilland, who nevertheless found Cukor willing to moonlight and help them with their parts.[69] Cameraman Lee Garmes was replaced by Ernest Haller.

Although Sidney Howard received full screenplay credit, various others, including Ben Hecht, F. Scott Fitzgerald and, of course, Selznick himself, worked on the script. William Cameron Menzies was instrumental in the production design.

Contenders for the Scarlett O'Hara part included Bette Davis, Joan Bennett, Miriam Hopkins, Jean Arthur, Lana Turner, and Susan Hayward. Davis had won an Academy Award for *Jezebel,* but Selznick explained to *New York Daily News* Hollywood columnist Ed Sullivan why he did not get her for *GWTW:*

> But certainly you ought to know that Warner Brothers wouldn't give up Bette Davis for a picture to be released through MGM, even had we wanted Miss Davis in preference to a new personality. Warner Brothers offered me Errol Flynn for Butler and Bette Davis for Scarlett if I would release the picture through Warners — and this would have been an easy way out of my dilemma. But the public wanted Gable, and I was determined that the public should have Gable. And Gable it is going to have, at the very earliest date it could have had him.[70]

For a spell Paulette Goddard had the inside track to play Scarlett. "I have looked at the new Goddard test — the one she made with Jeffrey Lynn — practically daily since it arrived, to see whether my first impression of the great improvement in her remained; and I must say that each time I see it I am more and more impressed. As much work as possible should be done with her."[71] There was a problem with Goddard's contract: Selznick wanted the standard seven years. The possibility that Goddard and Chaplin were not legally married was another fly in the ointment.

Selznick knew the public preferred a new face, and although he conducted a nationwide talent search, in the end he chose British actress Vivien Leigh when she appeared on the set of the burning of Atlanta and piqued his interest.[72] "Miss Leigh seems to us to be the best qualified from the standpoints of physical resemblance to Miss Mitchell's Scarlett, and — more importantly — ability to give the right performance in one of the most trying roles ever written. And this is after a two-year search."[73]

Sidney Howard wrote an immense script, which sat on a shelf till Selznick hired Ben Hecht and they rediscovered it and pared it down.[74] The film, a three-hour-plus tale of the antebellum South, the Civil War's effect on the home front, and Reconstruction, fulfilled most everyone's expectations.

> For, by any and all standards, Mr. Selznick's film is a handsome, scrupulous and unstinting version of the 1,037-page novel, matching it almost scene for scene with a literalness not even Shakespeare or Dickens were accorded in Hollywood, casting it so brilliantly one would have to know the history of the production not to suspect that Miss Mitchell had written her story just to provide a vehicle for the stars already assembled under Mr. Selznick's hospitable roof.[75]

Vivien Leigh seemed the embodiment of beauteous, fiery Scarlett. Before intermission she had delivered her most impassioned monologue.

> As God is my witness. As God is my witness, they're not going to lick me. I'm going to live through this and when it's all over, I'll never be hungry

In *Mr. Smith Goes to Washington* (Columbia, 1939), old Washington hands, Jean Arthur and Thomas Mitchell (right), are initially skeptical when the new senator (James Stewart) describes the wonders of democracy and the nation's capital.

again. No, nor any of my folk. If I have to lie, steal, cheat or kill—as God is my witness—I'll never be hungry again.

Mr. Smith Goes to Washington presented Jefferson Smith (James Stewart), an idealistic, naïve young senator. His mentor, Senator Joseph Paine (Claude Rains), attempts to discredit him when Smith learns that the senior senator is in the pocket of Jim Taylor (Edward Arnold). Dispirited and depressed, Smith plans to return to his hometown, but Clarissa Saunders (Jean Arthur) encourages him. Once he understands the technicalities of political life and gets the go-ahead from a sympathetic vice president (Harry Carey), he filibusters on the Senate floor.

> I guess this is just another lost cause, Mr. Paine. All you people don't know about lost causes. Mr. Paine does. He said once they were the only causes worth fighting for. And he fought for them once, for the only reason that any man ever fights for them. Because of just one plain simple rule: love thy neighbor. And in this world today full of hatred, a man who knows that one rule has a great trust. You know that rule, Mr. Paine, and I loved you for it just as my father did. And you know that you fight for the lost causes harder than for any others! Yes, you even die for them, like a man we both knew, Mr. Paine. You think I'm licked. You all think I'm licked! Well I'm not licked! And I'm gonna stay right here and fight for this lost cause even if this room gets filled with lies like these, and the Taylors and all their armies come marching into this place! Somebody'll listen to me. Somebody...

Wuthering Heights was based on Emily Brontë's tragic romance (1847) of waif Heathcliff (Laurence Olivier), who is brought into the Yorkshire home of Catherine Earnshaw (Merle Oberon). When Cathy dies, the grieving Heathcliff utters a curse:

> What do they know of Heaven or Hell, Cathy, who know nothing of life? Oh they're praying for you, Cathy. I'll pray one prayer with them. I repeat till my tongue stiffens: Catherine Earnshaw, may you not rest so long as I live on. I killed you. Haunt me then. Haunt your murderer. I know that ghosts have wandered on the earth. Be with me always. Take any form. Drive me mad! Only do not leave me in this dark alone where I cannot find you. I cannot live without my life. I cannot die without my soul.

Gunga Din featured Sam Jaffe as Rudyard Kipling's water carrier for the British troops (Cary Grant as Cutter, Victor McLaglen as MacChesney, Douglas Fairbanks, Jr., as Ballantine) in 19th-century India. The four squash plans for conquest by the fanatical Gura (Eduardo Ciannelli). The initial engagement between the three soldiers and their Indian troops against Gura's adherents, led by henchman Chota (Abner Biberman), is a marvel of action and an obvious inspiration to filmmakers like George Lucas and Steven Spielberg. The advertisements were packed with text. Usually the stars sold the film for a movie-mad America.[76]

> Here they come! . . . The reckless, lusty, swaggering sons of the thundering guns of Kipling's storied India . . . in the picture whose action sweeps the screen like a cyclone! . . . Armies and elephants . . . Love and laughter . . . Breathless adventure tuned to the rolling thunder of red drumfire in seething India . . . Staged On A Scale That Beggars Words!

The Four Feathers came from Britain. Harry Faversham (John Clements) declines active military service in what he feels is an unjust Sudanese war and is rejected by friend John Durrance (Ralph Richardson) and spurned by fiancée Ethne Buroughs (June Duprez). He receives the four feathers, the mark of a coward. Disguised as a mute Muslim, Harry travels to the Sudan, saves the sun-blinded Durrance's life, and assists British prisoners escape. In so doing he helps win the war against the Mahdi's fanatics. His courage is proved. Durrance and Ethne learn the truth.

Naturally, top star Shirley Temple was up for the role of Dorothy in *The Wizard of Oz,* but that necessitated a loan from Fox that was not accomplished, and MGM's own Judy Garland won the role. Dorothy leaves a tornado-wracked Kansas homestead for the colorful land of Oz, hoping the wizard will return her to black and white Kansas. In Oz she befriends the Cowardly Lion (Bert Lahr), who wants courage, the Tin Man (Jack Haley), who desires a heart, and the Scarecrow (Ray Bolger), who needs a brain. Bent on foiling their plans and regaining the magical red shoes are the Wicked Witch (Margaret Hamilton) and her terrifying flying monkeys. Dorothy triumphs over the witch and wakes as if from a dream, ecstatic to be home. "But anyway, Toto, we're home, home. And this is my room. And you're all here. And I'm not going to leave here ever, ever again because I love you all. Oh, Auntie Em, there's no place like home." The no-place-like-home theme fit studio head

Wuthering Heights (Samuel Goldwyn, 1939) was based on Emily Brontë's tragic romance. Laurence Olivier played Heathcliff, Merle Oberon Cathy.

L. B. Mayer's outlook. "Not since Disney's *Snow White* has anything quite so fantastic succeeded half so well."[77]

By 1939 Bette Davis had come far. Turned down like so many others for the Scarlett O'Hara role, she made a black and white quality clone, *Jezebel*, that beat *GWTW* into release by a year. In *Dark Victory* she elicited audience sympathy for a valiant woman dying from a brain tumor.

> Bette Davis won an Academy Award last year for her performance in *Jezebel*, a spottily effective film. Now it is more than ever apparent that the award was premature. It should have been deferred until her *Dark Victory* came along, as it did yesterday at the Music Hall. Miss Davis is superb. More than that, she is enchanted and enchanting.[78]

In *Beau Geste* the brothers Geste (Gary Cooper, Ray Milland, and Robert Preston) join the French Foreign Legion in this remake of the silent version of the Percival Christopher Wren novel. Brian Donlevy was the vicious Sergeant Markov, who whipped recruits into shape.

> I make soldiers out of scum like you, and I don't do it gently. You're the sloppiest looking lot I've ever seen. It's up to me to prevent you from becoming a disgrace to the regiment. And I will prevent that, if I have to kill half of you with work. But the half that lives will be soldiers. I promise you!

Drums Along the Mohawk was one of the sound cinema's few excursions into the Revolutionary War period. Henry Fonda and Claudette Colbert starred as frontier newlyweds in the John Ford adaptation of the Walter D. Edmonds novel. When war came to the Mohawk Valley and the British incited an Indian attack on the fort, Fonda ran for help, pursued by bloodthirsty Native American warriors. Edna May Oliver was hilarious as a matron who intimidated the savages intent on burning her home.

Two westerns of excellence emerged in 1939. *Stagecoach* became the standard by which future westerns would be measured and made John Wayne a star. *Destry Rides Again* paired the unlikely duo of peaceful, trusting James Stewart and dance-hall hellcat Frenchy (Marlene Dietrich), both menaced by villainous casino owner Brian Donlevy. The film saved Dietrich's failing popularity. Her rendition of "See What the Boys in the Back Room Will Have" became a trademark, and her saloon catfight with Una Merkel was much talked about. Stewart played a peace-loving lawman, slow to anger.

> Now hold on, hold on. Don't get excited here. I was just tryin' to tell ya that I ain't got any guns. See, if I woulda had a gun there why, one of us might got hurt, and mighta been me. I wouldn't like that. Would I?

Ninotchka starred Greta Garbo as the Russian Lena Yakushova, who comes west and learns of true love from capitalist Melvyn Douglas: "Now don't misunderstand me. I do not hold your frivolity against you. As basic material you may not be bad, but you are the unfortunate product of a doomed culture."

Most of these movies belied the fact that civilization was in dire peril in 1939. The bitter legacy of World War I was a communist Russia and a fascistic Central Europe, both anathema to freedom, privacy, civilization. The golden age of the English-language cinema was about to be terminated by those with revenge on their minds.

Chapter 4

The War Years, 1940–1945

> What comes off them [films of 30s and 40s], very strongly, is a remarkable innocence. No doubt the Hays Office and the British Board of Film Censors had something to do with it, but not all that much. It was, as I look back and remember, a very innocent time — even with the Depression and Hitler and the atom bomb, it was still innocent.
> — George MacDonald Fraser, *The Hollywood History of the World*

World War II began on September 1, 1939, when Germany invaded Poland. In that year's *Confessions of a Nazi Spy,* Martin Kosleck played Josef Goebbels, after which Germany's real propaganda minister threatened to make films divulging corruption in American government.[1] By the end of 1940, the Wehrmacht had occupied northern France. The closing of Continental European markets to its product was a severe blow to the American film industry.

WARNINGS: EXPATRIOTS AND REFUGEES

Like composer Franz Waxman and writer-director Billy Wilder, who had exited Europe in the mid–30s, Curtis Bernhardt came to the United States via Britain to escape Nazi Germany. But the freedom he had experienced making European films was not to be found in his new home. In a faster moving world, cinema was commerce as much as art and movies had to be churned out.

> The first thing that hit me here, and hit me hard, was that I no longer had the authority that I had had before. In Germany, France, and Italy before World War II, the director was in charge of the whole artistic side of the film including the script and the choice of the story. The producer had very little influence on actual filmmaking; he was only the business head of the organization.
>
> In America, I found that the producer was the number one man and that the director was supposed to take a script, make a few changes if he felt like it, and then shoot it. My earliest memory of Warner Brothers in 1940 is of somebody handing me a script and saying: "You start shooting Monday."

73

And I was used to having three, four, or five months' preparation: selecting the story, writing one shooting-script with the writers and then a second shooting-script, and when I was ready I went on to the stage and started shooting.[2]

In Fritz Lang's *Man Hunt* (1941), Walter Pidgeon played Captain Alan Thorndike, British game hunter stalking Hitler for fun on July 29, 1939. He is caught with the Führer in his rifle sights, however, and interrogated by the Gestapo (George Sanders). Although beaten, he refuses to sign a confession that he was working for the British government. The Nazis fake his death, pushing him off a precipice. But a tree breaks his fall, and he makes his way to the sea and by ship to England. Followed by a gaunt fellow posing as Thorndike (John Carradine) and other minions, the real Thorndike is assisted by a cockney woman (Joan Bennett). Fearing that if his presence were known, he would be turned over to the Germans, he makes his escape again, disposing of the bogus Thorndike in the Underground. To emphasize the intimidation of fascism, director Lang filmed the Nazis Berchtesgaden/Bavarian indoor scenes in spacious rooms with high ceilings and huge Nazi emblems.

Not unexpectedly, what with all the Continentals on hand, Hollywood knew all about Nazism in Europe (the 1940 *The Mortal Storm* explored its effects on a German family), including the plight of refugees and explored these themes in *So Ends Our Night* (1941) and *Hold Back the Dawn* (1941). In the British film *Pimpernel Smith* (1941), Leslie Howard played mild-mannered archaeologist Horatio Smith, who dabbled in the rescue of those condemned by the Nazis. "Don't worry, I shall be back. We shall all be back," says Professor Smith from the fog to the Nazi officer played by Francis L. Sullivan. In a stirring monologue he foresees the doom that will overtake them.

> You will never rule the world, because you are doomed. All of you who have demoralized and corrupted a nation are doomed. Tonight you will take the first step along a dark road from which there is no turning back. You will have to go on and on, from one madness to another, leaving behind you a wilderness of misery and hatred. And still you will have to go on, because you will find no horizon, and see no dawn, till at last you are lost and destroyed. You are doomed, captain of murderers, and one day, sooner or later, you will remember my words.

The possibility of fascism existing in America was tackled in Frank Capra's *Meet John Doe* (1941). "I don't think he was any fake. Not with that face." So spake Ann Doran of Gary Cooper's character, former bush league baseball pitcher Long John Willoughby who is talked into pretending he will take his own life on Christmas in return for a suit of clothes, a hotel suite, some food for him and his chum, the "Colonel" (Walter Brennan), and a trip to a doctor known as Bonesetter Brown. He'll get a ticket out of town on December 26. As Ann Mitchell, Barbara Stanwyck realizes she can make hay with the story and tells *Bulletin* editor Connell (James Gleason) how they can increase circulation:

> So?! So he writes me a letter and I dig him up! He pours out his soul to me, and from now on we quote, "I protest by John Doe." He protests against all

the evils in the world—the greed, the lust, the hate, the fear—all of man's inhumanity to man! Arguments will start! Should he commit suicide or should he not? People will write in pleading with him but no, no sir. John Doe will remain adamant! On Christmas Eve, hot or cold, he goes! See?

The fascistic oil tycoon and radio station owner D. B. Norton (Edward Arnold) promotes—with his own security force—Doe and nationwide John Doe clubs. When Doe finds out that he is being used for nefarious purposes, he tries to explain to his followers, but Norton's stooges disrupt the rally. An outcast, Doe plans to leap to his death in order to revive the movement. Ann, ill, rushes to the tallest building, knowing he will be there on Christmas Eve. Norton and his cronies are there, and the Colonel and some diehard Doe supporters are, too. If Doe jumps, Norton informs him, the mayor will have his body removed and buried in a potter's field. Ann persuasively argues that he must live to save the movement. "There you are, Norton. The people. Try and lick that!" says Connell. The ending posed such a dilemma for Capra and company that they even took suggestions from the public.

ESCAPISM

Recognized as great morale builders, all films, including low-budgeters and series, continued to be made during the war. *The Saint Strikes Back* had started at RKO in 1939. George Sanders and his brother, Tom Conway, both played in *The Falcon* (1941) and *The Falcon's Brother* (1942). *Detour* (1945) became the standard by which B movies would be measured and helped build a reputation for director Edgar G. Ulmer. Tom Neal plays a hitchhiker who gets involved with two women (Ann Savage and Claudia Drake) and gets more than he bargains for. He utters some priceless words: "That's the most stupid thing I ever heard of. Don't you know millions of people go out there every year and wind up polishing cuspidors? I thought you had better sense." While entertaining, it also merits the review, "On the whole, less than meets the eye."[3]

John Wayne and Marlene Dietrich were a team in the South Seas adventure *Seven Sinners* (1940) and were joined by Randolph Scott for *The Spoilers* and *Pittsburgh* in 1942. *The Spoilers* was Rex Beach's venerable story oft-told: an Alaskan western with a big, big fight scene. *Pittsburgh,* too, had its battle. Wayne and Ward Bond (and stuntmen) are also justly famous for a housewide brawl in the 1944 *Tall in the Saddle.*

War-related escapism was featured in *All Through the Night* (1942), in which American gangsters led by Humphrey Bogart demonstrated their patriotism by quashing Nazi agents. Of glossier mettle was *Casablanca* (1942). Apparently George Raft had no idea what a success this would be, just as he had mistakenly turned down the role that went to Bogart in *High Sierra.* Bogart played Rick Blaine, owner of Rick's Café Americain. Topicality helped its initial success—North Africa was in the news when the Allies invaded on November 8, 1942. Rich and Ilsa Lund (Ingrid Bergman) were lovers in Paris before the Nazis came ("The Germans wore gray, you wore blue"). Now Ilsa shows up in Casablanca on the arm of husband, Victor Laszlo (Paul Henreid).

Pianist Sam (Dooley Wilson) spies Ilsa first, and she makes him play "As Time Goes By." Rick comes storming out to berate Sam for the tune but spots Ilsa. Later he makes Sam play it again. "If she can stand it, I can. Play it!" Still, "Of all the gin joints in all the towns in all the world, she walks into mine." Memories trouble Rick, whose café is a watering spot for gamblers, agents, and refugees hoping to acquire passports to Lisbon and America. Free French Capitaine Renault (Claude Rains) indicates that he will take the orders of Nazi Major Heinrich Strasser (Conrad Veidt) and detain Laszlo, underground leader and escapee from a Nazi concentration camp. Although Rick states that "I stick my neck out for nobody," he relents and helps Victor and Ilsa. Ilsa believes she is staying with Rick, but he convinces her to board the plane with her husband in one of the screen's greatest moments: "Here's looking at you, kid." Strasser tries to stop the getaway, but Rick shoots him dead.Renault decides it's time to support the Free French; he tells his gendarmes that Strasser's been shot and that they should "round up the usual suspects." As Renault and Blaine walk off into the fog, Rick says, "Louis, I think this is the beginning of a beautiful friendship." For a film of little action, *Casablanca* hangs together, possessing all the atmosphere one could want, bridging war and escapism. The British reaction:

> Humphrey Bogart, who, as the owner of a night club, gives his usual deliberately flat performance of the sentimentalist masquerading as the cynic.... The incidentals of the film, however, are to be preferred to the main issue of visas, arrests, and escapes ... and at moments *Casablanca* seems genuinely to be trying to give expression to the emotions of those colonial French who were left bewildered by the fall of their country but did not lose their faith.[4]

At the Academy Awards ceremony studio mogul Jack Warner beat producer Hal Wallis to the stage to accept the best picture statuette.[5]

Taking place in a combat zone was *Five Graves to Cairo* (1943) in which Erich von Stroheim played German Field Marshal Erwin Rommel. Franchot Tone was a British soldier masquerading out of necessity as a waiter and spy at a coastal inn in Sidi Halfaya. It was Billy Wilder's second directorial outing, and he made the most of it.

Westerns could be used as escapism or feature messages applicable to the time. Historical inaccuracies permeated the 1940 film *Santa Fe Trail,* which, incidentally, had very little to do with any trail. Real-life characters Jeb Stuart (Errol Flynn) and George Armstrong Custer (Ronald Reagan) confound the violent actions of abolitionist John Brown (Raymond Massey), who seizes the arsenal at Harper's Ferry in 1859 West Virginia and are besieged by a host of men and batteries of cannon. (Massey also played *Abe Lincoln in Illinois* that year and would portray him again in 1963, in *How the West Was Won.* He would also play John Brown again in 1955, in *Seven Angry Men.*) In this first outing, his character gave an evocative monologue as he awaited execution.

> I am only walking as God foreordained I should walk. All my actions, even the folly leading to this disaster, were decreed to happen long ages before this world began. But I cannot remember a night so dark as to have hindered the

coming day, or a storm so furious as to prevent the return of warm sunshine on a country at peace. I, John Brown, am now quite certain that the crimes of this guilty land can never be purged away but with blood. Aye, let them hang me. I forgive them and may God forgive them, for they know not what they do.

Like *Santa Fe Trail, They Died with Their Boots On* (1942) was a Civil War film, a western, and a biography. This time Errol Flynn played George Armstrong Custer.[6] It remains the best of the Custer films. Max Steiner's score was excellent, with fine Indian motifs and a moving love theme that was especially effective during the parting of Custer and his wife, Libby (Olivia de Havilland). Uneducated mule-skinner scout "California" (Charley Grapewin) makes disparaging remarks about the "redskins." Native American grievances were voiced in Crazy Horse's recital of treaty breaking as well as in words printed over the action: "And so was born the immortal Seventh Cavalry, which cleared the plains for a ruthlessly advancing civilization that spelled doom to the red race."

Women and Children: While men were at war, films with women protagonists proliferated. They often suffered in the grandiose surroundings of beach houses and country estates. Definitive were Joan Crawford and Bette Davis vehicles. In 1945 Crawford could afford to thumb her nose at her old studio, MGM, after winning an Academy Award for Warner Bros.' *Mildred Pierce*. She played the long-suffering mother of the wicked Veda (Ann Blyth). *Now, Voyager* (1942) starred Bette Davis and Paul Henreid in an ill-fated romance. Wrote producer Hal Wallis,

> Our old nemesis, the Breen office, made ridiculous demands again. On April Fool's Day, 1942, Breen sent me a lengthy memorandum. He said that when Charlotte and a ship's officer climb out of a car in which they have been kissing, Charlotte's hair must not be mussed to suggest a close embrace. Despite the fact that the entire picture centered on the affair between Charlotte and her lover, Jerry, there must be no suggestion that they go to bed together. In a scene in which they are stranded for the night in a cabin in Brazil, it must be made clear that they are under separate blankets.[7]

This is the film famous for Paul Henreid's simultaneously lighting two cigarettes.

Popular screen children were Roddy McDowall, the cabin boy who helped Walter Pidgeon escape the Nazis in *Man Hunt* (1941) and the collie's owner in *Lassie Come Home* (1943). In 1944 the 12-year-old Elizabeth Taylor caught the public's eye in her second movie, *National Velvet*, where she played opposite Mickey Rooney. Margaret O'Brien scored big in *Meet Me in St. Louis* (1944).

Horror: Val Lewton, who had worked for David Selznick, produced many highly regarded horror films for RKO: *Cat People* (1943), *I Walked with a Zombie* (1943), *The Seventh Victim* (1943), *The Ghost Ship* (1943), *The Leopard Man* (1943), *Curse of the Cat People* (1944), *The Body Snatcher* (1945), *Isle of the Dead* (1945), and *Bedlam* (1946). There were no obvious monsters — imagination sufficed.

Universal had shot its bolt and was merely transferring 30s monsters into the 40s in mediocre sequels like *The Ghost of Frankenstein* (1942), *Frankenstein Meets the Wolf Man* (1943), and mummy films. Some remained entertaining, especially the more outlandish ones. *House of Frankenstein* (1945) featured Dracula (John Carradine), the Frankenstein monster (Glenn Strange), the wolf man (Lon Chaney, Jr.), a hunchback (J. Carrol Naish), and Boris Karloff, this time as the mad Dr. Niemann. *House of Dracula* (1945) again featured John Carradine, who played Dracula masquerading as Baron Latoes. "Yes, doctor, I am Count Dracula, but I am known to the outside world as Baron Latoes. You see before you a man who lived for centuries, kept alive by the blood of innocent people."

Science fiction? It needed A-bombs and saucer sightings to take off. *Dr. Cyclops* (1940) was one of the few true science-fiction films of the period. *Frankenstein* and a few predecessors had used bogus or slipshod science. In *Cyclops* bespectacled Albert Dekker shrank people. Almost all theatrical films that could be deemed science fiction involved mad scientists. Take Boris Karloff's Dr. John Garth in the 1940 *Before I Hang:* "This is a serum distilled from the cells, mixed in our own blood, which I inject directly into the heart. Of course it's true that I failed with the only human being I ever inoculated, but I know that I was on the right track!" And Bela Lugosi in Monogram's 1943 film *The Ape Man:* "What a mess I've made of things." Or George Zucco in 1943 PRC (Producers Releasing Corporation) movie *Dead Men Walk:* "We are all too quick to call 'insane' any mentality that deviates from the conventional. There have been many things in Heaven and earth undreamed of in our philosophy."

Biographies: The life stories of famous people continued to provide grist for the Hollywood mill. Gary Cooper followed his Academy Award–winning performance as World War I hero Alvin York in *Sergeant York* (1941) with a portrait of baseball star Lou Gehrig in *The Pride of the Yankees* (1942). Playing 2,130 consecutive games earned Gehrig his "Iron Horse" nickname. Ironically, he contracted the debilitating disease amyotropic lateral sclerosis and died at the age of 37 in 1941. Sam Goldwyn produced the tearjerker. The introductory portions of the retirement ceremonies at Yankee Stadium, with Dan Duryea in the press booth and the band marching around the field, prepared the audience for the famous farewell at Yankee Stadium.

> I have been walking on ballfields for sixteen years and I've never received anything but kindness and encouragement from you fans. I have had the great honor to have played with these great veteran ballplayers on my left — Murderers Row — our championship team of 1927. I have had the further honor of living with and playing with these men on my right — the Bronx Bombers — the Yankees of today. I have been given fame, and undeserved praise by the boys up there behind the wire in the pressbox — my friends the sportswriters. I have worked under the two greatest managers of all time — Miller Huggins and Joe McCarthy. I have a mother and father who fought to give me health. And a solid background in my youth. I have a wife, a companion for life, who has shown me more courage than I imagined. People all

say that I've had a bad break. But today, today I consider myself the luckiest man on the face of the earth.

As "Always" was heard, the wife (Teresa Wright) sobbed and Gehrig disappeared into the tunnel.

Edward G. Robinson was in two 1940 biographies. In *Dr. Ehrlich's Magic Bullet* he played the discover of the cure for syphilis, and in *A Dispatch from Reuters* began the famous wire service. *The Adventures of Mark Twain* (1944) starred Fredric March as America's greatest humorist.

Adventure: Doubtless they were not thought of at the time as anything other than escapist entertainment, yet several films of the period were so farfetched and had such wonderfully nonsensical dialogue that they would be designated "camp" in later years. In *South of Pago Pago* (1940) stage-trained veteran character actor Abner Biberman as Manuel propositioned Frances Farmer. "You sail with me, chiquita, and you can have a rope of pearls down to your knees."

Cobra Woman, a 1944 Universal release with big B stars Maria Montez and Jon Hall, was one of the most enjoyable pieces of tomfoolery ever made. Listen to Lois Collier as Veeda rejoicing: "Martok dead! Fire Mountain no longer angry with us! Cruelty and oppression ended here forever! We all now free — to live and believe as we please under rule of our rightful queen, Tollea!" That year's *Nabonga* was made at Poverty Row studio PRC and featured Buster Crabbe, who proposed the axiom that "crocodiles can sure give you a workout."

Salome, Where She Danced (1945) was a hybrid: part western, part adventure, all malarkey. Yvonne DeCarlo starred. This time Abner Biberman was the Asian Dr. Ling.

> The right road is always the hard one. When a man is redeemed, when he begins again, 'tis never the length of the road that dismays him. No, 'tis the thought of leaving the old comrades in arms, the thought of going it alone along the bitter path of peace. For ye have been bred for war and taught to fight and taught nothing else.

Others, too, spoke in parables and non sequiturs. "What way have I ever taken but the wrong way? Whenever I stood before two roads, I took the wrong one," says David Bruce as Cleve. "I ask your pardon, but mademoiselle is far too genuine to be wearing false feathers. The tropics of the Indian Seas have labored a million years to find a plume as worthy of your grace," Walter Slezak's Colonel compliments Salome. Salome rants, "No one can keep me here! I'll take to the road. I'll sing in every dance hall, in every saloon until I find Cleve!" Best of all was J. Edward Bromberg's tribute, "She was always a great artist, but above all — a woman."

Big budgets compromised any camp designations for a number of adventure films. Under Rouben Mamoulian's direction, Tyrone Power played Diego Vega, scion of a California family, in *The Mark of Zorro* (1940). The swordfight between Power and Basil Rathbone as Captain Esteban Pasquale is usually reckoned — along with that in *Scaramouche* (1952) — the screen's best duel.

Apparently a better swordsman in real life than were most of his opponents, Rathbone of necessity was punctured many times in film, for instance, in *Captain Blood* and *The Adventures of Robin Hood*.

The Sea Hawk (1940) starred Errol Flynn as Jeffrey Thorpe, one of Queen Elizabeth I's seadogs preying on Spanish shipping and Panamanian overland gold shipments. (Rafael Sabatini's novel placed the action in the Mediterranean amongst Muslim pirates.) Enhanced by Erich Wolfgang Korngold's music, the opening engagement between Thorpe's ship and Gilbert Roland's is the screen's finest piratical engagement. Claude Rains was the Spanish ambassador, Henry Daniell a worthy opponent for Flynn in the climactic sword-fighting scene. Flora Robson seemed the definitive Elizabeth, majestic in surroundings like the throne room.

The Black Swan and *Son of Fury*, both released 1942, starred Tyrone Power in seafaring adventures. Another big nautical film that year was *Reap the Wild Wind*, with John Wayne, Ray Milland, Paulette Goddard, and Susan Hayward and sterling support from crusty Lynne Overman. Wayne battled 19th century pirates and an octopus. During a more pleasant interlude, he complimented Goddard: "Nights on watch I'll see you like this, Loxie. With your hair catching fire in the sunset, and that look in your eyes — ten fathoms deep."

Musicals and Evocations of the Past: With war upon the world, it was tempting to view the past through rose-colored glasses. *Meet Me in St. Louis* (1944) featured Judy Garland, while the young and ingratiating Margaret O'Brien matched her in audience appeal. The studio had resisted making a film of Sally Benson's stories of growing up at the time of the Louisiana Purchase Exposition, the world's fair of 1903, because of their episodic nature.

> The people at Metro were very much against the idea I had of following the material to the letter. They insisted: "There's no story, nothing happens." But [Arthur] Freed and I were determined (and so was Judy Garland, who had hated the way the whole thing had been "written up") to preserve the autobiographical, series-of-sketches flavour.[8]

Songs included the title tune, "The Boy Next Door," "The Trolley Song," and the heartrending "Have Yourself a Merry Little Christmas," sung by Garland to an O'Brien distraught about an impending move to New York.

At 20th Century–Fox, backstagers and musical biographies were a staple. Alice Faye, Betty Grable, John Payne, Jack Oakie, Victor Mature, and Carole Landis were veterans of musicals whose music emanated from the stage, rarely from naturalistic settings that would come to mark MGM musicals in the next decade. *Lillian Russell* (1940) starred Alice Faye as the real-life songbird. *Dance Hall* (1941) featured Carole Landis, and *Footlight Serenade* (1942) Betty Grable, along with John Payne and Victor Mature. That same year Columbia's Rita Hayworth came over for *My Gal Sal*, with Mature. Grable, the G.I.'s other favorite pin-up girl, starred in *Coney Island* (1943) and *Pin Up Girl* (1944). The future producer of Mitzi Gaynor musical biographies, George Jessel, produced *The Dolly Sisters* in 1945, with Betty Grable and June Haver.

Tin Pan Alley (20th Century-Fox, 1940) featured Alice Faye (left) and Betty Grable in the "Sheik of Araby" number. In a few years Faye would retire from the screen to concentrate on her marriage to orchestra leader Phil Harris. Grable would become a favorite G.I. pin-up.

Nonmusical nostalgia was the concern of *Home in Indiana* (1944), with Lon McCallister, June Haver, and Jeanne Crain, Miss Long Beach of 1941. Walter Brennan reformed young Lon via harness racing. The film was remade as *April Love* in 1957.

Comedy: Comedy was a necessary morale booster during wartime. Bud Abbott and Lou Costello debuted in 1940 in *Night in the Tropics* and became the movies' premiere comedy team for Universal until supplanted by Dean Martin and Jerry Lewis at Paramount in the early 50s.

To Be or Not to Be (1942) from director Ernst Lubitsch poked fun at Poland's German conquerors. Jack Benny was hack Shakespearean actor Joseph Tura, who posed as a Nazi. "So they call me Concentration Camp Erhardt?" asked Sig Rumann. It was Carole Lombard's last film. Another brilliant director, Preston Sturges, brought his wit to *The Palm Beach Story* (1942) and two acclaimed 1944 items, *Hail the Conquering Hero* and *The Miracle of Morgan's Creek*.

Bob Hope came into his own via *The Ghost Breakers* (1940) and *Caught in the Draft* (1941). His first "road" film with Bing Crosby was *The Road to*

Italy, World War II: Robert Mitchum exceeds expectations in *The Story of G.I. Joe*
(United Artists, 1945). Burgess Meredith appeared as real-life war correspondent Ernie
Pyle.

Singapore (1940).[9] *My Favorite Blonde* was Madeleine Carroll in 1942. Later
came *My Favorite Brunette* (Dorothy Lamour, 1947) and *My Favorite Spy*
(Hedy Lamarr, 1951).

Ray Milland and Ginger Rogers played *The Major and the Minor* in 1942.
In *The More the Merrier* (1943), Jean Arthur shared a D.C. apartment during
wartime with Joel McCrea and Charles Coburn, who won a supporting actor
Academy Award.

War: Most films made about the war during the war naturally had a
propagandistic slant, which is why most of the best World War II films were
made after the conflict. *In Which We Serve* (1942) was the inspiring brainchild
of playwright Noel Coward. Coward produced, codirected with David Lean,
and wrote the screenplay. He also starred as Captain Kinross, with John Mills
as Shorty Blake and Bernard Miles as Walter Hardy. They manned the
destroyer *H.M.S. Torrin*. The doctor was played by James Donald, who would
be medical officer in *The Brigade on the River Kwai* (1957) and a POW again
in *The Great Escape* (1963). Other excellent war films about combat made during the war included *Air Force* (1943), *Sahara* (1943), *Destination Tokyo*
(1943), *Guadalcanal Diary* (1943), *The Way Ahead* (1944), *They Were Expend-
able* (1945), *The Story of G.I. Joe* (1945), *Pride of the Marines* (1945), and *The
Way to the Stars* (1945).

With Russia on the Allies' side as of June 22, 1941, when Germany invaded the Soviet Union, wartime movies portrayed the Soviet communists as brothers in arms. *The North Star* (also known as *Armored Attack,* 1943), was written by Lillian Hellman, and her master script was published in hardcover that year. *Days of Glory* (1944) showed Nazi atrocity and partisan resistance.

A supreme patriotic spiel was made in *Gung Ho!* (1943). Randolph Scott played Colonel Thorwald, leader of an attack on Makin Island. On the return submarine trip, he spoke to his men but, more importantly, to the stateside cinema audience:

> Men! It may seem too soon to talk of the Makin Island raid as finished, when we're seven days from home and Jap warships are closing in on us, but I'll take that chance. Raiders, you have shown the way. Whatever anyone may do in the days ahead, this was the first offensive action to be carried out. Our victory, however, has not been without the loss of men who were like brothers to us. But what of the future for those of us who remain? Our course is clear. It is for us at this moment, with the memory of the sacrifice of our brothers still fresh, to dedicate again our hearts, our minds, and our bodies to the great task that lies ahead. We must go further, and dedicate ourselves also to the monumental task of assuring that the peace, which follows this holocaust, will be a just, equitable, and conclusive peace. And beyond that lies the mission of making certain that the social order which we bequeath to our sons and daughters is truly based on freedom, for which these men died!

More virulent was *The Fighting Seabees* (1944). As Wedge Donovan, John Wayne proclaimed, "I have a contract here for an airfield on Island X214. I'm goin' there personally and take my best crew, and if Tojo and his bug-eyed monkeys get in our way, you and the Navy may find out you have a construction unit *and* a combat unit rolled into one!"

Desperate Journey (1942) was exciting nonsense about Allied pilots shot down over Europe. "Now for Australia and a crack at those Japs!" exclaims Errol Flynn to Ronald Reagan as they hightail it out of Nazi-occupied Europe in a captured plane after some amazing adventures.

Germans were sometimes treated more sympathetically. Cedric Hardwicke was a professional soldier merely obeying orders in *The Moon Is Down* (1943), based on the John Steinbeck novel of the Nazi occupation of Norway.

There was a furor in 1945 in Britain over *Objective, Burma!*

> This long film has met with objections from American service men, and it is indeed a little extraordinary for it to imply that the Burma campaign was fought almost entirely without the aid of the British. There is one reference to the Fourteenth Army; during the course of the action it is rashly presumed by one of the party of American parachutists that a British outpost may be somewhere about, but this suggestion is promptly snubbed, and for the rest Mr. Errol Flynn and the indomitable band he leads have it all their own way.[10]

On September 25, an article titled "Film and the Allies" maintained that because movies were seen by impressionable millions, it was imperative to get things right. Quoted from *Seac,* the publication of the South-East Asia Command, is Lieutenant-Colonel William H. Taylor of the U.S. Army Air Force, who said, "It is a disturbing thought that this meretricious hodge-podge, which implies that Burma was invaded and liberated by a force of American parachutists, American glider-borne troops, two Gurkha guides and a Chinese officer will be seen by thousands of men who know better."[11] And on September 26, 1945, was "Objective, Burma! Suspended." It was withdrawn from the Warner Cinema and would never reach the hinterland.

> In announcing this decision Mr. Max Milder, managing director of Warner Brothers Pictures, Limited, stated that criticisms accusing the producers of deliberately ignoring the major part played by the Fourteenth Army in the Burma campaign were without foundation. The film had set out to dramatize a single incident in the Burma war, and to give a realistic interpretation of conditions of jungle fighting. The foreword emphasized that experiences shown on the screen were shared by British, Indians, and Chinese forces who carried the campaign to its victorious conclusion.[12]

Milder was correct. With a plot similar to that of *Northwest Passage* (1940), *Objective, Burma!* is the saga of a small party of paratroopers whose mission is the destruction of a Japanese radar installation. It does not purport to be the history of the entire Burma campaign. Another criticism leveled at the film was that the American soldiers were aghast when they found some of their number butchered by the Japanese, even though they too had ambushed the enemy.

All in all, *Objective, Burma!* was one of the best World War II films made during the war. Critic and writer James Agee discerned its merits. "Often the camera prowls and veers along facades of vegetation which are freighted with the threat of imagination and possibility but which properly seldom turn out to contain any actual danger."[13]

A Walk in the Sun (1945), which focused on a small group of G.I.s in Italy, was perhaps the first film to use a ballad as musical accompaniment, although *High Noon* (1951) is usually credited for using the ballad accompaniment first, with "Do Not Forsake Me, Oh My Darling."

Alfred Hitchcock's *Foreign Correspondent* (1940) featured Joel McCrea as Johnny Jones/Huntley Haverstock, a reporter covering impending war in Europe. After spying on Nazis in a Dutch windmill, which entwines his coat in the gears, falling onto a hotel awning, stepping aside as an assassin tries to topple him from a roof, and surviving a plane crash at sea, he radios to America from a besieged Britain: "Keep those lights burning. Cover them with steel. Ring them with guns. Build a canopy of battleships and bombing planes around them. Hello, America! Hang on to your lights, they're the only lights left in the world!"

Alfred Hitchcock provoked comment about leadership in *Lifeboat* (1944). Adrift after a submarine attack were Tallulah Bankhead, William Bendix, Mary Anderson, John Hodiak, Henry Hull, Canada Lee, Hume Cronyn, Heather Angel, William Yetter, Jr., and, as the U-boat commander, take-charge Nazi Walter Slezak.

Mrs. Miniver (1942) starred Greer Garson and Walter Pidgeon as "typical" Britishers weathering the Blitz and won a best picture Academy Award. *Since You Went Away* (1944) was the biggest production dealing with the American

Errol Flynn leads parachutists against a Japanese radar station in the controversial but gripping *Objective, Burma!* (Warner Bros., 1945).

home front. Claudette Colbert was the mother, Jennifer Jones and Shirley Temple the daughters, Joseph Cotten and Robert Walker the military men on leave.

   Forever and a Day (1943) was made in the United States by British writers and performers. The former included C. S. Forester, Christopher Isherwood, James Hilton, and Claudine West. Among the latter were Jessie Matthews, Charles Laughton, Anna Neagle, Ida Lupino, June Duprez, Ray Milland, Cedric Hardwicke, Claude Rains, and C. Aubrey Smith. Their stories revolved around a London house, from 1804 till the German air blitz of 1940.

Downed American airmen are questioned by Japanese officer (Richard Loo, actually Chinese-Hawaiian) in *The Purple Heart* (20th Century–Fox, 1944). From left: Charles Russell, Dana Andrews, Farley Granger, Sam Levene, and John Craven.

Film noir: "Dark cinema" was a term applied by the French to Hollywood crime movies of a certain—but difficult to define—style and ambience that originated in the 1940s. *The Maltese Falcon* (1941) can be termed, with some accuracy, the first American entry. *Touch of Evil* in 1958 might be considered the last. These films were usually shot in black and white. The manipulation of light and shadow—white skin and platinum hair (Barbara Stanwyck in *Double Indemnity*)—contrasted with the dark interior of a soul or the modern city by night. This was truly cinematic art. There was a hard edge skillfully presented, and denouements were usually unpleasant. This distinguished *noir* from the regular cops and robbers story.

This Gun for Hire (1942) was based on a Graham Greene story and made Alan Ladd a star as Raven, the hired killer with the stone face. While entertaining, the plot was based on number of coincidences. Killer Raven (Ladd) finds the only empty seat on a train next to Ellen (Veronica Lake), who has just taken a nightclub job for Gates (Laird Cregar) while she is also spying for a senatorial committee. Raven wants to kill Gates, but Gates spots him first and wires the police. Raven sees the police first and escapes. Believing Ellen to be Raven's crony, Gates has her detained and prepared for drowning. Raven arrives at Gates' house while the investigating policeman (Robert Preston) is there, and the chauffeur tosses Ellen's pocketbook out the window in front of Raven. The policeman is Ellen's boyfriend!

Hitchcock's *film noir* candidate, *Shadow of a Doubt* (1943), disclosed an alternate side of the perceived idyll of small-town life when Uncle Charlie (Joseph Cotten) visits his niece Charlie (Teresa Wright). Questions and doubts about her uncle are heightened when he pulls her into a dive and rants,

> You live in a dream. You're a sleepwalker, blind. How do you know what the world is like? Do you know the world is a foul sty? Do you know if you rip the fronts off houses you'd find swine? The world's a hell. What does it matter what happens in it? Wake up, Charlie. Use your wit. Learn something.

This outburst only raises Charlie's suspicions that Uncle Charlie is the Merry Widow murderer, on the lam at his sister's house in Santa Rosa, California.

Director Jacques Tourneur, who would helm a definitive *noir* in *Out of the Past* (1947), worked for RKO, a studio familiar with *noir*. He described the help provided by the RKO family:

> Of course, the look of all these films at RKO was due to the wonderful work of the art department. This was one of the last family studios; normally in the studios there's a man and a half for every job, and if there's a cutting down of personnel, everyone hides, but at RKO everybody was exactly fitted to his job, and no one was after anyone else's. Each man was a specialist: there was a wonderful plaster shop, for instance; the best decorators; a wonderful property room: this was a family studio, like Disney's. Everyone had perfect taste; the art directors, Albert d'Agostino and Van Nest Polglase; the design man, Darryl Silvera.[14]

The Woman in the Window (1944) and *Scarlet Street* (1945) were both directed by Fritz Lang and had the same trio in the lead roles: Edward G. Robinson, Joan Bennett, and Dan Duryea. Bennett was the femme fatale. Only five years hence she would be a matron in *Father of the Bride*.

Otto Preminger directed *Laura* (1944), a mystery that became an audience favorite. It starred Dana Andrews as the detective, Gene Tierney as the mysterious, supposedly deceased title character, and Clifton Webb as mentor Waldo Lydecker. He would rather have Laura dead than in the arms of another man.

> The best part of myself, that's what you are. Do you think I'm going to leave it to the vulgar pawing of a second rate detective who thinks you're a dame? Do you think I could bear the thought of him holding you in his arms, kissing you, loving you?

Preminger used new techniques.

> Everything happens as if the characters had been created before the plot (it usually happens the other way round, of course), as if they themselves were constructing the plot, transposing it on to a level to which it never aspired. To accentuate this impression, Preminger thought up a new narrative technique (which moreover gave his film great historical importance): long sequences shot from a crane, following the key characters in each scene in their every move, so that these characters, *immutably* fixed in the frame (usually in close-up or in two-shot), see the world around them evolving and changing in accordance with their actions. Here was the proof that a thriller can also be beautiful and profound, that it is a question of style and conviction.[15]

Scarlet Street (Universal, 1945) was the second teaming of Dan Duryea and Joan Bennett, who made life difficult for Edward G. Robinson in this as well as 1944's *The Woman in the Window*. Fritz Lang directed both.

Double Indemnity (1944) starred Fred MacMurray as Walter Neff, insurance salesman for the Pacific All Risk Insurance Company. Barton Keyes (Edward G. Robinson) handled claims. Neff became involved with Mrs. Phyllis Dietrichson (Barbara Stanwyck in an unusual — for her — blond mane), whose allure loosened Neff's scruples to the extent that he agreed to help murder her callous husband. If Mr. Dietrichson were killed falling from a train, his spouse would collect $100,000 — thus the doubling of the original $50,000 accident policy. Naturally things went awry, and Phyllis was not all she seemed. "You're all washed up, Walter," says Keyes to a bleeding Neff near fadeout.

Murder, My Sweet (1944) was to have been titled *Farewell, My Lovely,* but it was learned that audiences expected the old, singing Dick Powell![16] The advertisements helped inform the spectators of the true nature of the film: "Congratulations, Dick Powell, You're terrific in your NEW tough role. . . . Forget That Feeling . . . she's got Murder in her heart! Trouble ahead, mister! That fellow who hired you to find his woman won't stop at murder . . . if you don't deliver! Neither will she . . . if you do!"

Powell was 6'2", but Moose Malloy (Mike Mazurki) was 6'4½". "So Dick walked in the gutter while Mike walked up on the curb, or Dick stood in his stocking feet while Mike stood on a box."[17] Marlowe was hired by Malloy to track down the long gone Velma (Claire Trevor). He began at Florian's bar. Jade got in the way, as did the big shot (Otto Kruger) who coveted it. Velma had been hiding at a beach house, where the protagonists met their—for some fatal—end. *Cornered* (1945) provided Powell with another tough guy role.

Mildred Pierce (1945) was ostensibly not a crime film, but self-sacrificing mother Joan Crawford killed in the name of her ingrate daughter, Veda (Ann Blyth). Crawford won an Academy Award. Oddly, she would make very few truly memorable films afterward. *Humoresque* (1946), *Johnny Guitar* (1954), and *What Ever Happened to Baby Jane?* (1962), with rival Bette Davis, might just be the only satisfying movies of her later years. The strength of her personality made and kept her a star.

Semidocumentaries, which may be said to have begun in earnest in 1945 with *The House on 92nd Street,* brought a bit more light to *noir*. This one was about the destruction of a U.S.-based Nazi spy ring.

REALISM

The 1945 Academy Award for best picture went to the Billy Wilder–Charles Brackett scripted, Wilder-directed *The Lost Weekend.* (In 1944, Academy Award best picture nominees totaled five for the first time; previously, there had been ten.) In a change of pace, debonair leading man Ray Milland played Don Birnam, failed writer and drunk. In addition to touching a heretofore taboo cinema topic, Wilder did much location work, also something of a novelty for Hollywood. Ray Milland wrote,

> For most of the work in New York the cameras were hidden. Holes were cut in the canvas tops of delivery trucks, or from the inside of a huge piano packing case strategically placed on the sidewalk before dawn or from the inside of a vacant store front. Therefore, nobody paid any attention to the unshaven bum staggering along Third Avenue looking for a pawnshop for his battered typewriter, an instance of protective coloring. To them I was normal.[18]

Whatever its faults—some think Milland's character should have died—*The Lost Weekend* and *Days of Wine and Roses* (1962) remain the best commercial statements about the evils of drink.

At Fox the decade began with *The Grapes of Wrath,* based on John Steinbeck's Pulitzer Prize–winning 1940 novel that told of the "Okies," farmers driven from their Oklahoma dust bowl homes by bank foreclosures. Many, including the Joad family, headed for the promised land of California.

> This here old man just lived a life and just died out. I don't know whether he's good or bad. Don't matter much. Heard a fella say a poem once. And he says all that lives is holy. Well I wouldn't pray this for the old man that's dead cause he's all right. If I was to pray I'd pray for folks that's alive and don't know which way to turn. Grandpa here, he ain't got no more trouble like that. He's got his job all cut out for him, so cover him up and let him get to it.

Henry Fonda was Tom Joad. He killed a cop who had bludgeoned itinerant preacher Casey (John Carradine) to death. Visiting his mother (Jane Darwell) before taking to the shadows, he made a stirring exit speech.

> Then it don't matter. I'll be all around in the dark. I'll be everywhere, wherever you can look, wherever there's a fight so hungry people can eat, I'll be there. Wherever there's a cop beatin' up a guy, I'll be there. I'll be in the way guys yell when they're mad, I'll be in the way kids laugh when they're hungry and they know supper's ready. And when the people are eatin' the stuff they raise, livin' in the houses they build, I'll be there too.

Director John Ford said,

> Gregg Toland did a great job of photography there—absolutely nothing but nothing to photograph, not *one* beautiful thing in there—just sheer good photography. I said to him, "Part of it will be in blackness, but let's photograph it. Let's take a chance and do something different." It worked out all right.[19]

Brief Encounter (1945) demonstrated the talent of British director David Lean. Married to others, a doctor (Trevor Howard) and a housewife (Celia Johnson) found a mutual attraction and kept a weekly rendezvous at a train station until they realized the affair could lead nowhere.

STARS

After 14 sound films, Greta Garbo called it quits. *Two-Faced Woman* (1941), an unsuccessful film, was her last.

Humphrey Bogart stepped out of James Cagney's shadow in 1941 in *High Sierra*. As ex-con Roy Earle, he planned a robbery but got involved with a club-footed woman (Joan Leslie), although he was loved by Marie, a harder dame, played by Ida Lupino. ("How was it? I mean, knowing you're in for life? I should think you'd go crazy.") Of course he was doomed and brought to bay on the side of a mountain. Then George Raft turned down *Casablanca,* and Bogart was Rick.

> The look of derision that sprung so easily to his battered features; his aggressive manner of kissing a girl, at the same time grasping her throat in a slightly menacing manner; or the cold hard stare, unblinking, into a foe's eyes; or the equally disturbing mannerism of tugging at the lobe of his ear, with a mockingly bemused expression in his eyes as his mouth slid automatically into a vacant half-grin. These and many other typical gestures project an extremely capable, confident man; a man who knew no fear, and could look after himself in any situation—the perfect hero, in spite of his lack of normal good looks, and what is generally considered to be charm.[20]

Ida Lupino, in retrospect, can be seen as more versatile, more affecting, than Bette Davis or Joan Crawford.

> The greatest pity about the Warner Brothers system was that in milking their contractees as frequently as was their custom, they depleted a player's talent or range. Thus Ida Lupino was always seen as a second string Bette Davis, bringing a steely, brittle intensity to her unsympathetic roles—and nobody explored her capacity for going insane on the screen more frequently than Ida—or brought a more delicate, tragic air to her sympathetic roles.[21]

Films—mostly by Warner Bros.—that merited such praise for Lupino included *The Light That Failed* (1940), *They Drive by Night* (1940), *High Sierra* (1941), *The Sea Wolf* (1941), *Out of the Fog* (1941), *Ladies in Retirement* (Columbia, 1941), *Moontide* (Columbia, 1942), and *The Hard Way* (1942).

Errol Flynn, who had come to the fore in 1935 in *Captain Blood,* had most of his best period pieces behind him but was frequently a surprisingly good westerner, as evidenced by *Dodge City* (1939), *Virginia City* (1940), and *They Died with Their Boots On* (1942).[22] In *Edge of Darkness* (1943), Flynn played a Norwegian Nazi fighter. Flynn lived the high life, but director Lewis Milestone remembered a different man.

> Maybe not enough people knew Flynn well. I not only admired him as an actor, I liked him very much as a person. I knew him as a perfect host, a marvellous connoisseur of good food and wine, and as a beautifully behaved guest in my home. His faults harmed no one except himself.[23]

Hollywood's most famous duo, Spencer Tracy and Katharine Hepburn, costarred for the first time in *Woman of the Year* (1942). That same year they made *Keeper of the Flame,* topical in its plot about the exposure of an American fascist.[24]

June Allyson—not Dorothy Lamour, Rita Hayworth, or Betty Grable—was the war's favorite pinup, suggests Fraser.[25] Could this be true? Saccharine though she was, June Allyson must have represented the real girl next door for many. But did she do cheesecake?

Margaret Lockwood, who had starred in Hitchcock's 1938 success, *The Lady Vanishes,* came to the United States briefly—for *Rulers of the Sea* at Paramount and for *Susannah of the Mounties,* with Shirley Temple, at Fox, both in 1939. Back home in Britain—often as a sympathetic bad girl—she became the number one draw in 1945 and 1946, getting there via *The Man in Grey* (1943) and *The Wicked Lady* (1945).

Neither tough nor exotic but rather sweet was Patricia Roc, who costarred with Lockwood in *Love Story* (1944) and starred in *Madonna of the Seven Moons* (1944) with Stewart Granger and Phyllis Calvert. Roc came to Hollywood to costar with Dana Andrews and Susan Hayward in *Canyon Passage* in 1946. Calvert was in *The Man in Grey,* with Lockwood and James Mason, and again with Mason in *Fanny by Gaslight* (1944), which featured another major British 40s leading lady, Jean Kent.

Although Robert Preston was the star, Alan Ladd's stone-faced killer in *This Gun for Hire* (1942) skyrocketed him to the top. After years of small parts and radio work, he received attention in the fan magazines.

> In the 1940s . . . every major studio maintained a department for the sole purpose of servicing fan magazines. Appearing on the cover of *Modern Screen* or *Photoplay* was considered a coup. It was a sure indication that a newcomer had "made it," that an established star was maintaining his or her popularity. Combined monthly circulation of these two publishing giants totaled nearly four million, which according to surveys came to an average readership of some twenty-five million people each month. Such an awesome-sized audience could easily insure an actor or actress's stardom, and justify the

Katharine Hepburn's charisma, wit, intelligence, talent and longevity make her arguably the movies' supreme star-actress. Her best actress Academy Awards came for *Morning Glory* (1933), *Guess Who's Coming to Dinner* (1967), *The Lion in Winter* (1968)
and *On Golden Pond* (1981).

> publication's constant promotion. It could also send him or her to oblivion,
> not by the magazine's commission of some scurrilous story but simply by
> omission of any story at all.[26]

Ladd and costar Veronica Lake, she of the peekaboo hairstyle, paired in several
other 40s films: *The Glass Key* (1942), *The Blue Dahlia* (1946), and *Saigon*
(1948).

Bing Crosby won a best actor Academy Award playing Father O'Malley
in *Going My Way*, the 1944 best picture winner. "Swinging on a Star" was his
hit tune from the film. Barry Fitzgerald was the older priest for whom O'Malley
was a breath of fresh air, and he won a supporting actor Academy Award. He
had been nominated in both that and the best actor categories.

New kids on the block included svelte Lauren Bacall, who debuted in
1944 in *To Have and Have Not* with the famous line to Bogart, "You know
you don't have to act with me, Steve. You don't have to say anything and
you don't have to do anything. Not a thing. Oh, maybe just whistle. You

The Wicked Lady (Gainsborough, 1945), a big hit in Great Britain, starred Margaret Lockwood and James Mason. They'd also starred in 1943's *The Man in Grey*.

know how to whistle, don't you, Steve? You just put your lips together and blow."

Gregory Peck, born in La Jolla, California, in 1916, began acting at Berkeley and debuted in *Days of Glory* (1944), an RKO film in which he played a Russian resistance fighter. It was probably his least interesting film till, possibly, *Shootout* (1971).

> It was exciting to work with people who loved moviemaking so much, each in their different ways. They all did—Jack Warner, L. B. [Mayer], Selznick, Zanuck, Harry Cohn. They had their different ways of going about it, but they all had this enormous appetite and love for moviemaking. So it was fun. And they generally put me in good pictures. I think I had about four academy nominations in my first six years in movies, and I didn't choose any of those stories. They were brought to me. . . . Zanuck was making 65 pictures a year. I said no to some scripts, and he never held it against me. He was just fantastically efficient in making the kinds of pictures that he was making in the '40s.[27]

Peck's Academy Award nominations were for *The Keys of the Kingdom* (1945), *The Yearling* (1946), *Gentlemen's Agreement* (1947), and *Twelve O'Clock*

High (1949). (He did not win until he played noble attorney Atticus Finch in the 1962 film *To Kill a Mockingbird.*) In addition to his Fox films, he worked at RKO, MGM, United Artists, and Selznick.

Peck's costar in *Spellbound* (1945) was Ingrid Bergman, who had come to the States à la Garbo from Sweden for *Intermezzo* (1939). Her second American film was the almost forgotten but excellent *Adam Had Four Sons,* in 1941. A run of outstanding movies followed: as a sexy lady opposite Spencer Tracy in the 1941 version of *Dr. Jekyll and Mr. Hyde;* Rick's former paramour in *Casablanca* (1942); Gary Cooper's lover in *For Whom the Bell Tolls* (1943); Charles Boyer's scarified wife in *Gaslight* (1944); and Gregory Peck's paramour in *Spellbound* (1945).

Van Johnson was a teen heartthrob, attracting attention and good roles in such as *Thirty Seconds Over Tokyo* (1944), following a serious injury in a March 1943 car crash. Thrown from his convertible, he suffered a head injury that necessitated the removal of muscle from his right arm to patch him up.[28]

Laurence Olivier made and starred in *Henry V* (1944), the first of a Shakespearean trilogy that included *Hamlet* in 1948 and *Richard III* in 1955. Olivier directed, and William Walton scored all three.

Stars were useful plugging for the war effort. Those who fought included Jackie Coogan, who received a Distinguished Flying Cross for manning gliders in Burma. Many traveled overseas to entertain service personnel in Europe and in the Pacific. Bob Hope and his company, which usually included Jerry Colonna, Martha Raye, and the latest leggy starlet or beauty contest winner, began his decades-long caravan to bolster troop morale. Back home, stars like Hedy Lamarr hawked U.S. Defense Bonds and Stamps at rallies and in parades.

Contract Breaking: Olivia De Havilland: Others had fought the system for better roles: James Cagney, Bette Davis. But Olivia De Havilland, often typed as a genteel lady although frequent screen companion of boisterous Errol Flynn, won. It received scant media attention at the time. A mere paragraph in the *New York Times* stated:

> The State supreme court today ruled that Olivia De Havilland, actress, does not have to work an additional twenty-five weeks for Warner Brothers Pictures, Inc. The actress had a seven-year contract with Warners during which she was suspended at various times for a total of twenty-five weeks in disputes about types of films. Upon expiration of the contract, Warners insisted Miss De Havilland work twenty-five weeks.[29]

Star Deaths: Brit Leslie Howard, his father Hungarian by birth, had been the star of Hollywood films *Of Human Bondage* (1934), *Romeo and Juliet* (1936), *The Petrified Forest* (1936), *Intermezzo* (1939), and *Gone with the Wind.* He worked diligently for the British war effort. In *The 49th Parallel* (1941) he complained, "So that's who you are! Nazis! That explains everything—your arrogance, your stupidity, your bad manners!" He was killed when the plane he was in was shot down by Nazis. "It is no exaggeration to say that no figure in British show business was so deeply mourned, or missed, during this century."[30] The *Times* reported on June 3, 1943, that there were 13 passengers and four crew on the flight between Lisbon and Britain. Howard had been lecturing in Spain on filmmaking for the British Council. "His visit was so successful that 900 Spanish cinemas agreed to show British documentary films. He arranged to return home four days ago, but postponed the journey to be present at the Lisbon premiere of his film *The First of the Few,* in which he played the part of Mr. R. J. Mitchell, the designer of the Spitfire."[31] A June 4 obituary said that Howard was

> an actor of great charm and intelligence whose death means a severe loss to the British theatre and to British film. He was 50 years of age.... He was really a man of four reputations: as a stage actor in England and America, as a film actor, a film director, and, finally, as a member of the B.B.C. Brains Trust, and all of them were founded on the same qualities. Howard played in a film of the *Scarlet Pimpernel,* and *Pimpernel Smith* was the title of another film which he directed and in which he played the leading part, and it is easy to understand why the character of a man who was by no means all that he seemed so appealed to him. For as the Pimpernel concealed a strength and tenacity of purpose behind a flippant air, so did Howard disguise an art conceived in terms of hard work and perfect timing behind the casual understatement, the off-hand approach, the quietly humorous habit of self-deprecation.... As a film director Howard was an invaluable acquisition to a British industry which has improved out of all recognition in the past few years."[32]

Carole Lombard died at age 33 in a domestic plane crash on January 16, 1942. Her widower was Clark Gable.

Laird Cregar, the Philadelphia-born Victor Buono of his day, who had lent an imposing presence to *The Black Swan* (1942), *The Lodger* (1944), and more than a dozen other films, died on December 9, 1944, at age 28.

CHARACTER ACTORS

Perhaps because they were too busy and worked for decades, character actors' autobiographies are few. A few of them and representative films follow.

Walter Brennan continued his reign as a supporting and character actor extraordinaire in *Meet John Doe* (1940), *Northwest Passage* (1940), *The Pride of the Yankees* (1942), and *To Have and Have Not* (1944). At Warner Bros. George Tobias was a contemporary, urban type in *City for Conquest* (1940) or a complaining serviceman in *Air Force* (1943) and *Objective, Burma!* (1945). Willie Best, now condemned for his scared, subservient Negro image, was still funny, especially as Bob Hope's manservant in *The Ghost Breakers* (1940), where he was no more frightened than Hope and Paulette Goddard. Wisecracking Roscoe Karns was a pleasure in *They Drive by Night* (1940) and *His Girl Friday* (1940). S. Z. "Cuddles" Sakall, sometimes called the "Hunky Donkey Man" by audiences, had fled the Nazis in 1939 and added charm and humor to *Ball of Fire* (1941), *Casablanca* (1942), and *Christmas in Connecticut* and *San Antonio* (both 1945). Henry Daniell was usually villainous, particularly in *The Sea Hawk* (1940) and *The Body Snatcher* (1945). "Ethnic type" Joseph Calleia was in *The Jungle Book* (1942), *The Glass Key* (1942), and *For*

His Girl Friday (Columbia, 1940).

Whom the Bell Tolls (1943). Paul Stewart was welcomed by audiences as a good or bad guy, for instance, in *Citizen Kane* (1941) and *Johnny Eager* (1942). George Zucco was almost always bad (*The Mummy's Hand* [1940], *The Mad Ghoul* [1943], and *Confidential Agent* [1945]). British-born Lionel Atwill, who had been a policeman with one arm courtesy of the Frankenstein monster in the 30s, was *The Mad Doctor of Market Street* (1942), Dr. Bohmer in *The Ghost of Frankenstein* (1942), Moriarty in *Sherlock Holmes and the Secret Weapon* (1942), the Mayor of Vasaria in *Frankenstein Meets the Wolf Man* (1943), Inspector Arnz in *House of Frankenstein* (1944), and Inspector Holst in *House of Dracula* (1945). Lynne Overman was the outdoorsy type in *North West Mounted Police* (1940), *Reap the Wild Wind* (1942), and *The Forest Rangers* (1942).

After *Love Affair* and *The Rains Came* in 1939, Russian-born Moscow Art Theater alumna Maria Ouspenskaya became a welcome American film mainstay in *Dance, Girl, Dance* (1940), *The Mortal Storm* (1940), *The Wolf Man* (1941), and *Kings Row* (1941). She died in 1949. Often a long-suffering mother, Beulah Bondi made *Our Town* (1940) and *Shepherd of the Hills* (1941). Another motherly type was Elizabeth Patterson. See her to advantage in *Tobacco Road* (1940), *I Married a Witch* (1942) and *Hail the Conquering Hero* (1944). Spring Byington, later popular as television's "December Bride," brought her considerate personality to a spate of films, including *Meet John Doe* (1941), *Heaven Can Wait* (1943), and *The Enchanted Cottage* (1945).

During the war, enemy types were in demand. Philip Ahn was featured in *China Girl* (1943), *The Keys of the Kingdom* (1944), *Dragon Seed* (1944), and *Blood on the Sun* (1945). Chinese-Hawaiian Richard Loo played in *Wake Island* (1942) and *Road to Morocco* (1942) as a Chinese announcer. Keye Luke, a Chinese American, was Charlie Chan's No. 1 son and also played in *Across the Pacific* (1942) and in *Dr. Gillespie's New Assistant* (1942). A major Nazi type was Kurt Kreuger; see his 1943 films, *Sahara* and *Edge of Darkness*.

ONE-MAN SHOWS

"Rosebud": Orson Welles and *Citizen Kane*: Wisconsin-born world traveler, magician, and performer Orson Welles came to RKO from theater and radio with his Mercury Theatre players after the unforeseen success and notoriety of *The War of the Worlds* radio broadcast on October 29, 1938. *Citizen Kane* (1941) would be his first film, based in some degree on the life of newspaper magnate William Randolph Hearst.

Investigating the life of the recently deceased Kane, Jerry Thompson (William Alland) tracks down friends, relatives, and associates of the newspaper magnate (*The New York Daily Inquirer*) cum art and bric-a-brac collector. "You know, Mr. Bernstein, if I hadn't been very rich, I might have been a really great man," said Kane. In the end, at palatial Xanadu, much of the stuff is crated or burned. Thompson tells his fellow reporters,

> Mr. Kane was a man who got everything he wanted, and then lost it. Maybe Rosebud was something he couldn't get or something he lost. Anyway it

Legendary director-actor Orson Welles and legendary cinematographer Gregg Toland on the set of *Citizen Kane* (RKO, 1941).

> wouldn't have explained anything. I don't think any word can explain a man's life. No, I guess Rosebud is just a piece in a jigsaw puzzle. A missing piece. Well, come on everybody. We'll miss the train.

Rosebud, a sled, is consigned to the flames after a shot that might have inspired the final crating in *Raiders of the Lost Ark*.

Contemporary reviewers were mostly perspicacious, "It must be stated here that no amount of advance publicity or ballyhoo could possibly ruin the effect of this remarkable picture. It is probably the most original, exciting, and entertaining picture that has yet been produced in this country, and although it may lack their subtlety it can certainly be placed in the same bracket as the very best pre-war French productions."[33] "Fortunately, this long-promised film survived the hazards of its pre-release fame, and emerged as an exciting work, vital and imaginative, full of the unbridled energy which Orson Welles brings to every new medium he invades. . . . It is also, when it has all been told, the picture of a man who is really not worth depicting, and here is the film's weakness. *Citizen Kane* depends for its importance on implications which are external to the movie itself."[34]

"Thanks to this quasi-musical conception of dialogue, *Citizen Kane* 'breathes' differently from most films."[35] Low-angle, wide-angle, long set-up shots — these would make the film a landmark. Deep-focus photography, or, as cinematographer Gregg Toland termed it, "pan-focus,"[36] allowed for a depth of field (focus) not previously achieved. Innovative as well was the construction of ceilings for the sets. As all cinematographers realized, lighting and camera placement were the keys to success.

François Truffaut wrote of Welles, "the sound cinema has given us only one, one single filmmaker whose style is immediately recognizable after three minutes of film, and his name is Orson Welles."[37] "Welles is not really the inventor of this [narrative originality, decomposition of time, multiplicity of points of view] in the cinema, and the procedure was obviously taken from novels. But he perfected its use and adapted it to the resources of cinema with a comprehensiveness that had never yet been achieved."[38]

Welles could never duplicate this movie's success, and "he has mostly wandered from place to place in Europe, realizing now and then one of the projects of his fertile imagination and making magnificent, *tour de force* appearances in other people's films. The problem for him has always been that he seems unable to adjust his copious capacities to the strait-jacket of commercial film-making, which alone can provide him with the resources he needs."[39]

Like composer Bernard Herrmann and editor Robert Wise, cinematographer Gregg Toland was instrumental in the film's artistic success.

> A cameraman is the hardest worker in a picture set-up. The actors have days off; the director can relax while each scene is being lighted. But the cameraman lines up each and every shot, shoots it when ready, follows through the laboratory processes. He is among the first to arrive on the set every morning, the last to leave the studio at night. Watch him at work and you will find him the one person who is never idle. Others can be seen sitting around at times but never the cameraman. Throughout all preparation for a scene, the entire stage staff is at his disposal. It is not unusual for him to have a crew of forty to fifty various technicians.[40]

Obviously *Citizen Kane* was a one-man show made possible by the efforts of many. Yet some understood the necessity for a guiding hand.

> In the past year enough one-man pictures have been both good and successful to make it evident to the most reluctant members of the industry that the

Walter Brennan (left) as a disoriented Hunk Marriner and Spencer Tracy as a confident
Major Robert Rogers make their way back to civilization during the French and Indian
War in *Northwest Passage* (Metro-Goldwyn-Mayer, 1940).

usual Hollywood system of distributing the various creative film jobs among
many people is impractical and artistically untenable.[41]

King Vidor: Like Welles, King Vidor was another director with a measure
of power. "Vidor's vitality seems ageless, and his plastic force is especially appropriate for partings and reunions, and the visual opposition of individuals
to masses, both social and physical."[42] *Northwest Passage* (1940) was a good
example. This was designed initially to be as big as *Gone with the Wind,* but
no one could script book 2 of Kenneth Roberts' massive 1937 historical novel.
Book 1 and the film detail the trek into Canada by Indian fighter Robert Rogers
(Spencer Tracy). In retaliation for raids during the French and Indian War, his
Rangers surprise and wipe out the encampment of the St. Francis tribe. Then
the Rangers skedaddle to safety—but many, beset by French and allied native
tribes and suffering from starvation, don't make it. At the conclusion, Herbert
Stothart's stirring music accompanies Rogers and his survivors and new recruits
as they begin a new trek into the uncharted interior. Rogers stands against the
sky at the crest of the road and waves farewell to artist Langdon Towne (Robert
Young). "I'll see you at sundown, Harvard." Filmed "on location" in Idaho,
the crew put up with ticks, fire, and raging water. *Northwest Passage* was

among a select few films concerned with North American history before 1800. Westerns seemed to have subverted studio resources from dealing with colonization, the French and Indian War, and the American Revolution.[43]

David O. Selznick and Alfred Hitchcock: Due to the international success of *The 39 Steps* and *The Lady Vanishes,* director Alfred Hitchcock was called to Hollywood by none other than David O. Selznick. For Selznick, Hitch directed four films between 1940 and 1948: *Rebecca* (1940), which won a best picture Academy Award, *Spellbound* (1945), *Notorious* (1946), and *The Paradine Case* (1948).

STUNT PEOPLE

Yakima Canutt was the scurvy fellow who menaced Scarlett O'Hara in her buggy in *Gone with the Wind.* He normally was unrecognizable but could be seen jumping from horse to horse in *Stagecoach* or performing in some other dangerous scene. Later he would head second units that filmed such scenes as the chariot race in the 1959 version of *Ben-Hur.* Other notable stuntmen were David Sharpe, Joe Canutt, Chuck Roberson, Dale Van Sickel, Chuck Hayward, Richard Talmadge, Dick Crockett, Loren James, Bob Rose, Red Morgan, Duke Green, Harvey Parry, Joe and Bill Yrigoyen, Gil Perkins, Cliff Lyons, Paul Baxley, Charles Horvath, the Mazetti Brothers, Fred Graham, Saul Gorss, and Rod Cameron. Cameron became a star of B movies, mostly westerns. Later Jock Mahoney would jump from the stairs of *The Adventures of Don Juan* (1948) to leading roles, including Tarzan, in the 60s.

Many women engaged in stunt work: Helen Thurston, Aline Goodwin, Opal Ernis, Loretta Rush, Frances Miles, Nellie Walker, Evelyn Smith, Jeanne Criswell, Babe Defreest, Vivian Valdez, Betty Danko, and Ione Reed. They made $35 per day, with stunts earning them extra.[44]

CENSORSHIP

Millionaire aviator Howard Hughes occasionally dabbled in film and actresses. When he took over RKO, he turned his mind to a Billy the Kid story. The result was *The Outlaw* (1943 and 1946, plus reissues), a pet project that stirred controversy because of the cleavage of Jane Russell in her first film and certain seemingly innocuous but naughty lines. Obscured by the furor was the fact that *The Outlaw* was not a good — or even watchable — film. Its real importance was its effect on censorship.

> Regardless of Hughes's motives, he brought some refreshing honesty to Hollywood's approach to sex. He made the American public laugh a little at its own prudery about the female breast. If ever a cinematic Rabelais emerges from Hollywood, he will be indebted to this unusual industrialist. Hughes lacked artistry. But he was not afraid to show, on a movie screen, that sex, even without a license, can be fun.[45]

Foreign films, even British ones, necessitated laundering by U.S. censors. Scenes were grudgingly reshot lest Googie Withers in *Pink String and*

Sealing Wax (1945) or Patricia Roc and Margaret Lockwood in *The Wicked Lady* (1945) inflame audiences with too much décolletage. Characters philandering without remorse and committing suicide to achieve an easy out were frowned upon.[46]

Chapter 5
Apogee, 1946–1947

Gable's back and Garson's got him! — Advertisement
for *Adventure* (1945) with Clark Gable and Greer Garson

Average U.S. theater attendance between 1945 and 1948 was a whopping 90 million when the total population of the United States in 1945 was approximately 140 million. In 1946 the "Big 8" studios totaled record profits of $122 million.[1] Inflated by the returning G.I.s, marines, sailors, and airmen, total boxoffice receipts that year were $1.7 million.[2] Nevertheless, danger was on the horizon.

THE HEROES RETURN

The Best Years of Our Lives premiered at New York's Astor theater at 8:30 P.M. on the night of Thursday, November 21, 1946. (Beginning Friday there would be six continuous performances.) Upon viewing the film, World War II General Omar Bradley, now head of the Veterans Administration, wrote a congratulatory letter to producer Samuel Goldwyn. "I cannot thank you too much for bringing this story to the American people.... You are not only helping us to do our job but you are helping the American people to build an even better democracy out of the tragic experiences of this war."[3]

Fredric March, Myrna Loy, Dana Andrews, and Teresa Wright were the Hollywood stars of the film, which covered the joy and pain of returning veterans. Wright was in the midst of a spate of excellent roles, such as Charlie in *Shadow of a Doubt*. "Like Frances Dee, she [Wright] has always been one of the very few women in movies who really had a face. Like Miss Dee, she has always used this translucent face with delicate and exciting talent as an actress, and with something of a novelist's perceptiveness behind the talent. And like Miss Dee, she has never been around nearly enough."[4] One cast member had been a real veteran: Harold Russell, whose prosthetic hooks substituted for the hands he had lost in the war. For his performance he received a supporting actor Academy Award.

William Wyler's *The Best Years of Our Lives* (RKO/Goldwyn, 1946) explored the lives of three returning war vets. In this scene Fredric March greets daughter Teresa Wright while wife Myrna Loy looks on.

FILM NOIR STEPS INTO STRIDE

The big war was over. The United States, relatively unscathed, was economically and politically dominant. Yet maybe all was not right with the world. The "dark cinema" came into its own.

One of the first postwar *noir* entries was *The Blue Dahlia* (1946). Raymond Chandler wrote its script under unusual circumstances. When Chandler was having trouble finishing, desperate producer John Houseman agreed to try the author's suggestion.

> Chandler told Houseman that the only way he could finish the script was under the stimulating influence of alcohol. He could write it drunk, or not at all. He would require two chauffeured limousines outside his home around the clock, available to bring the doctor to him for daily glucose injections, (since he would be eating no food) and to take finished script pages to Paramount. Also, he would require six secretaries, in shifts of two, for dictation and typing, and he also needed a direct, twenty-four-hour phone line to Houseman.[5]

It worked.

A more confusing but bigger and more entertaining *noir* of 1946 was based on Raymond Chandler's novel *The Big Sleep*. Director Howard Hawks,

The presence of Jane Greer spells big trouble for RobertMitchum in the film noir classic, *Out of the Past* (RKO, 1947).

with the assistance of heavyweight scriptwriters William Faulkner, Leigh Brackett, and Jules Furthman, provided a stimulating plethora of sexual innuendo and violence. Lauren Bacall played Mrs. Rutledge, Humphrey Bogart private eye Philip Marlowe. A sample of the dialogue runs as follows.

RUTLEDGE: You go too far, Marlowe.

MARLOWE: O-o-o-h. Those are harsh words to throw at a man, especially when he's walking out of your bedroom.

In retrospect, the best of *The Postman Always Rings Twice* (1946) was Hume Cronyn's defense attorney. Based on a James M. Cain novel, this was a rare *noir* entry from MGM. John Garfield became enamored of Lana Turner, who was married to Cecil Kellaway. They did away with the husband but found little peace.

Ernest Hemingway's short story provided the basis for *The Killers* (1946), which introduced Burt Lancaster, "the ex-circus acrobat with more vitality than a dozen normal men."[6] Although a weak film, *I Walk Alone* (1947) saw Kirk Douglas and Burt Lancaster in the first of many onscreen partnerships.

Kiss of Death (1947) gave Victor Mature one of his best roles and introduced New York stage actor Richard Widmark as psychotic killer Tommy Udo. As the hit man who pushed wheelchair-bound Mildred Dunnock down the stairs, Widmark made a stunning debut. "The fright and suspense of the closing sequences depend largely on the conception of the pathological Udo and

Dennis O'Keefe (formerly Bud Flanagan) had his best days in hard-hitting crime films like the semi-documentary *T-Men* (Eagle-Lion, 1947). Here's a publicity shot with Mary Meade.

on Richard Widmark's remarkable performance of the role. He is a rather frail fellow with maniacal eyes, who uses a sinister kind of falsetto baby talk laced with tittering laughs. It is clear that murder is one of the kindest things he is capable of."[7]

The film most often thought of when *film noir* is mentioned may be *Out of the Past* (1947), starring Robert Mitchum, Jane Greer, and Kirk Douglas. (It was remade in 1986 as *Against All Odds*.) Mitchum was Jeff, sent to locate

Whit's (Douglas) girlfriend Kathi (Greer). Jeff accomplishes his mission but falls for the dame. "I wouldn't kill a guy for a martini," says Jeff at one point. Not so the amoral Kathi. Ostensibly to help Jeff, she plugs an "associate" (Steve Brodie) who wants in on the action. Then Whit ends up dead. Jeff is caught in a nightmare. The ending is unpleasant for all concerned.

In *Nightmare Alley* (1947) Tyrone Power took a chance and played a carnival charlatan and, later, disgraced, a geek (man who eats the heads off live chickens).

> Scripter Jules Furthman and Director Edmund Goulding have steered a middle course, now and then crudely but on the whole with tact, skill and power. They have seldom forgotten that the original novel they were adapting is essentially intelligent trash; and they have never forgotten that on the screen pretty exciting things can be made of trash. From top to bottom of the cast, the playing is good. Joan Blondell, as the fading carnival queen, is excellent and Tyrone Power — who asked to be cast in the picture — steps into a new class as an actor.[8]

In *Lady in the Lake* (1947) 30s matinee idol Robert Montgomery, sire of future television luminary Elizabeth, took a cue from pretty boy turned tough guy Dick Powell and starred in and directed this version of Raymond Chandler's Philip Marlowe mystery. Critics complained that it was pretentious to have filmed from Marlowe's vantage point. In other words, the audience only saw Montgomery/Marlowe when he looked in a mirror. Nevertheless, the film was solid entertainment with lines suitably trenchant, the dame (Audrey Totter) more than suitably icy. "When it concerns a woman, does anybody ever really want the facts?" asked Montgomery/Marlowe.

T-Men (1947) was an early outing by soon-to-be-respected director Anthony Mann, combining *noir* and the semidocumentary style.

> Edward Small's production *T-Men*, which is based on a composite of cases showing how the Treasury Department goes after counterfeiters, is also strong on realism. In fact this well-knit film, directed by Anthony Mann, has stunning photography of several cities and a documentary atmosphere that make it seem like the real thing.... My main objection to this well made movie is that it carries realism a little too far at times, and some of the fights are too brutal to watch.[9]

Boomerang (1947) was about the murder of a clergyman, followed by the trial and acquittal of the accused. It had one of the decade's best casts: Dana Andrews, Jane Wyatt, Ed Begley, Lee J. Cobb, Karl Malden, Arthur Kennedy, and Robert Keith.

Noir would continue into the 50s, its end perhaps *Touch of Evil* (1958). Orson Welles, heavily made up, played a corrupt border town sheriff, Charlton Heston a Hispanic policeman trying to engage in a hassle-free honeymoon with Janet Leigh. Prefiguring Tony Perkins' *Psycho* (1960) character was the day motel manager jumpily portrayed by Dennis Weaver. "*Touch of Evil* confirms an idea which can be verified by *The Big Sleep, Kiss Me Deadly* and *Psycho:* filmed by an inspired director, the most ordinary thriller can become the most moving fairy tale."[10]

Although Universal's Sherlock Holmes films were programmers that transferred Arthur Conan Doyle's characters into contemporary times, *Dressed to Kill* (1946) gave Basil Rathbone a worthy opponent in Patricia Morison.

ATMOSPHERE

The atmosphere of *noir* was also present in other genres. The 1946 Sherlock Holmes film, *Dressed to Kill,* was one of the second-rank Holmesian films with Basil Rathbone as the master sleuth. Not up to the first two Rathbone-Holmes films released by Fox in 1939, *The Hound of the Baskervilles* and *The Adventures of Sherlock Holmes,* Universal's *Dressed to Kill* was solid and, thank goodness, no longer an anti–Nazi tract. (The series had brought Holmes to World War II in such films as the 1942 *Sherlock Holmes and the Secret Weapon.*) *Dressed to Kill* possessed "atmosphere," a quality that would shortly be lacking in films. Take the scene when Holmes and Watson (Nigel Bruce) go to a pub for out-of-work thespians. A man entertains the crowd with a ditty, "You Never Know Just Who You're Going to Meet." Smoke fills the room. Everyone seems appropriately attired. The bric-a-brac looks authentic. Even in a B movie like this, attention to background detail was splendid. Of course, extras were cheap.

Atmosphere, too, held sway in David Lean's adaptation of Charles Dickens' *Great Expectations* (1946). Anthony Wager played the young Pip, accosted by escaped felon Magwitch (Finlay Currie) in a much commented upon graveyard scene. John Mills played the adult Pip, with Valerie Hobson (once

The Razor's Edge (20th Century–Fox, 1946) was a valiant, mostly successful rendering of Somerset Maugham's story of Larry Darrell (Tyrone Power), seeker of life's true meaning. Isabel Bradley (Gene Tierney) loved but did not understand him.

the bride of Frankenstein) as the adult Estella (Jean Simmons played her as a child).

STARS

Clark Gable returned from shooting film and bullets over Europe. His best films were behind him, however, and it can be argued that after *Command Decision* (1948), he never again made a truly excellent film.

Director Frank Capra had spent the war years producing the impressive *Why We Fight* documentaries, while James Stewart had been promoted to Army Air Force colonel, an officer with seven battle stars and Distinguished Flying Cross for bombing missions over Germany.[11] Back in Hollywood, they collaborated on what was not a smash at the time but what became a Christmas classic, *It's a Wonderful Life* (1946). Loss of a company bankroll leads to all sorts of trouble for George Bailey (Stewart), who contemplates suicide until an angel named Clarence (Henry Travers) arrives in the nick of time and shows George how the lack of his presence in Bedford Falls would have made life so much more difficult for his wife, Mary (Donna Reed), and its citizens. As was his wont, Capra assembled a marvelous supporting cast that included Lionel Barrymore, Thomas Mitchell, Beulah Bondi, Frank Faylen, Ward Bond, Gloria Grahame, H. B. Warner, Frank Albertson, and Mary Treen.

The Marx Brothers showed some of their former magic in *A Night in Casablanca* (1946), which contained one of their best routines. Walter Slezak packs trunks preparatory to absconding, but the Marxes continually baffle his efforts. This scene alone was worth the price of admission. "It is logical that Groucho and company should prevent him by hiding in his room and *un*packing, in ways so wildly mysterious, including a walk-through wardrobe and a drop-through table, that the count thinks he's going mad. This is the kind of scene you wait to sit through again, even if you miss the last bus."[12]

Gene Tierney, who had reached the first rank in *Laura* (1944), consolidated her position in *Leave Her to Heaven* (1945) and *The Razor's Edge* (1946).

> On November 19, 1946, there was a party in New York to celebrate Clifton Webb's birthday, and mine, which coincided with the opening at the Roxy Theater of *The Razor's Edge*. In those days a New York premiere was as close to heaven as an actor could expect to get, and a great boost to the pictures selected for such treatment. It was part of the era of tumult and searchlights and huge crowds, an era long gone. . . . This was to be the first great postwar splash of Hollywood-made razzle-dazzle.[13]

Sleepy-eyed, laid-back Robert Mitchum had a fabulous 1947. *Pursued* was the first adult, psychological western, *Out of the Past* the definitive *film noir*, and *Crossfire* a bold step in tackling sensitive subject matter.

Jane Wyman surprised everyone with her performance as the deaf-mute girl in *Johnny Belinda* (1947). Raped by Locky (Stephen McNally), she bears his son. The new doctor in the rural Canadian community (Lew Ayres) is thought to be the father. When Locky tries to take his son, Belinda (Wyman) shoots and kills him, then stands trial.

Character actors of note included Cecil Kellaway of *The Postman Always Rings Twice* (1946), *Unconquered* (1947), and *Life with Father* (1947), and Edmund Gwenn, who played Kris Kringle and won a supporting actor Academy Award in *Miracle on 34th Street* (1947).

TAKING CHANCES: BEN HECHT'S SPECTER OF THE ROSE

Prolific screenwriter Ben Hecht sometimes got financing for his own projects. Virtually unknown today, *Specter of the Rose* (1946), a psychological study of a ballet dancer, was one such effort he wrote, produced, and directed for Republic. Although Leslie Halliwell called it "a rather hilarious bid for culture: hard to sit through without laughing, but unique,"[14] kinder words described it at the time: "what we rarely get from Hollywood: a mature story, artistically depicted"[15]; "the script has humor and literary flavor; the acting shows great talent; the direction exhibits a gift for the dramatic and subtle. What with beautiful dancing, in addition to everything else, we have a movie appealing to the esthetic sense as well as to the intellect. In this picture Hollywood, via Ben Hecht, has achieved a masterpiece"[16]; "a compelling development of a psychological theme, and I found myself thinking about it a great deal afterwards"[17]; "the importance of *Specter of the Rose* is that here,

Susan Hayward was just about finished with pin-ups when this shot helped publicize *The Lost Moment* (Universal, 1947). Soon she'd sign with 20th Century–Fox and become its number one dramatic actress.

as in *The Scoundrel* and *Tales of Manhattan*, Hecht uses the poetic cinematic image right on the main thoroughfare of film production."[18]

HOT TOPICS

When he left Warners in the 30s to come to 20th Century–Fox, Darryl F. Zanuck had brought his social consciousness—and sure-fire money-making instincts with him. One of his biggest triumphs was *Gentleman's Agreement* (1947), featuring Gregory Peck as Phil Green, who got an idea for a great story.

> I got it! The lead, the idea, the angle! This is the way, it's the only way! I'll, I'll be Jewish. I, I, all I gotta do is say it, nobody knows me around here. I can just say it. I can live it myself for six weeks, eight weeks, nine months, no matter how long it takes! Ma, it's right this time.... Listen, I even got the title: *I Was Jewish for Six Months.*

Anti-Semitism was also explored in that same year's grim *Crossfire,* the film with the three Roberts: Young, the policeman; Mitchum, the inquisitive G.I.; Ryan, the Jew-hating G.I. Part *noir,* part social consciousness, the story concerns the search for the murderer of a Jewish soldier (Sam Levene). It was based on Richard Brooks' novel, *The Brick Foxhole,* which had concerned itself with a bigot's murder of a homosexual. It cost a mere $500,000 to make.

> To strengthen its box-office potential and ensure quality performances, we decided to make the budget top-heavy on the talent side. That meant B-picture expenditure below the line, and a very short schedule — eventually fixed at 22 days. The above-the-line cost (story and talent) turned out to be double the below-the-line cost (sets, materials, and labor), just the reverse of the average film.[19]

James Agee praised it: "In part, I don't doubt, because the picture is *about* something, which everyone making it can take seriously, it is, even as melodramatic entertainment, the best Hollywood movie in a long time."[20]

WESTERNS

Another World War II veteran, John Ford, opened his postwar era with *My Darling Clementine* (1946), an evocative look at the West undergoing the civilizing influences of women and town building. Henry Fonda played Wyatt Earp; Victor Mature, Doc Holliday; Walter Brennan, Ike Clanton. The gunfight at the OK Corral was apparently closer to fact, if less rousing, than other film versions had been. But Fonda was a perfect Earp, and Victor Mature as the tuberculer Holliday proved he was more than just "the Hunk."

Duel in the Sun (1946) was David O. Selznick's attempt to outdo his own *Gone with the Wind.* As with *GWTW,* he went through more than one director. It was big enough, certainly, and quite watchable, with impressive star power: Gregory Peck as the amoral Lewt and Jennifer Jones as Pearl, a wanton half-breed in a total contrast with her Academy Award–winning 1944 holy outing in *The Song of Bernadette.* Joseph Cotten was the good brother, Lionel Barrymore the crippled father. As the "Sinkiller," Walter Huston had some choice advice for Pearl in the presence of Laura Belle (Lillian Gish).

> Then remember that the devil's always aimin' to hogtie ya! Sometimes he comes ghostin' over the plains in the shape of a sneakin' rustler and sometimes — beggin' your pardon, Laura Belle — he stakes out in the homes of the worthy and the God-fearin'! Pearl, you're curbed in the flesh of temptation. Resistance gonna be a darned site more difficult for you than for females protected by the shape of sows. Yessiree, bub, you gotta sweeten yourself with prayer! Pray till you sweat and you'll save yourself eternal hellfire! Do ya understand me, girl?

Top: Cecil B. DeMille directing Paulette Goddard on the set of *Unconquered* (Paramount, 1947), a fantastical historical pageant — and supremely entertaining. *Bottom:* Dorothy McGuire had an enviable list of film credits in the forties, including 1946's *The Spiral Staircase* and 1947's *Gentleman's Agreement*. In the fifties she had impressive mother roles. See *Friendly Persuasion* (1956).

Jennifer Jones and Gregory Peck relax on the set of the mammoth western, *Duel in the Sun* (Selznick International Pictures, 1946). The role of the wild Pearl Chavez was a change of pace for Jones, who had won an Academy Award as the visionary from Lourdes in *The Song of Bernadette* in 1943.

Pearl couldn't stick with it. "I guess I'm just trash—like my ma ... Trash. Trash, trash, trash, trash, trash!" To her Lewt was a "varmint!" It was entertaining yet ultimately disappointing. Any child could identify the flaw of amassing a horde of range riders, letting them ride hell bent for leather to confront an equally imposing cavalry mass at the boundary, and then having everyone get away without a fist thrown or a bullet fired.

Black and white blurred in adult westerns. The villain might not be as bad—or he might have a psychological quirk. Such films may trace their heritage to the 1943 *Ox-Bow Incident,* but Raoul Walsh's *Pursued* (1947) was the true progenitor. Novelist Niven Busch *(Duel in the Sun)* had his wife, actress Teresa Wright, in mind when he wrote the screenplay. The story concerns Medora Callum (Judith Anderson), who takes in Jeb Rand (Robert Mitchum) to raise with her own children, Thorley (Wright) and Adam (John Rodney). Always at odds, Jeb and Adam have it out and the missing father, Grant (Dean Jagger), returns to kill Jeb. Medora takes dramatic action.

BRITAIN

Postwar British stars included James Mason, Patricia Roc, Margaret Lockwood, Celia Johnson, Trevor Howard, Stewart Granger, Jack Hawkins, John Mills, Deborah Kerr, Alastair Sim, Phyllis Calvert, and the young Jean Simmons. Mason, Howard, Granger, Mills, Hawkins, Kerr, and Simmons would prove to have international appeal.

Internationally, two British directors came to the fore: David Lean and Carol Reed. Lean turned from the contemporary romance of *Brief Encounter* to brilliant evocations of Charles Dickens in *Great Expectations* and 1948's *Oliver Twist.* Critics look back on this period as his best. Like American George Stevens, he would shift toward epics in the 50s and 60s. Carol Reed made a worldwide impact when he directed *Odd Man Out* (1947) and followed in 1948 with *The Fallen Idol* and *The Third Man.*

Dead of Night (1946) was the original horror story compendium. Architect Walter Craig (Mervyn Johns) drives to Pilgrim's Farm, where a passel of other visitors tell odd stories. Awakened from this dream, Craig finds himself driving to the farm again. It was recognized both at the time and later as a classic.

> When an English picture is good, it is superlatively good. This happens to be the case with *Dead of Night,* in which each of four characters relates the most startling incident of his life. The stories are engrossing and intensely dramatic. As in so many English pictures, the mood of the film is created at the start, and one feels at once that the film will be of a high order.
>
> American audiences will get the lines readily, for the diction is unusually clear and distinct. At his best is Michael Redgrave; in fact, the entire cast is excellent. A middle-aged mother, who comes in for a brief moment, does a delicious bit of comedy.
>
> High praise should be awarded the directors for a most artistic job and to the script writers for dialog that has distinction.[21]

BLACKLISTING

The tensions that were beginning to start a Cold War between the West and the Soviet-led communist bloc scared certain Americans. The building of the Iron Curtain—a chain of walls, minefields, and barbed wire fences across Europe—the Berlin airlift, the successes of Mao Tse-tung's Chicoms, the imminent explosion of a Russian A-bomb (1949) thought to have hinged on spies—

Ida Lupino played a stuttering, winsome daughter of reclusive Henry Hull and Fay
Bainter in *Deep Valley* (Warner Bros., 1947). Jean Negulesco directed this bittersweet
gem.

all of this suggested to some people, like the American Legion, an internal rot.
Pressure was brought to bear on Hollywood to hire only right-thinking citizens,
although there was no evidence that communist infiltration of the cinema had
ever occurred, or if it had, that it had been "anti–American." Congress's Committee on Un-American Activities began investigating the movie industry for
subversive activities in the spring of 1947. Many writers were targeted. The
Hollywood Ten—writers Herbert Biberman, Alvah Bessie, Lester Cole, Ring
Lardner, Jr., John Howard Lawson, Albert Maltz, Samuel Ornitz, Dalton
Trumbo, producer Adrian Scott, and Edward Dmytryk, director of
Crossfire—were jailed for contempt and their job opportunities in Hollywood
squashed. The film industry would soon reel from another blow. A captive au-
dience was about to be freed by television.

Chapter 6

Seasons of Change, 1948–1955

It is hard to believe that absolutely first-rate works of art can ever again be made in Hollywood, but it would be idiotic to assume that flatly.   —James Agee, *Nation*, January 10, 1948

The 1950s in America and in its cinema is often viewed as a time of stagnation, an era of fear brought about by theater divestiture and the Cold War between Russia and the United States. The Soviet Union detonated an A-bomb in August 1949. Anticommunist witchhunters caused the blacklisting of artists for real or supposed communist affiliations — or personal vendetta. There were obvious anti–Red tracts like low budgeters *The Red Menace* (1949) and *The Whip Hand* (1951). On a larger scale were the 1952 films *My Son John* and *Big Jim McLain* as well as the much delayed *Jet Pilot* (1956), with Janet Leigh as a Russian pilot. The best one was probably *The Iron Curtain* (1948). None of these films was a big hit. On the positive side, the 1950s was a time of technical innovation. Processes were developed to combat the attractions of television and the other amusements taking up the people's leisure time. Additionally, midcentury heralded the golden ages of westerns, science fiction, and musicals.

PROBLEMS

Although no law forbade people from being communists, Wisconsin Senator Joseph McCarthy charged communist subversion in the Truman administration in 1950 and kept it up in the Eisenhower administration till he was discredited in 1954. He died in 1957. What it meant for Hollywood was a blacklist of those thought to be communist sympathizers. It did not take much to brand them. An accusation from an informer or a failure to testify before the House Committee on Un-American Activities put the kibosh on many careers: performers like Gale Sondergaard, Will Geer, Howard da Silva, and Jay Robinson, directors like Joseph Losey, writers like Dashiell Hammett and the Hollywood Ten. Some testified or informed on others to save their own professional lives. The 1952 *Annual Report of the Committee on Un-American*

117

Activities commended those individuals who revealed Communist party membership and supplied "facts relating to Communist efforts and success in infiltrating the motion-picture industry." Most of the ten-page document was a list of supposed communists and an adjacent list of those who had implicated them. It concluded with a section claiming many Los Angeles attorneys were communists and identified the National Lawyers' Guild as a Communist party supporter.[1]

As well as in Korea, where United Nations forces battled North Korean and Chinese armies from 1950 to 1953, onscreen wars could be fought and won against the atheistic demons. Oddly, the first to exploit this was no cut-and-dried Red-baiter, and his movies, especially *The Steel Helmet* (1951), demonstrated the insanity of war. Director Samuel Fuller, a World War II veteran, tackled the Korean War in a second film that year, *Fixed Bayonets!* Soldiers fight for each other. Sergeant Rock (Gene Evans) advises a young recruit (Richard Basehart):

> Look Denno, I know you're a brave Joe. It took guts to go down there and get Lonergan, no matter what your personal reason was. But it takes more than guts to stay alive in this business. You've gotta get over that big hump. There's eight bullets in that clip. That means eight dead Reds. I ain't askin' you to use a clip to kill eight men. I just want you to kill one man, even if you gotta use the whole clip—but kill 'im! Now get your tail down there.

Though mostly forgotten today, Elia Kazan's *Man on a Tightrope* (1953) was an altogether better stab at repression in Iron Curtain countries than were the Red scare films. Fredric March was the manager—owner in precommunist times—of a Czech circus. Tired of harassment, he and his cronies plan a breakout to the West. Problems arise from an informer; the plan goes ahead, but not without casualties, including March. Gloria Grahame was a sexy wife, Terry Moore, the daughter falling for a stranger (Cameron Mitchell) who turns out to be an American soldier trying to get back to West Germany.

Shack Out on 101 (1955) may be the most entertaining of the low-budget anticommie films. This time Frank *I Was a Communist for the FBI/Retreat, Hell!* Lovejoy plays a nuclear scientist who dates hashhouse waitress Kottie (Terry Moore) while he secretly searches for a spy. Lee Marvin plays short order cook Slob. "Don't make any deals with that garbage pail!" advises Kottie, who admonishes Sam (Lovejoy) for concentrating too much on work. "Sam, you've changed, we used to be together all the time! Now I only see you when you come to the shack, and then you spend most of your time talking to Slob and looking at shells!"

In addition to the fear of communism that inspired the blacklisting, theater divestiture, censorship, and television posed difficult problems for the cinema.

> This is how the art got made: by the size and wealth and power that the system gave the studios. When they divested themselves of their theatres, they shattered the innate balance of the structure. With no guarantee of exhibition, fewer movies could be made. The studios had to break their lots down to minimum personnel.[2]

Lee Marvin menaces Terry Moore in *Shack Out on 101* (Allied Artists, 1955), an anti-communist tract that seems to have become a cult film.

Starting in 1938, the Justice Department sued the Big 8 studios for monopolistic practices. On November 20, 1940, a consent decree was reached between the government and Paramount, Loew's (MGM), RKO, Warner Bros., and Fox. For the nonce, the majors had warded off interference. Litigation reactivated in 1944 reached the U.S. Supreme Court in 1948. It was argued February 9–11, 1948.[3] The decision was handed down on May 3, 1948, as the so-called Paramount decree, which abolished block booking, blind bidding, and price fixing. It was a severe blow that made Hollywood "like the South after the Civil War—the plantations wasted, the slaves emancipated, a way of life gone forever."[4] The Court had confronted the monopoly issue.

22. Monopolies 24(1)

"Block booking," which is practice of licensing or offering for license one motion picture feature or group of features on condition that exhibitor will also license another feature or group of features released by distributor during a given period, was properly enjoined as an improper enlargement of monopoly of copyright. Sherman Anti-Trust Act, Sections 1, 2, as amended, 15 U.S.C.A. Sections 1, 2; Copyright Act Section 1, 17 U.S.C.A. Section 1.[5]

Justice Douglas delivered the opinion.

[1,2] The District Court found that two price-fixing conspiracies existed—a horizontal one between all the defendants, a vertical one between each distributor-defendant and its licensees. The latter was based on express agreements and was plainly established. The former was inferred from the

A more lovable curmudgeon than Charles Coburn could hardly be imagined. He over-
came life's frustrations for himself as well as Jean Arthur and Robert Cummings in *The
Devil and Miss Jones* (1941), Arthur and Joel McCrea in *The More the Merrier* (1943),
Gene Tierney and Don Ameche in *Heaven Can Wait* (1943), and Piper Laurie and Rock
Hudson in *Has Anybody Seen My Gal?* (1952).

pattern of price-fixing disclosed in the record. We think there was adequate
foundation for it too. It is not necessary to find an express agreement in order
to find a conspiracy. It is enough that a concert of action is contemplated and
that the defendants conformed to the arrangement. Interstate Circuit v.
United States, 306 U.S. 208, 226, 227, 59 S. Ct. 467, 474, 83 L. Ed. 610;
United States v. Masonite Corp., 316 U.S. 265, 275, 62 S. Ct. 1070, 1076,
86 L. Ed. 1461.[6]

Next up was the problem of censorship. Although there had been 40s
films like *Citizen Kane, Out of the Past, Deep Valley, The Specter of the Rose*,
and *Crossfire*, Hollywood hoped that no film would offend anybody and that
all films could be enjoyed by the family. The increasing availability of more
realistic and adult European films threatened a Hollywood laboring under Production Code restrictions. Censorship would also hamper studios competing
with the geometrically escalating number of television stations and sets. Add
to that the "distractions" caused by postwar nighttime sports, veterans attending night school, and suburban living, and the industry was in trouble.

Jeanne Crain was one of the screen's greatest beauties. A former Miss Long Beach, she officially debuted in *Home in Indiana* (1944). A wealth of fine roles awaited her during her 20th Century-Fox contract years, but her career suffered when she started a large family and the studio system began breaking up in the 50s.

SOCIAL CONSCIOUSNESS CONTINUES

A postwar trend to investigate injustices continued. It was monetarily as well as socially remunerative. *All the King's Men* (1949) gave heretofore character actor Broderick Crawford the role of a lifetime as rustic turned big-time politician Willie Stark.[7] It was based on the Robert Penn Warren 1946 Pulitzer Prize–winning novel, a loose adaptation of the life of Louisiana governor Huey Long. John Ireland, Joanne Dru, and Mercedes McCambridge rendered able support. Robert Rossen produced and directed this best picture and best actor (Crawford) Academy Award winner.

From United Artists came Stanley Kramer's *Home of the Brave* (1949), in which James Edwards was Moss, a G.I. on a wartime Pacific island. In a stirring speech he rages against racism:

> I told you I heard something in the middle of the night once. It was some drunken bum across the alley yelling "Throw the dirty niggers out!" That was us. But I just rolled over and went back to sleep, I was used to it by then. Sure I was ten, that's old, that's old for a pickaninny! When I was six, my first

At the end of Billy Wilder's *Sunset Boulevard* (Paramount, 1950), madness overcomes faded screen star Norma Desmond (Gloria Swanson). Erich von Stroheim humors her in the greatest moment about film on film.

day in school, some kids got around me. White kids. They said, "Hey, hey you. Is your father a monkey?" I was dumb, I smiled and said no. Well they wiped that smile right off my face, they, they beat it off! I had to get beat up a coupla more times before I found out that if you're colored you stink! You're not like other people, you're not like white people at all. You're low, you're strange, you're something different—when you make us different. Whadaya want us to do, whadaya want us to be?!

Racism was also the theme of *Pinky* (1949), in which Jeanne Crain played a black girl passing for white. Elia Kazan directed for Fox. *Lost Boundaries* and *Intruder in the Dust* (1949) continued investigating the African-American issue. Joseph L. Mankiewicz' 1950 film, *No Way Out,* was another breakthrough. Richard Widmark was a vicious racist who, when injured, was attended to by a black doctor (Sidney Poitier).

While many of these films retain their power, the 1948 Fox Anatole Litvak production about mental collapse, *The Snake Pit,* does not. Olivia De Havilland underwent the "tortures" of a mental institution. Leo Genn, flanked by a portrait of Freud to remind the audience of his credentials, played her understanding psychiatrist. What put De Havilland in the institution was tame by later standards: when she was a child, her father sometimes took her

Robert Wise's *The Set-Up* (RKO, 1949) may be the best of all boxing films. From left: Robert Ryan, James Edwards, Wallace Ford.

mother's side. What was more, the mother had to divide her attention between her and a younger sister. There is one moving moment, however, when during an infrequent fraternization dance a woman sings the Dvorak-based "Goin' Home," and the male and female inmates join in.

Hollywood on Trial

Filmmakers were not loathe to examine their industry's failings from time to time. In the 30s *What Price Hollywood* and *A Star Is Born* had examined the price of film stardom.

Sunset Boulevard premiered in 1950, the result of a Billy Wilder–Charles Brackett script about the old and glamorous Hollywood in which a screenwriter (William Holden) becomes the kept man of faded screen star Norma Desmond (Gloria Swanson). It was black as only Wilder could do it; after Preston Sturges, he was the most sarcastic observer of people.[8] The *Newsweek* cover and three-page June 26, 1950, story aimed at Gloria and glamour: that's Hollywood.

The Bad and the Beautiful (1952) presented Kirk Douglas as a producer turned director. *The Star* (1953) was Bette Davis. A remake of *A Star Is Born* (1954) starred Judy Garland and James Mason in the roles originally played by Janet Gaynor and Fredric March. The updated version was a musical, of course,

Glenn Ford and Gloria Grahame starred in *The Big Heat* (Columbia, 1953), a hard-boiled cop picture famous for a scene in which Lee Marvin dashes scalding coffee in Grahame's face.

with impressive numbers by Garland. Kim Stanley would play a Marilyn Monroe–like character in *The Goddess* (1958).

DELINQUENCY

In the 1930s there were the Dead End Kids. Leo Gorcey, Huntz Hall, Billy Halop, Gabriel Dell, Bobby Jordan, Bernard Punsley had debuted in 1937 in

Dead End. Thereafter they had a B movies series to themselves. In 1949, *Knock on Any Door,* with John Derek as the troubled youth, was the postwar film of this ilk. Unlike *Dead End,* in which Humphrey Bogart was a bad influence, he played the understanding adult this time. *City Across the River* (1949) was Brooklyn, the home of teen hoodlums like Anthony (Tony) Curtis. *Blackboard Jungle* (1955) became more famous. Bill Haley and the Comets performed "Rock Around the Clock," Glenn Ford played the harassed teacher Richard Dadier ("Daddy-O"), Vic Morrow was a irredeemable punk in the Brando mold, and Sidney Poitier the redeemable Gregory Miller.

SEMIDOCUMENTARIES

Following the success of the 1947 *T-Men,* semidocumentaries continued with two engrossing 1948 films, *Call Northside 777* and *The Naked City.* Jules Dassin directed the latter, but the name he made in the late 40s could not help when the communist witch-hunters arrived. He left for Europe, where he made such seminal films as the 1956 crime caper *Rififi.*

THE GOLDEN AGE OF SCIENCE FICTION

Universal had dominated the 30s with its supernatural creatures like Dracula and the Frankenstein monster. Val Lewton's subdued horror entries for RKO were the peak of 40s horror. The genre was temporarily killed in 1948. *Abbott and Costello Meet Frankenstein* was a riotous send-off typified by the pursuit, during which Abbott and Costello block a door with a bed only to find the monster opening it outward. Why was this so funny? The audience could see it coming. Atom bombs and unidentified flying objects (UFOs) completed the demise of mere humanoid monsters and paved the way for technologically induced fright objects on a grand scale.

While flying near Mount Rainier in Washington State on June 24, 1947, pilot Kenneth Arnold observed airborne circular objects progressing at swift speed. The "flying saucer" was officially born, but *The Flying Saucer* (1950) does not qualify as the first true science fiction saucer movie because it was about a manmade vehicle. *Destination Moon* (1950), which won an Academy Award for special effects, inaugurated the modern outer space film. It was straightforward, logical. *The Man from Planet X* (1951) introduced the first alien, but two other aliens made a more impressive appearance that year. *The Thing* was filled with memorable scenes: the crashed saucer beneath the arctic ice, the defrosting of the ship's pilot by a thermite bomb, the melting block of ice within which lies the alien, the escaped creature's battle with sled dogs, the air force captain's greenhouse door confrontation with the monster, the haunting warning by newsman Scotty (Douglas Spencer):

> Tell General Fogarty we've sent for Captain Hendry. He'll be here in a few minutes. Over. Are there any newsmen there who can hear me? All right, fellows, here's your story. North Pole. November third. Ned Scott reporting. One of the world's greatest battles was fought and won today by the human race. Here at the top of the world a handful of American soldiers and civilians

The Thing! From Another World (RKO, 1951).

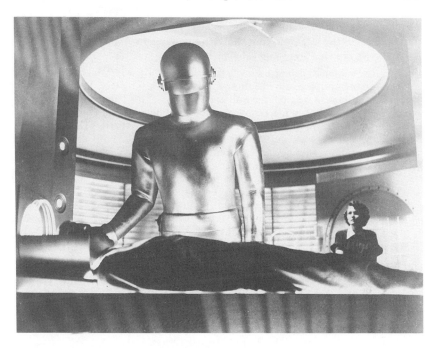

Klaatu (Michael Rennie, reclining) is tended by Gort (Lock Martin), his robotic servant and intergalactic policeman in *The Day the Earth Stood Still* (20th Century–Fox, 1951). Patricia Neal observes the healing process.

met the first invasion from another planet. A man by the name of Noah once saved our world with an ark of wood. Here at the North Pole a few men performed a similar service with an arc of electricity. The flying saucer which landed here—and its pilot—have been destroyed, but not without casualties among our own meager forces. I would like to bring to the microphone some of the men responsible for our success, but as senior Air Force officer, Captain Hendry is attending to demands over and above the call of duty. Dr. Carrington, the leader of the scientific expedition, is recovering from wounds received in the battle. And now before giving you the details of the battle, I bring you a warning. Everyone of you listening to my voice. Tell the world. Tell this to everybody wherever they are. Watch the skies. Everywhere. Keep looking. Keep watching the skies!

Direction credit went to Christian Nyby, but *The Thing!* was produced by Howard Hawks, who many believe was the guiding hand. His penchant for overlapping dialogue as well as for the presence of a group of men that included one feisty woman (Margaret Sheridan) were in evidence. Dimitri Tiomkin provided a chilling music score. *Variety's* review was not observant: "lacks genuine entertainment values. . . . Strictly offbeat subject matter."[9]

Variety was on target with the same year's *The Day the Earth Stood Still*: "fantasy and suspense are tinged with a sharply-pointed moral—that the nations of the earth will be destroyed if they don't put an end to their warfare . . .

plenty of exploitation angles."[10] The possibility of nuclear war was on people's minds. Besides the infamous line, "Klaatu birada nicto," Klaatu (Michael Rennie), like Scotty, had pungent advice:

> For our policemen we created a race of robots. Their function is to patrol the planets in spaceships like this one and preserve the peace. In matters of aggression we have given them absolute power over us. This power cannot be revoked. At the first sign of violence they act automatically against the aggressor. The penalty for provoking their action is too terrible to risk. The result is, we live in peace, without arms or armies, secure in the knowledge that we are free from aggression and war, free to pursue more profitable enterprises. We do not pretend to have achieved perfection, but we do have a system, and it works. I came here to give you these facts. It is no concern of ours how you run your own planet, but if you threaten to extend your violence, this Earth of yours will be reduced to a burned-out cinder. Your choice is simple: join us and live in peace, or pursue your present course and face obliteration. We shall be waiting for your answer. The decision rests with you.

In *Five* (1951), directed by oft maligned Arch Oboler, a Frank Lloyd Wright cliff house was used as a refuge of survivors of a worldwide holocaust who meet on the West Coast: a pregnant woman, a black bank guard, a New Yorker, a bank executive, and a fellow who crossed the Pacific after descending Mount Everest to find—no one. This last character was played by the ultimate American hick crumbum of the era, James Anderson. With a bizarre accent, he played an elitist! William Phipps was the good guy.

The past was served up in the 1951 B film *The Lost Continent,* starring Cesar Romero and John Hoyt (intriguingly playing a former Soviet in this Red-fearing era) as discoverers of a prehistoric world. Thought necessary to counter the lure of television, the advertisements combined pizzazz and exaggeration: "They Lived . . . 180,000,000 Years in Seven Days! Modern Man against Prehistoric Monster! . . . ZOOM at atomic speed to a NEW land of fantastic adventure! . . . SEE! Daring climb to a strange prehistoric world! SEE Violent upheaval of a prehistoric earthquake! SEE Breathtaking escape as an entire island explodes!"[11]

A better film of prehistoric life was *The Beast from 20,000 Fathoms* (1953), with Ray Harryhausen's first major stop-motion creature: a rhedosaur, a composite monster that had never existed. With a tyrannosauruslike head on a powerful body supported by tree trunk–size legs fore and aft, it had been thawed from polar ice by atomic testing. It swam southward to its ancient spawning grounds in underwater caverns off the coast of New York and came ashore, wreaking havoc in the metropolis. Shells wounded it, but its blood contained germs sickening the populace. What to do? How about a radioactive isotope?

The War of the Worlds (1953) was based on H. G. Wells' classic science fiction novel of 1898. George Pal's excellent special effects were compromised by a contemporary setting and a geographic change from London to Los Angeles (although Jules Verne's material was never updated). Pal did not make this mistake when he made Wells' *The Time Machine* in 1960.

The red planet sent more invaders that year. In *Invaders from Mars,* "From Out of Space . . . came hordes of green monsters! . . . Capturing at will the humans they need for their own sinister purposes! . . . A General of the Army turned into a Saboteur! Parents turned into . . . rabid Killers! Trusted police become Arsonists! Told in panorama of fantastic, terrifying COLOR." "Mu-tants. What would they want here?" asked psychologist Dr. Pat Blake (Helena Carter). (Oftentimes "mu-tant," not "mutant," was used in these films. The Metaluna mu-tant confronted inhabitants of *This Island Earth* [1955], and in *World Without End* [1956] the scientist termed his discoveries "mu-tates.") The well-known William Cameron Menzies was involved with *Invaders.* To some this is an irritating film. A child looks out his window one summer evening and observes a flying saucer sinking into the sand some distance away. His parents begin acting weird. Martians have landed and taken control of those foolish enough to investigate. Minions with bulging eyes do the bidding of the master Martian — a face with tentacles in a bubble. The army arrives and does battle beneath the earth. Pat is rescued before her neck receives the dreaded implant. (Compare also the 1956 *It Conquered the World* for aliens using implants.) What irks some viewers are the zippers in the minion suits, although they can be justified on the grounds that this is a child's dream.

There was another 1953 "dream" film, *Robot Monster.* This movie introduces the infamous "Ro-Man" of gorilla body and diving helmet head. Again, as a dream, it supposedly cannot be properly criticized.

There were ten men who repeatedly battled monsters — or became them — in 50s films: John Agar visited *The Mole People* ("Deep Inside The Earth . . . A Lost Civilization . . . A Million Years Old! . . . raging with hate, driven by wild revenge, clawing with savage fury at the heart of the world!"). Paul Birch was a vampiric alien *Not of This Earth.* Richard Carlson fought *The Creature from the Black Lagoon* and uncovered the secret of *The Maze,* Robert Clarke was *The Hideous Sun Demon,* Richard Denning survived the *Day the World Ended.* Peter Graves was captured by the *Killers from Space* and battled the horrendous Venusian in *It Conquered the World.* Arthur Franz combated the *Invaders from Mars* and made a *Flight to Mars* before becoming the *Monster on the Campus.* Marshall Thompson was not crying wolf about the *Fiend Without a Face* or *It, The Terror from Beyond Space.* Kenneth Tobey put electricity to *The Thing* and helped destroy the giant octopus in *It Came from Beneath the Sea* and the rhedosaur in *The Beast from 20,000 Fathoms.* Jeff Morrow played Exeter of *This Island Earth* and helped destroy *The Giant Claw.*

The Creature from the Black Lagoon (1954), from Universal, featured the most convincing humanoid creature since Jack Pierce's makeup in the studio's glory days of the 30s. The Gill Man was from the prehistoric Devonian age. Makeup artist Bud Westmore stepped in to help when the first monster suit proved a bust.

> The basic suit for the monster was made of liquid rubber baked onto the statue of Browning. Bud, [Jack] Kevan, and [Tom] Case made hundreds of

individual latex scales to glue on the suit, with some of the scales on the legs as much as an inch thick. To make it easier for Browning to swim, more pliant scales were added to the torso. But still the monster wasn't frightening enough, so Bud kept improvising. He devised a scaled and jagged dorsal fin, running all the way from the base of the skull down to the tailbone. A zipper and hooks and eyes were concealed inside the fin so Browning could get in and out of the suit. . . . The iguanalike head of the creature was separate from the suit. It, too, had individually applied scales and was surmounted by a matching spiny fin, also with a zipper inside. Bud built goggles into the head so that Browning's own eyes could be photographed wide open under water.[12]

Lead Richard Carlson had some trouble with this "monster."

We'd be shooting at midnight in freezing cold water, and suddenly this thing would swim toward me. It took all my discipline to hold my position and let it come near me. Bud Westmore had so completely captured the creature's personality that once inside the outfit Ricou Browning turned in one hell of a performance.[13]

Julie Adams, like Fay Wray before her, entranced the Gill Man, who mirrored her swimming from below in a sexy, scary sequence.

These films also had wonderful advertising lines. "Fury" was a popular word. Take *Revenge of the Creature.* "The City Flees In Terror . . . Before The Fury That Rages For Vengeance!" And *The Creature Walks Among Us:* "Fury stalks the streets and a city screams in TERROR!" Or *Tarantula:* "Towering Over Cities! Even Dynamite Can't Stop It! Thousands Flee Its Terror!" *This Island Earth:* "Hurtling Thru Outer Space They Challenged The Unearthly Furies Of An Outlaw Planet!" and "The Supreme Excitement Of Our Time!"

Them! (1954) was the definitive giant bug movie and demonstrated once again the concern over nuclear testing and radiation. The premise of an ant as big as a truck was made acceptable, the tension created gradually, the climactic battle in the Los Angeles sewer system rendered exciting — and possessed of a hard edge when James Whitmore is killed while rescuing a child.

B WOMEN

A stock company of actresses appeared regularly in these and other B films: Mari Blanchard (*Abbott and Costello Go to Mars,* 1953; *Rails into Laramie,* 1954; *Destry,* 1955), Marie Windsor (*Hellfire,* 1949; *Dakota Lil,* 1950; *The Tall Texan,* 1953; *Cat-Women of the Moon,* 1953), Marla English (*Shield for Murder,* 1954; *Desert Sands,* 1955), Beverly Garland (*Killer Leopard,* 1954; *New Orleans Uncensored,* 1955), Peggie Castle (*The Yellow Tomahawk* and *The White Orchid,* 1954), Mala Powers (*City That Never Sleeps,* 1953; *Bengazi* and *Rage at Dawn,* 1955), Coleen Gray (*Arrow in the Dust,* 1954; *Las Vegas Shakedown,* 1955). Powers and Gray had had A picture credits, the former in *Cyrano de Bergerac* (1950), the latter in *Nightmare Alley* (1947). Garland occasionally was the lead actress' best friend in an A production like *The Joker Is Wild* (1957).

In *The Narrow Margin* (RKO, 1952) tough dame Marie Windsor gives policeman-bodyguard Charles MacGraw a hard time. But she's not what she seems. A low-budget vehicle for young director Richard Fleischer became a B-movie classic.

CRACKS IN THE CENSORSHIP DIKE

> To compete more readily with TV, the Motion Picture Association of America took a deep breath and let out a notch or two in Hollywood's self-censorship production code. Permitted in feature films are such expressions as "hell," "damn," "fanny," "nerts." Miscegenation, "within the limits of good taste," is lawful grist for film-makers. Even jokes about traveling salesmen and farmers' daughters are permissible, if properly bleached.[14]

The miracle segment of Italian director Roberto Rosselini's 1948 film *L'Amore (Ways of Love)* was considered blasphemous in the United States. Anna Magnani played a peasant woman seduced by a shepherd. She believes her pregnancy the result of immaculate conception.

The Moon Is Blue (1953) was merely a cute Broadway-based comedy starring Maggie McNamara, William Holden, and David Niven, but it was a bombshell in the censorship wars. For employing heretofore forbidden words like *virgin,* it was denied a Production Seal. Producer-director Otto Preminger got it distributed anyway. Preminger must be commended for his stance on this and for making the first commercial narcotics-addiction film, *The Man with the Golden Arm* (1955).

From Here to Eternity (1953) was based on James Jones' immense and controversial novel about army life on Hawaii just up to and including December 7, 1941. "The Boldest Book Of Our Time," began the advertisement for the film starring Burt Lancaster as First Sergeant Milt Warden, toughest of the tough, fairest of the fair. Deborah Kerr, unexpectedly cast as Karen Holmes, played a neglected officer's wife ripe for an affair. In the film's most famous scene, she and Warden embrace on the sand as the tide rolls in. Montgomery Clift was Prewitt, the boxer who would not box, Frank Sinatra was Maggio, Donna Reed the prostitute Alma. Ernest Borgnine was a despicable stockade sergeant. Claude Akins and Jack W. Arden added to a fine supporting cast.

> From Here to Eternity is hardly an Army recruiting film. For civilian tastes it makes the Army seem tough and hazardous. . . . And yet this picture does help us to understand at the same time what would attract some people to the Army, and even grudgingly to admire — because now we know — some Regular Army types. As Prewitt justly observes at one point, "We may seem all alike. We ain't all alike." And it is this steady revelation of Army people, based upon the detailed observation of a writer who knew them at first hand, that makes this one of the most engrossing pictures of the year.[15]

For Sinatra this was a most important film. "The raucous laughs of those who consider Sinatra-as-Maggio a flagrant case of Hollywood miscasting haven't yet faded. But the cast and crew of Eternity predict that when he shows up on screen as the potato-peeling private, Frankie Boy will make the critics swoon."[16] "It is Private Maggio, and the actor is Frank Sinatra, who manages to make a fully rounded character from a minimum number of lines and convey all the ripe bravura of the original without any of its profanity."[17] From Here to Eternity (1953) resurrected his career after less than sterling outings in The Kissing Bandit (1948), Double Dynamite (1951), and Meet Danny Wilson (1952). He won a supporting actor Academy Award. He also received plaudits for his assassin in Suddenly (1954).

> In this tense and well-photographed thriller Frank Sinatra plays a psychopath who's been hired to kill the President of the United States. Mr. Sinatra gives quite a convincing performance — in an underplayed sort of way, and he raises an interesting point when he says: "If Booth hadn't been such a ham, he'd a made it." You feel quite sure that this killer won't even get the first part of his job done, to say nothing of the get-away.[18]

> Frank Sinatra, who proved in From Here to Eternity that he can act as well as he can sing, is cast as a killer in Suddenly, and he doesn't do at all badly in the role.[19]

In 1959 Sinatra starred in a sequel of sorts to Eternity, Some Came Running. (It was the third of James Jones' unofficial World War II trilogy, of which The Thin Red Line was the middle — and the last filmed.) Dave Hirsch returns to his Midwest home, confronting small town hypocrisy and his brother's problems, falling in love with a teacher (Martha Hyer) but attached to trampish waif Ginny (Shirley MacLaine) and gambler Bama (Dean Martin). Events came to a crashing halt at a carnival, where Ginny's pimp unloads his gun.

Maureen O'Hara and John Wayne starred in *The Quiet Man* (Republic, 1952), a much loved film that won director John Ford his fourth Academy Award.

ON-LOCATION "RUNAWAY" PRODUCTIONS

To combat the reality television presented, Hollywood turned to what had once been a futuristic marvel used in numerous serials of the 30s and 40s — it went on location with a vengeance. *The Black Rose* (1950) was filmed in Morocco, *The Quiet Man* (1952) in Ireland, *Untamed* (1952) in South Africa, *Mogambo* (1933) in the African jungles, *Three Coins in the Fountain* (1954) in Italy, *Soldier of Fortune* (1955) and *Love Is a Many-Splendored Thing* (1955) in Hong Kong, *Vera Cruz* (1954) and *Garden of Evil* (1954) in Mexico, *Green Fire* (1954) in South America, *Valley of the Kings* (1954) in Egypt, *House of Bamboo* (1955) in Japan, *A Prize of Gold* (1955) in West Germany.

A large-scale runaway production was *King Solomon's Mines* (1950), an acceptable adventure but a poor rendering of H. Rider Haggard's seminal African adventure novel. Stewart Granger played hero Allan Quatermain. The Englishwoman (Deborah Kerr) was manufactured for the film, there was no big battle between rival native legions, the witch Gagool was eliminated, and the treasure was a piddling amount indeed. Scenery and an animal stampede were mild substitutions.

The biggest of the early runaways was *Quo Vadis* (1951). Based on the Henryk Sienkiwicz novel of Nero's Rome that had been published in Italy in 1912, this version starred Robert Taylor, Deborah Kerr, Leo Genn, and Peter

Romantic leading man Robert Taylor proved conclusively in the fifties that he could handle he-man action roles with the best of them. In *Knights of the Round Table* (Metro-Goldwyn-Mayer, 1953) he played Lancelot. He also portrayed cowboys, an Indian, a Roman officer and a whaling man.

Ustinov as Nero. Marcus Vinicius (Taylor) returns to Rome after a successful campaign in Britain, falls in love with Lygia (Kerr), triumphs before Nero, and uses Petronius' suggestions to woo Lygia. Lygia is a Christian, however, and consigned to the arena for the fire Nero ordered but blames on the young sect. (The burning of Rome is the set piece and mighty impressive — recall MGM's experience burning Atlanta for *Gone with the Wind*.) Marcus, Ursus (Buddy

The Philistine idol topples onto George Sanders and minions in *Samson and Delilah* (Paramount, 1949), one of director Cecil B. DeMille's most entertaining Biblical pageants.

Baer), and some Praetorian guards who have had enough of Nero rescue her. Nero is helped to commit suicide, and Marcus and Lygia retire to the country. Critic Bosley Crowther called it a "monument to its unique and perishable type, to an item of commerce rendered chancy by narrowing markets and rising costs . . . a perfection of spectacle and of hippodrome display with a luxuriance of made-to-order romance in a measure not previously seen. Here is a staggering combination of cinema brilliance and sheer banality, of visual excitement and verbal boredom, of historical pretentiousness and sex."[20] *Quo Vadis* was a roadshow (two performances a day) at New York's Astor theater, but had continuous showings at the nearby Capitol.

Even Hitchcock, who in the 1948 *Rope* restricted his camera to one room and long takes, was frequently a location-loving filmmaker.

> Hitchcock's most successful films always seem to be the ones where real locations are used — the basic sense of geography and the wanderlust in his make-up come through in many of the pre-war films even when for financial reasons the studio was used to recreate the atmosphere. Many of the first Hollywood films (except *Shadow of a Doubt* which was shot mainly on location) lost this feeling of *genius loci* and floated in the limbo world of Hollywood phoneyness. But *Strangers on a Train* used real locations, and used them well, as integral parts of the story's development. The backgrounds are completely realistic and believable — the music shop where Guy argues

The Golden Horde (Universal, 1951) was a mini-epic starring, from left, Richard Egan, Henry Brandon and David Farrar. Brandon was one of the screen's great villains.

> with his impossible wife, the fairground and the island where Bruno kills her, the Washington diplomatic party, the tennis ground and the big trains thundering between New York and Washington.[21]

Like Cecil B. DeMille, Alfred Hitchcock was very active in this period and was in fact entering his halcyon age. Hitchcock used two superstar actors four times each: James Stewart (*Rope*, 1948; *Rear Window*, 1954; *The Man Who Knew Too Much*, 1956; *Vertigo*, 1958) and Cary Grant (*Suspicion*, 1941; *Notorious*, 1946; *To Catch a Thief*, 1955; *North by Northwest*, 1959).

Rear Window (1954) concerns Jeff (Stewart), who has broken his leg and is confined to his apartment, which fronts a courtyard. He begins using his Nikon and telephoto lens to observe his neighbors and comes to the conclusion that Lars Thorwald has murdered his wife. Lisa Fremont (Grace Kelly) helps him gather evidence. It was a multileveled Hitchcock masterpiece. Jeff is a voyeur, but he catches a criminal. *To Catch a Thief* (1955) was a more frivolous piece, filmed in VistaVision and Technicolor on the Riviera, where former cat burglar John Robie (Grant) works to convince the authorities and Frances Stevens (Grace Kelly again) that the local thefts are not his doing.

Backed by catchy zither music, *The Third Man* (1949) was a thriller shot on location in postwar partitioned Vienna by British director Carol Reed. Harry Lime (Orson Welles), an expatriate American, brokers bad penicillin. Old chum Holly (Joseph Cotten) finds him out. There is a chase by British police in the sewers. Welles is not onscreen much but dominates the story and has the best lines:

> Holly, what fools we are talking to each other this way. As though I'd do anything to you, or you to me. You're just a little mixed up about things in general. Nobody thinks in terms of human beings. Governments don't, why should we? They talk about the people and the proletariat. I talk about the suckers and the mugs. It's the same thing. They have their five-year plan, so have I.

> I still do believe in God, old man. I believe in God and mercy and all that but the dead are happier dead. They don't miss much here, poor devils. What do you believe in?

> Don't be so gloomy. After all, it's not that awful. Remember what the fellow said. In Italy for thirty years under the Borgias they had warfare, terror, murder, and bloodshed but they produced Michelangelo, Leonardo da Vinci, and the Renaissance. In Switzerland they had brotherly love. They had five hundred years of democracy and peace, and what did that produce? The cuckoo clock. So long, Holly.

The Treasure of the Sierra Madre (1948) was based on the novel by B. Traven. Slumming in Mexico, Fred C. Dobbs (Humphrey Bogart) joins grizzled prospector Howard (Walter Huston) and newcomer Curtin (Tim Holt) in a search for gold. They find it, and bandidos under the leadership of Goldhat (Alfonso Bedoya, known in Mexico as "the face that kills") find them. Asked for his credentials when he poses as a *federale,* Goldhat responds in one of the three or four most oft-quoted lines in movie history, "Badges? We ain't got no badges. We don't need no badges. I don't have to show you any stinkin' badges."

> It is amazing how seldom the movies go in for realism—the one property they are best qualified to display. But when a director does employ honest realism plus sufficient invention to interpret it, he is likely to make a film that can be spoken of as cinematic art. Such a film is *Treasure of the Sierra Madre.* The credit for this movie, like most good films, must be divided among many people: Henry Blanke for the excellent production; John Huston for direction that stands with the best of recent years and is reminiscent of the forceful style used by Eric von Stroheim in *Greed;* John Huston (again) for the remarkable script he wrote from the novel by B. Traven (that mysteriously unidentified writer who also deserves a share of the praise); photographer Ted McCord; art director John Hughes and several other artists, technicians and staff members whose work is less obvious but whose contributions often prove so important. And the cast in this good movie deserve applause—applause that they usually get anyway for most audiences remember and praise the actors when actually it is the director who is most often responsible for an outstanding performance.[22]

James Agee, who admired director John Huston for his work and obviously for his stand against blacklisting, and who would script Huston's *The Red Badge of Courage,* praised it:

> *The Treasure* is one of the very few movies made since 1927 which I am sure will stand up in the memory and esteem of qualified people alongside the

Joan Collins was the deliciously evil Princess Nellifer in Howard Hawks' *Land of the Pharaohs* (Warner Bros., 1955). Few would forget the sealing of the pyramid.

best of the silent movies. And yet I doubt that many people will fully realize, right away, what a sensational achievement, or plexus of achievement, it is. You will seldom see a good artist insist less on his artistry; Huston merely tells his story so straight and so well that one tends to become absorbed purely in that; and the story itself—a beauty—is not a kind which most educated people value nearly enough, today."[23]

The Treasure of the Sierra Madre (Warner Bros., 1948).

TECHNIQUES

In 1952 *This Is Cinerama* mesmerized audiences. Three cameras filmed a rollercoaster, a sailing ship, and the like, and the film was projected onto a screen by three projectors. It was the number one hit of the year, but the innovation temporarily died when theaters would not equip for it. The 1953

Walt Disney holds a model of the submarine *Nautilus* used to film one of his most successful live-action movies, *20,000 Leagues Under the Sea* (Buena Vista, 1954).

African adventure *Bwana Devil,* starring Robert Stack, introduced 3-D. Many followed, including *House of Wax, Hondo, Kiss Me, Kate,* and *The Charge at Feather River.* Special cardboard glasses with one frame green, the other red, were handed out in the theater. It was a craze quickly dead, so soon that many of the films made in the process were released "flat." *Inferno* (1953) is now generally regarded as the best 3-D film. A wealthy man (Robert Ryan), his leg broken, is left in the desert to die by his wife (Rhonda Fleming) and her lover (William Lundigan). He makes a splint and a rope to lower himself over mesas, finds a prospector, and survives. The 3-D touches include a lantern thrown at the bad guy, a rattlesnake striking, and a rockslide. The movie stands without 3-D because of Ryan, the scenery, and the film's sense of humor.

A more durable process was CinemaScope. Frenchman Henri Chretien developed it during World War I. An anamorphic lens squeezed the horizontal image to half size, and another lens expanded it when projected. CinemaScope was not welcomed by many American and British critics, and some of the public expected 3-D effects. Subsequent to viewing *The Robe,* even an insightful critic like Hollis Alpert could write,

> The new wide, curved screen, in common with all technical innovations of the past year or so, is disappointing. I found not the slightest illusion of depth in it. If anything, the images appear to be flatter than those of the ordinary screen, although this impression may have been created by the widespread use of painted backdrops to simulate vistas of Rome and Galilee. The screen used is eighty feet in width and portions of it have a way of going blurry every now and then. This may have been due, however, to faulty projection. One immediately misses the lively pace and movement of old-fashioned movies; the slowdown is probably due to the necessity to set up scenes for long takes. The huge screen must always appear to be filled.... At the end of the picture, when Richard Burton and Jean Simmons advance toward the audience, their heads filling the whole screen, their eyes as big as picture windows, I was undeniably frightened.[24]

Time said,

> The CinemaScope screen is handsomely utilized for swordplay, torture chambers and a thundering chase sequence as well as for dramatic shots of the Way of the Cross and Christ's entrance into Jerusalem the week before the Crucifixion.... *The Robe* would have been a good movie in two-dimensional black and white.... Obviously, Hollywood has finally founded something louder, more colorful and breathtakingly bigger than anything likely to be seen on a home TV screen for years to come.... But it has not found the answer to all of Hollywood's ills. Moviegoers may not want to be inundated with furious sight and sound every day of the week. And, impressive as is the wide CinemaScope screen, it is also curiously oppressive for eyes trained to the simpler demands of "flat," ordinary films. Can Cinema-Scope be used for anything except ponderous spectacles and chorus lines? Twentieth Century–Fox's Production Chief Darryl Zanuck thinks it can, and will attempt to prove his point with the soon to be released *How to Marry a Millionaire,* a lightweight comedy starring Marilyn Monroe. In fact, Zanuck has placed $35 million worth of eggs in his CinemaScope basket by scheduling a total of 14 pictures for wide-screen production.[25]

There was enthusiasm from one quarter. The French had a better handle on the promise of CinemaScope.

> We shall have to wait for the shooting of a film in CinemaScope to be as natural an occurrence as an ordinary flat black and white film before directors can enjoy the same kind of freedom. We must recognize that if CinemaScope is a commercial REVOLUTION it is also an aesthetic EVOLUTION. If you agree that every stage of perfection must of necessity be an effective increase in realism, then CinemaScope is a stage in that perfection, the most important one since the introduction of sound.[26]

No, I'm not going to attempt to describe this cinema—not what it will be an hour from now, far less tomorrow. I am making a statement: CinemaScope, Abel Gance's triple screen, Cinerama—whatever; they are always that same desire to break out of the antiquated frame and, more than that, the desire for the kind of sudden opening-out of the screen that is like the blossoming of a Japanese paper flower plunged in running water.[27]

Above all, let us rejoice that the advent of CinemaScope also means the definitive arrival of colour. What fallacies abound there too! Not to speak of all the nostalgics who miss their cherished lighting effects, and their even more cherished back lighting. . . . I recognize the need for an initial selection of tones—strangely, all wrong in *The Robe*—but with certain precautions the most vivid colours, like those found in nature, should run no risk of clashing. Expressive colour should be something not judged according to the criteria of the painter. I can think of no better example than *Niagara* itself. Its colour is alive, it speaks, even if it is a shade on the vulgar side. But this shrillness is about something new, and I find it very exciting.[28]

BIG AND LITTLE BUSINESS

In 1954 came the CinemaScope color film from Fox, *Woman's World.* Automotive plant chief Clifton Webb interviews three executives from the hinterland for a top job: Van Heflin, Fred MacMurray, Cornel Wilde. As it transpired, whether the man gets the job depends on the merits of his spouse: Arlene Dahl, Lauren Bacall, June Allyson. "She's a woman. Prime Texas beef with New York steaks in exactly the right places," said Bacall of Dahl. The same year MGM offered the black and white big biz epic *Executive Suite,* with another powerhouse cast: William Holden, June Allyson (the "perfect" wife yet again!), Barbara Stanwyck, Fredric March, Paul Douglas, Louis Calhern.

In 1955 a "little" film won the best picture Academy Award: *Marty.* Like Broderick Crawford before him in *All the King's Men,* Ernest Borgnine had a career role as a butcher who found love after years of heartbreak: "Ma, leave me alone! Ma, what do ya want from me, what do ya want from me? I'm miserable enough as it is. All right, so I'll go to the Stardust Ballroom, I'll put on a blue suit and I'll go. And you know what I'm gonna get for my trouble? Heartache, a big night of heartache." It was a revelation, but if one checks the other nominees, it becomes clear that none was an "epic": *Love Is a Many-Splendored Thing, Picnic, Mister Roberts,* and *The Rose Tattoo.*

THE EXOTICS

Darryl F. Zanuck began introducing—mostly unsuccessfully—exotic European actresses in 20th Century–Fox's product: the Polish-French Bella Darvi in two 1954 entries, *The Egyptian* and *Hell and High Water* (1954), and French Juliette Greco in *The Sun Also Rises* (1957) and *The Roots of Heaven* (1958).

Other countries provided leading ladies for the English-language cinema: Eva Bartok, Hungarian (*The Crimson Pirate,* 1951); Hildegarde Neff (originally Hildegard Knef), German (*Decision Before Dawn,* 1951; *Diplomatic*

Courier, 1952); Denise Darcel, French, and Sarita Montiel, Spanish (both in *Vera Cruz,* 1954); Corinne Calvet, French (*The Far Country,* 1955); Jeanmaire, (*Hans Christian Andersen,* 1952); Taina Elg, Finnish (*The Prodigal,* 1955; *Les Girls,* 1957; *Imitation General,* 1958). Precursors had been the French Annabella and the Spanish Margo in the 30s and 40s, the Italian Alida Valli in the late 40s.

More successful on the international scene would be two Italian actresses. Sophia Loren had a bit part in 1951 in *Quo Vadis* but in 1957 would star with Hollywood's finest in *Legend of the Lost* (John Wayne), *The Pride and the Passion* (Cary Grant and Frank Sinatra), and *Boy on a Dolphin* (Alan Ladd). Gina Lollobrigida's first English-language film was the 1954 *Beat the Devil,* with Humphrey Bogart and Jennifer Jones. She came on strong in *Trapeze* (1956), *Solomon and Sheba* (1959), and *Come September* (1961).

THE GOLDEN AGE OF WESTERNS

Robert Warshow explained the western's appeal.

> It is an art form for connoisseurs, where the spectator derives his pleasure from the appreciation of minor variations within the working out of a pre-established order. One does not want too much novelty; it comes as a shock, for instance, when the hero is made to operate without a gun, as has been done in several pictures (e.g., *Destry Rides Again*) [1939], and our uneasiness is allayed only when he is finally compelled to put his "pacifism" aside. If the hero can be shown to be troubled, complex, fallible, even eccentric, or the villain given some psychological taint or, better, some evocative physical mannerism, to shade the colors of his villainy, that is all to the good. Indeed, that kind of variation is absolutely necessary to keep the type from becoming sterile; we do not want to see the same movie over and over again, only the same form.[29]

Red River (1948) was the next classic. Tom Dunson (John Wayne) and chum Groot (Walter Brennan) plan to leave a wagon train heading west and strike off on their own. Tom must take leave of Fen (Coleen Gray). She makes it difficult.

> Too much for a woman? Put your arms around me, Tom. Hold me, knead me, Tom. Do I feel weak, Tom? I don't, do I? You'll need me. You'll need a woman. You'll need what a woman can give you to do what you have to do. Listen to me, Tom, listen with your head and your heart, too. The sun only shines half the time, Tom, the other half is night.

Tom manages to leave, later learning that the wagon train has been attacked by Indians, Fen killed. He and Groot are attacked during the night but survive and arrive in Texas. On the way he picks up a wandering boy, Matthew Garth (Montgomery Clift), and his cow. They plan to establish a ranch. A Mexican gunman and outrider for a Spanish landowner unsuccessfully tries to dissuade Dunson. He explains to Matt how he won the draw: "By watchin' his eyes, remember that." Years pass. Times are bad. Dunson must find a market for his herd. A huge drive is undertaken, the destination a railhead in Missouri. Plagued by men and the elements, Dunson becomes a tyrant, and Matt must act.

Backed by Joanne Dru, Alan Ladd intimidates his enemies in *Hell on Frisco Bay* (Warner Bros., 1955). Like Robert Mitchum and Humphrey Bogart, Ladd frequently sported a trenchcoat.

The Gunfighter (1950) continued an adult trend. Aging gunman Jimmie Ringo (Gregory Peck) arrives in town, confiding his fears of a useless life on the run from those who would match their six-shooting prowess against his. Frustrated, he mounts to leave and is backshot by punk Hunt Bromley (Skip Homeier).

The golden age of the western had begun. Both B and A westerns thrived,

Left: Red River (United Artists, 1948) was director Howard Hawks' ultimate cattle drive movie and the film that catapulted John Wayne to superstardom. As rancher Tom Dunson he gave one of his greatest performances. *Right:* Dean Jagger was a character *and* a supporting actor. For his performance as Major Stovall in *Twelve O'Clock High* (20th Century-Fox, 1949), he won a supporting actor Academy Award.

as did the white men who played Indians (Michael Pate, Pat Hogan, Frank DeKova, Eduard Franz, Keith Larsen, Henry Brandon, plus those who went on to become major stars, Charles Bronson and Jack Palance).

By contrast, the Indians in *Little Big Horn* (1951) were mosty hidden, as they were in *The Tall Texan* and *Garden of Evil.* This is eminently scarier. The last two films, released in 1953 and 1954, respectively, were about gold fever. At least one reviewer recognized the merits of B movie *Texan.* "Marie Windsor as the woman who shifts her loyalties, Lloyd Bridges as the Tall Texan on his way back to jail, and Luther Adler as an oily villain handle their assignments well. Director Elmo Williams uses the New Mexico locale magnificently."[30] Hardly anyone took note of *Garden of Evil,* which remains the most underrated A western of the 50s. It had an imposing score by Bernard Herrmann and impressive Mexican locations around the recently active Paricutin volcano. The cast was small but charismatic: Gary Cooper as Hooker, Susan Hayward as Leah Fuller, Richard Widmark as Fiske. Cameron Mitchell, Hugh Marlowe, Victor Manuel Mendoza, and, in a small part, Rita Moreno comprised the rest of the noteworthy ensemble.

High Noon (1952) has detractors and proponents, both with valid points. Producer Stanley Kramer frequently gets boos from critics who find his films too simplistic. For example, they did not like the clock ticking off the time. The title tune, "Do Not Forsake Me, Oh My Darling," became the song responsible for the rage in movie tunes, to the detriment of the whole score.

For some, like John Wayne, a plot in which a sheriff fails to receive help from the citizens when they learn that an old nemesis and his gunmen are coming to town for revenge does not make sense. (Wayne's 1959 film for Howard Hawks, *Rio Bravo*, seems to be a reply, although the help comes more from outsiders—drunk Dean Martin, new kid in town Ricky Nelson, coot Walter Brennan—than from normal townsfolk.) On the positive side, *High Noon* is riveting, the villains (Ian MacDonald, Lee Van Cleef, Sheb Wooley, Robert J. Wilke) hard to beat, the gunplay superbly choreographed, the acting fine (Gary Cooper's Will Kane won him a second Academy Award. Grace Kelly impressed as a Quaker bride). Dimitri Tiomkin's score was another in this Russian-born composer's exceptional western repertoire. Master director Fred Zinneman helmed it.

George Stevens' *Shane* (1953) was the ultimate in western mythmaking. Set in a valley beyond which rise Wyoming's Grand Tetons, the film presents both the rancher and farmer sides of nation building. Emile Meyer's Ryker roughly but eloquently explains the cattleman's viewpoint to sodbuster Starrett (Van Heflin), his wife, Marian (Jean Arthur), and son, Joey (Brandon DeWilde). Ryker related the rough times he and his kind experienced, fighting Indians and rustlers, when they first came to the territory. Starrett would not budge, so Ryker's men antagonize the farmers. Shane, a mysterious stranger in buckskin, arrives in the valley and takes a job with Starrett. Both men wage a barroom brawl with Ryker's henchmen after Shane whips Chris (Ben Johnson) in a fair fight. Shane shows Joey how to shoot. "And there are some who like two guns, but one's all you need if you can use it." Marian protests the instruction. Shane replies, "A gun is a tool, Marian. No better, no worse than any other tool. An ax, shovel, or anything. A gun is as good or as bad as the man using it. Remember that." Ryker sends for a hired gun, a man in a black hat by the name of Wilson (Walter Jack Palance), whom even the dogs shun. He guns down Torrey (Elisha Cook, Jr.). Shane buckles on his gun and, as Joey watches, wages the battle of good and evil in Grafton's saloon. Knowing that there's no living with a killing, he rides away, wounded, as Joey calls his name. The Victor Young score, the setting, the role of a career for Ladd ("He is larger than life, more heroic than legend, the kind of man who is feared by men and loved by women, children and dogs."),[31] and the conscious and successful attempt to distill myth created a western classic. *Shane* probably has more set pieces than any other western: the two-man brawl, the multiman brawl, the victory over nature in the removal of the stump, the gun lesson, Wilson's killing of Torrey, the shootout between Shane and Wilson. And then there are the static scenes that under the director's placement bring tears to the eyes: Shane in the rain, Marian looking at him from the window; Shane telling Joey he has to leave; a closeup of Ben Johnson's face after he's been knocked onto his backside. Director Stevens had spent some of his youth in the Cody, Wyoming, area, learning to ride and shoot.[32]

Director John Sturges came to the fore after years of apprenticeship in various genres with the 1953 *Escape from Fort Bravo*, one of those western

Raised in Petrolia, Texas, and Buffalo, New York, Reed Hadley supplied the voice of Red Ryder on radio and narrated 1945's semi-documentary, *The House on 92nd Street.* Among his many film appearances were *Little Big Horn* (1951) and *Big House U.S.A.* (1955).

subgenre films about Confederate prisoners and Yankee wardens holding the frontier together.[33] Sturges was to become master of gunfighting scenes. In *Bravo* the "well-staged Indian attack was the first convincing demonstration Sturges had made of what was to become his greatest knack as a director: the staging of violent action."[34]

Director John Ford began his cavalry trilogy in 1948 with *Fort Apache. She Wore a Yellow Ribbon* followed in 1949 and may be the definitive cavalry epic. Captain Nathan Brittles endeavors to prevent an Indian uprising. In 1950 Ford capped the trilogy off with *Rio Grande.* John Wayne had starred in all three as well as Ford's other 1948 western, *Three Godfathers.*

Novelist Borden Chase scripted many westerns, including *Red River* (1948), *Winchester 73* (1950), *Vera Cruz* (1954), *Man Without a Star* (1955), and *Backlash* (1956).

Richard Widmark comforts Susan Hayward as Victor Manuel Mendoza and Gary Cooper tend the arrow-riddled body of Hugh Marlowe. The film is *Garden of Evil* (20th Century-Fox, 1954), the terrain the "Lost World" around Mexico's Paricutin volcano.

Randolph Scott—who had played serviceman, coalminer, "other" man—welcomed westerns as a staple diet. Between 1948 and 1962 he appeared in 35. Compatriot Joel McCrea made 23 westerns in the same spell.

Native Americans had received some respect as early as 1934 in *Massacre*.[35] Now, in MGM's *Devil's Doorway* (1950), Robert Taylor is a Civil War medal winner who must fight a losing battle for his homeland. That same year's more famous entry was Fox's *Broken Arrow,* based on Elliot Arnold's novel of the real-life Tom Jeffords and Apache chief Cochise. As essayed by James Stewart and Jeff Chandler, respectively, they proved an admirable duo. In *Apache* (1954) Burt Lancaster and Jean Peters refused to be sent to a reservation.

Director Anthony Mann depicted "extreme men stretching out beyond their reach,"[36] often using James Stewart as the tortured hero. *Winchester 73* (1950) was the initiation of Stewart. Dodge City, July 4, 1876: A rifle contest will net the winner "One of a Thousand," a repeating Winchester rifle. Lin McAdam (Stewart) is in town tracking "Dutch Henry Brown" (Stephen McNally), later learned to be his brother, who killed their father. He pursues him to Tascosa, fights off another badman, Waco Johnny Dean (Dan Duryea), and shoots it out with Dutch among the cliffs. The film marked a distinct change of character for Stewart, who would play these types again for director Mann.

After his criminal roles, Richard Widmark (left) had a stint as a serviceman. In *Halls of Montezuma* (20th Century-Fox, 1951) he commanded a platoon of which one member was the highly-decorated World War II veteran Neville Brand.

It was important as a training ground for Tony Curtis and Rock Hudson, who had small roles as a cavalry man and Native American chief, respectively.

James Stewart also got a percentage of the profits from his Universal pictures. His next westerns were *Bend of the River* (1952) and *The Naked Spur* (1953). "For a western, the acting is uncommonly good; also uncommon for a western, the issues are not clearly outlined in black and white. At times the changing patterns in the plot seem contrived, but they are never without suspense."[37]

Janet Leigh was female lead in *The Naked Spur,* shot near Durango, Colorado. "The fear we registered was genuine," she wrote of cliff climbing.[38] She admired James Stewart's professionalism:

> Howard Koch, the A.D., dismissed Jimmy for the day, since his work was done. Jimmy, as only he can, said, "Well, I can't do that, you see, because, well, that just wouldn't be right, now would it? I think I'll just—hang around—and be off camera—for my friends there." And he stayed the entire tedious afternoon, only to play the scene in back of the camera, while it was focused on us.[39]

The other Stewart 50s westerns were *The Far Country* (1955), *The Man from Laramie* (1955), and *Night Passage* (1957).

Johnny Guitar (1954) was the most bizarre of the era's westerns. The mysterious Vienna (Joan Crawford) runs a saloon, which irritates "decent" townsfolk, including the repressed Emma Small (Mercedes McCambridge). Former lover Johnny Guitar (Sterling Hayden) comes to town and assists Vienna and her cronies, including the Dancin' Kid (Scott Brady), against her enemies. The fabulous supporting cast included Ward Bond, Ernest Borgnine, John Carradine, Paul Fix, Royal Dano, Ian MacDonald, and Denver Pyle.

THE GOLDEN AGE OF MUSICALS

On the Town (1949) continued the tradition of "spontaneous" musicals. The songs were sung anywhere they fit the mood, not realistically on a stage or performed on a piano for the houseguests. Gene Kelly, Frank Sinatra, and Jules Munshin were sailors on leave in New York. They met and caroused with Betty Garrett, Vera-Ellen, and Ann Miller. Songs like "New York, New York," "Prehistoric Man," and "Miss Turnstiles" were written by Adolph Green and Betty Comden, who based the screenplay on the stage musical. Gene Kelly and Stanley Donen directed. Arthur Freed was the producer, naturally.

At MGM Freed was the guiding force behind what would become known as the golden age of musicals. People tend to forget Warner Bros. 1930s Busby Berkeley extravaganzas and RKO's Astaire-Rogers romances when speaking of Hollywood's best musicals. Still, the best and brightest musical talents were groomed at or moved to MGM, as Astaire did. At MGM, "the Freed Unit showed its strength not in originality as much as in the freedom with which its artisans made use of tools invented by their predecessors. . . . However, the material itself varies as at no other studio at any time from Edison to the collapse of the Golden Age. One never quite gets a bead on Freed's series *as a series*; one must consult the whole abacus."[40]

"With the general collapse of the studio setup, it was the Freed Unit that played MGM's last cards of power and polish."[41] The best was *Singin' in the Rain* (1952), a tuneful satire of the end of the silent era, the start of sound. *An American in Paris* won the best picture Academy Award for 1951 but could have used more tunes. Howard Keel, Kathryn Grayson, Jane Powell, Gene Kelly, Cyd Charisse, Debbie Reynolds, and Leslie Caron were among the MGM mainstays. Fred Astaire came over from RKO.

Astaire made his last film with Ginger Rogers in 1948, *The Barkleys of Broadway.* In the 50s he had a second career as a middle-aged gent who nevertheless attracted the young ladies: Cyd Charisse, Leslie Caron, Audrey Hepburn, Jane Powell. He had, of course, escorted dancers and stars other than Rogers in the 40s, among them Rita Hayworth and Paulette Goddard.

The oddest musicals of this era were the pyrotechnic aquacades starring Esther Williams. A champion (but not Olympic) swimmer herself, Williams played real life swimmer Annette Kellerman in *Million Dollar Mermaid* (1952). (Annette Kellerman had played herself in the 1914 version!)

At Warner Bros. Doris Day became a star in her first movie by replacing Betty Hutton in *Romance on the High Seas* (1948). Day previously had been lead singer with the Les Brown and Bob Crosby bands. She made musicals like *I'll See You in My Dreams* (1951). There was an unfortunate emphasis on the

The Far Country (Universal, 1955) was one of seven gritty, scenic westerns that along with his three Hitchcock films, rabbit fancier *Harvey,* defense attorney in *Anatomy of a Murder,* and folk hero roles in *The Glenn Miller Story* and *The Spirit of St. Louis* made James Stewart star of the decade.

adults in *On Moonlight Bay* (1951) and its 1953 sequel, *By the Light of the Silvery Moon,* both of which were based on Booth Tarkington's Penrod stories. Billy Gray played the youth Wesley, Day's brother. In the larger scale musical biography *Love Me or Leave Me* (1955) she played Ruth Etting opposite James Cagney's Martin Snyder. Later came such hits as the sprightly *The Pajama Game* (1957).

Offbeat casting featured ballerina Leslie Caron, fresh from her triumph in *An American in Paris,* opposite tough guy Ralph Meeker in *Glory Alley* (Metro-Goldwyn-Mayer, 1952), a boxing movie set in New Orleans.

Many of the Fox musicals were still backstagers. Mitzi Gaynor was promoted in not very good musical biographies: *Golden Girl* (1951) and *The I Don't Care Girl* (1952). (Bigger and better bios of the era starred Susan Hayward — as Jane Froman in the 1952 *With a Song in My Heart* and as Lillian Roth in the 1955 *I'll Cry Tomorrow.*) "Mitzi Gaynor flashed but briefly on cinema screens, a happy, chirpy girl seemingly hurt once musicals stopped

Sets, costumes and the dancing of Moira Shearer were the overriding strengths of *The Red Shoes* (The Archers, 1948). That's Robert Helpmann in the rear, top.

being staple product at each studio."[42] Although Gaynor did obtain the plum musical role of the decade as Nellie Forbush in *South Pacific,* she could have been Vera-Ellen at MGM (although Vera-Ellen's voice was often dubbed by such singers as Anita Ellis and Carole Richards).[43] Gaynor did make one stylish MGM musical, *Les Girls* (1957).

Costume/Adventure

Doing what the little screen could not, Universal produced miniepics with Rock Hudson, Tony Curtis, Piper Laurie, Janet Leigh, and Jeff Chandler. Full of memorable lines, they included *The Black Shield of Falworth* (1954), *The Prince Who Was a Thief* (1951) ("Hah, a likely tale to hear from such as you, lowborn," says Hayden Rorke as Basra. Later Curtis as Jalna/Prince Hussein praises Piper Laurie's character: "With the most brave and most beautiful princess in all Islam—Princess Tina."), *Son of Ali Baba* (1952), *Captain Lightfoot* (1955), Chandler vehicles *Yankee Buccaneer* (1952), *Sign of the Pagan* (1954), and *Yankee Pasha* (1954). Dialogue was typically western. In *Son of Sinbad* (1955) Dale Robertson retorted, "It's always too late to surrender to Tamerlane!" Even larger scale epics like Fox's *Prince Valiant* (1954) contained silly dialogue, such as this line by Janet Leigh's Aleta: "Ooh, father's right about those blasted Vikings."

Better than any of the previous films was the 1952 *Scaramouche,* which

Roles in Universal swashbuckler and Arabian Nights mini-epics like *The Golden Blade* and *Son of Ali Baba* made Piper Laurie popular enough that paper dolls of her likeness were produced. The pert image was dropped for hard-edge comeback roles in 1961's *The Hustler* and as Sissy Spacek's mom in 1976's *Carrie*.

concluded with a seven-to-eight-minute duel between 18th century swords-man-actor Scaramouche (Stewart Granger) and a noble (Mel Ferrer). Eleanor Parker and Janet Leigh were radiant as the love interests.

ACTORS AND STARS

Antiheroes and rebellion equaled ambivalence and imperfection. The Actors Studio's "method acting" technique, by which actors "became" the character, received much publicity. Marlon Brando, James Dean, Rod Steiger, and Montgomery Clift were method actors.

Brando had come to film after a triumph at the Ethel Barrymore Theater in 1947 in *A Streetcar Named Desire*. *The Men* (1950) was his first film. The ad proclaimed: "Meet Marlon BRANDO who shocked Broadway in *A Streetcar Named Desire* . . . now reaches out for your hate . . . love . . . and fears—as no screen personality ever has . . . in his screen debut as one of *THE MEN*." Reviews were good.

For her portrayal of the worldly-wise yet vulnerable Blanche Dubois in *A Streetcar Named Desire* (Warner Bros., 1951), Vivien Leigh won her second Academy Award as a Southern belle. Back to the camera is the brutish Stanley Kowalski (Marlon Brando).

> I don't suppose anyone could improve on Mr. Brando's performance in *The Men*. Even as a handicapped veteran, he seems so authentically overpowering physically that he makes most standard Hollywood heroes look like flyweights, and he certainly succeeds in convincing one of the tragic immobility of his legs.[44]

Brando reprised his Stanley Kowalski role in *A Streetcar Named Desire* (1951), directed by Elia Kazan:

> Compliments to women about their looks, I never met a dame yet didn't know if she was good lookin' or not without bein' told, and they're some of them that give themselves credit for more than they've got. I once went out with a dame who told me I'm the glamorous type. She says, I am the glamorous type. I said, "So what?"

A Streetcar Named Desire (1951) proved that films can be aimed at a specific audience—in this case adults. Alex North composed the innovative jazz score. "Richly coloured with the sound of New Orleans jazz, the music wailed and stung, it pointed up Brando's coarse Kowalski and tinged the delusion and despair of Vivien Leigh's Blanche."[45]

In *The Wild One* (1954), Brando played Johnny, motorcycle gang leader whose troop wreaks havoc on a small town. Mary Murphy asks for his views on picnics. He replies,

> A picnic! Man, you are too square. I'm, I'm, I have to straighten you out. Now listen, you don't go any one special place. That's cornball-style. You just go!

In *Desiree* (20th Century-Fox, 1953), Marlon Brando essayed the role of Napoleon in what was really a Jean Simmons vehicle. Both would co-star again — and do their own singing — in 1955's *Guys and Dolls*.

> A bunch gets together after all week. It builds up. You just — the idea is to have a ball. Now if you're gonna stay cool you got to wail. You got to put somethin' down, you got to make some jive. Don't you know what I'm talkin' about?

The British banned the film in the United Kingdom till 1968.

> Any film first shown publicly nearly 15 years after it was made is bound to seem a trifle embalmed. Naturally it would, if it did not, why would our

censors have second thoughts about allowing us to see it? And certainly in the light of what we nowadays accept as the norm for screen violence and all that, Laslo Benedek's drama of the motor-cycle gangs and their girls seems perfectly innocuous. Worth seeing, though. It was made with a lot of gusto which survives intact, and contains one of Marlon Brando's most magnetic performances — Methody, but heavily charged with personality and not merely fidgety and perverse as so many of his recent appearances have been. And by now, even the dated side of the film has acquired a certain charm, the swinging jazz score in early Shorty Rogers style, the heroine wandering round in those early 1950s skirts which made women look as though they were wading waist-high through a swamp. So period, so period — and after all, at the rate these things move today, the Fifties should be coming up as the new period craze any moment now.[46]

Rumor has it that *The Wild One* was welcomed into the Soviet Union because it would prove how decadent American society was. Ironically, audiences thought the United States couldn't be that bad — after all, even a punk could own a motorcycle.

On the Waterfront (1954) paired Brando with Elia Kazan again. Brando was Terry Malloy, dockworker, club fighter who "mighta" been somebody if his brother, labor racketeer shyster Charlie (Rod Steiger) hadn't let boss man (Lee J. Cobb) tell him to make Terry take a fall.

Brando showed his versatility in 1955. He did his own singing, as did Jean Simmons, in *Guys and Dolls*.

Montgomery Clift made *Red River* first, but *The Search* was released earlier, in 1948. He followed as the callous lover of Olivia De Havilland in *The Heiress* (1949) and the doomed lover of Elizabeth Taylor in *A Place in the Sun* (1951).

James Dean had bit roles in *Fixed Bayonets!* (1951), *Sailor Beware* (1952), and *Has Anybody Seen My Gal?* (1952). Before a car crash ended his career, he blazed forth in three major and influential films, *East of Eden* (1955), *Rebel Without a Cause* (1955), and *Giant* (1956). In *Eden*, based on John Steinbeck's novel, he played the tormented Cal, son of Adam (Raymond Massey). Elia Kazan directed the young Nebraskan.

> Dean had no technique to speak of. When he tried to play an older man in the last two reels of *Giant*, he looked like what he was: a beginner. On my film, Jimmy would either get the scene right immediately, without any detailed direction — that was ninety-five percent of the time — or he couldn't get it at all. Then I had to use some extraordinary means — the Chianti, for instance.[47]

Kazan thought Dean got through the film because of Julie Harris, who was "goodness itself with Dean, kind and patient and everlastingly sympathetic."[48] Even more tormented — or, as Kazan thought, even though he admitted to helping create the image in *Eden*, "self-pitying, self-dramatizing, and good-for-nothing"[49] — Dean, as Jim in *Rebel*, raged against his parents (Jim Backus and the ubiquitous Ann Doran): "You're tearing me apart!"[50] At his new school he was harassed by classmates but comforted by Judy (Natalie Wood) and befriended by Plato (Sal Mineo). In *Giant* he was Jett Rink, poor boy who hit

Montgomery Clift and Elizabeth Taylor starred in George Stevens' *A Place in the Sun* (Paramount, 1951), based on Theodore Dreiser's novel *An American Tragedy*. Clift and Taylor co-starred again in *Raintree County* (1957) and *Suddenly, Last Summer* (1959).

paydirt with an oil gusher and challenged neighboring cattle baron Bix (Rock Hudson) for prestige and his wife (Elizabeth Taylor).

These three method actors—Brando, Clift, and Dean—were not inter-changeable. "Could you see Dean as Stanley Kowalski or Marc Antony?"[51]— Brando's roles in *Streetcar* and *Julius Caesar*.

A nonmethod actor, William Holden, was having an outstanding decade. After years as the "golden boy," and despite his own fear that he was not a real actor, he became one in *Sunset Boulevard*, *Sabrina*, *Executive Suite*, *The Bridges at Toko-Ri*, *Love Is a Many Splendored Thing*, *Picnic*. His fortune was assured when the 10 percent of the gross he took on *The Bridge on the River Kwai* in 1957 was paid out at $50,000 per year.

Sometimes a rebel, Kirk Douglas was unsympathetic in William Wyler's *Detective Story* and Billy Wilder's *Ace in the Hole*, both (1951).

It is possible to count on the fingers of one hand the films that have come from Hollywood with an utter disregard for box-office values or potentialities. There have been Von Stroheim's *Greed*, John Ford's *The Informer*, John

Huston's *The Treasure of the Sierra Madre,* perhaps one or two more. *Ace in the Hole* gleefully dissects human beings at their worst.[52]

Ace, retitled *The Big Carnival* in an attempt to get an audience, details the biggest story of Douglas' reporter character's life as he covers a man trapped in a southwestern cave. He gets the story *and* the man's wife (Jan Sterling).

Audie Murphy, the most decorated U.S. serviceman of World War II, debuted in *Beyond Glory* (1948) and made 43 films before his death in 1971. Most were B westerns. The best were John Huston's *The Red Badge of Courage* (1951), his own story, *To Hell and Back* (1955), and *The Unforgiven* (1960), in which he plays Burt Lancaster's brother.

June Allyson must be considered "the" Hollywood wife. She played the model spouse in *The Stratton Story, The Glenn Miller Story, The McConnell Story, Woman's World, Executive Suite,* and *Strategic Air Command.*[53]

Audrey Hepburn, Brussels born and dance trained, had appeared in British films including *One Wild Oat* (1951) and *The Lavender Hill Mob* (1951) before an outstanding international coming out party in *Roman Holiday* (1953), for which she won an Academy Award. William Wyler's newcomer had more than proved her worth. *Sabrina* costarred her with Humphrey Bogart and William Holden. As Linus Larrabee, Bogart has one of the best lines for his brother (William Holden):

> Your office is on the twenty-second floor. Our normal work week is Monday through Friday. Our working day is nine to five. Should you find this inconvenient, you are free to retire under the Larrabee Pension Plan. Having been with us one year, this will entitle you to sixty-five cents a month for the rest of your life.

Judy Garland made the most of George Cukor's 1954 musical remake of the 1937 *A Star Is Born,* which had been inspired by *What Price Hollywood* (1932). "The Man That Got Away" became part of Garland's repertoire. She played Esther Blodgett/Vicki Lester, whose fame came to outshine that of her husband, Norman Maine (James Mason).

John Wayne was in the first big nondisaster epic, *The High and the Mighty* (1954). It had a catchy title tune, whistled onscreen by Wayne himself. As Dan Roman, almost-has-been copilot, he keeps pilot Robert Stack in line on a Pacific flight. Flashbacks detail the lives of most of the passengers: Jan Sterling, Claire Trevor, Douglas Fowley, Laraine Day, David Brian. Former pilot William Wellman was at the directorial control board. Here's another tune that captured a national audience. The plane landed safely. Contrast this with future catastrophe cinema.

Robert Mitchum would play crazed preacher Harry Powell in *Night of the Hunter* (1955), thus adding yet another outstanding character to his repertoire. Carved on one hand's fingers were "L O V E," on the other "H A T E." He married widows, murdered them, and absconded with their money. He pursued John (Billy Chapin) and Pearl (Sally Jane Bruce) through a nightmarish, surrealistic landscape in the only film directed by Charles Laughton. As Rachel Cooper, Lillian Gish put the fear of God into him with a load of buckshot.

Burt Lancaster played Dardo in the Robin Hood–like adventure, *The Flame and the Arrow* (1950). "You can't make a prince out of a peasant." By *Come Back, Little Sheba* (1952), he had become an actor as well as a peasant.

Bette Davis made a comeback of sorts in *All About Eve* (1950), full of lines from writer-director Joseph L. Mankiewicz. "What a story. Everything but the bloodhounds snappin' at her rear end" and "I never played Fort Sumter," said Thelma Ritter. And from Davis a scathing attack on Anne Baxter's Eve:

> I want everybody to shut up about Eve. Just shut up about Eve. That's all I want. Give Karen more wine. Never have I been so happy. Isn't this a lovely room? The Cub Room. What a lovely, clever name. Where the elite meet. Never have I seen so much elite, all with their eyes on me, waiting for me to crack that little gnome on the noggin with a bottle. But not tonight. I'm forgiving tonight. Even Eve. I forgive Eve. There they go. There goes Eve. Eve Evil. Little Miss Evil. But the evil that men do. How does that go, Groom. Something about the good they leave behind. I, I played it once in rep in Wilkes-Barre.

BLONDS AND REDHEADS

Judy Holliday played the dumb blond in *Adam's Rib* (1949), then made it definitive when she reprised her Broadway role as Billee Dawn in *Born Yesterday* (1951).

"Some sweet kid," Louis Calhern called Marilyn Monroe in *The Asphalt Jungle* (1950). After another small but noticeable part in *All About Eve,* she showed off a leg to Cary Grant in *Monkey Business* (1952). Even a dreadful outing as a semipsychotic baby-sitter in *Don't Bother to Knock* (1952) could not ruin her. She lived up to promise when playing flighty roles in two 1953 films, *Gentlemen Prefer Blondes* and *How to Marry a Millionaire.* In the latter she was given star billing over both Betty Grable and Lauren Bacall—proof of her standing. *Niagara* (1953) gave her a dramatic role she was suited for: the cheating wife of Joseph Cotten. *River of No Return* in 1954 was no great shakes—she was poor—but *The Seven Year Itch* (1955) was made to order. Although the stage character was a less provocative girl, MM's part as the sweet but sexy upstairs neighbor of Tom Ewell was just right for her. Needless to say, Ewell as the married man alone for the summer and Robert Strauss as custodian Kruhulik helped make the whole thing work. MM would make only five more films, the best being *Some Like It Hot* (1959).

Miss Deepfreeze, Kim Novak, was manufactured by Harry Cohn at Columbia to compete with and replace G.I. pinup girl Rita Hayworth, now a mature woman and demanding star. Cohn succeeded. In 1955 Novak was getting $75 per week at Columbia, but Otto Preminger had to pay Columbia $100,000 for her services in *The Man with the Golden Arm.*[54] For an icelike nonactress termed somnambulistic, she held her own in a raft of big productions through the decade after introductory parts in her two 1954 films, *Pushover,* opposite Fred MacMurray, and *Phffft,* with Judy Holiday and Jack Lemmon. *Five Against the House* was a satisfying casino heist film in which she costarred with Guy Madison and Brian Keith.

By the mid-fifties Marilyn Monroe was a sex symbol for the ages. Best at comedy, she was suited for dramatic roles in *Niagara* (1953) and *Bus Stop* (1956).

Redhead (or chestnut hued) Elaine Stewart (Elsie Steinberg) was a top model, appeared on *Life*'s cover, and played supporting roles or leads in seven 1953 films: *The Bad and the Beautiful, Rogue's March, Code Two, Young Bess* (as Ann Boleyn), *Desperate Search, A Slight Case of Larceny,* and *Take the High Ground.* Opposite Richard Widmark and Karl Malden in the last, it was also her most important part.

Eleanor Parker continued a fine career, starring in, among others, *Escape from Fort Bravo* (1953) and *The Naked Jungle* (1954). She received Academy Award nominations for *Caged* (1950), *Detective Story* (1951), and *Interrupted Melody* (1955).

Until Marilyn Monroe rose to prominence, Susan Hayward was 20th Century–Fox's most popular leading lady, ranking in the Quigley Publications poll ninth in 1952 and 1953, tenth in 1959. (MM made the top ten in 1953, 1954, and 1956.) Acting honors would still go to Hayward, who received Academy

Cheaper by the Dozen (20th Century–Fox, 1950).

You're Never Too Young (Paramount, 1955) with Jerry Lewis and Dean Martin was a remake of 1942's *The Major and the Minor*. Martin had the Ray Milland part, Lewis the Ginger Rogers role.

Award nominations for *With a Song in My Heart* (1952) and *I'll Cry Tomorrow* (1955) and won in 1958 for playing real-life call girl Barbara Graham in *I Want to Live!*

COMEDIANS AND CHARACTER ACTORS

Alec Guinness had become a versatile master of comedy and drama in Britain. In the 1949 *Kind Hearts and Coronets,* Guiness, who had performed the role of Fagin in *Oliver Twist* and a small part in *Great Expectations,* played eight roles: the Duke, Banker, Parson, General, Admiral, Young Ascoyne, Young Henry, and Lady Agatha. In *The Man in the White Suit* he played the inventor of an indestructible fabric. "The combination of Ealing Studios and Alec Guinness has clicked again."[55] Other jewels in his crown were *The Ladykillers, The Promoter* (aka *The Card*), *All at Sea, The Captain's Paradise,* and *The Horse's Mouth* (1958). Many of Guinness' films were comedies for Ealing Studios, the most famous name in 50s British film comedy.

> The country was tired of regulations and regimentation, and there was a mild anarchy in the air. In a sense our comedies were a reflection of this mood . . . a safety valve for our more anti-social impulses. Who has not wanted to raid a bank *(The Lavender Hill Mob)* as an escape to life of ease; commit mayhem on a fairly large scale to get rid of tiresome people in the way *(Kind Hearts and Coronets);* make the bureaucrat bite the dust *(Passport to Pimlico* and

The 30s' number one gangster, James Cagney (center between Edmond O'Brien and Virginia Mayo), made a tour-de-force comeback in *White Heat* (Warner Bros., 1949). He was vicious, he was mother-loving, he was insane as Cody Jarrett and blew himself up on an oil tank. "Made it, ma! Top of the world!"

Titfield Thunderbolt)? The comedies gave us the opportunity to tell our stories almost exclusively in cinematic and visual terms. They were not, with the exception of *Whiskey Galore*, stories taken either from novels or plays. They started as ideas designed from the outset in screen terms.[56]

Hollywood drained Britain of actors like Guinness and actresses who were deemed to possess an international appeal. Contrast with the British Film Invasion of the 60s, in which the actors had more leverage after the decline of the studio system and the end to mandatory long-term contracts.

Character performers distinguishing themselves at this time included Thelma Ritter *(Pickup on South Street)*, Paul Stewart *(Kiss Me Deadly, Carbine Williams, Deadline U.S.A.)*, Frank Faylen *(Hangman's Knot, Riot in Cell Block 11)*, Barry Jones as Claudius in *Demetrius and the Gladiators*. In 1954 Nestor Paiva appeared in six films: *Jivaro* (as Shipley), *Creature from the Black Lagoon* (as Lucas), *Casanova's Big Night* (as Gnocchi), *Four Guns to the Border* (as Greasy), *The Desperado*, and *Thunder Pass*. Paiva, it seemed, could play anything.

A NEW VICIOUSNESS

While James Cagney had not retired from the screen, his 40s roles were not so numerous as they had been in the 30s. As if to reinforce his standing, he starred as Cody Jarrett in *White Heat* (1949), playing the half-maniacal son of a warped Ma Barker–style mother (Margaret Wycherly). His gang robs a train. He must deal with rebellious henchman (Steve Cochran) and his own floozy wife, Verna (Virginia Mayo). Going to prison to avoid prosecution for another crime, Jarrett learns of his mother's death while dining in the cafeteria. An animalistic cry wells up his throat and he goes berserk, felling guards till overcome by their numbers. Escaping, he kills his competition and is finally brought to bay during a new robbery attempt. His gang has been infiltrated by Frank Fallon (Edmond O'Brien). Climbing atop a gas storage tank, he is filled with holes but will not go down. "Made it, Ma. Top of the world!" The tank goes up. The reviewers said:

> There is then the matter of Cagney's death, which turns out to be not an execution but an apotheosis.... Cagney's performance in *White Heat* is certainly his most brutal, and very probably his most convincing. Margaret Wycherly, as the insane mother of an insane son, gives a chilling impression of perfectly controlled madness.[57]

> In several of our new films crime and violence are carried to extremes of vividness of portrayal. The pictures try desperately to justify their scenes of realistic brutality; but we can't help wondering if the raw sequences of sadism are not thrown in more for their shock value than for any real understanding of the characters involved. In *White Heat* James Cagney gives a superb performance of a gang leader who is ruthless in his methods ... exciting cinema.[58]

It remained a peak time for *film noir*. Orson Welles directed and starred in *The Lady from Shanghai* (1948), with Rita Hayworth and Everett Sloane. The denouement, with Hayworth and Sloane blasting away at each other in a mirror maze, is justly famous. *Kiss Me Deadly* (1955) was Robert Aldrich's contribution. Ralph Meeker played Mike Hammer, somewhat amoral, or at least not so moral as Philip Marlowe. He was not averse to smashing valuable record albums to elicit information. "Aldrich is the Devil's travel agent, inviting us on what promises to be a regulated voyage up a charted river. But we wake on the third morning and the guide is gone and the map is no good and the river is bounded by jungle on both sides."[59]

HEIST FILMS

Although there had been criminals virtually from day one of the silent cinema and western bank and train robbers in profusion in the sound cinema, the true heist film was a post–World War II phenonenon. In these films the planning and execution of the robbery became the raison d'être. *Criss Cross* (1949), with Burt Lancaster and Dan Duryea as partners in an armored car robbery, may be the first in this subgenre. It was followed by a lesser relation, *Armored Car Robbery*. The first classic was John Huston's *The Asphalt Jungle* (1950). Alonzo D. Emmerich (Louis Calhern) needs cash, some of which he will spend on his mistress (Marilyn Monroe). He hires Doc Riedenschneider (Sam Jaffe) to mastermind the bank robbery. Dix Handley (Sterling Hayden) is the muscle. (Hayden would also play the lead in Stanley Kubrick's 1956 racetrack robbery film *The Killing*.) As usual in these films, there is a glitch, and the protagonists came a cropper. With girlfriend Doll Conovan (Jean Hagen), the wounded tragic figure of Dix heads for Kentucky.

Chapter 7

The Last Great Days of Moviegoing, 1956–1974

Different had become a genre, and the 1960s was becoming a genre in its own time.
— Ethan Mordden, *Medium Cool: The Movies of the 1960s*

The Hollywood studio system disintegrated gradually. Loss of the theater chains and the competition from commercial television, foreign films, and sports were factors that could but cause a long-term decline. And studio breakup, when it happened, did have its benefits. A blacklist would be more difficult to institute and the filmmakers would not be forced to make ninety-minute movies meant to play from morning till night. More devastating to the studios as the 60s passed into the 70s were inflation and escalating wage and labor costs, which cut down the number of films that could be made and stifled variety. Epic moviemakers like Cecil B. DeMille died, and who could afford to hire thousands of Spanish extras to play Roman legions or medieval crusaders? Nor could big-budget musicals recoup the cost of production and promotion.

ROADSHOWS

The 30s may have been the golden age of moviemaking. But moviegoing? Audiences of the 50s and 60s, especially the baby boom generation, who called film art, had the past and present of film. Retrospectives abounded. Studios sold older films to television. And the roadshow made moviegoing an extraspecial event.

Roadshows were usually three hours or more in length. They premiered in one center city theater and stayed there for months or, in the case of a movie like *Cleopatra* or *The Sound of Music,* a year. Patrons purchased reserved seats by mail or several hours before the shows, which normally played at 2:00 and 8:00 P.M. During intermission patrons could purchase deluxe programs in the lobby for a mere buck.

Besides *The Birth of a Nation* (1915) and *Gone with the Wind* (1939), there were few roadshows before the mid–50s. *Quo Vadis* (1951) played twice a day at New York's Astor but continuously at the nearby Capitol.

It wasn't until 1956 that regular gigantism set in. King Vidor directed Henry Fonda and Audrey Hepburn in *War and Peace* in Italy, and George Stevens directed Rock Hudson, Elizabeth Taylor, and James Dean in Edna Ferber's tale of Texas, *Giant*. Cecil B. DeMille's *The Ten Commandments* featured a cast of thousands, the parting of the Red Sea, and Charlton Heston as Moses, Yul Brynner as Pharaoh. Mike Todd produced *Around the World in 80 Days* on worldwide locations with David Niven, Mexico's Cantinflas, Shirley MacLaine, and an all-star cast.

A brief respite occurred before *Ben-Hur* (1959) heralded a new roadshow rush. Director William Wyler tackled Civil War General Lew Wallace's "tale of the Christ" novel for the sound era. Wyler was a major director who not long ago was dismissed for not evincing an auteuristic bent. Like Victor Fleming, he lent his hand to any number of diverse stories. Recently his reputation has been somewhat restored. In any case, *Ben-Hur* was *the* epic of 1959, and the chariot race the set piece. Charlton Heston was Judah. Stephen Boyd, who "wore Roman armour as though it belonged to him,"[1] played Messala, who had a great death scene after the chariot race. It won 11 Academy Awards, the record.

The roadshow took firm hold in 1960 and ran a course of ten years, petering out in the early 70s. Whatever their artistic worth, these films helped make that period a golden age of *movie watching*. In chronological order, the roadshows of the sixties were *The Alamo, Exodus, Pepe, Spartacus, El Cid, King of Kings, West Side Story, How the West Was Won, Lawrence of Arabia, The Longest Day, Mutiny on the Bounty, The Wonderful World of the Brothers Grimm, Cleopatra, It's a Mad, Mad, Mad, Mad World, The Fall of the Roman Empire, My Fair Lady, The Agony and the Ecstasy, Battle of the Bulge, The Greatest Story Ever Told, The Hallelujah Trail, Doctor Zhivago, The Sound of Music, Those Magnificent Men in Their Flying Machines, or How I Flew from London to Paris in 25 Hours and 11 Minutes, The Bible, The Blue Max, Grand Prix, Hawaii, Is Paris Burning? A Man for All Seasons, The Sand Pebbles, Khartoum, Camelot, Far from the Madding Crowd, Doctor Dolittle, The Happiest Millionaire, Gone with the Wind* (1967 reissue), *The Taming of the Shrew, Thoroughly Modern Millie, Chitty Chitty Bang Bang, Finian's Rainbow, Funny Girl, Star! Half a Sixpence, Ice Station Zebra, The Lion in Winter, Oliver! 2001: A Space Odyssey, Paint Your Wagon, Sweet Charity, Goodbye, Mr. Chips,* and *Hello, Dolly!* In the 70s only a few attained roadshow status: *Patton, Lost Horizon,* and *Fiddler on the Roof. Nicholas and Alexandra,* released in December 1971, and *Man of La Mancha,* released in December 1972, were roadshows, although the latter was shown three times per day simultaneously in three New York theaters.

Several roadshows deserve mention. *Spartacus* (1960) starred Kirk Douglas as the Thracian slave who led a gladiators' revolt against Rome, circa

In *Spartacus* (Universal, 1960), Kirk Douglas (left) battles Woody Strode for the edification of offscreen Laurence Olivier. The epic of ancient Rome cost a then fabulous $12 million.

70 B.C. Laurence Olivier played a decadent Crassus, who finally conquered the slave army with the assistance of Pompey's forces. Jean Simmons was slave Varinia, Peter Ustinov the gladiator school owner Batiatus, Charles Laughton a senatorial enemy of Crassus, Tony Curtis a poet member of the slave army. The film cost $12 million. Douglas selected young Stanley Kubrick for the directorial chair. Dalton Trumbo, heretofore blacklisted and writing under a

pseudonym (as Robert Rich he had won a screenplay Academy Award for the 1956 film *The Brave One*) was restored to Hollywood respectability. Alex North's score may be the best ever for a historical pageant, more sparing than, say, one by Rozsa or Tiomkin, especially in the prelude to the final battle as the Roman legions form before the slave horde. Among the instruments North used were the ondioline, an electronic instrument that simulated woodwinds, mandolin, and percussion; a sarrousophone, a wind instrument; the kythara, a Roman lyrelike stringed instrument; bagpipes; and a dulcimer.

> I strove for a barbaric quality ... which was exemplified in the cold, brutal inhumanity of General Crassus. A violin was not used until the thirteenth reel when the love story blossoms between Spartacus and Varinia. There is a simple, universal theme for the slaves, a liberation theme after their breakout from the gladiator school and typical period music when the slave army trains and prepares for battle which uses an odd ⅝ meter, early Greek style, never written contemporarily.[2]

After some impressive but rather naive opening narration about the disease of slavery (Rome lasted another five hundred years), Spartacus is seen laboring in the Libyan salt mines. Sent to a gladiator school in Italy, he leads a revolt that attracts thousands of slaves. They defeat Roman forces and decide to deal with pirates for transportation to a better world. Sadly for them, they must fight a battle against Crassus' legions and a second army. Defeated, the survivors, including Spartacus, are crucified. Spartacus' lover, Varinia, and their child are saved by the grace of a senator and her former owner, Batiatus. Deemed too erotic or violent at the time, scenes featuring Crassus and Antoninus in the former's bath as well as bloodletting (a severed hand) were reinstalled in the restored version in 1991. The best scenes depict the gladiators' school and the impressive formations of the legions. Kubrick, like other filmmakers, disappoints when the final battle is joined. It quickly becomes a single combat issue. This was not how Roman armies defeated their enemies.

El Cid (1961) was made at Samuel Bronston's Spanish studios with seven thousand Spanish extras providing warring Moors and Castillians in the 12th century. Second unit director Yakima Canutt helmed the rousing action scenes: the joust at Calahorra, the battle with 13 knights, the siege of Valencia. Star Charlton Heston previewed it on November 16, 1961.

> I ran *El Cid* and was very disappointed, though I'm sure it will make a lot of money. The plus values are an impeccably tasteful physical presentation, as well as some very good performances. The whole last third of the film is extremely good. The flaws are excessive length, one minute too much footage in each fight scene, and ten feet too much in each silent close-up of Sophia (who is very good). I'm very good in the last, a bit stiff in the opening, patchy in the middle till I get into the beard scenes.[3]

Lawrence of Arabia received almost unqualified critical applause, a best picture Academy Award, and financial success. David Lean's crew had captured the Arabian desert as had none before them. Filming took place 150 miles from water east of Aqaba at Jebel Tubeiq, as well as in Spain and Morocco.[4] A stage veteran but film newcomer, Peter O'Toole was a sensation as the enigmatic

Elizabeth Taylor undergoes a costume test during the filming of *Cleopatra* (20th Century-Fox, 1963).

British officer who helped engineer Arab freedom from the Turks during World War I.

Cleopatra (1963) has taken heat for allegedly being an expensive bomb, for stirring gossip, and for not being true Shakespeare. At a cost of some $40 million, it did need a big audience to succeed financially. The casting department at 20th Century–Fox had originally proposed the ideal boxoffice team of Cary Grant as Caesar, Elizabeth Taylor as Cleopatra, and Burt Lancaster as

Antony. Other possible Cleos were Brigitte Bardot, Marilyn Monroe, Jennifer Jones, Kim Novak, Audrey Hepburn, Sophia Loren, Gina Lollobrigida, and, more seriously, Susan Hayward, a favorite of producer Walter Wanger. Younger contract actresses were also considered: Joan Collins, Dolores Michaels, Millie Perkins, Barbara Steele, Suzy Parker.[5] In retrospect, this seems a relic of a past studio age. This *Cleopatra* would exceed in press, expense, and opulence any of the prior film outings for the Queen of the Nile.[6]

During filming the offscreen romance between Richard Burton and Elizabeth Taylor filled the tabloids. Critics complained. All in all, the film was a fairly literate epic of colossal proportions. For the average moviegoer, its only faults may be the faults of many epics: the battle scenes are too short or too disorganized. Nor was it the financial bust predicted. By 1970 it had made $28 million in the United States and Canada.[7] The story begins *after* Caesar's defeat of Pompey at Pharsalus (48 B.C.), a battle scene Rex Harrison had offered to finance.[8] Still, like the scene in the northern woods in *The Fall of the Roman Empire* (1964), where Emperor Marcus Aurelius waged war against nomadic tribes, this one had a ring of authenticity, of what it may have been like. Following is Caesar's pursuit of Pompey to Egypt, his meeting with Cleopatra, their romance and entry into Rome, Caesar's assassination, Marc Antony's passion for the Egyptian queen, their affair and fall from power after Octavian's forces defeat them in the sea battle of Actium.

Watching over the filming were the publicists. From Rome on December 13, 1961, Jack Brodsky wrote to his copublicist Nathan Weiss back in New York,

> Today was the kind of day that makes some of these trials and tribulations seem worth it. We shot a nude scene of Miss Taylor being rubbed by one of her handmaidens on a marble slab in her apartment. The set was ordered closed, with only a minimum number of technicians allowed. I just happened to stroll on and stood next to Bob Penn, who was told that his negatives were to be given directly to [Walter] Wanger. I waited for someone to chase me, and I already had my story prepared about how important it was to my work, but Mank probably figured, "Give the kid a break." Anyway, Liz was adjusted by Eddie [Fisher] himself and the crew seemed to be occupied with what they were doing. Bob Penn snapped away and I sort of shuffled from one foot to another, trying to look business-like. My Adam's apple seemed to be straining at my throat.[9]

> But yesterday was really too much. That vast set, Rome in all its grandeur, thousands and thousands of everything—people, animals, props, you name it; the Sphinx being hauled under the arch to Caesar's feet, and then our girl Liz a little shakily descending that golden staircase that tongues out of the Sphinx. With Joe [Mankiewicz] sweating and screaming from his crane, while Roman society 1962 fans itself from that grandstand behind the cameras and the whole world seems to be going mad.[10]

What did the critics think? Hollis Alpert did not like Taylor, but "the film has its impressive moments, and it is not a disaster. Nor is it any kind of triumph."[11]

Solomon and Sheba (United Artists, 1959) was as famous for Gina Lollobrigida's barely accoutered figure as Yul Brynner's king or its battles.

Gone with the Wind was rereleased in 1967. It had been reissued before, but this time it was given extraspecial treatment: the original 35mm negative with a 1.33:1 aspect ratio was turned into a 70mm print at a 2.2:1 frame ratio. Some of the sound was rechanneled for six-track stereo. This all cost a quarter of a million dollars. It "remains today a powerful, breath-taking spectacle. A triumph 28 years ago, the David O. Selznick production even now puts into the shade most contemporary films. It remains a gem, of many facets.... As for the film's current physical form, time has exacted its toll in many of the subtler image contrasts and color registration."[12]

Famous last words: "Industry feeling is that the future of roadshows, though somewhat expensive, is secure. And its security does, in fact, rest on the very costliness of the product."[13] All 1969 roadshows were musicals: *Goodbye, Mr. Chips, Sweet Charity, Hello, Dolly!* and *Paint Your Wagon.* None

Before Monty Python there was the "Carry On" gang, charter members of which were (from left) Charles Hawtrey, Kenneth Williams and Kenneth Connor, seen here in *Carry On Teacher* **(Governor Films, 1962). They also poked fun at nurses, doctors, sergeants and Cleopatra.**

was an unqualified critical or commercial success. By the mid–70s roadshows were no more. Center city theaters were razed, and suburbanites would go no farther than a new mall theater. It had been a splendid phenomenon nonetheless. A few facts: MGM distributed ten roadshows in the 60s, United Artists and Fox nine each. Nine were released in 1968. The next most prolific year was 1966, when eight were released. Julie Andrews was in four. The greatest percentage were musicals.

OTHER EPICS

The Vikings (1958) was, surprisingly, the first commercial production to tackle the Norsemen of the Middle Ages. Kirk Douglas, Tony Curtis, Janet Leigh, and Ernest Borgnine starred. In this film, Einar's half-brother Eric (Curtis) must kill him. (In *Spartacus,* Douglas kills Curtis.) Filmed in Europe, the movie also benefited from Mario Nascimbene's score and Jack Cardiff's cinematography.

Taras Bulba (1962) featured eight thousand Argentinian Pampas horsemen dressed as Poles or oppressed Cossacks under the leadership of Bulba (Yul Brynner). Tony Curtis played his son and was killed by the father.

Top: The Vikings (United Artists, 1958) was the best of the few films about the Norsemen who terrorized Europe during the Middle Ages. Here the barbarians attack the English castle of Aella. It is actually a fort in Britanny. *Bottom: Zulu* (Embassy, 1964) was a meticulous reconstruction of the Battle of Rorke's Drift, where about a hundred Welshmen defended a South African river crossing against thousands of Zulus in 1879.

Actor Stanley Baker and director Cy Endfield coproduced *Zulu* (1964), made on location in South Africa. Based on the siege of Rorke's Drift, the meticulously filmed epic featured thousands of Zulu warriors besieging a hundred-odd Welsh soldiers under the command of Lt. John Chard (Baker) and Lt. Gonville Bromhead (Michael Caine) on January 22, 1879. Nigel Green, a dominating character and sometimes supporting actor of the 60s, was most impressive as calm Color-Sergeant Bourne. John Barry's score gave him a break from his work in James Bond films. Welshman Richard Burton narrated. "Men of Harlech," a traditional Welsh tune, added to the drama.[14]

The War Lord (1965) was a more thoughtful spectacle but the critics disliked it anyway. Charlton Heston played Norman knight Chrysagon, sent to the Frisian lands to maintain order and battle invaders. The action scenes were violent and Richard Boone was excellent as Chrysagon's shadow, but the ending, in which the wounded knight comforts his beloved Bronwyn (Rosemary Forsyth), is suspiciously like Gary Cooper's farewell to Ingrid Bergman in *For Whom the Bell Tolls* (1943). Much was made of Forsyth's "nude" scene, but water covered all private parts.

The Last Valley (1971) was from writer, now director, James Clavell. The critics did not like this one either, even though it featured only dozens, or perhaps scores, but at least not the thousands of extras held in contempt by most critics. It concerned the devastating Thirty Years' War in Europe, 1618–1648. Michael Caine was a German mercenary, Omar Sharif a renegade priest, Nigel Davenport the chief of the secluded village where the mercenaries wintered. There was war, plague, witchcraft, and another beautiful score by John Barry.

WESTERNS

The golden age of westerns continued with a classic. John Ford's *The Searchers* (1956), based on Alan LeMay's grim novel, was not accorded this status when it premiered, but over the years its claim to eminence has been recognized. Some discerned its value when it was released. It was "really a rip-snorting Western, as brashly entertaining as they come ... toughness of leather and the sting of a whip.... John Wayne is uncommonly command-ing."[15] The story begins with the return of Civil War veteran Ethan Edwards (John Wayne) to his brother's Texas ranch. Leaving to track raiding Coman-ches, Ethan comes to realize that they are on a wild goose chase: his brother's ranch is to be attacked in their absence. He whips the sheath off his rifle and rides back—too late to prevent the raid by Comanche chief Scar (Henry Brandon) and his band.

> The massacre of the Edwards family is one of the most terrible ever filmed— not because of what is seen, but because of what is not seen. The details are not shown—only the sickened reactions of Wayne and Hunter. Ford shows the moments before the attack—but not the attack.[16]

All Ethan can do is rescue his brother's two girls. He and half-breed Marty (Jeffrey Hunter) undertake an epic, five-year journey, during which Ethan

Filmed on spectacular western locales, *Running Target* (United Artists, 1956) was one of the fifties' best B-movies. Richard Reeves (left) confronts the sheriff (Arthur Franz) during their escaped convict manhunt.

becomes increasingly bitter. Knowing that only Debbie is left alive, he also knows he will kill her because in his eyes she has become a Comanche. Posing as traders, they meet Scar. "You speak pretty good American—for a Comanch," says Ethan. Debbie (Natalie Wood), now a young woman, is there in the wickiup. Rangers raid the Comanche camp, Scar is killed—and Ethan proceeds to scalp him before seeking Debbie. Marty is brushed aside, but with a change of heart, Ethan lifts his niece high. "Let's go home, Debbie." At fadeout Ethan is framed in the doorway as he was at the outset, an outsider once again. The audience hears the Sons of the Pioneers sing "Ride Away, Ride Away." Ethan Edwards' journey has been "ultimately interior."[17]

Run of the Arrow (1956) starred Rod Steiger as a Confederate who cannot bear the fact of Union victory. He heads west and joins the Sioux (including a chief played by Charles Bronson) and continues his war against the whites. Ralph Meeker is a despicable Union officer who, in one of the grisliest scenes in film history, is skinned alive. Only the first cut is shown, but his screams are so unnerving that the Reb ends his misery with a bullet to his skull.

Gunfight at the OK Corral (1957) "contains the historically fastest and loosest, but longest and most sustained and exciting rendition of the confrontation."[18] Like *Duel in the Sun* and *The Big Country,* there is something missing, but like those films it is eminently watchable.[19] *OK's* success was dependent on locations, Dimitri Tiomkin's score and Frankie Laine's rendition of the title tune, the exciting final gunfight, the star combo of Lancaster and Douglas,[20] and the notable cast of supporting and character actors: John Ireland as Ringo, Ted de Corsia as Shanghai Pierce (a real person who would surface in Larry McMurtrey's novel *Lonesome Dove*), Lyle Bettger as Ike Clanton, Dennis Hopper as Billy Clanton, Kenneth Tobey as Bat Masterson, and nasty henchmen Jack Elam and Robert J. Wilke.

The Big Country (1958) was a slightly disappointing grand-scale western from director William Wyler. Perhaps classic westerns must be made by masters in the form: John Ford, Sam Peckinpah, Howard Hawks, Anthony Mann. Only George Stevens *(Shane)* was a nonwestern master who created a western classic. Range war over water rights between the Terrills (Charles Bickford and Carroll Baker with top hand Charlton Heston) was mediated by ex–sea captain James McKay (Gregory Peck) and maid-in-the-middle Julie Maragon (Jean Simmons). As grandpapa of the Hannessey clan, Burl Ives won a supporting actor Academy Award. Chuck Connors was suitably scummy as Buck Hannassey, plugged by dad for cheating during a duel. Best of all was Jerome Moross' score, arguably the finest ever to grace an oater. This film featured typically great United Artists gunshots.

Warlock (1959) was a big, long, and quite good adult western with Henry Fonda, Richard Widmark, and Anthony Quinn. The townsfolk of Warlock needed to rid their community of rowdies and hired gunman (Fonda) and his pal (Quinn). In some ways this role presages Fonda's more villainous one in Sergio Leone's Italian epic *Once Upon a Time in the West*.

> One of the most effective suspense-in-action scenes that can be staged is the callout, with its fast-draw climax. We had several in our film. I was ready to try every trick known to get really quick gun action—undercranking the camera, double-cutting the film, using experts as doubles—but none of these proved necessary. When I rehearsed the first such scene, I found that Fonda could draw almost faster than the camera could register, though he professed himself to be unaware of it. I wound up looking for ways to slow up the action so the audience could savor it properly, and not miss it with the blink of an eyelid.[21]

In 1960 John Huston entered the western field with *The Unforgiven,* an almost epic tale of Kiowa-white relationships. Unwelcome harbinger Abe Kelsey (Joseph Wiseman) brings word that Rachel Zachary (Audrey Hepburn) might be Indian. The Kiowas hear this, too, and want her for their own, attacking the ranch of Rachel's brother Ben (Burt Lancaster) and setting fire to the house. Cash Zachary (Audie Murphy) returns to help.

The Magnificent Seven (1960) was the most satisfying western of these years. Akira Kurosawa's film *The Seven Samurai* was its inspiration. A sterling cast of veterans like Yul Brynner, beautifully attired in black—an ironic twist because he was a noble gunslinger—Vladimir Sokoloff, and Brad Dexter were surrounded by up-and-coming stars like Steve McQueen, James Coburn, Robert Vaughn, and Charles Bronson. The select seven ride south of the border under the leadership of Chris (Brynner) to defend a peasant village from

Gunfight at the OK Corral (Paramount, 1957) featured Kirk Douglas as Doc Holliday (left) while John Ireland played badman Jimmy Ringo. Ireland had played Billy Clanton in the 1946 Wyatt Earp-Doc Holliday saga, *My Darling Clementine.*

bandidos. Bandit leader Calvera (Eli Wallach) is urged to "ride on" as Vin (McQueen) explains that "we deal in lead, friend." Calvera responds as his men ready their weapons, "Generosity, that was my first mistake. I leave these people a little bit extra and they hire these men to make trouble. Shows you, sooner or later you must answer for every good deed." Kabamm! Driven out of the village, the bandits come back and get the goods on the seven. Instead of killing the seven, they release them for fear a host of gringos will ride south to avenge their deaths. Outside town, Britt (Coburn) speaks for

Bandit leader Calvera (Eli Wallach) leaves a hot reception provided by *The Magnificent Seven* (United Artists, 1960). A western version of Akira Kurosawa's *The Seven Samurai,* it spawned a couple of mediocre sequels.

the rest: "Nobody throws me my own guns and says run. Nobody." Returning, the seven engage in a to-the-death struggle. Shot and dying, Calvera cannot believe it: "You came back. To a place like this. Why? A man like you. Why?" Of the seven, three survive: Chris, Vin, and Chico (Horst Buchholz). Britt (Coburn), O'Reilly (Bronson), Lee (Robert Vaughn), and Harry Luck (Brad Dexter) don't make it.

It was still respectable for big stars to appear in westerns. Marlon Brando starred in and directed *One-Eyed Jacks* (1961). As Rio, he was betrayed by fellow gunman Dad Longworth (Karl Malden). When he broke out of the prison he came to extract revenge—from a Longworth who was now a town sheriff.

For director Howard Hawks it was a "let's make it again" period. The trio of *Rio Bravo* (1959), *El Dorado* (1967), and *Rio Lobo* (1970) all starred John Wayne and all were dominated by men with one dominant woman in attendance—Angie Dickinson, Charlene Holt, and Jennifer O'Neill, respectively. The story: the few against the many. *Rio Bravo* achieved the highest reputation and deserves it. Whether it deserves the classic status awarded it by some critics is another matter.

After *The Deadly Companions* (1961), Sam Peckinpah emerged as a western master with the critically acclaimed *Ride the High Country* (1962). Two old-timers (Randolph Scott and Joel McCrea) guard a gold shipment and must thwart a gang of cutthroats at risk to the daughter (Mariette Hartley) they have saved from fanatical preacher-man father (R. G. Armstrong). The success of this film allowed Peckinpah a crack at an epic, *Major Dundee*. Flawed but impressive, this 1965 film starred Charlton Heston as a Union officer who gathered a motley crew, including Southerners from a prison camp, for warfare in Texas and Mexico against the Indian chief Sierra Charriba (Michael Pate). Peckinpah gave the audience a taste of what was to come in cinematic violence. "Pony soldier, I am Sierra Charriba. Who you send against me now?" asks Charriba of a tortured soldier. A woman lies pierced with arrows. A man hangs from a rope over a smoldering fire. James Coburn was one-armed scout Samuel Potts among a sterling supporting cast that included Ben Johnson, Warren Oates, John David Chandler, Dub Taylor, Slim Pickens, L. Q. Jones, R. G. Armstrong, and Brock Peters. Peckinpah howled that studio interference had marred the film, believed to run over four hours in its original version. In the final rendering the Senta Berger interlude still drags. Nonetheless, a plethora of topics was covered: South versus North, the betrayal of friends for advancement, politics, race (Native Americans and blacks).

MUSICALS

Mammoth musicals had been inaugurated in 1955 when Fred Zinnemann directed Rodgers and Hammerstein's *Oklahoma!* Although some chances were successfully taken—Gloria Grahame playing Ado Annie, method actor Rod Steiger playing Jud—the substitution in a ballet sequence of James Mitchell for Gordon MacRae and Bambi Linn for Shirley Jones was jarring. *Carousel,* also with MacRae and Jones, and *The King and I* followed in 1956, *South Pacific* in 1958. Distracting coloring by cinematographer Leon Shamroy and director Joshua Logan was a valiant mistake. As in all the Rodgers and Hammerstein plays, the songs were the thing, and there were so many good ones: "Oh, What a Beautiful Mornin'," "Poor Jud," "Many a New Day," "The Surrey with the Fringe on Top," and "I Can't Say No" *(Oklahoma!)*; "A Cockeyed Optimist," "A Wonderful Guy," "Younger Than Springtime," "Some Enchanted Evening," and "There Is Nothing Like a Dame" *(South Pacific)*. The most successful—financially and from an entertainment standpoint—of all these Rodgers and Hammerstein screen translations was *The Sound of Music* (1965). It rapidly overtook *Gone with the Wind* as the number-one boxoffice attraction of all time. "Edelweiss," "Do-Re-Mi," "Climb Every Mountain," "Sixteen Going on Seventeen"—these great songs, the Austrian locales, the incredibly popular new star Julie Andrews, not-too-obnoxious children, a resplendent Christopher Plummer, and a sarcastic Richard Haydn (a Clifton Webb type) made for an exhilarating roadshow experience.

Gigi (1958) was the last gasp of Arthur Freed's musical factory at MGM. Leslie Caron was radiant as Colette's heroine, and Maurice Chevalier was

As nun Maria become governess and later wife of Baron von Trapp, Julie Andrews became a superstar in 1965's *The Sound of Music*. The best film version of a Rodgers and Hammerstein musical play, it replaced *Gone with the Wind* as the top grossing movie of all time.

delightful as narrator and performer ("Thank Heaven for Little Girls"). The other great songs—"The Night They Invented Champagne," "Gigi," "Say a Prayer"—helped obscure the lack of dancing. *Gigi* was a multiple Academy Award winner, including one for best picture.

  West Side Story (1961) equaled the Rodgers and Hammerstein musicals in number of outstanding songs. Codirected by Robert Wise and choreographer Jerome Robbins, this Romeo and Juliet modernization with the marvelous Leonard Bernstein–Stephen Sondheim score attracted an audience never before interested in musicals. High schools promoted it on music room bulletin boards. And it had a hard edge; witness detective Simon Oakland's retort to Puerto Rican gang members: "Aw, yeah, sure. I know. It's a free country and

Gene Kelly and Mitzi Gaynor performed "Why Am I So Gone About That Gal?" a motorcycle gang parody, in *Les Girls* (Metro-Goldwyn-Mayer, 1957).

I ain't got the right. But I got a badge. Whadda you got? Things are tough all over. Beat it!"

From the opening overhead shots of New York City to its tragic conclusion, the film was fabulously entertaining and gripping. The meeting of Tony (Richard Beymer) and Maria (Natalie Wood) during the gym dance is unforgettable, as are Tony's homeward journey singing "Marie," the rooftop "America," and Rita Moreno's outburst after almost being terrorized by the

Left: Tony (Richard Beymer) and Maria (Natalie Wood) were the Romeo and Juliet-like lovers of *West Side Story,* 1961's groundbreaking musical. *Right:* A child actress become a woman of exceptional beauty, Natalie Wood achieved superstardom during Hollywood's last halcyon days in the 60s.

Jets in Doc's candy store: "Bernardo was right. If one of you was lying in the street, bleeding, I'd walk by and spit on you!" Moreno and George Chakiris won supporting actress and actor honors, and the film won best picture and seven other statuettes.

Natalie Wood had been in the business since she was five years old, but she had been a child actress rather than a child star. Immediately following *West Side Story* came *Gypsy* (1962), in which the young Louise (Wood) became the stripper Gypsy Rose Lee, whose stage mother Rose (Rosalind Russell) had lavished most of her attention on the sister. Catholic church bulletins urged parishioners to shun the film. Did any Legion of Decency arbiters see it? Perhaps it was the subject matter about which they had misgivings, because the language was clean and Wood's bare back was the only flesh displayed. Promotion for *Gypsy* included two-page magazine ads promoting a Baby Ruth and Butterfinger Contest. Ten people would win three trips for two to Hollywood if they wrote a fourth line for the jingle,

> I'd like to be an honored guest,
> I'd like to have a date
> With movie stars and chauffeured cars,

Age 24, Natalie Wood was a glamour queen of Hollywood. "Sitting in a plush Beverly Hills restaurant she was the center of all eyes in a full-length mink coat and a décolletage that left no doubt that Natalie was indeed a movie star."[22]

Looking better now than it did in 1966, Richard Lester's transfer of Broadway's *A Funny Thing Happened on the Way to the Forum* was a satire

The epic musical peaked with *Oliver!* (Columbia, 1968), a critical and commercial success. The "I'd Do Anything" number featured, from left: Jack Wild, Shanni Wallis, Mark Lester, and Sheila White.

featuring stage and movie veterans like Zero Mostel and Phil Silvers, newcomers like Michael Crawford, even silent era great Buster Keaton. The set piece was the "My Bride" entrance into the city of the legionary commander come to claim his betrothed. His troops find the welcome a mixed blessing. Vegetables are thrown at them, the drummers fall and disrupt the march. Miles Gloriosus is oblivious. (Like Jesse Pearson in *Bye Bye Birdie*, Leon Greene as Miles Gloriosus made the most of a rare cinematic appearance. He was perfect as the self-important "slaughterer of thousands." "He raped Thrace thrice?" asked an incredulous Pseudolus [Mostel].)

How to Succeed in Business Without Really Trying (1967) allowed Robert Morse to re-create his role as J. Pierpont Finch, a part he had played in 1961 in Broadway's 46th Street Theatre. It may have been the most fully realized musical in the 60s, balancing cinematic flow with stage songs like "The Company Way," "Been a Long Day," "I Believe in You," "A Secretary Is Not a Toy," and "Brotherhood of Man."

Musicals were frequent best picture Academy Award winners in the 60s: *West Side Story, My Fair Lady, The Sound of Music, Oliver!* Note that *My Fair Lady*, at one time thought to have actually lost money, made $34 million in the United States and Canada alone.[23]

Oscar (John McMartin) leads Charity Hope Valentine (Shirley MacLaine) out of the
parking garage where they've just heard Sammy Davis, Jr., lead his flock in the
"Rhythm of Life." The film is *Sweet Charity* (Universal, 1969).

Cabaret (1972), based on Christopher Isherwood's *Berlin Stories,* was
brought to the screen as straight drama in 1955 as *I Am a Camera,* with Julie
Harris, Laurence Harvey, and Ron Randell. Choreographer Bob Fosse, who
had directed *Sweet Charity* in 1969, achieved financial success and critical ac-
claim with this second outing. Starring were Liza Minnelli, Michael York,
Helmut Griem, and Joel Grey as the cabaret's master of ceremonies. "*Cabaret*
is a great movie musical, made, miraculously, without compromises. It's
miraculous because the material is hard and unsentimental, and until now
there has never been a diamond-hard big American movie musical."[24]

SCIENCE FICTION, HORROR, AND FANTASY

Youth and Science Fiction: Roger Corman, a now legendary name,
gained fame with the Edgar Allan Poe series of films he directed for Jim
Nicholson and Sam Arkoff at American International Pictures: *House of Usher*
(1960), *The Pit and the Pendulum* (1961), *Tales of Terror* (1962), *The
Premature Burial* (1962), *The Raven* (1963), *The Masque of the Red Death*
(1964), *The Tomb of Ligeia* (1965). Richard Matheson and Charles Beaumont
contributed most of the screenplays. "Cormanesque all-film-is-artifice-anyway
syndrome, which, for some critics, makes a virtue out of expediency. The very
lack of polish is seen as endearing; it makes movies less finished but somehow

American International gave Ray Milland a second career in fantasy films, and he almost became the next Vincent Price — but Price never retired. Here Milland prepares Hazel Court for *The Premature Burial* (AIP, 1962).

purer."[25] He makes every buck get on the screen and look like two bucks."[26] How much directorial talent Corman had is questionable. Can anyone sit through more than once the movie made in three days, *The Terror* (1963)? What is not debatable is the training ground he provided for future screen notables: Jack Nicholson, Francis Ford Coppola, Peter Bogdanovich.

Double features were still common in theaters and drive-ins. Horror and science fiction double bills proliferated: *War of the Colossal Beast* and *Attack of the Puppet People* (1958), *The Killer Shrews* and *The Giant Gila Monster* (1959), and *The Wasp Woman* and *Beast from Haunted Cave* (1960).

Blobs were introduced in 1956 in *The Creeping Unknown* (in Britain, *The Quatermass Xperiment*), based on writer Nigel Kneale's BBC serial about Professor Quatermass. The movie concerned a rocket returned to earth with only one of three original crew on board. What happened to the others? The survivor, Victor Carroon (Richard Wordsworth) escapes custody, and Dr. Quatermass (Brian Donlevy) learns that the man is infected by an outer space virus that consumes his mind and body, turning him into something akin to an octopus that is cornered in Westminster Abbey. The film spawned good sequels, *Enemy from Space (Quatermass II)* (1957) and *Five Million Years to Earth (Quatermass and the Pit)* (1967), as well as a pseudo-television finale.

X the Unknown followed the same year, and the United States then caught up. No one but Saturday afternoon matinee fans caught the 1957 *The Unknown Terror,* during which even the youngsters roared at a protagonist who entered a cave containing fungus-covered humans and ran *toward* the monsters. The film that caught the public's fancy was a 1958 U.S. entry, *The Blob.*

> Though it is done with some wit and sophistication, the story is quite serious. Apparently the idea was to make a film with a simple, direct story line, and a simple, direct monster; filming it in color made it distinctive and more salable. Furthermore, the production company apparently hired Steve McQueen on the basis of his *acting* ability, certainly an unusual idea at the time. *The Blob* has the feeling of intelligent people making a film in a disreputable genre, trying to do something they could be proud of. They don't seem to have realized that films like this almost never dealt with characters, but with stereotypes. There's hackneyed material in *The Blob,* to be sure, but the writers' attempt to characterize people does raise the film above the level of the usual teenagers-versus-monsters story.[27]

The Blob had a sequel, *Beware! The Blob (Son of Blob),* in 1972 and a remake in 1988. Other fungi films included *Spacemaster X-7* (1958), Japan's scary *The H-Man* (1958), *First Man into Space* (1959), Mexico's *Caltiki, The Immortal Monster* (1960), *The Creeping Terror* (1964), *Mutiny in Outer Space* (1965), Japan's *The Green Slime* (1969), and *The Stuff* (1985). Remember that *The Slime People* were not slimy but squamous.

Consummately outrageous was William Castle's *The Tingler* (1959). Did you know that in all of us lurks a Tingler, a squishy "creature" that looks like the spinal cord and can become tangible if a person cannot scream to release fear? In this story a mute woman (Judith Evelyn) is scared to death by her husband (Philip Coolidge). During the autopsy, a Tingler is removed and, of course, gets away. In a movie theater Vincent Price as Dr. William Chapin warns the audience:

> Ladies and gentlemen. Please, do not panic, but scream! Scream for your lives! The Tingler is loose in this theater, and if you don't scream it may kill you. Scream! Keep screaming! Scream for your lives! ... Ladies and gentlemen, the Tingler has been paralyzed by your screaming. There is no more danger. We will now resume the showing of the movie.

The Fly (1958) "was almost *The Exorcist* of its day, with lines waiting to get in, the eager audience primed for the horrifying scenes."[28] Again, Price was on hand, not this time as the bad guy but rather as François, brother of scientist André Delambre (Al Hedison), who invents a matter transmitter. Naturally, things go awry and a fly shares the booth with Andre when he is transmitted. The sight of a man with a fly's head and arm and a fly with a man's head shocked the audience. The most disturbing and revolting scene — one that lives in the minds of countless adults who saw this as teenagers — involves the half-insect in a spider web, the arachnid about to pounce. Inspector Charas (Herbert Marshall) crushes both with a rock.

The Gothic Returns: With science fiction film in decline, supernatural horror regained its preeminent position in the fantastic cinema. The rebirth occurred in England at Hammer's Bray Studios in 1957.

Hammer had been a minor company for years but the success of the black and white science fiction film *The Creeping Unknown* generated a brainstorm. Why not resurrect gothic horror—in color, to shock audiences with red blood? This scheme was so successful that "it is certainly doubtful whether any other film company in the world has a *name* with as much selling power as Hammer."[29]

The Curse of Frankenstein initiated the cycle in 1957. Basing their film within legal limits on the Universal characters of the 1930s, Peter Cushing became Dr. Frankenstein, Christopher Lee his creation, Hazel Court the romantic interest. Terence Fisher became Hammer's mainstay director after his work on this movie.

> Despite occasional complexities, Fisher is always at pains to preserve the inner coherence of his films; they contain few flashbacks, virtually no dream sequences, no self-parody and no great psychological insight. Instead they have a quality of robustness, a peculiarly bizarre and English form of logic within fantasy and a powerful atmosphere augmented by an underlying sexuality. The formula is certainly comparable to that of the best Gothic novelists.[30]

Cushing and Lee were but the most famous members of a growing stock company. Peter Cushing had appeared in *The Man in the Iron Mask* (1939), *Hamlet* (1948), and, in the 50s, in *Moulin Rouge* and *Alexander the Great.* "His slightly fussy manner at first confined him to mild roles, but since allying himself with the Hammer horror school he has dealt firmly with monsters of all kinds."[31] Cushing and Christopher Lee costarred in a dozen films. Gaunt Lee had also appeared in numerous previous movies, but his appearance as the vampire Count in *Horror of Dracula* (1958) gave him a new lease on film life. Ranked by many as the best version of Bram Stoker's novel, it has several brilliant scenes, including the impalement of the female vampire who turns into a hag and the disintegration of Dracula as the sunlight streams into his castle.

Other Supernatural Horror and Fantasy: American Dana Andrews starred with Briton Peggy Cummins in the 1957 film *Night of the Demon* (U.S. title, *Curse of the Demon*), a scary rendering of M. R. James' short story "Casting the Runes." Some felt the visible presence of the demon at the end ruined the tone. Others have reconsidered.

> Critics used to blame the monster's appearance at beginning and end; these were allegedly added just before release because box office prospects were thought to be a trifle dim, and the pressure is supposed to show. All I can say is that a medieval demon can't be easy to animate, and this one scares me every time I see it. Besides, something to gawk at does no harm to a movie which otherwise sets its sights on the cerebral rather than the visual.[32]

Darby O'Gill and the Little People (1959) was an enchanting Disney production with the then unknown Sean Connery as the romantic interest opposite spunky Janet Munro. Albert Sharpe played Darby, who captures the king of the leprechauns. A generation of moviegoers was scared silly by the banshee and the death coach come to take Katie, then Darby away.

The 7th Voyage of Sinbad (1958) was in the estimation of many the best

Christopher Lee expresses dissatisfaction with minion Valerie Gaunt in *Horror of Dracula* (1958), Hammer Studios' second installment in the blood red color resurrection of gothic horror.

film using Ray Harryhausen's stop-motion special effects, called Dynamation. Kerwin Matthews played Sinbad, called upon to locate and rescue Parisa (Kathryn Grant), made-miniature captive of Sokurah (Torin Thatcher). Sinbad was assisted by boy genie Barani (Richard Eyer), whom he summoned by using the words "From the land beyond beyond, from the world past hope and fear, I bid you, genie, now appear." A two-headed roc, a cyclops, and a dragon posed almost insurmountable threats to the expedition. *Citizen Kane's* composer and a frequent Alfred Hitchcock associate Bernard Herrmann was not averse to scoring fantasy, and his music added immeasurably.

Mysterious Island (1961) added Harryhausen creatures to the Verne sequel to *20,000 Leagues Under the Sea*. Herbert Lom surfaced as Captain Nemo, who hoped to fix the *Nautilus* with the help of the Civil War prisoners who had escaped their confines in a balloon only to be blown in a gale to his island. *Jason and the Argonauts* (1963) was another Harryhausen extravaganza and, with *The 7th Voyage of Sinbad,* considered his best. Appearing again, and more plentifully, the skeleton animation was superb.

Journey to the Center of the Earth (1959) was a crowd-pleaser based on a Jules Verne story. James Mason led a small expedition down an extinct volcano, found a world of dinosaurs, and escaped via a volcanic eruption that propelled an insulating rock projectile. Bernard Herrmann provided this score, too.

The Time Machine (1960) featured Rod Taylor as H. G. Wells' hero who traveled past world wars into the far future, the year 802,701. He encountered the subservient above-ground dwellers the Eloi, fed upon by hideous subterranean mutants, the morlocks.

Back to Basics — *Night of the Living Dead*: *Chicago Sun-Times* syndicated columnist Roger Ebert complained of the lack of a MPAA rating for *Night of the Living Dead* (1968), which meant children could see it.[33] George Romero filmed this low-budget black and white film in the vicinity of Pittsburgh. Flesh-craving ghoulombies/zomboulies rose from the grave, slavering after human flesh, and besieged people in a farmhouse. It was gross — and successful. These zombies were more formidable than most: they had to be shot in the brain to be killed for good.

Sequels were forthcoming, but not right away. Perhaps that is one reason the series was eminently more successful on an aesthetic level than the series spawned by *Friday the 13th, Halloween,* or *Nightmare on Elm Street.* Usually the original films possess quality but their offspring come under the care of hack directors who go for gore and gross-out techniques in a triumph of technique over plot and character.

Dawn of the Dead (1979) and *Return of the Living Dead* (1985) actually explained the revival of the flesh-eaters. More startling were the pursued, who used common sense and developed techniques and weapons to deal with the monsters. The supernatural was brought into the explanation; *Friday the 13th* and *Halloween,* on the other hand, offer little or no explanation.

Mental Aberration: *Peeping Tom* (1959) examined the deleterious effects of a psychoanalytic father making his son (Karl Boehm) his subject. Grown, the son impales women on the tripod of his camera, filming them as they die and they witness their own deaths in a mirror attached to the camera. Previously respected director Michael Powell was virtually blacklisted for what was then perceived as trash but which has been resurrected as important commentary. It is brilliantly directed. British clones, or at least titles of similar nature, included *Scream of Fear* (1961), *Maniac* (1962), *Paranoiac* (1963), *Die! Die! My*

Darling (1965) (which was in "Stabbing Color!"), *The Nanny* (1965), and *Hysteria* (1965).

Peeping Tom presaged *Psycho* (1960), which is now considered something of a put-on by Alfred Hitchcock, who used his television series crew and filmed in black and white. Having Janet Leigh killed off early was also unusual and, equally disturbing—even though we see it coming—is the attack on Martin Balsam at the top of the stairs. Norman Bates (Anthony Perkins) became a household name.

Janet Leigh was pleased to get the role of Marion, even if she was annihilated rather early in the story. Audiences were not used to seeing the heroine and a major star get the ax. (See Wendy Padbury's sacrifice to the demon in the 1971 film *The Blood on Satan's Claw* for another instance of unexpected destruction of the beautiful.) On the set Hitchcock told funny tales then made people serious with "mother's" corpse. "I would return from lunch, open the door to the dressing room, and propped in my chair would be this hideous monstrosity," said Leigh.[34] As for the shower scene,

> What I was to wear in the shower gave the wardrobe supervisor migraines. I had to appear nude, without being nude. She and I pored over striptease magazines, hoping one of their costumes would be the answer. Every male on the set tried to donate his services in the search. We had popular literature. There was an impressive display of pinwheels, feathers, sequins, toy propellers, balloons, etc., but nothing suitable for our needs. Finally the supervisor came up with a simple solution: flesh-colored moleskin. Perfect! So each morning for seven shooting days and seventy-one setups, we covered my private parts, and we were in business.[35]

American clones included *Homicidal* (1961), a low-budget feature from William Castle that was not without its shocks. *What Ever Happened to Baby Jane?* (1962), which teamed Bette Davis with long-time rival Joan Crawford, was a big Robert Aldrich hit. Lesser entries were *The Couch* (1962), *Lady in a Cage* (1964), *Straight-Jacket* (1964) (whose ad read "WARNING! *Straight-Jacket* Vividly Depicts Ax Murders!"), *Hush . . . Hush, Sweet Charlotte* (1965), and *Berserk* (1967). Hollywood veterans Joan Crawford, Bette Davis, and Olivia De Havilland competed for these roles.

Hershell Gordon Lewis' 1963 opus *Blood Feast* pointed the way toward what would become known as "splatter" films. It opens with a woman in her bathtub who is stabbed in the eye and has her left calf removed—a schlock homage to *Psycho*, perhaps, and this time in good color. (Soon color and technical proficiency would accrue to all; unfortunately, the stories would not improve.) The murderer turns out to be—no mystery for the audience—one Fuad Ramses (Mal Arnold), exotic caterer. Signed to serve Egyptian fare at the party of comely blond Suzette Fremont (*Playboy's* June 1963 Playmate, Connie Mason), he scours the neighborhoods, annihilating young women who have joined a book club offering *Ancient Weird Religious Rites*. The advertisement read, "You'll Recoil and Shudder as You Witness the Slaughter and Mutilation of Nubile Young Girls—in a Weird and Horrendous Ancient Rite!" From each victim he extracts a portion of her anatomy to be boiled or baked for the

Kim Novak played Judy cum Madeline opposite James Stewart in *Vertigo* (Paramount, 1958), perhaps the most lustrous jewel in director Alfred Hitchcock's crown.

goddess Ishtar. Needless to say, the police are impotent until Suzette's boyfriend, detective Pete Thorn (Thomas Wood), connects the book, Ishtar, and Suzette's party. "Holy smoke, Frank! We gotta get over to the Fremont house. They're havin' a dinner party tonight and Fuad Ramses is the caterer!" cries Pete to his superior. Frank responds, "Fuad Ramses! Well let's get goin'. Roberts, Nicholson, Harris! Get on that phone! Call the Fremonts! For Pete's sake, tell 'em not to eat anything!" Fuad's sacrifice is unsuccessful, and he is pursued to a dump and crushed in a garbage truck. Director Lewis followed this schlock masterpiece with *Two Thousand Maniacs* (1964), again starring Mason. Despite the gore, and in contrast to what was to come, Lewis' heroine escapes. Evil would later triumph.

Anthology horror films became popular: *Torture Garden* (1968), *The House That Dripped Blood* (1971), *Asylum* (1972), *Tales That Witness Madness* (1973), and *Vault of Horror* (1973). Perpetually busy horror stars like Cushing and Lee were joined by newcomers to the genre who were or had been mainstream stars, such as Britt Ekland, Kim Novak, and Joan Collins.

Hammer Studios' Karnstein Trilogy was comprised of *The Vampire Lovers* (1970), *Lust for a Vampire* (1971), and a prequel, *Twins of Evil* (1972). This vampire saga was initiated by the studio to equal the revenue that the now anemic Dracula series had generated throughout the 60s. Added ingredients were nudity and overt sex. Ingrid Pitt played the lesbian Mircalla Karnstein in

Ingrid Pitt had her greatest impact as Mircalla/Marcilla/Carmilla Karnstein in *The Vampire Lovers* (Hammer/AIP, 1970). She played vampire types again in *The House That Dripped Blood* and *Countess Dracula.*

The Vampire Lovers. Having officially passed on in 1546, as a vampire she rose to feed on the living in 19th century Styria, calling herself Marcilla or Carmilla. *Carmilla,* by J. Sheridan LeFanu, was the basis for what was likely the most beautifully photographed Hammer film.

Where Roman Polanski failed when he tried to be funny about homosexual vampires, in *The Fearless Vampire Killers,* scenarist Tudor Gates and director

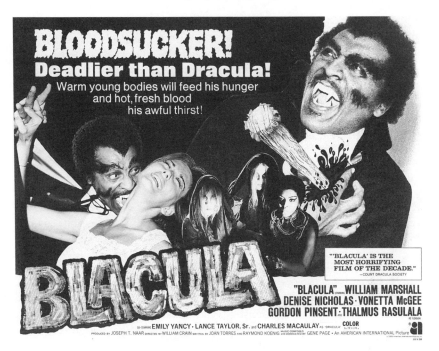

Blacula (American International Pictures, 1972).

Roy Ward Baker succeed because they are in dead earnest . . . a luscious film for enthusiasts . . . refreshment comes in the overlay of culture, in the "civilized" country-home atmosphere where the vampiress reads her intended victim to sleep from a romantic novel, where the skeptical governess pauses in mid–German tutoring to yield her charge to the visitor. . . . "Vampires are intelligent beings," one authority remarks. They are also, in this film, gorgeous, as are their victims. Ingrid Pitt, Dawn Addams, Pippa Steele, Madeleine Smith and Kate O'Mara are absolutely yummy. And everyone plays it straight—right down to the last decapitation, stake-drive and erotic innuendo.[36]

Yutte Stensgaard played Mircalla in *Lust for a Vampire,* and Katya Wyeth appeared briefly as Mircalla in *Twins,* whose real stars were Mary and Madelaine Collinson of *Playboy* fame.

The Blood on Satan's Claw (1971) was not Hammer, but rather Cannon/Tigon, and took a different era for its setting. In the 17th century a ploughman (Barry Andrews) discovers a horrible visage in a furrow. Soon villagers and farmers go mad, are murdered, or disappear. A hairy clawed hand reaches up from attic floorboards. Angel Blake (Linda Hayden) attempts to seduce the minister. Cathy (Wendy Padbury) is sacrificed by a coven led by Angel. The demon needs human skin to become whole again. Finally a studious judge (Patrick Wymark) puts an end to its reign of terror. Director Piers Haggard used freeze frame and slow motion to good effect and created a disquieting horror. Also nontraditional was *The Wicker Man* (1974), a high-class British horror set in contemporary times on a Scottish isle, where Lord Summerisle (Christopher Lee) rules a pagan cult. Edward Woodward was the police inspector sent from the mainland to investigate a murder. Britt Ekland, Diane Cilento, and Ingrid Pitt costarred.

The Exorcist (1973) was based on William Peter Blatty's best-seller. William Friedkin directed the big budget film that appealed to horror addicts and general cinemagoers. In the Washington, D.C., Georgetown section a teenage girl, Regan (Linda Blair), manifests peculiar behavior, levitating and speaking in tongues. Father Karrass (Jason Miller) intervenes, but his own guilts and fears interfere, and he seeks the help of Father Merrin (Max von Sydow). They exorcise the demon, Pazuzu, but only after Merrin's death and Karrass' exhortation to the demon to come into him. (He returns, relatively subdued, in 1990 in *Exorcist III*. Regan had confronted the demons again in John Boorman's *Exorcist II* in 1977.)

Science Fiction's Pinnacle: On the science fiction front, *Forbidden Planet*, *Invasion of the Body Snatchers,* and the first fungi film, Britain's *The Creeping Unknown,* made 1956 the last great year of science fiction's golden age. *Forbidden Planet* detailed United Planets Cruiser C-57-D's 23d century rescue mission to Altair IV. Two survivors of a past crash of the *Bellerophon* are found, a Prospero-like Morbius (Walter Pidgeon) and his daughter, Altaira (Anne Francis). A robot attends their every need, and they have few. Morbius guides the unwelcome rescuer skipper (Leslie Nielsen) to the underground laboratories of the long-gone Krell. Members of the rescue team are mysteriously killed. An invisible monster? Laser-like beams illuminate this strange creature, which can topple trees and melt metal doors—it's a monster from the id of Morbius. Providing comic relief was Robby the Robot, who quickly became an icon and appeared in *The Invisible Boy* (1957) and on television.

"You're next!" *Invasion of the Body Snatchers* was based on Jack Finney's novel *The Body Snatchers*. Dr. Miles Bennell arrives home in Santa Mira, California. A budding romance with Becky Driscoll (Dana Wynter) is interrupted by strange occurrences. A child complains that his mother is not really his mother, and large pods are discovered in the greenhouse of Jack and Teddy Belicec (King Donovan and Carolyn Jones). Splitting open, they reveal half-formed duplicates of nearby humans. Miles determines that humans disappear as the pod creatures fully form. These beings have no emotions. As the town becomes infested, Miles and Becky hide in his second-floor office and observe trucks delivering pods to the town square. They are to be spread throughout the area and the world. How to escape and stop them? The original ending left the audience hanging. A subsequent one featured psychiatrist (Whit Bissell) calling the FBI. Either way, it's one of the scariest films ever made and better than the 1978 color remake for one very good reason: viewers intuitively realize that it is harder to escape pod people in a small town than in San Francisco.

The Worst Movies Ever Made: Although there are other contenders, such as *Robot Monster,* director Ed Wood's *Plan 9 from Outer Space* (1959), with its humanoid aliens, vampires (Bela Lugosi, Vampira, Tor Johnson), the psychic Criswell, and hubcap flying saucers, has become generally known as the worst movie ever made. Wood's *Bride of the Monster* (1956) could also vie for the title. Dr. Eric Vornoff (Bela Lugosi) spouts priceless dialogue:

> Twenty years ago I was banned from my homeland, parted from my wife and son, never to see them again. Why? Because I had suggested to use the atom elements for producing super beings, beings of unthinkable strength and size. I was classed as a madman, a charlatan, outlawed in the world of science, which previously had honored me as a genius! Now here in this forsaken jungle hell I have proven that I am all right. No, Professor Strowski, it is no laughing matter.

Harvey B. Dunn uttered the immortal lines "He tampered in God's domain" and "You just weren't born for swamp duty, Marty."

Other films vied for junk masterpiece: *The Astounding She-Monster* (1958), *The Slime People* (1963), and *The Horror of Party Beach* (1964). In the first film, people block a door even though a smashed window stands open to the alien woman. In *The Slime People* Susan Hart scampers over hill and dale in spike heels as she totes an enormous handbag. William Boyce plays a Marine named Calvin who is floored by sudden love: "Gee whiz. Ya know as long as you're settin' here, I don't even wanna think about slime people." In *Party Beach* atomic waste turns drowned sailor skeletons into hideous and hilarious scaly creatures who can be defeated only by sodium — that is, salt. There is one horrifying scene, obviously unintentional: a host of creatures ascends from a quarry in fast motion as the horrified heroine watches immobilized, her leg caught between rocks. These films were in black and white, but by the mid–60s even trash was well photographed— in color—and the sound seemed to have been recorded some place besides in a barn. *The Incredibly Strange Creatures Who Stopped Living and Became Crazy Mixed-Up Zombies* (1964) was a transitional piece.

DRAMAS

Baby Doll (1956) was yet another well-made film of a Tennessee Williams play. Williams contributed the screenplay, while Elia Kazan directed. "And some people of Benoit, Mississippi," played themselves, reminiscent of Kazan's 1950 movie *Panic in the Streets,* filmed in New Orleans. Karl Malden, Carroll Baker, and Eli Wallach had the leads. Malden was trying to generate enough money from his cotton gin to refurbish an old mansion, but lack of ready cash led the furniture company to remove everything but what was in the nursery, where Baby Doll (Baker) slept in a crib. Although married to Archie (Malden), she refused to consummate the relationship till her twentieth birthday. Cotton syndicate boss Silva Vacarro (Eli Wallach) comes along, has his plant burned up by Archie, tries to get the goods, and possibly seduces Baby Doll. Mildred Dunnock was wonderful as a half-crazed aunt cooking up greens. Needless to say, the Legion of Decency and Production Code Administration were bothered by the material. The Legion condemned it, although it received a Production Code seal. In 1969 the film was given a R rating by the Motion Picture Association of America.[37]

Peyton Place (1957) was based on Grace Metalious' "scandalous" best-selling novel of life in a smallish New England community. Hollywood turned it into a handsome, tasteful production starring Lana Turner, Lee Phillips, Hope Lange, Arthur Kennedy, Terry Moore, and much ballyhooed newcomer Diane Varsi.

Twentieth Century–Fox gave deluxe treatment to Ernest Hemingway's best novel, *The Sun Also Rises,* but the cast was too old for their roles as World War I's lost generation. The best elements were Errol Flynn's performance and Hugo Friedhofer's score, the overture an unforeseen dirge for the impending premature deaths of Tyrone Power (1958) and Flynn (1959).

The Defiant Ones (1958) was a breakthrough film for race relations on the screen and for Tony Curtis, pretty boy who proved he could act in this as well as in *Sweet Smell of Success,* released the previous year. In *Defiant,* he and Sidney Poitier, chained together, make a break from their Southern penal gang. To survive they must put animosities aside.

I Want to Live! (1958) featured Johnny Mandel's jazz score as backdrop for Robert Wise's treatment of the true life case of Barbara Graham, B-girl executed for a murder she did not commit. Susan Hayward had honed herself for this role with long-suffering parts, especially in the 1955 *I'll Cry Tomorrow.*

The greatest trial movie of all time might be *Anatomy of a Murder* (1959). Courtroom dramas had a long cinematic history, comprising a dramatic sub-genre most all of whose entries were memorable—*They Won't Forget, Trial, Witness for the Prosecution, Twelve Angry Men.* James Stewart added another superb performance to his repertoire. Lee Remick was suitably sexy as the ravished wife of Ben Gazzara. George C. Scott made an impressive motion picture debut as the prosecuting attorney, Dancer, and Eve Arden and Arthur O'Connell added excellent support. Joseph N. Welch, instrumental in revealing Senator Joseph McCarthy as a real life fraud, was ingratiating and witty as Judge Weaver.

Elmer Gantry (1960) starred Burt Lancaster as Sinclair Lewis' protagonist, a preacher on the make who assists the tent show revivalism of Sister Falconer (Jean Simmons).

> Sin! Sin! Sin! You're all sinners! You're all doomed to perdition! You're all going to the painful, stinkin', scaldin', everlastin' tortures of a fiery hell created by God for sinners! Unless! Unless! Unless you repent. Repent with Sister Falconer!

Shirley Jones cast off her wholesome image to play a prostitute and won a supporting actress Academy Award.

WAR

A revisionist view of war was presented in Robert Aldrich's *Attack* (1956). During the last months of World War II in Europe, Lieutenant Costa (Jack

Between his dance man days and hit television series in the 60s and 70s, Buddy Ebsen, like James Whitmore, made an outstanding screen G.I. seen here in *Attack* (United Artists, 1956). Ebsen fought the Pacific campaign that same year in *Between Heaven and Hell*.

Palance) determines that Captain Cooney (Eddie Albert) is a weakling and a coward who has cost the lives of too many men. Although he sympathizes, Colonel Bartlett (Lee Marvin) refuses to oblige Costa by giving Cooney a headquarters desk job. Costa warns Cooney before they head to the front after a German counterattck. "You double-cross me like you did Ingersoll. You, you play the gutless wonder just once more and I'll come back and I'll get you, Cooney. I'll shove this grenade down your throat and pull the pin!" Fox Company must probe a town. Costa and Sergeant Tolliver (Buddy Ebsen) converse upon approaching it.

> TOLLIVER: Looks quiet.
> COSTA: So does a graveyard.
> TOLLIVER: Yeah, that's right, Lieutenant.
> COSTA: You know those cowboy movies, the one joker says, "Mighty quiet out there. Too quiet," he says. Same thing every time. It's too quiet.
> TOLLIVER: It is too quiet.

During an ensuing battle, Costa's arm is crushed by a tank. Reeling into the cellar where his men are taking refuge, he tries to kill Cooney but falls dead. Cooney decides that the better part of valor is surrender to the Nazis, but the men realize what they must do. When it's over, Tolliver tells the other officer, "Look, Lieutenant, if ever a man needed killin' it's that no good putrid piece a trash lyin' there."

The Bridge on the River Kwai (1957) was a superproduction based on Pierre Boulle's novel and directed by David Lean. Ceylon provided the Burma-like locations. Alec Guinness was Colonel Nicholson, commanding officer of the British in a Japanese POW camp. Charged with building a railway bridge, Colonel Saito (Sessue Hayakawa, who had also been camp commandant in the 1950 film *Three Came Home*) had to convince the prisoners to do a proper job. Nicholson refuses to let officers do manual labor and is tortured. Refusing to break, he manages to extract a concession that in return for allowing his officers to supervise, the bridge will be built properly. One prisoner, the American Shears (William Holden), escapes and is convinced, against his will, to accompany Major Warden (Jack Hawkins) back to the Kwai to destroy the bridge. The first time the film crew tried to blow up the bridge with the train on it, the engine roared across too fast and crashed on the other side. The film won seven Academy Awards, including best picture and best actor (Guinness). William Holden received a percentage that made him wealthy.

Western master Anthony Mann proved to be competent helming *Men in War* (1957), a grim Korean War saga. A lost platoon must fight to its lines. Lieutenant Benson (Robert Ryan) and Montana (Aldo Ray) survive; Robert Keith, James Edwards, Vic Morrow, Nehemiah Persoff, and others do not.

Pork Chop Hill (1959) featured Gregory Peck as the real-life Lieutenant Joe Clemmons, who leads his company up the afore-named hill as the Korean War grinds to a close. Capturing and holding the hill will presumably convince the North Koreans and Chinese that the United Nations forces are serious about carrying on the war.

Equally intolerable was thirty-year-old director Stanley Kubrick's exploration of corruption within the French command in World War I. *Paths of Glory* (1958) told the tale of French soldiers (Ralph Meeker, Timothy Carey, Joe Turkel) made scapegoats for a misguided attack on the German "mole hill" and executed for cowardice. After unsuccessfully defending them, Major Dax (Kirk Douglas) confronts his superior (Adolphe Menjou):

> I apologize for not being entirely honest with you. I apologize for not revealing my true feelings. I apologize, sir, for not telling you sooner that you're a degenerate, sadistic old man! And you can go to Hell before I apologize to you now or ever again!

Paths of Glory is usually accorded the lofty status of *All Quiet on the Western Front*. Some had reservations: "It is so relentless in its determination to condemn war that it becomes at times almost unbearable to watch. Even a well-made picture needs first to win audiences if it wants to put over its worthy theme."[38]

With *The Longest Day* (1962) 20th Century–Fox chief Darryl F. Zanuck scored an immense hit with this re-creation of D-Day, June 6, 1944, the Allied

Kenneth More was the most likable of 50s British leading men. If Americans did not see his English films *Genevieve, Reach for the Sky,* or *A Night to Remember,* they did see *Northwest Frontier (Flame Over India)* and *Sink the Bismarck!*

invasion of Europe. Most criticism was leveled at the casting because it seemed like every major male star of North America and Europe was involved, from John Wayne to Robert Mitchum, Gert Frobe to Irina Demich, Peter Lawford to Kenneth More, even the almost known Sean Connery. Black and white filming gave it the air of authenticity. There was little of the real World War II footage that often mars a nondocumentary, however.

Merrill's Marauders (1962), Samuel Fuller's Warner Bros. entry, was, like the 1945 *Objective, Burma!* about the southeast Asian theater — and even used music from the earlier film. Retelling the story of three thousand G.I.s battling the Japanese from front and rear, Fuller had many impressive large-scale set pieces, including the battle in a black concrete maze before massive storage tanks.

A low-budget but compelling nuclear holocaust movie was American International's 1962 production *Panic in Year Zero*. Here Ray Milland and Frankie Avalon discover a ravaged Joan Freeman.

> My favorite scene in the picture is when the officer climbs on top of the stones after the battle. I make a 360-degree turn with him as he's looking at the dead, and he can't distinguish between the Americans and the enemy. They're all mixed up. That's what I'd like to hit on more than anything else. If people like war, they should just take a look when the fighting's all over.[39]

Filmed in the Philippines, there was no mistake this time. The British and other nationalities were noted by the narrator as participating in the war to oust the Japanese from Burma. Jeff Chandler played the real life General Frank Merrill, who led three thousand men deep behind Japanese lines—to Walawbum, Shaduzup, and Myitkyina in 1944. The supporting cast featured Warner Bros. contract television stars Ty "Bronco" Hardin, Peter "Lawman" Brown, Will "Sugarfoot" Hutchins. Claude Akins made a great sergeant, and John Hoyt bore a resemblance to General Stilwell.

Hell Is for Heroes (1962) starred Steve McQueen as a private with a problem: he was so used to killing the enemy, that was all he was good for. His squad, pretending to be more numerous than they are, is left facing a portion of the Siegfried Line. The Germans probe. McQueen is more than a match, helping his sergeant (Harry Guardino) maintain the ruse.

PT 109 was one of two large-scale 1963 World War II films. Cliff Robertson got plenty of publicity for portraying John F. Kennedy during his wartime stint

When her Disney contract expired, Janet Munro returned to England for a lead role in *The Day the Earth Caught Fire* (Universal, Pax, 1962), a thoughtful examination of what might happen if nuclear testing altered the earth's orbit.

in the Pacific. John Sturges proved again his mastery of an all-male action film. When he filmed Paul Brickhill's book *The Great Escape* (1963), he reteamed Steve McQueen, James Coburn, and Charles Bronson from *The Magnificent Seven* (1960), McQueen and Coburn from *Hell Is for Heroes* (1962), and added James Garner, Richard Attenborough, David McCallum, and Donald Pleasence to re-create the largest escape of Allied prisoners in World War II. (Only three made it out of Nazi territory.) McQueen was "Cooler King" Hilts, constantly given solitary for trying to escape. Filmed in Germany, it followed the tradition of prison escape movies like the British films *The Wooden Horse* (1950), *The Colditz Story* (1954), *The One That Got Away* (1957, with Hardy Kruger as a German POW), and *A Coming Out Party* (1961), and the U.S. production *Stalag 17* (1953).

> Steve McQueen stands for something the movies seem to have lost, along with everything else that once made them so important in our lives: the power of iconography. The way he smiles his trademark smile, the way he leans against a building or tosses a baseball, the way he squints at the sun. The motorcycle.
> Of course, he's *merely* playing himself, another lost and underrated art.[40]

In the midst of a raging Vietnam conflict, with antiwar protesters rallying throughout the land, a seemingly traditional war film had something original to say about warfare and the men who control it. *Patton* (1970) began with World War II's commander of the Third U.S. Army stepping up before a screen-filling flag to harangue unseen troops (the audience) on the merits of a good fight and how the soldier will know what to do when he sees his buddy turned into a bloody mess from a Nazi shell. George C. Scott *was* Patton, a man who lived for battle, who felt he had been a warrior centuries before. Scott won the Academy Award but refused to attend the ceremony and accept it.

STARS

Dean Martin, who split as Jerry Lewis' straight man after *Hollywood or Bust* (1956), played gambler Bama opposite Frank Sinatra's Dave Hirsh in *Some Came Running* (1959). Martin was Sinatra's rat pack buddy offscreen, as was Shirley MacLaine, here playing the first of her lovable, love-starved but love-deserving bimbo roles ("I got nothin' agin' Ginnie, nothin' at all, but even she knows she's a pig," says Martin's Bama) that she'd season in *Irma La Douce* and perfect for audience sympathy in *Sweet Charity* (1969).

Solo, clownish Jerry Lewis met success with *Rock-A-Bye Baby* (1958) and *The Nutty Professor* (1963). In the latter retelling of the Dr. Jekyll and Mr. Hyde story, he was college professor Julius Kelp transformed into cool dude "Buddy Love." Stella Stevens played Miss Stella Purdy. Eventually Buddy reverts, and the reel and real audiences learn that it is best to be oneself.

In the scenario of his career, playing a romantic lead in *Love in the Afternoon* (1957) was not new for Gary Cooper. He had essayed such roles in the 30s in Lubitsch's *Desire, Bluebeard's Eighth Wife,* and *Design for Living.* Cooper had range; he was not merely a rustic or cowboy. It just seemed a mite odd to see the older man opposite Audrey Hepburn here and former model Suzy Parker in *Ten North Frederick* (1958).[41]

Cary Grant continued his association with director Alfred Hitchcock in the classic espionage chase film *North by Northwest* (1959); used his comic timing perfectly in the wartime comedy *Operation Petticoat* that same year ("We sunk a truck!"); partnered Doris Day in the comedy *That Touch of Mink* (1962); and escorted Audrey Hepburn through Paris and its spies in *Charade* (1964). Although his last films were mild—*Father Goose* (1964) and *Walk, Don't Run* (1966), the latter a remake of *The More the Merrier*—Grant's career includes more quality films than any other male star's.

Jack Lemmon was a 20th century urban man who proved able to play drama as well as comedy. Comedies came first: *Pfffht* (1954) and *You Can't Run Away from It* (1956). He won a supporting actor Academy Award for his role as Ensign Pulver in *Mr. Roberts* (1955) and played in another service comedy, *Operation Mad Ball* (1957), with Kathryn Grant and Ernie Kovacs. In *Days of Wine and Roses* he played the alcoholic husband of Lee Remick. Lemmon's first teaming with Walter Matthau was *The Fortune Cookie* (1966).

Tony Curtis, then out of his cut-rate Universal swashbuckler phase, had some memorable costarring stints with Lemmon: *Some Like It Hot* and *The Great Race* (1965). With Sidney Poitier he costarred as an escaped convict in *The Defiant Ones* (1958). Much was made of his selection to play *The Boston Strangler* (1968). He did well, the movie was solid, no more.

Walter Matthau was an interesting case. He began as a supporting actor, often as a bad guy, as in his 1955 film debut in *The Kentuckian,* when he regretted using his whip on Burt Lancaster. In *Strangers When We Meet* (1960) he went after Kirk Douglas' wife, Barbara Rush. Previously, he had comforted Rush when James Mason went off the deep end in *Bigger Than Life* (1956). *The Fortune Cookie* made his fortune by winning him a supporting actor Academy Award that led to starring roles.

Although the film was rather old-fashioned, Barbra Streisand scored a triumph in *Funny Girl* (1968). *Hello, Dolly!* was next up, a more enjoyable film overall but less of a personal or financial success.

Funny man and entertainer of various dimensions, Danny Kaye contributed one last classic: *The Court Jester* (1956). Kaye starred with Glynis Johns, Basil Rathbone, Robert Middleton, and the redoubtable Mildred Natwick in this medieval spoof famous for the poisoned vessel with the pestle.

A broad-shouldered, square-jawed leading man of the 30s and 40s, cast against type impressively in *Double Indemnity* (1944), Fred MacMurray did medium-budget westerns in the 50s as well as items like *Pushover* (1954) and *The Apartment* (1960). He was reborn as a father figure at Disney in *The Shaggy Dog* (1959), *The Absent-Minded Professor* (1961), and its 1963 sequel, *Son of Flubber* (flying rubber). (He was also the father on the hit television series "My Three Sons," which premiered in the fall of 1960.) He also made for Disney *Bon Voyage* (1962), *Follow Me, Boys!* (1966), and *The Happiest Millionaire* (1967).

Noticed by only a few when he debuted opposite John Saxon in the 1962 Korean War film *War Hunt,* Robert Redford copped leading man roles opposite Natalie Wood in *Inside Daisy Clover* (1965) and *This Property Is Condemned* (1966). In Arthur Penn's *The Chase* (1966) he was an escaped con whom Marlon Brando's sheriff sought to save from townsfolk savagery. In 1967 he had a bigger hit opposite Jane Fonda in *Barefoot in the Park.* The breakthrough film was *Butch Cassidy and the Sundance Kid* (1969), with Paul Newman. They were paired again in 1973 in the hit *The Sting.* Redford balanced his Hollywood activities with conservationism.

ELIZABETH TAYLOR, THE BRUNETTE LOVE GODDESS

"I'm not *like* anyone, I'm me," said Elizabeth Taylor's character Gloria Wandrous in *Butterfield 8* (1960). Besides her beauty (see *Beau Brummell, Raintree County,* and so many others), scandal and illness kept the public abuzz. Showbiz wonder Michael Todd, the producer of *Around the World in 80 Days* and Liz' husband, was killed in a plane crash. She became enamored of singer Eddie Fisher, who was married to Debbie Reynolds. Liz got Eddie, thus turning the Reynolds following against her. However, double pneumonia prompted a 1959 life and death situation, and she regained popularity. She won an Academy Award for *Butterfield 8.* Many thought it should have come for *Cat on a Hot Tin Roof* (1958), in which her character, Maggie, rejuvenated Paul Newman and stood up to Big Daddy (Burl Ives). *Suddenly, Last Summer* (1959) was an obtuse film in which she costarred with Katharine Hepburn and,

The Disney Studios created one of the screen's great action sequences when the pirates attacked the *Swiss Family Robinson* (Buena Vista, 1960).

for the third and last time, Montgomery Clift. She demonstrated her ability again in *Who's Afraid of Virginia Woolf?* (1966), one of the many times she starred with Richard Burton, whom she married in 1964. They were paired in *The V.I.P.s* (1963), *The Sandpiper* (1965), *The Taming of the Shrew* (1967), *The Comedians* (1967), *Boom!* (1968), *Dr. Faustus* (1968), and *Hammersmith Is Out* (1972).

TARZAN

After Lex Barker and some substandard Gordon Scott Tarzan outings ("The curse of Mongu on you, Tarzan," cried James Edwards in the 1958 film *Tarzan's Fight for Life*), Britain provided Scott with two outstanding opportunities, *Tarzan's Greatest Adventure* (1959) and *Tarzan the Magnificent* (1960). Both took place in contemporary times. In the latter, Scott's nemesis was Jock Mahoney, who had once played Tarzan himself. In the former, Sean Connery is one of the villains, with Sara Shane supplying gritty support. Both films bear favorable comparison with the Weissmuller-O'Sullivan epics. Current opinion ranks these two and *Tarzan and His Mate* as the all-time best of the series.

In Nicholas Roeg's Australian-lensed *Walkabout* (20th Century–Fox, 1971), Jenny Agutter shares a branch with David Gumpilil. Agutter was apparently the last actress to receive an Elizabeth Taylor-style contract from Metro-Goldwyn-Mayer.

LOW-BUDGET GANGSTER FILMS

From 1957 to 1961 appeared some mostly grade B gangster films set in the Depression: *Baby Face Nelson, Machine Gun Kelly, Al Capone* (Rod Steiger), *Murder, Inc., Pay or Die,* and *Underworld U.S.A.* Although the budgets were small, there was a conscious attempt to make the films authentic. Of *The Rise and Fall of Legs Diamond,* cinematographer Lucien Ballard said,

> Yes, we wanted to go for an authentic atmosphere for the 1920s where the
> film was showing. So after seeing some of the rushes, the producer went to

[Budd] Boetticher and said, "I thought you said Ballard was a great cameraman — this looks like it was shot in 1920!" And Budd said, "It's *supposed* to look like it was shot in 1920!"[42]

Said director Budd Boetticher,

I didn't like working with our producer on that film. He thought we were really shooting junk. On the third day of the picture, he came up to me and said, "I thought you said that Lucien Ballard was a great camerman." I said, "He's a genius!" He said, "But good God, this stuff looks like it was shot in 1920!" Well, how do you compete with that? So I just said, "Go away. Let us finish the picture."[43]

This Unhappy Breed with the Secret Code (Jazz): Kitchen Sink Cinema

Any investigation of British films unearths class consciousness. Based on John Osborne's play, *Look Back in Anger* (1959) was a seminal film in this group that endeavored to uncover malaise and describe middle or working class life in supposedly realistic terms. Richard Burton was angry young man Jimmy Porter. He plays jazz trumpet for fun, mans a market stall for a meager income, and taunts his wife, Alison (Mary Ure), and her actress friend, Helena Charles (Claire Bloom). He likes only Cliff (Gary Raymond) and his former landlady (Edith Evans). There were real black and white backdrops: a graveyard next to trestle bridges and tire heaps.

No good fooling about with love, you know. You can't fall into it like a soft job without dirtying up your hands. Takes muscle and guts. If you can't bear the thought of messing up your nice, tidy soul, you'd better give up the whole idea of life and become a saint. Cause you'll never make it as a human being. It's either this world — or the next.

Room at the Top (1959), which won Simone Signoret a best actress Academy Award, was probably the most important of these films internationally. Other important ones were *No Love for Johnnie* (1961), *Saturday Night and Sunday Morning* (1961), *The Loneliness of the Long-Distance Runner* (1962), *A Taste of Honey* (1962), *A Kind of Loving* (1962), *This Sporting Life* (1963), and *The L-Shaped Room* (1963).

No-No Sex Comedies

The simplest equation: Doris Day + Rock Hudson or James Garner + Tony Randall and/or Gig Young = a bunch of films, 1959 to 1964.

Pillow Talk (1959) was the first of three teamings for Doris Day, Rock Hudson, and Tony Randall. The ensuing entries, *Lover Come Back* (1962) and *Send Me No Flowers* (1964), were just about as funny and naive. ("Roly-Poly" was a song sung in a club that now irritates many viewers.) Note that in *Flowers* Day is *not* a virgin but Hudson's wife. *That Touch of Mink* (1962) featured Cary Grant, Day, Gig Young in the Tony Randall role, as well as Al's Motel, where you bring your own lightbulbs. Later James Garner paired with Day in *The Thrill of It All* (1963) and *Move Over, Darling* (1963), a remake of *My Favorite Wife* (1940). In this version Edgar Buchanan, a veteran character actor,

The Buccaneer (Paramount, 1958) featured Claire Bloom in another Hollywood period piece. Like fellow Brit Jean Simmons, Bloom could essay ancient *(Alexander the Great)* or modern *(Look Back in Anger)* roles.

played a judge. His query of Chuck Connors, "What's your story, Tarzan?" can still elicit a laugh. Such veterans provided much of the amusement in these films. Most of these films have a southern California or a (usually) summertime New York setting — it is sunny, bright, and cheerful, and everything will be all right in the end.

Day also starred in *Teacher's Pet* (1958) opposite Clark Gable (and Gig Young), and in *The Tunnel of Love* (1958) opposite Richard Widmark (and Gig Young). *Ask Any Girl* (1959) featured Shirley MacLaine put upon by New York bachelors like David Niven, Rod Taylor (and Gig Young). In *Boys' Night Out* (1962) behavioral psychology student Kim Novak investigated the male libidos of James Garner, Tony Randall, Howard Duff, and Howard Morris. Short fantasy sequences helped make this film palatable. Without such episodes, *For Love or Money* (1963) was mild and could not be saved, even by Thelma Ritter. *Sex and the Single Girl* (1964) had a funny taxi ride; *Good Neighbor Sam* (1964) a funny car ride. *A Very Special Favor* (1965), with Rock Hudson and Leslie Caron, may be chiefly remembered for Hudson's retort to Caron's comment that most men do not care about the size of women's breasts: "What men?"

The familiar presence of Edward Andrews graced *Fluffy* (Universal, 1965). Andrews could play dramatic roles, witness *Tea and Sympathy* (1956), but most often was featured in comedies. He appeared in three 1963 films and in seven in 1964.

Neil Simon, Broadway writer, supplied material — scripts or the theatrical material — for a string of very successful comedies, from *Come Blow Your Horn* (1963) to *Barefoot in the Park* (1967), *The Odd Couple* (1968), *Plaza Suite* (1971), and to many more into the 80s and 90s.

Elaine May, writer and comedienne who paired opposite Mike Nichols on stage and television, acted in the 1967 films *Enter Laughing* and *Luv,* then acted in and directed the riotous 1971 film *A New Leaf.* "Have you tasted Mogen David's Extra Heavy Malaga Wine with soda and lime juice?" asks nerdy but rich biologist Henrietta Lowell (May). Walter Matthau, a cad gone broke, believes he has discovered the woman who can once again allow him to enjoy the finer things in life. May remained behind the camera for *The Heartbreak Kid.* Lenny (Charles Grodin) marries Lila (Jeannie Berlin, May's real-life daughter) but on their Miami honeymoon falls for corn-fed midwestern blond Kelly Corcoran (Cybill Shepherd). He leaves his sunburned bride to woo Kelly at college, attempting to soft-soap her father (Eddie Albert) by complimenting the "honest" food at the Corcoran's table.

Walter Matthau and Elaine May played playboy and "feral" biologist in the underrated comedy *A New Leaf* (Paramount, 1971). May directed.

BILLY WILDER

Director Billy Wilder was reaching another peak with three hits in a row. *Some Like It Hot* (1959) was set during the Prohibition. Tony Curtis and Jack Lemmon witness a gangland killing, are seen, and flee to Florida. On the train they masquerade as women and bunk with an all-girl band featuring Sugar Kane (Marilyn Monroe), who wows them with her rendition of "Running Wild."

The Apartment (1960) was humorous in minor incidents but masked a gloom in corporate life. Elevator operator Shirley MacLaine was the kept girl of married executive Fred MacMurray. Junior executive Jack Lemmon rescued her.

With I. A. L. Diamond, Wilder coscripted *One, Two, Three* (1961), a buzzsaw commentary on the Cold War, which would feature James Cagney's final film performance until the 1981 *Ragtime*. Cagney was MacNamara, a Coca-Cola representative in West Berlin. His goal was to market the soda to the Eastern bloc: "Look at this Schlemmer. All virgin territory. Three hundred million thirsty comrades. Volga boatmen and Cossacks, Ukrainians and Outer Mongolians panting for the pause that refreshes." Trouble comes in the form of his boss's marvy daughter, Scarlet Hazeltine (Pamela Tiffin), who acquires an East German boyfriend named Piffle (Horst Buchholz).

HEIST AND CHASE

Heist films almost always delivered the goods, and in this era there were many good ones, including *Odds Against Tomorrow* (1959), *Seven Thieves* (1960), *The League of Gentlemen* (1961), *How to Steal a Million* and *Gambit* (1966), *$* and *The Anderson Tapes* (1971), and *The Hot Rock* (1972).

The Lineup (1958) was a progenitor, but in *Bullitt* (1968) British-born director Peter Yates followed up his 1967 British film, *Robbery*, with the seminal chase film. Steve McQueen was San Francisco detective Frank Bullitt, intent on solving a murder case involving a man who had robbed the mob. The auto pursuit over the San Francisco hills became the standard by which all future auto chases would be measured. Just about as thrilling was the finale, when McQueen tracks his man on the runways and in the airport terminal.

The French Connection (1971) starred Gene Hackman as New York policeman Popeye Doyle out to bust a drug ring with his cohort Roy Scheider. A thrilling chase involved Popeye's auto pursuit of a killer (Marcel Bozzuffi) in an elevated train.

TELEVISION INFLUENCES

Henry Fonda narrated "Hollywood and the Stars," an early 60s television series of half-hour shows. Hour-long specials included "The Golden Years" (silents) and "The Fabulous Years" (30s). One of the most important film events of the 60s occurred on September 23, 1961, at 9:00 P.M., when NBC and announcer Don Rickels (not comedian Don Rickles) inaugurated "Saturday Night at the Movies," the first national airing of semirecent theatrical movies in primetime. It was a smash hit that led ABC and CBS to follow suit.

All of the initial 1961–62 NBC films were 20th Century–Fox features. In order they were: *How to Marry a Millionaire, The Snows of Kilimanjaro, Titanic, Garden of Evil, The Desert Fox, There's No Business Like Show Business, Soldier of Fortune, Halls of Montezuma, Demetrius and the Gladiators, Dreamboat, Broken Arrow, Man on a Tightrope, Destination Gobi, O. Henry's Full House, On the Riviera, What Price Glory? People Will*

Talk, Five Fingers, Cheaper by the Dozen, The Frogmen, With a Song in My Heart, Monkey Business, Stars and Stripes Forever, The Day the Earth Stood Still, The Black Rose, Where the Sidewalk Ends, No Highway in the Sky, Bird of Paradise, It Happens Every Spring, and *Diplomatic Courier.* Gary Cooper, Susan Hayward, Tyrone Power, Clifton Webb, and Richard Widmark gained new, young fans from this exposure.

On April 8, 1962, ABC aired the "Hollywood Special," which became "The Sunday Night Movie." Its first offering was the 1958 film *Run Silent, Run Deep,* with Clark Gable and Burt Lancaster. Relating the tale of a U.S. submarine traversing the Bungo Straits made for a pleasurable school lunchtime for many youngsters on Monday. Some of the mostly United Artists films that played first season were *The Indian Fighter, Shake Hands with the Devil, Pork Chop Hill, Witness for the Prosecution, Man of the West, The Wonderful Country, Men in War, The Kentuckian, Marty, Not as a Stranger, Johnny Concho,* and *The Pride and the Passion.*[44]

THE RETURN OF JEAN HARLOW

Carroll Baker, heretofore a serious method actress who had appeared in Elia Kazan's *Baby Doll,* grasped for Marilyn Monroe's sex symbol crown in *The Carpetbaggers* (1964) and *Harlow* (1965). In the latter, she played the 30s platinum blond bombshell Jean Harlow. Harlow had died in 1937 but had been resurrected in Irving Shulman's biography. She, like her successor Marilyn Monroe, had starred with the late Clark Gable. The new films, however, were failures as art, boring even as entertainment. *The Carpetbaggers* did accrue $15 million in its initial run, helped by readers of the Harold Robbins best-seller.[45]

There was another *Harlow* the same year, which starred Carol Lynley and was filmed quickly in something called Electronovision. Litigation ensued, but both were released to unenthusiastic reviews and receipts.

THE CURSE OF ELVIS

Rock idol Elvis "The King" Presley had debuted in 1956 in *Love Me Tender,* thereafter making a string of successful movies for fans more interested in hearing him sing than in plots. Some did have good stories, in particular the 1960 Don Siegel western *Flaming Star.* But more and more plotless musicals followed. Even Barbara Stanwyck could not add much to *Roustabout* (1964), although that particular picture had quite good songs — none of which were promoted as singles. Male viewers could at least cheer for the fight scenes and the exquisitely beautiful actresses. Elvis was paired with Yvonne Craig (*It Happened at the World's Fair,* 1963, *Kissin' Cousins,* 1964); Joan O'Brien *(It Happened at the World's Fair);* Joan Blackman (*Blue Hawaii,* 1961, *Kid Galahad,* 1962); Anne Helm (*Follow That Dream,* 1962); Jocelyn Lane (*Tickle Me,* 1965); Stella Stevens *(Girls! Girls! Girls!* 1962); Ann-Margret (*Viva Las Vegas,* 1964); Deborah Walley (*Spinout,* 1966); and Joan Freeman *(Roustabout).* Only those like Stevens and Ann-Margret, who had already started their careers, progressed. Appearance in an Elvis movie was almost a

The floozy with a heart of gold was a Stella Stevens specialty and accomplished exceedingly well in Sam Peckinpah's least violent outing, *The Ballad of Cable Hogue* (Warner Bros., 1970). Jason Robards attends the bath.

kiss of death for some; for others, it may not have harmed, but it did not help.

It might be noted in passing that Pat Boone was a cinematic rival for Elvis for a brief time. Perceived as more acceptable to adults, Boone, the crooner of "Love Letters in the Sand," debuted in 1957 in *Bernardine* and *April Love*. The latter was a remake of the 1944 harness-racing story, *Home in Indiana*.

COMEDY-DRAMAS

The 60s had a fair share of quality comedy-dramas. *The Courtship of Eddie's Father* (1963) starred Glenn Ford as a widower seeking a wife and mother for his son (Ronny Howard). Shirley Jones, Stella Stevens, and Dina Merrill were the candidates.

Soldier in the Rain (1963) is a little-known gem about the peacetime army and is full of great lines. Jackie Gleason as Sergeant Maxwell Slaughter: "Let me tell you something my friend. Being a fat narcissist isn't easy." And, "And I'm not getting any younger. I'm in the twilight of my years and every minute is precious, every second counts. Of necessity, my very existence depends on prompt and immediate action. To wait is to ponder, to ponder is to waste. And Eustis, to waste is a mortal sin. Do you understand?" Tuesday Weld as Bobby Jo Pepperdine: "I think it's sad. I think fireworks are the saddest thing in the whole world. The, the way they just disappear. They should make 'em so they just hang up there all night." Steve McQueen was Eustis, soldier with a soft spot in his heart for his dog, Donald. There is a marvelous barroom fight.

Other excellent comedy-dramas of the 60s were *The World of Henry Orient* (1964), with pianist Peter Sellers bothered by teens Merrie Spaeth and Tippy Walker, and *A Thousand Clowns* (1965), with Jason Robards, Martin Balsam, and Barbara Harris. *A Fine Madness* (1966) was an early change of pace for Sean Connery, who played a life-loving New York poet not unlike the Jason Robards character in *A Thousand Clowns.*

The Jokers (1967) starred Oliver Reed and Michael Crawford. "Favorable word of mouth can be established by deliberate, but not overdone, promotion of the pic in smaller theatres catering to students. It could become a sleeper on this circuit, after which careful nursing in more general, but still small, houses would expand the market."[46] The story: two brothers plan to steal the Crown Jewels as a joke, but the younger feigns innocence when the plot is uncovered.

ANACHRONISMS

Director Michael Curtiz, who had made so many notable movies, from Errol Flynn swashbucklers to *Casablanca,* passed on. His last two films were released in 1961 and were reminiscent of the studio age, which was also failing. *Francis of Assisi* was an old-fashioned Hollywood pseudo-epic with Bradford Dillman as the man becoming the saint. Told traditionally, *The Comancheros* was a rousing, scenic western, with John Wayne and Stuart Whitman and a great supporting cast, including Lee Marvin and Jack Elam.

The change in movies was nowhere more evident than in *Madison Avenue* (1962). Multi–Academy Award nominee Eleanor Parker, popular leading man of the 40s and 50s Dana Andrews, the beauteous Jeanne Crain, who was really in her prime, starred in this black and white small film about advertising. It is not without interest, but it resides in between the old and new.

B westerns were a dying breed due to competition from television, where they held sway with such popular 60s series as "Rawhide," "Gunsmoke," "Have Gun, Will Travel," "Cheyenne," "Bonanza," "The Virginian," and "Maverick." A. C. Lyles continued churning out theatrical westerns, however. Shot in color, filled with old-timers, they contained too many close-ups but were still enjoyable. These included *Waco, Black Spurs,* and *Town Tamer.*

Frothy but cute Broadway adaptations abounded. Jane Fonda's apprenticeship was served in *Period of Adjustment* (1962), *Sunday in New York* (1963), *Any Wednesday* (1966), and *Barefoot in the Park* (1967). Like some of the remakes of 30s films, there were often plenty of small scenes to make the whole worthwhile.

DOOMSDAY 1964

"The Wild Hot-Line Suspense Comedy!" read the advertisement. *Dr. Strangelove, or How I Learned to Stop Worrying and Love the Bomb* came out in February and was the blackest of black comedies from director Stanley Kubrick and writer Terry Southern. Sterling Hayden played General Jack D. Ripper, who sent Major T. J. "King" Kong (Slim Pickens) off to bomb the Soviet Union.

> He said war was too important to be left to the generals. When he said that — fifty years ago — he might have been right. But today, war is too important to be left to politicians. They have neither the time, the training, nor the inclination for strategic thought. I can no longer sit back and allow communist infiltration, communist indoctrination, communist subversion, and the international communist conspiracy to sap and impurify all of our precious bodily fluids.

Peter Sellers played a triple role — President Muffley of the United States, Group Captain Lionel Mandrake, and consultant Dr. Strangelove. George C. Scott was General "Buck" Turgidson. Keenan Wynn played Colonel "Bat" Guano, sent to deter Ripper. Encountering Mandrake, he said, "If you try any perversions in there, I'll blow your head off." As the crippled, wheelchair-bound Strangelove, Sellers cries out as the holocaust begins, "Mein Führer, I can walk!"

Fail-Safe, also from Columbia, hit the theaters in September. Henry Fonda played the president, Walter Matthau was Groeteschele, a Edward Teller–like scientist ("Those who can survive are the only ones worth surviving!"), and Dan O'Herlihy, Frank Overton, Edward Binns, and Fritz Weaver provided excellent support. In this scenario, a bomber is mistakenly sent into the Soviet Union and the president tries to recall it — to no avail. To prevent Russian retaliation and a worldwide calamity, the president proposes to destroy New York.

YOUTH AND REBELLION

After *Rebel Without a Cause,* there was no turning back. Independents and small studios like American International jumped on the bandwagon rolling for the young and drive-in audiences. *Dragstrip Girl* starred Fay Spain in 1957. Yvonne Lime and Jana Lund were *High School Hellcats* in 1958. Lime was part of *Dragstrip Riot* (1958).

The 60s was the Paul Newman decade when he made his "H" films: *The Hustler,* (1961), *Hud* (1963, "Paul Newman is 'Hud'!" and "The Man with the Barbed Wire Soul!"), *Harper,* and *Hombre* (1967, "Paul Newman is Hombre!" and "How you gonna get down that hill!"). *Cool Hand Luke* (1967) was a real rebel film, and, even if silly in the final analysis, what chain gang film isn't riveting? ("What we've got here is a failure to communicate," were the immortal words of Strother Martin's "Captain," which became the motto of a generation.)

England's rock group, the Beatles (Paul McCartney, John Lennon, Ringo Starr, George Harrison), toured the States to ecstatic response in 1964, singing "I Wanna Hold Your Hand" and "She Loves You." Movies beckoned the Liverpool lads immediately. The director of *A Hard Day's Night* (1964), American Richard Lester, was a veteran of television commercials, a musician, and the

Harper (Warner Bros., 1966) was one of 17 films Paul Newman made in the 60s. The other "H" movies were *The Hustler, Hud* and *Hombre.*

director of the "Goon Shows" in Britain. "No film-maker in this decade appeared more punctually when his hour struck; and for a long time he succeeded marvellously in synchronising himself to its every trend and eruption."[47] *A Hard Day's Night* was in black and white, yet. No matter—the teenage audience ate up this bizarre tracking of the quartet playing themselves. *Help!* (1965) was just about as good.

   Beach Movies: Two 1959 films may be credited with creating a preliminary "beach" craze: *A Summer Place* and *Gidget.* In the former, Sandra Dee and Troy Donahue were the youths misunderstood by Dorothy McGuire and Richard Egan. In retrospect, this execrable movie is memorable only for the title tune. Dee was also *Gidget.* Her mother's sampler would come to haunt women: "To Be a Real Woman is to Bring Out the Best in a Man." James Darren as Moondoggie romanced Gidget, while Kahuna (Cliff Robertson) was the mature beach bum. *Where the Boys Are* (1961) was a masterpiece in comparison to its 1984 remake. It starred George Hamilton, Jim Hutton, Dolores Hart, Paula Prentiss, Yvette Mimieux, Connie Francis, and Frank Gorshin. The title tune, sung by Francis, became a standard.

Beach Party (1963) from AIP starred Frankie Avalon and Annette Funicello and some old-line stars, Robert Cummings and Dorothy Malone. Stock characters that would appear in most of the ensuing films included Harvey Lembeck as the incompetent motorcycle gang leader Eric Von Zipper, Bobbi Shaw, Candy Johnson, Sally Sachse, Jody McCrea, Aron Kincaid, and a bevy of *Playboy* Playmates like Jo Collins, Sue Hamilton (Williams), Karla Conway, Donna Michelle. This series' ultimate importance may be the sets done by rock, soul, and pop performers before the advent of music videos. Eric Burdon and the Animals and the Dave Clark Five are featured in *Get Yourself a College Girl* (1964), while James Brown and Lesley Gore perform in *Ski Party* (1965).

Cycle Flicks: Whereas *The Wild One* (1954) was the first major film about motorcycle gangs, this genre did not really take off until the 1966 film *The Wild Angels* ("He's wasted," says Nancy Sinatra of Bruce Dern). Although Adam Roarke (*The Savage Seven,* 1967, *Hell's Belles,* 1969) was often called king of the bikers, the more imposing William Smith was the true hetman. He starred in *Run, Angel, Run!* (1969), a revenge chase melodrama in which all of the 60s lingo was run out: "groovy," "bag," "dig," "blast," "That's where it's at, man!"; *The Losers* (1970, "William Smith as the leader of the cyclists is all muscle and wonderfully photogenic");[48] *Chrome and Hot Leather* (1971, "Gabriel, can't you see we're menacing someone?"); and *C.C. and Company* (1970). Smith could carry modern Bs like *Invasion of the Bee Girls* (1973) and *Seven* (1979) or be an imposing bad guy in *Darker Than Amber* (1970) or a good-bad guy in *Any Which Way You Can* (1980). *Easy Rider* (1969), the most famous of the cycle flicks, in turn spawned antiestablishment youth movies like *The Strawberry Statement* (1970), *Getting Straight* (1970), and *Move* (1970).

Permissiveness: While author Kingsley Amis, *Esquire's* critic of the art of the cinema, declared "how bloody awful most non–American films were,"[49] European, Japanese, and Indian films were making inroads into American and British markets.

> The main reason that the films of foreign producers and directors have dominated American art houses is not that the directors are more brilliant than the best of Hollywood. It is because they do not suffer from pre-censorship. They are willing to carry through to the end an idea that sparked their enthusiasm. They are not frightened by the unusual or intimidated by the possibility of failure.[50]

> The Hollywood cinema, up to the end of 1965, was still clamped rigidly between the hypocrisies of the Production Code and the ratings administration on the one hand and, on the other, the pressure-groups, secular and religious, who were still trying to impose a consensus attitude on a society that was everywhere disintegrating into a sensation-seeking culture.

The Trouble with Angels (Columbia, 1966) was perhaps Hayley Mills' best film away from the Disney Studios. She and June Harding (right) made life difficult for the Mother Superior (Rosalind Russell).

The changing mood of America was visible everywhere except in the home-produced movies. Anyone studying the film-industry periodical *Variety* in, say, 1964–65 will be amazed by the swelling civic indignation—sometimes genuine, sometimes fomented—engendering by American films that dared deviate from a restrictive set of thou-shalt-nots that the Production Code represented.[51]

Rating System Changes in Late 60s: MPAA, 1968: *The Pawnbroker* (1965) was instrumental in forcing a liberalization of the Production Code. A serious film about a concentration camp survivor trying to survive in New York, its producer appealed and got Code approval even though in one scene a prostitute briefly displayed bare breasts. Yet nudity would not be common until the new rating code was implemented in 1968. First came the strong language of Edward Albee's *Who's Afraid of Virginia Woolf?* transferred faithfully to the screen in 1966 by new director Mike Nichols.

The Graduate (1967), from writer Buck Henry and director Mike Nichols, captured the angst of a generation. Dustin Hoffman played Benjamin, recent college graduate who does not know what to do with his life — he is hardly interested in entering the plastics field. Suffering suburban ennui, Mrs. Robinson (Anne Bancroft) seduces him, but he falls for her daughter (Katharine Ross). Dave Grusin provided the instrumental score, but the Simon and Garfunkel songs "Sounds of Silence," "Scarborough Fair," and "Mrs. Robinson" made the album a hot seller and convinced studio bosses that contemporary tunes could sell future films.

In *Here We Go Round the Mulberry Bush* (1968), Jamie (Barry Evans) thinks life would be just peachy if he could score with a luscious "bird." He fails with three (Angela Scoular, Sheila White, and Adrienne Posta), makes it with two others (Vanessa Howard and Judy Geeson), but finds it is not all it was cracked up to be. But at the end he spies another bird (Diane Keen), and his heart is aflutter once more. A rock score by Traffic and the Spencer Davis Group mirrors his doings. Album notes from the film's director Clive Donner must have flustered traditional film score composer Elmer Bernstein.

> Never before has the musical score for a film been created the way this one was. I decided all the background music would be pop songs, performed by top groups just as if they were regular discs available to the record buying public. Sometimes treating them electronically and mixing in way out sound effects as is [*sic*] the hero's "Daydreams."
>
> It was a gamble. Not on the songs as songs, because of the talents of the people concerned. But not having a conventional score and an experienced film composer meant I was dependent on their responding to the story of the film, digging the characters and situations in it and writing the sort of material I wanted.
>
> I talked — they may plead I jabbered my head off — to them at fantastic length; they listened — silently, reacting very little — then went away, composed, performed, recorded and delivered. Successfully — the gamble had come off.
>
> This group of popular songs of to-day makes a unique film score and mirrors something of the feelings of those who are young to-day, and for those who have been and will go Round the Mulberry Bush of Love.[52]

"Recommended for Adults Only," read the *HWGRTMB* advertisement. (The MPAA letter code would be instituted later that year.) The National Catholic Office for Motion Pictures gave it a condemned rating because it was "marred by the unnecessary introduction of offensive elements, notably a prolonged nude sequence."[53]

Some termed it the golden age of the R rating for female nudity: Jo Ann Harris in *The Beguiled*, Stella Stevens in *Slaughter*, Ingrid Pitt in *The Vampire*

It becomes clear to Katharine Ross (center) that Benjamin (Dustin Hoffman) has had an affair with her mother, Mrs. Robinson (Anne Bancroft). Mike Nichols' *The Graduate* (Embassy, 1967) was a key film for disaffected youth.

Lovers, Mary and Madelaine Collinson in *Twins of Evil,* Yutte Stensgaard in *Lust for a Vampire,* Mimsy Farmer in *Road to Salina,* Katherine Justice in *The Stepmother,* Linda Hayden in *The Blood on Satan's Claw,* and Britt Ekland in *The Wicker Man* (1974). As the years passed, foul language would be suf-fiient to earn a film an R rating.

A ratings test case occurred in 1974 when a district federal court in Chicago ruled that the PG rating of *Papillon* was not misleading and denied a father's suit for $7 million in compensatory damages and $250,000 in punitive dam-ages from the MPAA, Allied Artists, and General Cinema Corporation. The father said the film was not suitable for his three daughters, ages 14, 11, and 7, whom he had taken to see it. The film had originally been rated R. This was the first legal test of the MPAA's voluntary rating system.[54]

FOUR DIRECTORS

Britisher Tony Richardson had scored with *Look Back in Anger* (1959), *A Taste of Honey* (1961), and *The Loneliness of the Long-Distance Runner* (1962), then hit it tremendously big in 1963 with *Tom Jones,* which won the best picture Academy Award. His antiwar revisionist epic of 1968, *The Charge of the Light Brigade,* was a moderate failure.

Ken Russell, the Britisher, made what some thought were increasingly

Vanessa Howard was the first British "bird" bedded by Barry Evans in *Here We Go Round the Mulberry Bush* (Lopert, 1968). Fast on the heels of *The Graduate,* Clive Donner's film also incorporated a rock score (Traffic and the Spencer Davis Group). Vanessa's career continued in *Corruption* and *Girly.*

excessive films: *Women in Love* (1970), *The Devils* (1971), *The Boy Friend* (1971), *The Music Lovers* (1971).

Arthur Penn had directed the critically acclaimed Billy the Kid opus *The Left-Handed Gun* in 1958, following in 1962 with the broader appeal of *The Miracle Worker. Mickey One* (1965) was a puzzle for select audiences. *The Chase* (1966), with Marlon Brando, Robert Redford, and Jane Fonda, while not critically praised, was a rousing hothouse Southern melodrama and police show. Then came *Bonnie and Clyde* (1967), *Alice's Restaurant* (1969), and *Little Big Man* (1970).

Robert Altman had helmed the low budget *Countdown* and *That Cold Day in the Park* (1969) before *M*A*S*H* (1970) was made at the right time — the height of the Vietnam War. More nontraditional films followed: *Brewster McCloud* (1970), *McCabe and Mrs. Miller* (1971), *Images* (1972), and *Nashville* (1975).

007 AND SPIES OF THE 60S

"Blast him! Seduce him! Bomb him! Strangle him! Target: The unkillable James Bond 007," proclaimed the advertisement for the second James Bond film, *From Russia with Love* (1964; U.K., 1963). The obscure, to

James Bond (Sean Connery), Ian Fleming's agent with the license to kill (007), was unleashed on an unsuspecting world in *Dr. No* (United Artists, 1962). Eunice Gayson played girlfriend Sylvia.

say the least, Scottish-born actor Sean Connery had been given the role of Ian Fleming's agent with a license to kill for *Dr. No* (1962). In this film set in the Caribbean, Bond investigated agents' murders and uncovered the fiendish plot of Dr. No (veteran actor Joseph Wiseman), who would start a world war by redirecting an American rocket. Bond was almost killed by a spider, an armored, flame-spewing vehicle, and No's minions. Of the latter, Anthony Dawson deserves note. With a hard edge little evident in later films, Bond dealt a form of justice to the incompetent assassin.

From Russia with Love opened with the apparent stalking and strangulation of Bond by Red Grant (Robert Shaw). But it was merely a man in the mask, a test case for the international assassination-espionage network known as Spectre. Later on, Grant would have the real opportunity in a hair-raising fight in a train cabin where Bond guarded a Russian Lektor cipher machine. Fighting gypsy women, Istanbul locations, and villains like Grant and Rosa Klebb (Lotte Lenya) made this Connery's best Bond film.

Although *From Russia with Love* was profitable, *Goldfinger* (1965) became *the* breakthrough Bond film. More beautiful women, like Pussy Galore (Honor Blackman) and the ill-fated golden gal (Shirley Eaton), a worthy villain's henchman Oddjob (Harold Sakata), a master villain (Gert Frobe), a scheme to knock over Fort Knox, the popular theme sung by Shirley Bassey, and gimmicks from Q (Desmond Llewellyn) served to make this one a big, big hit.

Thunderball (1965) and *You Only Live Twice* (1967) ("Sean Connery *Is* James Bond") followed for Connery. Tom Jones sang the former's title song, Nancy Sinatra the latter. The main title sequences by Maurice Binder were artworks in themselves, sometimes serving to refresh the audience's memory, as was most evident in *On Her Majesty's Secret Service* (1969). Connery had wanted out, so Australian George Lazenby replaced him. Lazenby apparently told the producers after he had been selected to play Bond that he had no interest in continuing the series. The film did not get the publicity it normally would, and Lazenby took flack for lack of talent. Ironically, *OHMMS* was the equal of *From Russia with Love*. Gimmicks were held to a minimum, and the female lead was Bond's equal: the beautiful and steel-strong Tracy Draco (Diana Rigg, late of "The Avengers" television series, where she played agent Emma Peel). Angela Scoular was a delicious temptress in Blofeld's hideaway. Three chases enthralled the audience: car, ski, and toboggan. John Barry's score was among his best, and Louis Armstrong provided "We Have All the Time in the World." The best line in all of the Bond films was voiced by Telly Savalas: "All right, we'll head him off at the precipice." Another possible contributing reason the film was not as popular as previous Bonds was word of mouth. Audiences were visibly shocked when Blofeld machine-gunned the car Bond and Tracy drove off in on their honeymoon.

Connery came back on board for *Diamonds Are Forever* (1971). He got 12½ percent of the gross rentals, an anticipated $6 million.[55] He then left the series and was replaced by Roger Moore but returned for *Never Say Never Again* (1983), a virtual remake of *Thunderball*. Roger Moore was not as physically imposing as Connery and, for the most part, his films were gadget-infested. *For Your Eyes Only* (1981) was the best.

Casino Royale (1967) was released by Columbia, competing directly with United Artists' *Thunderball*. *Royale* was a send-up which at the time seemed to have too many cooks spoiling the broth. In retrospect it can be enjoyed as the farce it is—or something that could only have been made in the 60s.

Other studios were keen to emulate the success of the James Bond series. Even broader was *Our Man Flint* (1966), featuring James Coburn as Derek Flint, who worked for ZOWIE (Zonal Organization World Intelligence Espionage). A group of scientists on an isolated island aimed to control world weather to force international disarmament. They developed the electrofragmentizer and for some reason converted comely young women into Pleasure Units, branding them with serial numbers. One venue was a bogus drive-in, where men and PUs necked. Although successful, only one sequel emerged, *In Like Flint* (1967). Dean Martin portrayed Matt Helm beginning in *The Silencers*, a good spoof. But the series became increasingly unwatchable as *The Ambushers* (1967), *Murderers' Row* (1968), and *The Wrecking Crew* (1969) attest. *The Ipcress File* presented a protagonist agent of normal dimensions.

sions. Michael Caine played Harry Palmer in this and the two sequels, the good but incoherent *Funeral in Berlin* and the ludicrous *Billion Dollar Brain*, in which Ed Begley led a snowmobile invasion of Russia. Richard Johnson resurrected Bulldog Drummond and played him in modern times in *Deadlier Than the Male* (1967) and *Some Girls Do* (1968). Neither was first-rate, although the former's Elke Sommer was a beautiful assassin. *The Spy Who Came in from the Cold* (1965) with Richard Burton, Claire Bloom, and Oskar Werner was considered the most serious and truthful espionage film. Also critically well received but publicly ignored was *The Deadly Affair* (1967), with James Mason.

Espionage oriented were *Charade* (1964) with Cary Grant, *Mirage* (1965), and *Arabesque* (1966), with Gregory Peck. *North by Northwest* (1959) was reissued with a 60s spy-slant ad.

BRITISH INVASION (ON THEIR TERMS)

For union and tax reasons, American filmmakers like Stanley Kubrick holed up in Britain, but British stars found it financially advantageous to live and work overseas. They were much in demand. In contrast to previous decades, when British performers were lured away from Britain, in the 60s they invaded the United States on their own terms and initially in British films (sometimes financed by U.S. companies). To name a few who made big impressions: Susannah York, Julie Christie, Julie Andrews, Richard Harris, Terence Stamp, Tom Courtenay, Oliver Reed, Sean Connery, Michael Caine, Albert Finney, Samantha Eggar. Dirk Bogarde was virtually the only British leading man who did not make a "Hollywood" film. Bogarde chose to stay east, working in a number of well-regarded Continental films.

Tom Jones (1963) symbolized the new, internationally popular British cinema. As Henry Fielding's good-natured rake, Albert Finney wowed everyone, critics and public alike. Susannah York was lovely. Hugh Griffith got another over-the-top meaty role. The chicken eating scene between Finney and Joyce Redman was immediately famous. "Just when the 'new realism' was dropping for want of refreshment, its energies were revived by *Tom Jones* and redirected away from a scene that had staled from over-familiarity and repetitiveness. The sense of having a 'good time' spilled out of every frame of *Tom Jones* and, in the phrase then in vogue, audiences found themselves 'switched on' by it."[56]

At the 1967 Academy Award telecast host Bob Hope said, "To the Redgrave family all the world's a stage — and they're playing all the parts." Lynn was in *Georgy Girl* (1966), *Smashing Time* (1967), and *The Deadly Affair* (1967); Vanessa in *A Man for All Seasons, Morgan!* and *Blow-Up* in 1966, *Camelot, Isadora,* and *The Sailor from Gibraltar* in 1967; Corin in *A Man for All Seasons* and *The Deadly Affair;* father Michael in *The 25th Hour* (1967).

SUPERCALIFRAGILISTICEXPIALIDOCIOUS

In 1964 Audrey Hepburn played Eliza Dolittle in *My Fair Lady*. Many critics were outraged that Julie Andrews was not chosen to reprise her stage

Red Sky at Morning (Universal, 1971) was an episodic (in the best sense) film about coming of age during World War II. In the car are Claire Bloom, Richard Crenna and Richard Thomas. Gregory Sierra played the sheriff.

role. But who knew Julie Andrews? Hepburn was a natural choice, even if Marnie Nixon did the singing (as she had done for Deborah Kerr in *The King and I* and for Natalie Wood in *West Side Story*). Hepburn did not get an Academy Award nomination, but Andrews did — and won for *Mary Poppins,* which had been released in September 1964. (In October her second film, *The Americanization of Emily,* came out.) *Mary Poppins* was Disney's biggest hit and provided a springboard to superstardom for Andrews. Live action, animation, excellent original songs like the Academy Award–winner "Chim-Chim-Cheree" plus "A Spoonful of Sugar," "I Love to Laugh," "Step in Time," "Feed the Birds," and "Fly a Kite," and the screen presence of Andrews made for enchantment. Next up was *The Sound of Music* (why no outcry for Mary Martin to reprise?), which turned out to be the best screen adaptation of the Rodgers and Hammerstein "Big Five": *Oklahoma! Carousel, The King and I, South Pacific.* Andrews opened the roadshow from a high Alpine hill, singing the title song. It was a sensation and took from *Gone with the Wind* the title of top grosser of all time. Some critics complained that there was too much sugar. With Nazis? The first half was undoubtedly better; after her splendiferous marriage to a resplendent Christopher Plummer, Andrews' character became matronly and prim.

For three years Andrews was the hottest star around. *Hawaii* (1966) was a moderate success, *Thoroughly Modern Millie* (1967) was a hit, but the 1968 biography of Gertrude Lawrence, *Star!* sank so low it was unsuccessfully retitled *Those Were the Happy Times*. *Darling Lili* (1970) was good but no smash, and it was not till the 80s that Andrews reemerged in successful films like *S.O.B.* (1981) and *Victor, Victoria* (1982). In *S.O.B.* she eschewed her saintly image for all time by baring her breasts.

SEX SYMBOLS

Earthy, bosomy Continental actresses proliferated as the Production Code was reformed and the Legion of Decency became moribund. Senta Berger had gained some attention in Richard Widmark's 1961 Cold War film, *The Secret Ways*, but both she and Elke Sommer found the 1963 antiwar film *The Victors* the stepping stone to international stardom. Sommer was in *The Prize* that same year and *A Shot in the Dark* in 1964. Berger came to Hollywood for two 1965 westerns, a major one, *Major Dundee*, and a lesser entry, *The Glory Guys*. She made a good spy movie (*The Quiller Memorandum*, 1966), and a poor spoof (*The Ambushers*, 1967). Irina Demich, a Darryl F. Zanuck protégé, was noticed in *The Longest Day* (1962). Swedish Britt Ekland married Peter Sellers and starred with him in *The Bobo* (1967) and the splendid 1968 tribute to the bygone days of vaudeville and burlesque, *The Night They Raided Minsky's*. Claudia Cardinale made hay after *The Pink Panther* (1964) by starring with John Wayne that same year in *Circus World*, with Anthony Quinn and George Segal in *Lost Command* (1966), and opposite Burt Lancaster and Lee Marvin in the western *The Professionals* (1966), in which she played a Mexican. Virna Lisi came on strong in *How to Murder Your Wife* (1965) and *Not with My Wife, You Don't!* (1966). The exotic Ursula Andress mastered the bikini in *Dr. No* (1962), starred with Anita Ekberg, Frank Sinatra, and Dean Martin in *Four for Texas* (1963) and as *She* (1965). Gila Golan, from Israel, filled a bikini just as well in *Our Man Flint* (1966). Giovanna Ralli was never so well known but was James Coburn's female lead in *What Did You Do in the War, Daddy?* (1966) and Michael Caine's accomplice in *Deadfall* (1968). Equally forgotten now, Rosanna Schiaffino was another *Victors* alumnus who costarred in *Arrivederci, Baby!* German Romy Schneider, also from *The Victors*, was in *The Cardinal* (1963) and *Good Neighbor Sam* (1964). Eva Renzi starred with Caine in *Funeral in Berlin* (1966), Camilla Sparv with Robert Redford in *Downhill Racer* (1969).

American-made sex symbols included Carroll Baker in *The Carpetbaggers* (1964), *Station Six—Sahara* (1964), and *Harlow* (1965). Brunette Raquel Welch was a triumph of publicity whose films will never make retrospectives, except for *One Million Years B.C.* (1967), which will undoubtedly be seen at special effects master Ray Harryhausen tributes. *100 Rifles* (1969) caused a mild stir from its advertisement, which showed Welch hugging Jim Brown. Sharon Tate was in *Valley of the Dolls* and *The Fearless Vampire Killers* (both 1967), the latter directed by husband Roman Polanski.

Bullitt (Warner Bros., 1968) was a no-nonsense, how-things-work crime drama with Steve McQueen. Its car chase through San Francisco became the standard by which cinematic auto pursuits would be gauged.

From the United Kingdom came Jacqueline Bisset (*The Grasshopper, Bullitt,* 1968) and Julie Christie, who after her Academy Award for the 1965 *Darling,* could call her own shots on both sides of the Atlantic. She played Thomas Hardy's heroine Bathsheba Everdene in the 1967 roadshow *Far from the Madding Crowd.* Samantha Eggar was in demand after *The Collector* (1965). After *Tunes of Glory* in 1960, *Freud* in 1962, and *Tom Jones* in 1963, Susannah York made a number of films all over the globe, including *The 7th Dawn* (1964) in the Far East and *Sands of the Kalahari* (1965) in Africa.

GLOSSY REMAKES

In *Imitation of Life* (1959), Lana Turner reprised the Claudette Colbert role. In *Back Street* (1961) and *Stolen Hours* (1963), Susan Hayward played the

Irene Dunne/Margaret Sullavan role in the first, the Bette Davis role in the second, which was a color remake of *Dark Victory*. "Glossy" was an oft-used term for these remakes—or "zombified descendants" of their comedy-drama progenitors.[57] Producer Ross Hunter took heat for some of these. They were invariably inferior to the originals, perhaps because the stories had suited a different age.

Some remakes succeeded, in particular *An Affair to Remember* (1957), a color version of *Love Affair* (1939). Nickie Ferrante (Cary Grant) meets Terry McKay (Deborah Kerr) on an ocean passage; they fall in love and agree to meet at the top of the Empire State Building. Terry is paralyzed in a traffic accident and cannot make the appointment. Later Nickie locates her, and much against Terry's will, learns the truth. "The denouement of *An Affair to Remember* may mark the last time a writer [Delver Daves and Leo McCarey], a director [McCarey], an a pair of actors [Cary Grant and Deborah Kerr] could plumb the ludicrous shallows of the weepie and emerge deliriously triumphant—and the last time Hollywood had the strength to believe in the dreams that made it great."[58]

VIOLENCE

Beach Red (1967) was a fairly big-budget attempt by star Cornel Wilde at an antiwar statement. During the invasion of a Pacific Island during World War II the audience is treated to an arm blown off in the surf. But where was spurting blood? Instant cauterization, perhaps?

Bonnie and Clyde (1967) initiated the ultraviolence of American cinema when Warren Beatty as Prohibition era bank robber Clyde Barrow pointed his pistol to the car window and shot his pursuer on the running board in the face. At the end Clyde and Bonnie (Faye Dunaway, in her first substantial role) are blown away in slow motion by Denver Pyle and his deputies. The violence disgusted many critics. Old guard dean of critics Bosley Crowther said, "It is a cheap piece of bald-faced slapstick comedy that treats the hideous depredations of that sleazy, moronic pair as though they were as full of fun and frolic as the jazz-age cut-ups in *Thoroughly Modern Millie* . . . strangely antique, sentimental claptap."[59] But the public was entranced, and some critics revised their original opinions; others had pegged it right the first time.

> Two things trouble me about most of the argumentation of the "anti-violence" proponents up to now. One is that they make no distinction, or make unconvincing ones, between gratuitous violence that merely panders to base instincts, and violence that is set in a firm enough dramatic context so that it can have a purging effect. Learning to distinguish between the two and assisting others to tell the difference is a reasonable goal. Expecting to eliminate violence from the screen is not.
>
> My other "problem area" is that implicit in most denunciations of the excesses of the present is the assumption that things used to be better at some unspecified time in the past. I am convinced, however, that our present upheavals are the direct result of evils that were allowed to fester untended and often unrecognized in any and all past ages. Perhaps one reason I admire

Bonnie and Clyde is that it effectively forecloses our option to look with idealized nostalgia on one era of the immediate past.[60]

Mostly enthusiastic, Wilfrid Sheed objected to the gobs of simulated blood: "Converting this into the Siege of Dienbienphu seemed out of key."[61]

Assassination was the topic of John Frankenheimer's controversial 1962 Cold War thriller *The Manchurian Candidate,* featuring Frank Sinatra and Laurence Harvey as repatriated Korean War prisoners. Harvey, however, was far from through with his ordeal. He had been programmed by the Reds, and presidential assassination was his goal. The movie "disappeared" after its initial release, prompting comments that it had been yanked because of the Kennedy assassination. Not true, said Frankenheimer on public radio; it had in fact appeared on television but until the VCR explosion had fallen in the cracks.

President John F. Kennedy was assassinated November 22, 1963, his brother Robert Kennedy on June 6, 1968. Martin Luther King was killed on April 4, 1968. Peter Bogdanovich's *Targets* (1968) played on this theme. Seemingly normal son (Tim O'Kelly) murders family, climbs on storage tanks to snipe at freeway cars. That night he fires into cars from behind the Reseda Drive-in screen. The other plot has Baron Orlok (Boris Karloff) debating the merits of making a personal appearance promoting his latest horror film — at the Reseda Drive-In. In the midst of the commotion he spies the killer searching for bullets. The killer sees him there, and there — up on the screen. Mind akilter, he cannot figure it out and is bludgeoned into a sniveling heap by Orlok.

Pretty Poison (1968) featured Anthony Perkins, who in contrast to his *Psycho* role, this time was the victim of a woman, played by Tuesday Weld, who killed her mother (Beverly Garland).

The Wild Bunch (1969) were Sam Peckinpah's antiquated western gunmen fighting authoritarianism and remaining true to their own code. Only later do they adapt to survive.[62] It is 1914 and the gang rides into a sleepy border town to rob a bank but is ambushed by former gang member Deke Thornton and the scummy bounty hunters (including Strother Martin as Coffer and L. Q. Jones as T. C.) the railroad has hired. Caught in a crossfire, temperance union townsfolk are victims. Some of the gang get away, namely Pike Bishop (William Holden), Dutch (Borgnine), Tector Gorch (Ben Johnson), and Lyle Gorch (Warren Oates). They skedaddle to Mexico, pick up Angel (Jaime Sanchez), then rob a U.S. train for weapons for Generalissimo Mapache (Emilio Fernandez). The posse, the warlord, and his German advisers — these are the villains of the piece. Pike and his men have a code. When Tector says he's gonna get rid of Sykes (Edmond O'Brien, totally unrecognizable as a gruff old coot), Pike makes his spiel for harmony: "You're not gettin' rid of anybody. We're gonna stick together just like it used to be. When you side with a man you stay with him, and if you can't do that you're like some animal! You're finished! We're finished! All of us!" The gang, shorn of Angel by the General, goes berserk and takes on the whole Mexican "army" in a masterpiece of mayhem. Deke and Sykes come late and survey the carnage.

Not only bystanders but the villains of this era get violence done to their persons—in spades. Recall the quick justice for the bad guy in past films like *Dodge City* (1939). Errol Flynn and Alan Hale shot Bruce Cabot and Victor Jory at long range in a rather disappointing finale. In *Cape Fear* (1962) Robert Mitchum's Max Cady was a genuine terror ("Shocking degenerate. I've seen the worst, the dregs, but you. You are the lowest. Makes me sick to breathe the same air," said Gregory Peck) but received only a good thrashing at the finale. Compare the vengeance here with that of *Deliverance* (1972). Ned Beatty was sodomized, and Burt Reynolds and Jon Voight put arrows into Bill McKinney and "Cowboy" Coward. *Variety* complimented the production but found it hardly important or relevant.[63]

In the same year in *The Cowboys* John Wayne was killed after pulverizing Bruce Dern in a fistfight. Wayne's teen cowpunchers took their revenge on the Dern herd rustlers, eliciting cries of outrage from concerned parents. Other villains of this era who mostly received their just deserts included Donald Pleasence in *Will Penny* (1968), Anthony Zerbe in *The Omega Man* (1971), Andy Robinson in *Dirty Harry* (1971), Jessica Walter in *Play Misty for Me* (1971), and Richard Boone in *Big Jake* (1971).

SERVED HIS TIME

"No, not for nothing. Sometimes you've gotta lose before you finally win," said Clint Eastwood's Reb Keith Williams in the 1958 *Ambush at Cimarron Pass*. After years at Universal, noticeably as the pilot who napalmed *Tarantula* and as a lab assistant in *Revenge of the Creature,* Clint Eastwood steadily rose to the top. In the early 60s he costarred with Eric Fleming in the hit television oater "Rawhide," then traveled to Italy, where he became the international star of Sergio Leone's spaghetti westerns *A Fistful of Dollars, For a Few Dollars More,* and *The Good, the Bad and the Ugly.* (Eastwood is an example of those who started their careers in feature films, then ventured into television, and finally became movie stars. Actors and actresses who endeavored to parlay television success into big screen fame almost always failed. Actresses like Elizabeth Montgomery and Lindsay Wagner, who concentrated on television movies, became mired in them.) Back in the States, Eastwood made *Hang 'Em High* (1968), *Coogan's Bluff* (1968), and *Where Eagles Dare* (1969). Although Richard Burton was top cast in the latter, when Eastwood's name appeared on the screen, audiences applauded. He had arrived. In *Kelly's Heroes* (1970) Eastwood led misfits and get-rich-quick G.I.s behind German lines to grab a gold horde. The best elements were the vintage German Tiger and American Sherman tanks, courtesy of the Yugoslavian army. Contrast these with the modern tanks used in *Patton.*

Dirty Harry (1971) was every bit as good as the safer Academy Award–winning crime film that year, *The French Connection.* Directed by Don Siegel, it confirmed Clint Eastwood's star power. Before the credits, the camera pans a monument to the dead of San Francisco's police force. A rooftop swimmer is seen through the telescopic sight of a high-powered rifle. Inspector Harry

Top: In John Boorman's *Deliverance* (Warner Bros., 1972), Herbert "Cowboy" Coward (left) and Billy (later Bill) McKinney played backwoods primitives who terrorized Ned Beatty and Jon Voight until Burt Reynolds put an arrow through McKinney. *Bottom:* Anton Diffring (right), often a movie Nazi, followed his lead role in *The Man Who Could Cheat Death* (1959) with another grand guignol performance in *Circus of Horrors* (American International Pictures, 1960). More significantly perhaps was the presence of Donald Pleasence (left), soon to become a very familiar face to moviegoers.

One of several significant roles Rosalind Cash had in the early 70s was that of jive-talking, cycle-riding survivor of a biological holocaust opposite Charlton Heston in *The Omega Man* (Warner Bros., 1971).

Calahan (Eastwood) is put on the case, finds the empty shell casing on an adjacent skyscraper and a note attached to an antenna. Signed Scorpio, it demands that he receive $100,000 or he will kill a person a day. Then Calahan's lunch is spoiled by a nearby bank robbery. Cornering one of the robbers, he offers him a choice:

> I know what you're thinking. Did he fire six shots or only five? Well, to tell the truth, I kinda forgot myself in all the excitement. But bein' this is a forty-four Magnum, the most powerful handgun in the world, and will blow your head clean off, there's only one question you should ask yourself . . . "Do I feel lucky?" Well, do you, punk?

Back on the sniper case, Calahan and new partner Chico (Reni Santoni) stake out a cathedral. Scorpio shows but is sent packing by Calahan's Magnum rifle.

The police agree to meet his demands after he kills a black youth. Calahan runs the money around town to the monumental cross in Mt. Davidson Park, where the ski-masked Scorpio batters him with intent to kill. Harry stabs his concealed knife into the maniac's leg, eliciting the howl of a wounded animal. Pursued to Kesar Stadium, Scorpio is run to the ground, wounded, and stomped as Harry endeavors to learn the location of a teenage girl his man had kidnapped. Scorpio gets off on a technicality, commandeers a school bus, but is pursued by Calahan to a quarry. Reminiscent of the ending of *High Noon*, Harry tosses Badge 2211 into the drink after the shootout.

Eastwood responded to critics who complained that Calahan was a fascist circumventing the letter of the law to get his man.

> I think the appeal of the Dirty Harry type character is that he's basically for good, and he's got a morality that's higher than society's morality. He hates bureaucracy and he thinks that the law is often wrong. If that's being called fascistic, as several critics have called it, they're full of it.[64]

Dirty Harry was a success whose sequels *(Magnum Force, The Enforcer, Sudden Impact, The Dead Pool)* sadly told us little about Harry's past, although *Magnum Force* showed Harry in his room with a picture of the late wife he had mentioned in *Dirty Harry*.

A valiant commercial but not artistic failure for Eastwood that year was *The Beguiled*. Later on Eastwood would form Malpaso Productions, and direct himself and others (William Holden in 1973 in *Breezy*, Forest Whitaker in 1988 in *Bird*) as well as form an unofficial stock company of versatile actors like Bill McKinney, Geoffrey Lewis, John Larch, John Vernon, Woodrow Parfrey, and Sondra Locke.

SERVED HER TIME

"You've come a long way, Annie," could describe Anne Bancroft in 1962. It had been a journey from her flying trapeze in *Gorilla at Large* (1954) to the role as Annie Sullivan in *The Miracle Worker* (1962). Her portrayal of mentor to Helen Keller (Patty Duke) gave Bancroft "instant" credibility, stardom, and an Academy Award. She chose roles with care and thus did not make a great number of films. *The Pumpkin Eater* (1964) was one of her critically acclaimed ones.

SERVED HIS TIME II

Charles Bronson tied with Sean Connery as the Hollywood Foreign Press Association's 1971 World Film Favorite — Male. Like Eastwood, Bronson had plenty of 50s experience in small roles (originally under his real name, Charles Buchinsky). In 1954 he played Indians in *Apache* (1954) and *Drum Beat* (1954) and a gang member in *Vera Cruz*. In 1958 he was *Machine Gun Kelly* in a low-budget gangster film, and played the lead in a 1958 B western, *Showdown at Boot Hill* ("Nothing to be proud about in an outlaw"). In the 60s he started getting noticed in important supporting roles in *The Magnificent Seven, The Great Escape,* and *The Dirty Dozen*. Again like Eastwood, he went abroad,

Andy Robinson begins the rampage that will involve the San Francisco Police Department, in particular one Inspector Calahan (Clint Eastwood). The film: *Dirty Harry* (Warner Bros., 1971).

where his rough-hewn visage made him a star in *Once Upon a Time in the West* and *Red Sun*. His U.S. breakthrough film was *Death Wish* (1974), which touched a nerve, as had *Dirty Harry*. Protagonist Roy Kersey was a vigilante blowing away muggers in payment for his wife's murder and daughter's rape. The film engendered contradictory opinions. In *Variety* "Murf." wrote that it was "unmarred by any script intelligence . . . very strong potential in the yahoo and popcorn trade . . . a few idea germs . . . but at least script lets him [Bronson] manifest a third dimension."[65] A full-page advertisement in the July 31, 1974, issue of *Variety* contained nine rave review extracts from such critics as Judith Crist, Gene Shalit, and the almost always favorably inclined Rex Reed. Rarely interviewed, Bronson made sequels and other ultraviolent films, often with his wife, actress Jill Ireland.

SERVED HIS TIME III

Like Eastwood and Bronson, Lee Marvin had spent most of the 50s in supporting and character roles. A wounded veteran marine of World War II, he began his film career in the 1951 Gary Cooper service comedy *You're in the Navy Now*. (Bronson was also in this film.) *Hangman's Knot* in 1953 gave him a good villain role. The same year he drew attention by splashing hot coffee in Gloria Grahame's face in *The Big Heat*. After a successful television series,

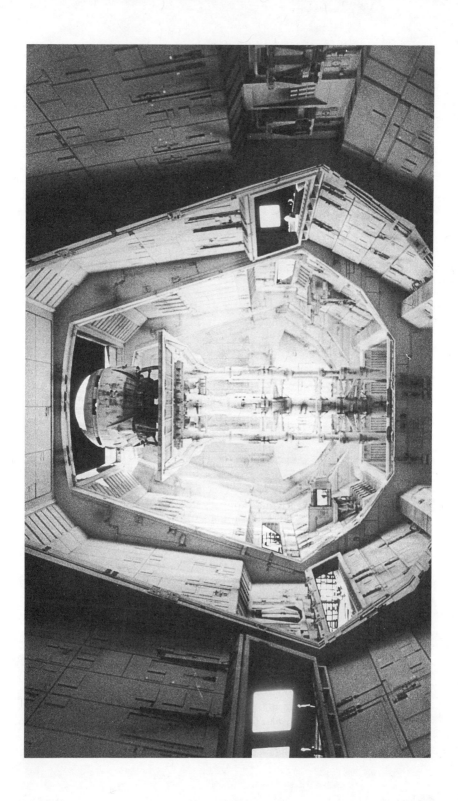

"M Squad," in the late 50s, he was back on film, scoring in *The Man Who Shot Liberty Valance* (1962). He again costarred with John Wayne in *The Comancheros* (1961) and John Ford's *Donovan's Reef* (1963), but nothing prepared him or the audience for his dual role of gunfighter and drunken gunman in the 1965 *Cat Ballou*. He won a best actor Academy Award and became an icon in *The Professionals* (1966), *The Dirty Dozen* (1967), and *Point Blank* (1967).

SERVED HIS TIME IV

Before *Five Easy Pieces* (1970), Jack Nicholson was the star of American International Pictures horror films like *The Terror* (1963), low-budget westerns like *The Shooting* (1966), and antiestablishment films like *Psych-Out* (1968). He wrote some of the screenplays. Then came *Easy Rider* (1969), in which he registered in a supporting role, which led to his big part as a self-made outcast in *Five Easy Pieces*. "I am not a piece of crap," exclaimed girlfriend Rayette Dipesto (Karen Black) before he abandoned her. After 1970 Nicholson was never at a loss for good roles.

ALSO SPAKE ZARATHUSTRA: 2001: A SPACE ODYSSEY

The Randolph Theater on Chestnut Street, center city Philadelphia, May 25, 1968. (Man would land on the moon at 10:56 P.M. on July 20, 1969.) Matinee intermission. A man at the water fountain shakes his head in disbelief. He wanted monsters from *2001: A Space Odyssey,* not a cerebral, mystifying exercise. What would one expect from science fiction writer Arthur C. Clarke and director Stanley Kubrick? Kubrick had begun in the 50s with small films, *Fear and Desire* (1953) and *Killer's Kiss* (1955). *The Killing* (1956) was his first major production, then came *Paths of Glory* (1958), *Spartacus* (1960), *Lolita* (1962), and *Dr. Strangelove* (1964). Like David Lean, Kubrick took pains and time and did not make traditional films.

There were three segments. "The Dawn of Man" described primitive bipeds who discovered a huge black monolith. One has the courage to touch it. Not long afterward his tribe confronts another at the waterhole, and he uses a bone to smash the skull of his enemy. A tool and weapon has been created. Intelligence implanted by the monolith? The apeman tosses his bone skyward to become a rocket ship in the late 20th century (segment two). Mysterious signals have been received from the moon's crater Tycho. Dr. Heywood Floyd (William Sylvester) investigates. A black monolith is found. It is signaling Jupiter. Jump to 2001. The *U.S.S. Discovery,* an immense spermlike, nuclear-powered craft approaches Jupiter. Awaiting the day they must awake three other astronauts from suspended animation, astronauts Dave Bowman (Keir Dullea) and Frank Poole (Gary Lockwood) exercise, send messages to earth,

Opposite: In Stanley Kubrick's *2001: A Space Odyssey* (Metro-Goldwyn-Mayer, 1968) special effects for an outer space film reached state of the art status. From this moon base the investigators journeyed to Tycho crater's black monolith.

converse, and play chess with computer HAL 9000. HAL is having second thoughts about the voyage. What is their mission anyway?

Critical reaction was mixed. Famous last words were written by "Robe." in *Variety*, "Big, beautiful but plodding sci-fi epic. Superb photography major asset to confusing, long-unfolding plot. But should do biz in initial release. . . . But *2001* is not a cinematic landmark."[66] HAL 9000 (Douglas Rain) was reckoned the most human, in a pathetic scene reacting to its dismantling by Dave.

> Just what do you think you're doing, Dave? Dave, I really think I'm entitled to an answer to that question. I know everything hasn't been quite right with me, but I can assure you now, very confidently, that it's going to be all right again. I feel much better now. I really do. Look, Dave, I can see you're really upset about this. I honestly think you ought to sit down calmly, take a stress pill, and think things over. I know I've made some very poor decisions recently but I can give you my complete assurance that my work will be back to normal. I've still got the greatest enthusiasm and confidence in the mission, and I want to help you. Dave, stop. Stop, will you? Stop, Dave. Will you stop, Dave? Stop, Dave. I'm afraid. I'm afraid, Dave. Dave, my mind is going. I can feel it. I can feel it. My mind is going. There is no question about it. I can feel it. I can feel it. I can feel it. I'm—afraid. Good afternoon, gentlemen. I am a HAL 9000 computer. I became operational at the H-A-L plant in Urbana, Illinois, on the twelfth of January 1992. My instructor was Mr. Langley and he taught me to sing a song. If you'd like to hear it, I can sing it for you.

"Not everyone attended *2001*—but just about everyone under thirty did, solemnizing the development of a youthful audience as the decisive element in a firm's success and forcing a shift in producers' tactics that is felt yet today."[67]

Planet of the Apes was also released in 1968 and was an immediate hit. Charlton Heston commented upon the grueling nature of filming the chase early in the film.

> June 29 [1967], Fox Ranch. I spent the entire day pattering barefoot (bare*foot!?,* bare *ass,* for God's sake!) through the undergrowth, picking up more than a touch, I fear, of poison oak; it was luxuriating on every hand. A chase sequence is always easy to act, no matter how complicated it may be to shoot. The fugitive syndrome must lie very near the surface in all of us, ready to burst into the open, panic-stricken.[68]

Oddly, the ape makeup won an Academy Award, whereas the man-apes in *2001* really engendered the questions, "Can these be apes? How did they do it?"

THE GOLDEN AGE OF THE MOVIE SOUNDTRACK

Like the multiplying literature on film, movie music enjoyed a heyday of availability in the late 50s and throughout the 60s. Jazz scores added force to a number of films, including *I Want to Live!* and *Odds Against Tomorrow*. Prolific composers included Elmer Bernstein (steadily improving since *Robot Monster* and *Cat-Women of the Moon* in 1953 to create scores for *The Magnificent Seven* and *The Great Escape*), Henry Mancini (*The Pink Panther,*

Charade, Dear Heart, Man's Favorite Sport, A Shot in the Dark—all in 1964), Jerry Fielding *(The Wild Bunch)*, John Barry *(Zulu, The Wrong Box)*, Jerry Goldsmith *(The Sand Pebbles)*, Lalo Schifrin *(Bullitt)*, and Maurice Jarre *(Lawrence of Arabia, Dr. Zhivago)*. Veteran composers like Miklos Rozsa *(El Cid, The Private Life of Sherlock Holmes)*, Franz Waxman *(Taras Bulba)*, Max Steiner *(A Distant Trumpet)*, Alfred Newman *(Nevada Smith)*, and Dimitri Tiomkin *(The Alamo, The Fall of the Roman Empire)* remained active. Alex North composed his austere but excellent music for the epics *Spartacus* and *Cleopatra*. Deluxe boxed albums that included a hardbound souvenir program were provided for select MGM roadshows: *Mutiny on the Bounty, The Wonderful World of the Brothers Grimm, Ben-Hur,* and *How the West Was Won.*

Contemporary films increasingly featured a signature song in the score. Henry Mancini's scores usually had one, such as *Breakfast at Tiffany's* "Moon River" and the title tune to *Dear Heart*, both popularized by Andy Williams. Burt Bacharach and Hal David wrote the hit song for *Alfie* (1966) and "Raindrops Keep Falling on My Head" for *Butch Cassidy and the Sundance Kid* (1969).

REBELS, MAVERICKS, AND EXPATRIATES

John Cassavetes, sometimes a leading man *(Edge of the City,* 1957, *Rosemary's Baby,* 1968), sometimes supporting actor *(The Dirty Dozen,* 1967) aimed to be creative and produced a cycle of non–Hollywoodish films. In 1968 he wrote and directed *Faces*, starring his wife Gena Rowlands. In 1970 he wrote and directed *Husbands*, which featured himself and his pals Ben Gazzara and Peter Falk.

Forties matinee idol Cornel Wilde directed and produced, often using his wife, Jean Wallace, as his leading lady. They costarred in *The Big Combo* (1955) and *Sword of Lancelot* (1963). *The Naked Prey* (1966) was his best—a thrilling chase film set in Africa. He produced and directed but did not star in *No Blade of Grass* (1970).

George Montgomery, a serviceable leading man of Hollywood action movies and husband of Dinah Shore (1943–60), made the Philippines his home away from home. *Huk* (1956) was one of the many action films he made there. He directed, produced, and coscripted *The Steel Claw* (1961), *Samar* (1962), and *Guerrillas in Pink Lace* and *From Hell to Borneo* (both 1964).

THE LAST GREAT YEAR: 1969

Like 1939, this end of decade year provided a harvest of films, and a variety that would fail to be repeated. *The Wild Bunch* was the last western masterpiece, joining the ranks of *Stagecoach, Red River, High Noon, Shane,* and *The Searchers*. The year was a banner one for oaters. *Butch Cassidy and the Sundance Kid* starred Paul Newman and Robert Redford as lovable train and bank robbers. They loved the same woman, Etta Place, played by Katharine Ross, who was almost fresh from her triumph in *The Graduate* (1967). The

In *The Sand Pebbles* (20th Century-Fox, 1966) Steve McQueen severs the boom the Chinese have set to block the American gunboat's passage. Robert Wise directed the powerful tale set in mid–20s China.

trio traveled to Bolivia when they knew their days as U.S. outlaws were over.

No less entertaining and filmed on equally vivid but greener western locations, near Montrose, Colorado, was *True Grit*. Cinematographer Lucien Ballard photographed both *True Grit* and *The Wild Bunch*.

> But we had great locations on *True Grit*, those beautiful aspen trees, with the natural back-lighting. But we got snowed out of Colorado, snowed out of Lone Pine, and ended up working all over. We were lucky in getting the snow we wanted for the last scene, though—we'd tried to time it that way, and sure enough it snowed the night before we were to shoot it. We had luck, but it was all planned out that way.[69]

As the whiskey-swilling, one-eyed marshal Rooster Cogburn, Wayne escorted Mattie Ross (Kim Darby) in pursuit of her father's killer Tom Chaney (Jeff Corey). A young Texas Ranger (Glen Campbell) accompanied them. Robert Duvall was Lucky Ned Pepper, leader of the outlaw gang. Strother Martin appeared as a horse dealer, making this his third western of the year. Elmer Bernstein's score was yet another of his great western soundtracks (incredibly, the soundtrack album is a jazzed up version). Other 1969 westerns, in descending order of quality, were *The Stalking Moon, The Good Guys and the Bad Guys,* and *Mackenna's Gold*.

Where Eagles Dare was an incredible but highly enjoyable World War II adventure. An Allied officer must be rescued from an Alpine German *schloss* before he divulges secrets of D-Day. Richard Burton and Clint Eastwood are entrusted with the mission. They masquerade as Germans and, with the aid of a female commando (Mary Ure) and barmaid Heidi (Ingrid Pitt), succeed after much derring-do.

> *Where Eagles Dare* is a textbook of techniques, a guide to movie methods in its blending of location photography (great, snowswept mountain vistas) with studio artifice (process and glass shots, miniatures), which are no less effective even when one is being consciously amused by them. This kind of awareness can be enriching when the methodology is so classic, representing, as it does, a direct line of descent from Melies. The methods employed to keep the story moving are no less classic. There are fights on top of cable cars, people hanging perilously over precipices, double and triple twists of plot (which prompt such character comments as "This is incredible!"), guns jammed at key moments, sheer walls to be climbed. It is a movie of almost constant destruction—vehicles, bridges, trees, faces, people, aircraft, with not much differentiation made among them.[70]

The end of the roadshow was assured when not one of the four 1969 mammoth musicals was an unqualified hit. Only *Hello, Dolly!* was a moderate success. *Paint Your Wagon* had fine songs like "They Call the Wind Moriah" but was not as adventurous in a physical sense as it needed to be. *Goodbye, Mr. Chips*, updated to World War II, was unfavorably compared with its straight predecessor of 1939. The best roadshow musical was Bob Fosse's initial directorial outing, *Sweet Charity*. It *did* garner some excellent notices at the time. "Not since *West Side Story* has dance been given the opportunity of contributing so much ambience to a film, and *Sweet Charity* proves even more than its predecessor that the choreographed camera and the kinetic impulse generate a vibrant and viable cinema style."[71] *Variety* praised it but watched others' reactions.[72] Shirley MacLaine perfected her lovable loose-woman character here, John McMartin was funny as an insurance actuary, Ricardo Montalban suave as matinee idol Vittorio Vitale. Sammy Davis was on hand for one number, "Rhythm of Life," that offended some matrons, who found it blasphemous. It was in reality a true 60s film—flower children cheered Charity at the climax: "And she lived hopefully ever after." The movie did not, only recently receiving a favorable reevaluation.

One critic called *Bob and Carol and Ted and Alice* "pretty terrific for a Hollywood comedy,"[73] and advertisement reviews suggested that this Paul Mazursky film was a laugh riot. But some audiences, not recognizing the film as satire, wondered why they were not rolling in the aisles. In truth, it did elicit a number of yucks—for Dyan Cannon's expressions of disbelief when Carol (Natalie Wood, in her first film since the 1966 *Penelope*) shares the news that Bob (Robert Culp) had an affair during a business trip.

The Love Bug was a Volkswagen with a soul that became a big hit for Disney. Another comedy, *Take the Money and Run*, marked Woody Allen's emergence as an auteur. An historical pageant, *Anne of the Thousand*

Days starred Richard Burton as Henry VIII and Genevieve Bujold as Anne Boleyn.

Contemporary, urban malaise was confronted in John Schlesinger's *Midnight Cowboy.*

> *Midnight Cowboy,* sometimes amusing but essentially sordid saga of a male prostitute in Manhattan, should do business as shock, sensation, sex, curiosity, dispute, and the popularity of Dustin Hoffman appearing in his first film since *The Graduate.* . . . It is never easy to work up a liking for either of the two main bums in this pantheon of lost souls . . . is of the modern moment moderne.[74]

Jon Voight was Joe Buck, occasionally haunted by his Texas past, who sought fortune in New York as a male prostitute for ladies who expected *him* to pay.

Past malaise was depicted in *They Shoot Horses, Don't They?* Jane Fonda, Michael Sarrazin, Susannah York, and Bruce Dern performed in a marathon dance emceed by Rocky (Gig Young, the former support for Grant, Gable, Niven, in a supporting actor Academy Award performance).

> Puffy-eyed, unshaven, reeking of stale liquor, sweat and cigarets, Young has never looked older, worse, or acted better. But Miss Fonda, as the unremittingly cynical loser, the tough and bruised babe of the Dust Bowl, gives a dramatic performance that turns her own previous career as a sexual bon-bon upside down and gives the film a personal focus and an emotionally gripping power.[75]

Easy Rider starred Peter Fonda and Dennis Hopper on a motorcycle trip to discover America. Jack Nicholson was lawyer George Hanson.

> 'Course don't even tell anybody that they're not free 'cause they gonna get busy killin' and maimin' to prove to you that they are. Oh yeah, they gonna talk to you and talk to you and talk to you 'bout individual freedom. But they see a free individual it's gonna scare 'em.

Other films included *If,* Lindsay Anderson's not exactly realistic but riveting picture of a British boys school in rebellion. Malcolm McDowell starred. Based on Philip Roth's novel, *Goodbye, Columbus* was almost another *Graduate.* Newcomers Richard Benjamin and Ali MacGraw were the ill-suited lovers. In *The Prime of Miss Jean Brodie,* Maggie Smith reprised her stage role as the iconoclastic, inspiring, but ultimately wrongheaded teacher at the Edinburgh, Scotland, Marcia Blaine School for Girls. Rod McKuen supplied a marvelously evocative score that captured the 30s setting. *The Sterile Cuckoo* was a breakthrough for Liza Minnelli, essaying the role of kookie but lovable Pookie Adams, "outrageously adorable, collegiate gamin who comes on like gangbusters and breaks your heart like Garbo at the fade-out."[76] Wendell Burton was the square lad she seduced and loved and lost.

RODEO CRAZE?

For some reason, Hollywood studios released a rash of rodeo films in 1972. Not one was a big success, though some had charms. *JW Coop* was probably the best. An ex-con (Cliff Robertson) tries to compete on the circuit without benefit of a plane. Sam Peckinpah's *Junior Bonner,* with Steve McQueen, has its champions. *The Honkers,* with James Coburn and Lois Nettleton, was

For the film version of Muriel Spark's serio-comic novel, *The Prime of Miss Jean Brodie* (20th Century-Fox, 1969), most of the more amusing elements were deleted. Nevertheless, Maggie Smith and real-life husband Robert Stephens made it engrossing.

average. *Pocket Money* was too leisurely to be popular, even if it did have Paul Newman and Lee Marvin. *When the Legends Die* explored the Indian question with rodeo as a background. Then there was *Black Rodeo.*

CULT MOVIES

Harold and Maude (1971), a black comedy directed by Hal Ashby and scored by Cat Stevens, was perhaps the definitive cult movie of its time. Displeased that his mother (Vivian Pickles) finds it necessary to invite prospective dates to his home, Harold (Bud Cort) flusters them by fake suicides and mutilations. He sets himself on fire in one scene, chops off his hand in another. He converts a Jaguar into a hearse and falls in love with Maude (Ruth Gordon), eccentric senior citizen resident of a converted railroad car. At her wit's end,

Harold's mother makes an appointment with his army officer uncle (Charles Tyner). With humor not wasted on G.I. audiences, the officer espouses the merits of army life, of combat and duty to country. Having had his right arm blown off, he has rigged the sleeve to salute.

FILM AS ART

Like soundtracks, books about film proliferated in the 60s. *Screen World* had been around in selected bookstores since the late 40s. Attracting renewed attention in the 60s were Marilyn Monroe, W. C. Fields, the Marx brothers, Jean Harlow, Greta Garbo, and especially Humphrey Bogart, who had died on January 14, 1957, but became the existential spokesperson for a generation.

Critic Andrew Sarris developed his auteur theory of the director. (Does auteur equal dogmatist? Were John Huston and William Wellman auteurs or undogmatic men who lent their skills to whatever caught their fancy?)[77] Many young directors, even those who were but hacks who could promote themselves, got carte blanche from studios who believed these people were in tune with the younger generation. Auteur might well equal dogmatist.

Was method acting necessary for cinematic art? Hitchcock, when making *I Confess,* had been disappointed with Montgomery Clift's method.[78] James Mason gave his opinion in 1970:

> Strasberg has taught a false gospel to a certain extent because he hasn't persuaded and taught people that acting is a great creative art, without limits, that a properly equipped actor can not only be a versatile entertainer but he can create characters which are beyond the average imagination. I believe he limits his people and he makes them terribly egotistical and self-centered with the greatest smug regard for their little clique. To hear these actors talking is unbelievable, the way they brag about a marvelous little scene they improvised.[79]

ALL-TIME CHAMPS

According to *Variety,* January 7, 1970, the top money-making films of all time as far as U.S. and Canadian receipts were concerned were *The Sound of Music* ($72,000,000), *Gone with the Wind* ($71,105,300), *The Graduate* ($43,100,000), *The Ten Commandments, Ben-Hur, Doctor Zhivago, Mary Poppins, My Fair Lady, Thunderball,* and *Cleopatra.*[80]

DISASTERS

Disaster epics began again in a big way with *The Poseidon Adventure* (1972). Hollywood had plenty of experience with these in its heyday: *In Old Chicago* (fire), *San Francisco* (earthquake), *Suez* (sandstorm), *The Hurricane.* For those choosing to analyze it further, *Poseidon* was irritating, the best characters killed off gratuitously: Gene Hackman, Stella Stevens, and Shelley Winters. The title song, "The Morning After," sung by Maureen McGovern, should have been sung during the survivors' trek from the top to the bottom of the ship. It was better by far, however, than *Beyond the Poseidon Adventure* (1979).

NEW LIGHTS

With *The Last Picture Show* (1971) director Peter Bogdanovich made headlines with this black and white Larry McMurtry tale of coming of age, sex, and old age in midcentury Texas, where the 1948 *Red River* film was the last picture show.

> The spiritual erosion that seems more likely to take place in small towns than anywhere else is a frequent subject of American cinema. Right now, . . . I can think of no director who has conveyed it better than Peter Bogdanovich in *The Last Picture Show*. . . . We find, moreover, the most accomplished demonstration of how to depict tedium without becoming tedious. . . . What *The Last Picture Show* avoids is the glamour which Hollywood often purveyed in the era it represents. Its intelligently monochromatic photography [Robert Surtees] is clear but never glossy; more often it is on the grainy side, looking more realistic than any colour movie because of the actuality connotations.[81]

American Graffiti (1973) was George Lucas' breakthrough film. Richard Dreyfuss, Paul LeMat, Ronny Howard, Cindy Williams, Charlie Martin Smith, and Candy Clark starred in a popular, nostalgic look at the last summer day and night before high school grads opted for college, a job, or the military. Dreyfuss loses his heart to a blond (Suzanne Somers) in a sportscar he cannot trace. Howard wonders if he should go to college or stay with Williams. Clark has an eventful evening with Smith. The most touching relationship was between teenybopper Mackenzie Phillips and her unwilling baby-sitter, the drag strip king (LeMat). Bo Hopkins provided seriocomic relief as head of the Pharaohs. Wolfman Jack appeared as the DJ he actually was. Innumerable songs were heard in the background, from "Book of Love" to Buddy Holly's "Maybe, Baby." The future Indiana Jones, Harrison Ford, had a small role as LeMat's challenger.

BLAXPLOITATION

Paul Robeson had not been a Hollywood star, exactly, but he had been a presence. Those who followed him in Hollywood were mostly supporting and character actors and actresses: Ethel Waters, Juano Hernandez, James Edwards, Ossie Davis, Brock Peters, Lena Horne.

Harry Belafonte was the next black leading man. He starred in *Carmen Jones* (1954), *Island in the Sun* (1957), and two 1959 films, *The World, the Flesh and the Devil* and *Odds Against Tomorrow*.

In the 50s came Sidney Poitier in important roles in *No Way Out* (1950), *Blackboard Jungle* (1955), *Edge of the City* (1957), and *Something of Value* (1957). He "arrived" in 1963 when he played Homer, who helped the nuns in *Lilies of the Field,* and won a best actor Academy Award. He was a gunslinger in *Duel at Diablo* (1966), and a doctor in *Guess Who's Coming to Dinner?* (1967).

If He Hollers, Let Him Go! (1968) starred Dana Wynter, Kevin McCarthy, Raymond St. Jacques, and Barbara McNair. The advertisement read, "Positively No One Under 18 Admitted To This Theatre During The Showing Of This Torrid Sock-It-To-Me Movie."

Richard Dreyfuss strikes a typically belligerent pose in *The Apprenticeship of Duddy Kravitz* (Paramount, 1974). Dreyfuss needed age to make him lovable. See *Stakeout* (1987).

Then came blaxploitation: action films for an urban audience. *Shaft* (1971), with Richard Roundtree, was primitively filmed but exciting and a big hit. "Now be cool, man." "You ain't so white, baby." "Right on." "Don't ever threaten me again! And don't call me Judas!"

Funded by Harlem businessmen, *Superfly* premiered at the Loews State II and Cine houses in New York and achieved word-of-mouth plugs that made it a hit. "*Super Fly* Goes Through N.Y. Roof on Black Trade," said a *Variety* headline on August 9, 1972. Many blacks objected to this tale of a drug dealer who makes good. It made a star — briefly — of Ron O'Neal. NAACP Hollywood branch president Junius Griffin protested and resigned.[82]

Melinda (1972) with Rosalind Cash, Calvin Lockhart, and karate man Jim Kelly, was "loaded with raw and commercial violence."[83] *Cotton Comes to Harlem* and its sequel, *Come Back, Charleston Blue,* costarred Godfrey Cambridge and Raymond St. Jacques.

Some were not exploitation. *Halls of Anger* (1970) examined ghetto school problems. *Lady Sings the Blues* starred former Supreme Diana Ross in the tragic story of jazz singer Billy Holiday. It was a big, classy production. *Sounder* (1972) featured Paul Winfield, Kevin Hooks, and Cicely Tyson as

Something of Value (Metro-Goldwyn-Mayer, 1957) with Sidney Poitier and Rock Hudson concerned friendship at risk during Kenya's Mau-Mau uprising. It was re-released in the mid–60s under the title *Africa Ablaze* to cash in on Poitier's popularity.

sharecroppers during the Depression and "transcends space, race, age and time."[84]

Jim Brown, the National Football League super fullback of the Cleveland Browns, had retired from the NFL in 1964 after nine sterling seasons. Before leaving he costarred in *Rio Conchos*. Then he landed an important role as one of *The Dirty Dozen*. Next he was a leading man in *The Split* (1968). In *Slaughter* (1972) Brown starred as a former Green Beret and avenger back in the States. "Stella Stevens, naked and clothed, adds to the scenery . . . will appeal to the rough trade."[85] Jim Brown himself wrote,

> I've been asked how far love scenes go. Some go nearly all the way. But some love scenes are overly orchestrated, they look it, watching ESPN is more

Dana Wynter was another lovely British brunette in international films during the 50s. See *Something of Value* (1957), *Fraulein* (1958), *Shake Hands with the Devil* (1959).

exotic. Sometimes in a love scene, you're on your own. The director throws a man and a woman together, tells them to deal. That's what they said to me and Stella Stevens in the movie *Slaughter*.

Stella was blonde and buxom, with full, pouty lips. For our love scene they cleared the room, except for the essential individuals: director, script guy, camera operator, a few necessary crew members. The camera started rolling around the bed, director said, "I'll leave it up to you two." It was the sexiest, hottest, most realistic love scene I've ever done. Stella Stevens was unbelievable. Had they not said Cut, we might have done it.[86]

MARTIAL ARTS: THE OLD MIRROR TRICK

The martial arts saga was initiated by Bruce Lee, tentatively in 1968 in *Marlowe,* when he harassed James Garner and took a mistimed flying leap off a tall building, more fully in the best of the genre, *Enter the Dragon* (1973). At a cost of $550,000, the film had grossed an estimated $10 million as of September 19, 1973.[87] Lee, who would die soon at age 32, Jim Kelly, John Saxon, and Ahna Capri starred in this international production made by British director Robert Clouse and *Bullitt*'s composer, Lalo Schifrin. The story concerns an island near Hong Kong infiltrated during a tournament of martial arts experts. The infiltrators' goal: to destroy a drug ring.

Tom Laughlin, who might have been remembered for small parts as a pilot in *South Pacific* and *Tall Story,* had essayed the title role of avenging 'Nam vet Billy Jack in the primitive 1967 cycle flick, *Born Losers.* In *Billy Jack* (1971) he used his martial arts skills to save wild horses, Native Americans, and underprivileged folk out West. The time was right, and he made lots of money.

Hammer Studios got into the act with *The Legend of the 7 Golden Vampires* (1973). Titles are often deceiving—this was one good film with Dracula gone East but still pursued by Van Helsing (Peter Cushing). There was plenty of action and chills as the bad guys rode or shambled into the village (shades of *The Magnificent Seven!*). Even heroine Julie Ege (late of *Creatures the World Forgot*) suffered an unusual fate worse than death.

South Africa's *Kill or Be Killed* (1980) and *Kill and Kill Again* (1981) starred James Ryan. Most martial arts films were poorly dubbed Hong Kong–produced kung-fu, ninja, or karate martial arts films. Before long Saturday afternoon television substituted these for horror fare.

The biggest martial arts star of the 80s was Chuck Norris, some of whose films were *Missing in Action* (1984), *Missing in Action II* (1985), and *Code of Silence* (1985).

WOODY ALLEN

Take the Money and Run (1969) was his first real film. *What's Up, Tiger Lily?* (1966) had been a set-up job: Woody Allen had taken an Asian film, redubbed it, and inserted himself. He was Jimmy Bond in the 1967 spoof *Casino Royale.* "*Take the Money and Run* is a joy. It's wry and sardonic and Allen's apologetic Virgil Starkwell is a genuine original. . . . There are few belly-laughs. Allen's humour, except in a couple of instances, is firmly anchored in the offbeat and the sly nudge."[88] Amid the lunacy are a chain gang, a misunderstood bank robbery note ("gub," not "gun," says the teller), a mother and father interviewed while wearing Groucho Marx disguises, and a man who literally turns into a rabbi while in prison.

In *Bananas* (1971) Allen was Fielding Melish. He joins a rebel Latin American army, becomes a leader, and, during one campaign, acquires take-out lunches for guerillas. Marx brothers style, the owner is unaware who his customers are until the bill is rejected. "Rebels are we. Born to be free. Just like the fish in the sea," sings Jacob Morales as Esposito. Once the revolution is successful, the new leader lets power go to his head. He makes underwear regs—they must be worn on the outside. In many ways these films are funnier than Allen's later, more critically acclaimed comedy-dramas.

PRODUCT DECLINE

A cursory glance at *Screen World* in the mid–70s can be misleading. There seem to be as many movies as ever, but counting finds that one hundred are

X-rated. *Variety* was filled with articles on cinema pornography: "Expect Film Biz To X-Out Its X" (May 7, 1970); "No Matter How Far Sex in Pix Has Gone, 'You Ain't Seen Nothing Yet'" (June 3, 1970); "Pornopix Tolerance Extensive in N.Y. but Recent Judicial Attack on Gay Orgy Clearer" (May 10, 1972); "Danes' Porno Policy Retreat: Tired of Rep as Smut Mart" (December 13, 1972); "Pornopic Trade in N.Y. Slumpo" (December 18, 1974).

Mike Nichols directed the overrated *Carnal Knowledge* (1971), which became important in the censorship wars. In 1973 in *Miller v. California,* the U.S. Supreme Court said juries should use "community standards" in obscenity tests. The film had been ruled obscene in Georgia, but the U.S. Supreme Court reversed the decision.

> We hold that the film could not, as a matter of constitutional law, be found to depict sexual conduct in a patently offensive way, and that it is therefore not outside the protection of the First and 14th Amendments because it is obscene. No other basis appearing in the record upon which the judgment of conviction can be sustained, we reverse the judgment of the Supreme Court of Georgia.[89]

Violence came in for harsher treatment as time progressed.[90]

There were few musicals, no roadshows, and the few westerns are heralded by antiwesterns like the 1971 releases *Doc, The Hired Hand,* and *McCabe and Mrs. Miller.*

Grosses, if not variety, were up by 1974, a record boxoffice year. *The Godfather, Part II, The Longest Yard, Earthquake, The Trial of Billy Jack,* and *Airport 1975* helped the industry take in between $1.625 and $1.650 billion.[91] *The Godfather, Part II,* was just as long and as good as its predecessor. It cost over $15 million to make and ran for two hundred minutes.

> *The Godfather, Part II* far from being a spinoff followup to its 1972 progenitor is an excellent epochal drama in its own right providing bookends in time — the early part of this century and the last two decades — to the earlier story. Al Pacino again is outstanding as Michael Corleone, successor to crime family leadership.... There should be very few criticisms that the latest film glorifies criminality since the script never lets one forget for very long that Pacino as well as Robert DeNiro, excellent as the immigrant Sicilian who became the crime family chief as played by Marlon Brando in the first pic, and all their aides are callous, selfish and undeserving of either pity or adulation. Yet, at the same time, there's enough superficial glory in the panoramic story structure to satisfy the demands of less discriminating filmgoers. Hence Coppola has straddled the potential audience and therefore maximized the commercial potential.[92]

Product decline affected women severely. In 1974 at the Donnell Library Center in New York a symposium was held: "Filmmaking U.S.A.: A World Without Women." Eleanor Perry, screenwriter for *David and Lisa* (1962), *The Swimmer* (1968) and *Diary of a Mad Housewife* (1970), was the moderator. Speakers included actress Joan Hackett and critic Molly Haskell.[93]

Chapter 8

Getting Serious — and Silly, 1975–1993

It would be wrong, however, to imply that before the late sixties all Hollywood pictures ended in the same warm glow of factitious "bliss." There were many big-budget movies that did not end as the movies do today: a fact that we would recognize at once if any of those earlier films were remade now. Today Rhett and Scarlett would patch things up and have a baby, Shane would come back, Charles Foster Kane would find his sled, Tom Joad would get to be a CEO, and Mildred Pierce would send her daughter out for counseling (and the two of them would end up in a freeze-frame, hugging).

— Mark Crispin Miller,
"Advertising: End of Story," in *Seeing Through Movies*

For many moviegoers, the last quarter of the century has become a feel-good age of anorexic actresses and steroid-enhanced musclemen in movies designed to pitch consumer products. Comic book heroes solve real problems of the present. By the mid–70s there are no roadshows, and most center city movie palaces are razed. Malls, cars, production costs, cable television and other leisure time activities cut into the audience base. Ticket prices escalate, deterring some viewers and making it seem as if the most recent blockbuster is seen by more people than viewed *Gone with the Wind*. Westerns and musicals virtually disappear. Increasingly inane sequels proliferate. Techniques are state of the art but storytelling suffers. Posters become less naïve — but less entertaining. Television advertisements take up the slack.

Videocassette recorders, generally available by the early 80s, become a double-edged sword. The study of film history is facilitated, but until the 90s — when "letterboxing" is more common for films presented on television and video — audiences suffer from movies confined to a small screen and from household distractions. There are few theatrical reissues beyond an occasional restoration such as *Lawrence of Arabia* or *Spartacus* or a 50th anniversary showing of *Citizen Kane*. Hollywood's knowledge of marketing and publicity must be questioned by the decision to present these films in a select few urban theaters. Cutting off one's nose to spite one's face, a new NC-17 rating for the restored version of *The Wild Bunch* aborts a planned 70mm theatrical reissue.

It is easy to condemn film in this era, but it may be too soon to evaluate it reasonably.

DISASTER II

Spawned by *Airport* (1970), a "Grand Hotel" of the sky that proved there was an audience for a traditional, old-fashioned story with a multitude of engaging characters, the modern disaster cycle had begun in style with *The Poseidon Adventure* (1972), and continued through *Earthquake* (1974) and *The Towering Inferno* (1974) to *Airport 1975* (1974), *Two-Minute Warning* (1976), and *Black Sunday* (1977). Gratuitous violence marred some of these stories. Was it really necessary for Jennifer Jones to fall to her death from an outside elevator in *The Towering Inferno?*

SEQUEL-ITIS

Can one imagine *The Robe II* rather than *Demetrius and the Gladiators?* *Broken Arrow II* rather than *Taza, Son of Cochise?* Moviemakers had often made sequels to films, but they usually gave the public some credit. After *Rocky* (1976) greed prompted movie promoters to make certain even a moron recognized a sequel. Not even "The Return of. . ." but rather roman numerals were deemed necessary. *Rocky* itself was rather charming. Rocky Balboa (Sylvester Stallone), "club" fighter — a journeyman with no shot at the title — gets a title bout when heavyweight Apollo Creed (Carl Weathers) decides to create a bicentennial extravaganza in Philadelphia. Rocky trains hard, jogging the streets of Philly and heroically ascending the steps of the Museum of Art. When mousy girlfriend Adrian (Talia Shire) visits Rocky in his apartment, women in the audience swooned at the sight of the muscles rippling beneath the he-man's T-shirt. Rocky did not win the fight, but he went the distance. The film's success was enhanced by a best picture Academy Award.

Rocky was followed by *Rocky II, III, IV,* and *V*. Rocky won a return bout with Creed, had Creed train him to fight Clubber Lang (Mr. T), battled a Russian bionic goliath (Dolph Lundgren), and in a street brawl leveled an ingrate great white hope (Tommy Morrison). The level of punishment meted out by each boxer was unbelievable, and as with Stallone's *First Blood* (which opened the *Rambo* series), the ensuing entries became cartoons.

In the realm of psychological and supernatural horror there are series aplenty that owe their proliferation to the success of John Carpenter's *Halloween* (1978). Carpenter introduced the masked murderer Michael Myers, who in this and its immediate sequel (of five) menaced Jamie Lee Curtis (scioness of Janet Leigh and Tony Curtis) in Haddonfield, Ohio, on October 31. Myers managed to annihilate most everybody except Curtis. *Halloween* and *The Texas Chainsaw Massacre* (1974) may be said to have created the "splatter" film. *Friday the 13th* (1980) and it innumerable sequels carried annihilation further, specifically to the butchery of sexually active teenagers at summer

Rarely garbed this skimpily, Carrie Fisher is rescued by Mark Hamill in *Return of the Jedi* (20th Century-Fox, 1983), the third of the *Star Wars* trilogy.

camp. Usually a "Final Girl"[1] survived to kill the menace—until next year. *Nightmare on Elm Street* (1984) introduced Freddy Krueger into the dreams of teenagers. Its director, Wes Craven, had succeeded with the 1972 low budget shocker *Last House on the Left*. In the hands of a Craven or a John Carpenter, first films in a series were worthwhile. There was no rationale in most progenitor splatter films — not even a passing comment by a character — that the imperviousness of the murderer suggested the presence of a preternatural being.

The excellent modern day adventure set in Latin America, *Romancing the Stone* (1984), with Michael Douglas and Kathleen Turner, was followed in 1985 by its inferior sequel, *The Jewel of the Nile*. Representative of proliferating misleading titles, the Nile, betokening adventure in darkest and greenest Africa, was of no importance in a sand-blasted adventure.

Sometimes the numeral trend was bucked. George Lucas' *Star Wars* trilogy, began in 1977 and included *The Empire Strikes Back* (1980) and *Return of the Jedi* (1983). Steven Spielberg eschewed roman numerals for the Indiana Jones trilogy: *Raiders of the Lost Ark* (1981), *Indiana Jones and the Temple of Doom* (1984), and *Indiana Jones and the Last Crusade* (1989).

In the final analysis, these sequels can be put into perspective: they are the modern serial. Alexander Walker's view applies: "At the best of times Hollywood is not really a creative place: it is an imitative industry in which only a few creative people are tolerated at any one time. What is imitated is the last big success; and in these jittery times, one man's success the night before could be another man's imitation the morning after."[2]

Bespeaking a real lack of imagination in Hollywood, a number of remakes were of foreign-language films: *Sommersby* (1993) of *The Return of Martin Guerre* (1982); *Scent of a Woman* (1992) of a 1974 film; *Point of No Return* (1993) of *La Femme Nikita* (1990); *The Vanishing* (1993) of *The Vanishing* (1988).

SCIENCE FICTION AND FANTASY CARRY THE DAY: "MAY THE FORCE BE WITH YOU!"

After the silliness of *Logan's Run* (1976), one might have expected a lull in science fiction and fantasy. *Star Trek: The Motion Picture* (1979) was hardly the smash expected, and the story was considered a disappointment, a bore. Sequels did follow in the 80s, possibly spurred by the success of another space opera film series.

George Lucas' *Star Wars* stunned the entertainment world when it debuted in 1977. Rapid pace, John Williams' majestic music score, and Dolby sound contributed mightily to its impact. Although they unaccountably eschewed stop-action miniature photography for the most part, Industrial Light and Magic achieved remarkable special effects.

> Like a breath of fresh air, *Star Wars* sweeps away the cynicism that has in recent years obscured the concepts of valor, dedication and honor. Make no mistake—this is by no means a "children's film," with all the derogatory

Nicholas Clay (left) played Lancelot to Nigel Terry's Arthur in John Boorman's erotic, exciting *Excalibur* (Orion, 1981).

overtones that go with that description. This is instead a superior example of what only the screen can achieve, and closer to home, it is another affirmation of what only Hollywood can put on a screen.[3]

The story: Luke Skywalker (Mark Hamill), Princess Leia (Carrie Fisher, Debbie Reynolds' daughter), and Han Solo (Harrison Ford) foil for the nonce the nefarious plans for galactic conquest by the Empire, whose troubleshooter is the imposing Darth Vader (David Prowse, voice by James Earl Jones).

After directing the cult television movie *Duel* and achieving critical plaudits for *The Sugarland Express* (1974), George Lucas' pal Steven Spielberg made a fortune with the popular phenomenon *Jaws* (1975), based on Peter Benchley's best-selling novel about a great white shark terrorizing a New England community. The huge and successful but ultimately disappointing UFO search, *Close Encounters of the Third Kind* (1977), was his first epic science fiction entry. His second became the biggest commercial success in the history of the cinema: *E.T. — The Extraterrestrial* (1982).

Sword and sorcery had their ups and downs. John Boorman's *Excalibur* (1981) was the cream, a violent and erotic rendering of the Arthurian legend. There was also much dross, including *The Sword and the Sorcerer* (1982) and *Legend* (1985). Better were *Labyrinth* (1986) and *The Beastmaster* (1982), better still *Dragonslayer* (1981).

Comic book paeans began with a vengeance in 1978 when *Superman* inaugurated a tribute to superheroes of yesteryear. As usual, this first one was the best of the pack. Who can forget the first time Clark Kent (Christopher Reeve) changes into the superhero and rescues Lois Lane (Margot Kidder) from a helicopter about to topple from a tall building? It had a sense of humor, although Gene Hackman's Lex Luthor and flunky Otis (Ned Beatty) were a bit too broad for the late 20th century. Some found *Flash Gordon* (1980) acceptable as camp. *Swamp Thing* (1982), though not a success for Wes Craven, the director of *Last House on the Left* and the forthcoming *Nightmare on Elm Street*, was an exciting, humorous evocation of a pulp magazine tragic hero. The voluptuous Adrienne Barbeau was a spunky heroine and, as Arcane, Louis Jourdan made a great villain who spouted Nietzscheisms while working to create a superrace from a plant-animal formula.

Perhaps the approach of the millennium caused the making of films about time travel, benevolent (*Always,* 1989, *Ghost,* 1990) and nonbenevolent ghosts (*Poltergeist,* 1982), and body transference (*Chances Are,* 1989, *Made in Heaven,* 1987, *Like Father, Like Son,* 1987, *18 Again,* 1988). Good, not great, but certainly successful, *Back to the Future* (1985) gave time travel films a boost, but *Peggy Sue Got Married* (1986) may have been the best of this subgenre. Of the others, none was worth a second viewing. As for spirits, *Ghost* at least had chilling demons from hell.

TEENS

The R rating allowed for plenty of "teen sex" films. Most were dreadful. Some, like *The Last American Virgin* (1982), turned from outright comedy to downbeat drama. Some critics praised *Valley Girl* (1983), but it was dull. *Where the Boys Are '84* made its 1961 predecessor look like a gem. For some reason, *Penthouse* Pet Corinne Alphen kept her clothes on in the awful *Spring Break* (1983). *My Tutor* (1983) had its moments, especially those with Kitten Natividad. Even Franco Zeffirelli's big scale production, *Endless Love* (1981), was a hoot. As literature it might have worked, but as a film it was utterly unbelievable.

The trend had been building since Elvis and the Beatles: rock and roll stars began replacing movie stars as teen idols. A hot property was always jumped on by filmmakers to make a fast buck. Sixties beach movies had featured sets by up and coming or currently popular rock idols. *Don't Knock the Twist* (1962) and others cashed in on a craze. *A Hard Day's Night* (1964), with the Beatles, was the breakthrough and pinnacle. Later more dramatic parts were given to the likes of James Taylor (*Two-Lane Blacktop,* 1971) and Kris Kristofferson (*A Star Is Born,* 1976). Prince, Sting, Madonna, and the Bangles' Susanna Hoffs tried their hands in film in the 80s and 90s. Most were forgotten a week after their run finished. For all their musical achievements, these performers still considered movie stardom the zenith.

A film about youth and music that stood out was *Saturday Night Fever* (1977), which benefited from and enhanced the disco craze. John Travolta played a Brooklyn lad, lothario, and dance king who found a partner (Karen Lynn Gorney) who helped him evolve on the dance floor and in the real world.

Posing beside some surviving creations, Ray Harryhausen was the master of stop-motion photography for two generations of moviegoers. His special effects usually over-shadowed plot and direction, from *The Beast from 20,000 Fathoms* in 1953 to *Clash of the Titans* in 1981.

Travolta, who had had a small role in *Carrie* (1976), shot to the top, and the movie was a smash. The album battled Fleetwood Mac's *Rumours* for number one. The Bee Gees provided most of the music ("Stayin' Alive," "Night Fever," "You Should Be Dancing," "How Deep Is Your Love?") with able support from Yvonne Elliman ("If I Can't Have You"), the Trammps ("Disco Inferno"),

Woody Allen starred in and directed the Academy Award-winning *Annie Hall* (United Artists, 1977). Frequent Allen co-star Diane Keaton was the title character.

and Tavares ("More Than a Woman"). David Shire composed and arranged "Manhattan Skyline."

In the 80s youthful stars known as the brat pack included Molly Ringwald, Kevin Bacon, Charlie Sheen and his brother Emilio Estevez, Judd Nelson, Ally Sheedy, and Demi Moore. (Sometimes they were interchangeable; Sheedy could have played the role Moore had in *Ghost.*) John Hughes often directed films with these folks. His best were two Molly Ringwald movies, *Sixteen Candles* (1984) and *The Breakfast Club* (1985).

The crazy cast of *Monty Python and the Holy Grail* (Cinema 5, 1975) was, from left: Graham Chapman, Eric Idle, Michael Palin, Terry Jones, John Cleese. Kneeling is the American, Terry Gilliam.

COMEDY

The comedic highlights of this era were provided by Woody Allen, a former stand-up comic directing movies for liberal arts majors. After modifying the Japanese film *What's Up, Tiger Lily?* in 1966 and acting in other people's productions like *Casino Royale* in 1967, Allen wrote, directed, and starred in a string of popular and critical successes: *Take the Money and Run* (1969), *Bananas* (1971), *Sleeper* (1973), *Love and Death* (1975). Paired as he frequently was with Diane Keaton, he touched a nerve with *Annie Hall* (1977), a tale of love won and lost. Alvy Singer: "Probably on their first date, right? Probably met by answering an ad in the *New York Review of Books*. 'Thirtyish academic wishes to meet woman who's interested in Mozart, James Joyce, and sodomy.'" Annie: "Oh, well. La-dee-da, la-dee-da. La-la, yeah." Alvy: "Just don't take any course where they make you read *Beowulf*." In perhaps the funniest scene, the New Yorker satirizes Los Angeles lifestyles, questioning buddy (Tony Roberts) when the latter dons bizarre driving gear. "Max, are we driving through plutonium?" The film won Academy Awards for picture, director (Allen), actress (Keaton), and original screenplay (Allen and Marshall Brickman). *Manhattan* (1979) was *Annie Hall*'s equal. Allen has yet to slow down, although personal problems tarnished his reputation.

Competition for Allen as auteur in the comedy realm was provided by Mel

Brooks and Albert Brooks. Mel was often crude though sometimes quite funny in *Blazing Saddles* (1974), *Silent Movie* (1976), *High Anxiety* (1977), and the 1983 *To Be or Not to Be* remake. The parody of *Star Wars*, *Spaceballs* (1987), was years too late. The most controlled was *Young Frankenstein* (1974) because Brooks obviously knew all the conventions of the 30s horror cycle.

Albert Brooks was never as well known to the general public. Sometimes an actor (*Private Benjamin,* 1980, *Broadcast News,* 1987), he directed and starred in *Modern Romance* (1981) and *Lost in America* (1985). In *Defending Your Life* (1991) he gave Meryl Streep a welcome chance to be silly.

Several funny scenes do not a feature film make. Many comedies were funny but not funny enough. It seems that writers are often unable to produce laughs throughout the entire length of a film. Take *Animal House* (1978), *Revenge of the Nerds* (1984), *Overboard* (1987), *My Blue Heaven* (1990), and *Hot Shots* (1991). Comedy sequels followed *Porky's* (1981), *Revenge of the Nerds* (1984), and *Police Academy* (1984). Often only one scene was really funny, for example, Bob Goldthwait maintaining that a vicious fall down the stairs in *Police Academy* did not hurt. While one or two rollicking sequences could not save a film, sometimes the presence of one accomplished supporting actor could make a film worthwhile. In the generally dismissed *Paternity* (1981) Beverly D'Angelo starred with Burt Reynolds, but as a cruise boat passenger with constant advice about hospitals, Mike Kellin stole the show. As a fabric salesman, he did even better in the same year's *So Fine.*

Several comedy hits—*Home Alone* (1990) and *City Slickers* (1991)—were fantasies, dramas with lessons masquerading as comedies. Advertisements for the former misrepresented the film as a laughfest about a boy who prevents two thieves from burglarizing his home. That was only a segment of the film, whose real theme was family harmony; witness the convergence of mom and dad at the end as well as the elderly man down the block who reunites with his children and grandchildren. *City Slickers* was about male bonding. Each film was contrived, the comedy incidental and ultimately phony.

Child rearing appeared, frequently as a theme in such films as *Mr. Mom* (1983), *Baby Boom* (1987), *Three Men and a Baby* (1987), *Look Who's Talking* (1989), *Parenthood* (1989), *Little Man Tate* (1991), and *Curly Sue* (1991). In their attempts to parody corporate structures, filmmakers—perhaps unaware of the real business world—steered clear of any reality in their comedic barbs. *Working Girl* (1988) was, like the 1980 *Nine to Five,* a fairy tale. Melanie Griffith was promoted from the secretarial pool to a management position in one fell swoop.

SERIOUS BUT NOT SERIOUS ENOUGH

While many comedies had hidden dramatic agendas, many dramas and thrillers were equally false. *The Big Chill,* the 1983 look at a reunion of Vietnam War–era types with coming stars like William Hurt, Meg Tilly, JoBeth Williams, Glenn Close, Jeff Goldblum, and Kevin Costner (whose character is deceased and unseen) was a big hit. The use of old rock music was often praised. It was entirely watchable — even more than once — but shallow.

Fatal Attraction was an even bigger commercial and critical success in 1987. Michael Douglas and Glenn Close costarred in the biggest B movie of them all. Psychotic Close attempted to break up Douglas' marriage, even killing the family rabbit. Later, after presumably drowned in the bathtub, she emerges knife in hand until a bullet ends her rampage. Some critics saw this as a significant discussion of adultery — even though Douglas suffered standard Hollywood retribution for his transgression. Worse, there was no explanation how such an unstable, vicious woman as Close could hold her spiffy, upscale job. This film was no more than a glossy melodrama that had been done more plausibly by Clint Eastwood and Jessica Walter in 1971 in *Play Misty for Me.* Close had made a better thriller, *Jagged Edge* (1985), that did not really become popular till word of mouth spurred video rentals.

Somewhat similar was *Sleeping with the Enemy* (1991), with Julia Roberts as the battered wife of a well-heeled but anal retentive Wall Streeter. Like the Close character in *Fatal Attraction,* Patrick Bergin was highly successful and inexplicably homicidal. Padding the film was a segment in which the camera lovingly photographed Roberts (the face of the 90s?) as she tried on a variety of stage costumes.

The female buddy film *Thelma & Louise* (1991), with Susan Sarandon and Geena Davis, was the object of much analysis. Did anyone trace its ancestry to the 1971 *Vanishing Point* or perhaps even the 1958 *Thunder Road?* On a literal level it was nonsense. Viewed symbolically or metaphorically, it might be otherwise.

Male buddy films proliferated in the 80s. The 1982 film *48 Hours* featured Nick Nolte and that hot comedian from television's "Saturday Night Live," Eddie Murphy. *Beverly Hills Cop* (1984) and *Beverly Hills Cop II* (1987) featured now superstar Murphy and cop Judge Reinhold. The *Lethal Weapon* trilogy that began in 1987 paired Australia's Mel Gibson and Danny Glover. In *Stakeout* (1987), Richard Dreyfuss, partnered by Emilio Estevez, was never so lovable. Bounty hunter Robert DeNiro and prey Charles Grodin complemented each other perfectly in the 1988 *Midnight Run.*

TITLES

Misleading titles accrued to *The In-Laws* (1979), *Nine to Five* (1980), and *Working Girl* (1988) — which is not to say that some of these were not funny. *The In-Laws* was hilarious, made so by the FBI agent (Peter Falk), innocent dentist Sheldon Kornpett (Alan Arkin), and dictator General Garcia (Richard Libertini).

One-word titles proliferated, especially with director Ron Howard, for example, *Willow* (1988), *Parenthood* ("From the opening salvo, however, it also moves further and further away from real life. . . . By comparison, the Addams family [Uncle Fester and all] seem like down-home Americana"),[4] *Splash,*

In *Taxi Driver* (Columbia, 1976) Robert DeNiro gave a chilling performance as Travis Bickle, would-be assassin and befriender of teen prostitute Jodie Foster. "Are you talking to me?"

Oscar. One-word titles were not new. Recall, for example, those British films of the 60s — *Accident, Performance, If.*

VIETNAM

At the height of the Vietnam War — 1969 — producer-director-writer Carl Foreman spoke at UCLA and NYU, suggesting there would probably never be a major film company release representing anti–Vietnam War feelings in the United States.[5] It took time but did occur a decade later, when a Jane Fonda, Jon Voight, and Bruce Dern film explored the issue in *Coming Home* (1978). Oliver Stone's *Born on the Fourth of July* (1989) featured Tom Cruise as paraplegic Ron Kovic.

As for combat films, there was a plethora after the simplistic debacle in 1968 of *The Green Berets*. Few were aware of *Go Tell the Spartans* (1978), with Burt Lancaster, but that same year Michael Cimino's *The Deer Hunter* (1978), with Robert DeNiro, Christopher Walken and Meryl Streep, won Academy Awards. *Apocalypse Now* (1979) was Francis Ford Coppola's fascinating modernization of Joseph Conrad's novel *Heart of Darkness*. It gave Marlon Brando an important role, as it did to Robert Duvall and Martin Sheen. *Rambo* (1985) was cartoonish, a sequel to Sylvester Stallone's rather good *First Blood*. Oliver Stone's *Platoon* (1986), with Charlie Sheen, copped a best picture Academy Award. In 1987 *Hamburger Hill* was overshadowed by Stanley Kubrick's *Full Metal Jacket,* which gave the audience plenty of food for thought as it posed moral dilemmas for Marine Corps recruits in basic training and during the North Vietnamese Tet offensive of 1968.

A Very Brief History of Porn

Russ Meyer had directed the unexpected hit blue movie *The Immoral Mr. Teas* in 1959. In the 60s Meyer had continued financial success with more ambitious projects like *Vixen,* featuring a typically well-endowed Meyer heroine, Erica Gavin. Concurrent with the youth and permissiveness movement spawned in great measure by *Easy Rider* (1969) and on the heels of his successful 1968 skinflick, *Finders Keepers, Lovers Weepers,* Meyer was courted by a major studio. Twentieth Century–Fox let him direct a Grade A "X" film, *Beyond the Valley of the Dolls* (1970). It should have been R-rated because it had nudity, not sex, and Meyer's herky-jerky style never let the camera linger on the flesh of ex–*Playboy* Playmates Dolly Read or Cynthia Myers, who played female rock singers. A better reason for the X rating was the violence. Meyer had a penchant for annihilating his women. Myers was beheaded and Erica Gavin, half asleep, had her brains blown out while sucking on a pistol. Meyer followed with *The Seven Minutes* (1971), a standard courtroom melodrama based on Irving Wallace's novel. His day at the top was over; it was back to items like *Beyond the Valley of the Ultra-Vixens.*

Other filmmakers had gotten into the act — not with major studios to be sure, but the necessity for product and the new freedom allowed independents to show copulation onscreen in major movie houses in cities and suburbs. Before the 80s, with the demise of most adult theaters due to VCRs that returned sex to its proper place — the privacy of the home — porn purveyors had the chutzpah to suggest that established actresses would be disrobing and engaging in onscreen coitus.

Flak *was* taken. Porn star Harry Reems was hauled into court on obscenity charges. *Variety* ran countless articles on porn and its combatants, for example,

Matthew Modine is followed by Adam Baldwin in *Full Metal Jacket* (Warner Bros., 1987), director Stanley Kubrick's disturbing version of Marine Corps training and the 1968 Tet offensive in Vietnam.

"Sex as a Spectator Sport: Liberal Professors Shrug; Incest, Bestiality Treated" (January 8, 1975). *Variety* reviewed X films along with legitimate entries, even complimenting on occasion. A few kudos were lavished on *Expose Me, Lovely* (a 1976 takeoff on the private eye film *Murder, My Sweet,* remade under the book's real title, *Farewell, My Lovely,* with Robert Mitchum in 1975).

> The snail's pace evolution of hardcore pornography into a quasi-fictional form incorporating credible plot is evident in this entry from producer-director-scripter Armand Weston. . . . *Expose Me, Lovely* is porno but for that genre, above run-of-market. Jennifer Welles portrays the voluptuous ex-wife of the detective, and is an asset.

But if *Expose Me, Lovely* was the best X could be, it was light years from quality as either eroticism or storytelling. The amateurish fight scene must be seen to be believed. Queen bee of porn, the mature and lovely, blond Jennifer Welles, did not appear till the very end of the film. Most X films remained plotless, however, and remain footnotes in the history of the commercial cinema.

The best thing about the films became the titles that were often takeoffs on legitimate ones: *Creme Rinse, Beach Blanket Bango, For Your Thighs Only, On Golden Blonde, The Whore of the Worlds, Strangers When We Mate.* Female stars of these opuses took almost equally fascinating monikers: seventies stars like Rene Bond, Annette Haven, Andrea True (whose 1976 disco tune "More, More, More" was a top ten single), Linda Lovelace, Georgina

Film veterans of the 40s and 50s, both Lloyd Bridges (left) and Robert Stack achieved television eminence in the 60s and were given new leases on cinematic life in the disaster movie spoof *Airplane* (Paramount, 1980).

Spelvin, and Marilyn Chambers gave way to 80s-90s porn video queens Christy Canyon, Annie Sprinkle, Lana Burner, Amber Lynn, Ginger Lynn, and Porsche Lynn.

THE FEEL-GOOD AGE

Conglomerates whose real interest was selling other products continued to purchase film studios. Because consumer goods must not be associated with negative images, most movies ended happily, with even the bystanders in the films applauding the denouement. Note that the ending of the stage version of *The Best Little Whorehouse in Texas,* in which the madam leaves, is changed in the 1982 film version, where she *and* the sheriff leave together. All genres were affected and only a few independent films, like Stanley Kubrick's *Full Metal Jacket* (1987), bucked the trend.

> It is natural, when seeking to influence people, to offer an attractive example of the desirable state of affairs, to demonstrate, in dramatic form, the benefits of its working. Yet to show an exemplary world is, in a sense, to assert its actuality; and many people will take it that this splendid state of affairs already prevails. Conversely films which never affirm without first criticizing may be felt as nihilistic; may sometimes intensify an amorality and apathy altogether opposed to their creator's hope that a robust and bracing pessimism could lead to more thoughtful and efficacious action. The interlocking problems can be solved, but if we all solved them the same way art would be very monotonous.[7]

A reworking of *The Big Clock* (1948), *No Way Out* (Orion, 1987) was a fine suspense film that allowed Kevin Costner to validate his status as a compelling leading man.

In *Stripes* (Columbia, 1981) veteran character actor, sometimes star Warren Oates (left) played a drill sergeant in charge of unlikely star Bill Murray, an alumnus of television's "Saturday Night Live." Murray's charm lay in looking normal but acting weird.

STARS

It became more difficult to build a body of work because fewer films were made. Yet some performers were constantly in demand. Although he starred in the occasional bomb like *Ishtar* (1987), Dustin Hoffman built an enviable filmography, including *All the President's Men* (1976), *Tootsie* (1982), and *Rain Man* (1988). Lambasted by most critics, *Hook* (1991) with Robin Williams as a contemporary adult Peter Pan opposite Hoffman's pirate, was a fair financial success. Williams brought his inimitable craziness to *The Fisher King* (1991). Jeff Bridges, scion of actor father Lloyd and brother of actor Beau, was Williams' costar and a relatively unsung actor who had quietly built a reputation in good films like *Starman* (1984) and *Tucker* (1988).

Kevin Costner was a reversion to American stars of yesteryear.

> The romantic tradition is alive and well in Hollywood, embodied in the ambitious presence of Kevin Costner. Like Gary Cooper or Jimmy Stewart, he cannily converts self-effacement into a larger-than-life moral statement. The modest ingrown decency of the heroes he played in *Bull Durham, The Untouchables* and *Field of Dreams* allowed him to reach for the grand gesture without embarrassment. Encased neither in cynicism (like Bruce Willis or Eddie Murphy), superheroic musculature (Schwarzenegger, Stallone) nor dewy youth (Cruise), he's set about reinventing the tradition of diffident nobility.[8]

Costner's greatest success came, unexpectedly, with an entry in what was perceived as a moribund genre — the western. Until the film Costner directed

Top: Cynthia Rhodes (left) helps Jennifer Grey partner Patrick Swayze. The number: Eric Carmen's "Hungry Eyes." The film: the unexpected smash *Dirty Dancing* (Vestron, 1987). *Bottom:* James Spader's vacuum cleaner gift is viewed with some surprise by Susan Sarandon in *White Palace* (Universal, 1990). Sarandon had acted for years before achieving renown as a sexy, gutsy earth mother in *Bull Durham,* this, and *Thelma & Louise.*

as well as starred in, *Dances with Wolves* (1990), Clint Eastwood's *The Outlaw Josey Wales* (1976) was the last epic western. *Heaven's Gate* (1980) had not even received a wide release. *Silverado* (1985) tried but failed. Costner succeeded. The success of *Dances with Wolves* allowed Costner to call his shots. A safe film followed: *Robin Hood* (1991). Controversial was *JFK* (1991), an Oliver Stone film that examined the John Kennedy assassination. (Lest we forget, *Executive Action* had touched on the subject in 1973.) This was followed by yet another safe — and successful — film, *The Bodyguard* (1992).

After a spate of less than successful films, including *The Rookie* (1990), which included elements from *Dirty Harry* (1971), Clint Eastwood reached a goal. The one-time lab assistant *(Revenge of the Creature)*, napalmer *(Tarantula)*, and star of Italian spaghetti westerns was honored with best director and best film Academy Awards for the 1992 *Unforgiven*. He dedicated it to two directors who were influential in his career: Sergio Leone and Don Siegel.

Bill Murray became a star after the primitive but funny *Meatballs* (1979) and the service comedy *Stripes* (1981). After *Ghostbusters* (1984) his financial future was secure, and he dabbled in more serious fare: In *The Razor's Edge* (1984) he essayed the Larry Darrell role Tyrone Power had played in the 1946 version of the Somerset Maugham novel. Although it was a noble effort, the audience had difficulty believing Murray in a straight role. He had come off better in a supporting role in *Tootsie*. Other Murray films often fell into the "funny but not funny enough" category, but the intriguing and gentle *Groundhog Day* (1992) was a critical and commercial success.

Patrick Swayze became a heartthrob in *Dirty Dancing* (1987), had a couple films nobody saw, like *Next of Kin,* then scored again in *Ghost* (1990). Mel Gibson came out of Australia's Mad Max series to become a number one hunk and marketable star, achieving huge success in *Lethal Weapon* (1987) and two sequels. An attractive rebel reminiscent of Montgomery Clift, Tom Cruise scored with younger audiences in 1983 in *Risky Business*. Bigger financial success accrued to *Top Gun* (1986) and *Rain Man*. He was the defense attorney in the 1992 military courtroom drama *A Few Good Men*. Another heartthrob, Richard Gere, did not make that many films. But some were immense successes, like *An Officer and a Gentleman* (1982) and *Pretty Woman* (1990).

Steven Seagal took Chuck Norris's martial arts crown. Stories took a backseat to incredibly violent melees in *Hard to Kill* (1990) and *Marked for Death* (1990) ("You know the feeling — another evening of maiming and killing evil drug lords, and you haven't got a thing to wear."),[9] and villains suffered plenty. In *Hard to Kill* Seagal thrusts a broken pool cue into an already incapacitated scoundrel's chest. A better story and cast accompanied *Under Siege* (1992).

Arnold Schwarzenegger, the former world champion bodybuilder from Austria, acquired a rabid international following. His film origins included a supporting role in *Stay Hungry* (1976) and the excellent 1977 documentary on bodybuilding, *Pumping Iron*. His sense of humor helped his films, which were of variable quality, from the plain dumb *Commando* (1985) and *Kindergarten*

Director and star Clint Eastwood (left) starred with Morgan Freeman in *Unforgiven* (Warner Bros., 1992), a grim western that garnered awards from many quarters.

Cop (1990) to action masterpieces like *The Terminator* (1984), *Predator* (1987), and *Total Recall* (1990).

From England, Anthony Hopkins inherited Richard Burton's mantle: respected actor of stage and screen. His novice movie days included a secret service agent in *When Eight Bells Toll* (1971), based an Alastair MacLean's novel. For some, his first big impression was as the sympathetic Dr. Frederick Treves in David Lynch's *The Elephant Man* (1980). Hopkins enjoyed making big American films. He won a best actor Academy Award for *The Silence of the Lambs* (1991), in which he played the intellectual serial killer Hannibal Lector. He was in two 1992 hits: *Howards End* and the Francis Ford Coppola version of Bram Stoker's *Dracula*.

Remaining on the edge, Jack Nicholson could do what he pleased, whether as the star of *Prizzi's Honor* (1985) or *The Witches of Eastwick* (1987), or in impressive supporting roles like the Joker in *Batman* (1989). Like Nicholson, Robert Redford had enough clout to do what he liked, when he liked. Some were big successes: *The Natural* (1984), *Out of Africa* (1985). Some were not: *The Milagro Beanfield War* (1988). Sometimes Redford directed, as in *A River Runs Through It* (1992). Warren Beatty, like Nicholson and Redford, had enough power to space out his projects. His biggest critical success came with *Reds* (1981), in which he played the real life American correspondent John Reed covering the Russian Revolution. *Dick Tracy* (1990) featured Beatty as the comic strip hero.

Beatty's sister Shirley MacLaine had a renaissance of sorts, winning an

Tom Burlinson and Sigrid Thornton starred in *The Man from Snowy River* (20th Century-Fox, 1982), an Australian film that found an international audience.

Academy Award for *Terms of Endearment* in 1983. She would also contribute to ensemble efforts like *Steel Magnolias* (1989). In *Postcards from the Edge* (1990), MacLaine costarred with Meryl Streep, who showed versatility by singing and dancing here and in *Death Becomes Her* (1992). Streep, "the face of the 80s," followed *Kramer vs. Kramer* (1979) with large-scale movies tailored for her: *The French Lieutenant's Woman* (1981), *Sophie's Choice* (1982), and *Out of Africa* (1985). Nonetheless, an emphasis on action films (with no language barrier for worldwide distribution) meant that few women achieved superstardom. This lack of product meant a dearth of women in film.[10]

Barbra Streisand acted rarely, sang less, but directed and costarred in *Yentl* (1983) and *The Prince of Tides* (1991). Kathleen Turner was the sexiest big star, stirring comment in *Body Heat* (1981) and controversy in *Crimes of Passion* (1984). Susan Sarandon, whose film days go back to the 1970 film *Joe,* became a sexy earth mother in *Bull Durham* (1988), *White Palace* (1990), and *Thelma & Louise* (1991). Debra Winger had a run with three successful movies, *Urban Cowboy* (1980), *An Officer and a Gentleman* (1982), and *Terms of Endearment* (1983). *Black Widow* (1986) was a moderate hit. Although Winger never looked better or more appealing than in *The Sheltering Sky* (1990), the film was too strange to attract a big audience.

With so few good women's roles it became easy for Streep, Sally Field, and Jodie Foster to rack up Academy Awards. Goldie Hawn prospered, surviving mediocre films and those "funny but not funny enough." Another 60s survivor

Top: Former actor Richard Attenborough directs Ben Kingsley in *Gandhi* (Columbia, 1982), an award-winning international triumph. *Bottom:* The year before Sigourney Weaver received so much praise for foiling *Alien,* Genevieve Bujold proved equally resourceful in the suspense thriller *Coma* (United Artists/Metro-Goldwyn-Mayer, 1978).

Academy Award-winning actor Daniel Day-Lewis *(My Left Foot)* played Hawkeye in Michael Mann's epic treatment of James Fenimore Cooper's *The Last of the Mohicans* (20th Century-Fox, 1992). This tale of the French and Indian War was one of a very few cinematic excursions into 18th century North American history.

was singer Cher, who demonstrated acting ability in *Silkwood* (1983) and won an Academy Award for *Moonstruck* (1987). It became a case of fitting the actress to the role rather than the role to the actress, as had been done in Hollywood's heyday.

There were a number of "underappreciated" actresses. These included Kate Nelligan (*Eye of the Needle*, 1981), Beverly D'Angelo (*National Lampoon's Vacation*, 1983), and Theresa Russell (*Impulse*, 1990). There was more room for women in low budget films. Donna Speir and Cynthia Rothrock had followings, but when she chose to work, Linda Blair was the exploitation queen. The 12-year-old subject of *The Exorcist* (1973) and the poorly received *Exorcist II: The Heretic* (1977), the adult Blair retained a childlike voice that marked her as a victim. Her pièce de résistance was *Chained Heat* (1982). In this execrable but entertaining prison film, Linda was jailed for unknowingly helping her boyfriend in a heist. Stella Stevens was a vicious head guard who engineered the drowning of warden — and Linda's rapist — John Vernon in his fish tank. Bisexual Sybil Danning — another B queen[11] — befriended Linda even though she had spurned a shower seduction. Even veteran bad guy Henry Silva was on hand briefly to help in a breakout. *Savage Streets* (1984) gave her more credentials. In this "good trash," Linda used a crossbow to skewer the slime who had killed a girlfriend.

In keeping with a lessening of product, the supporting and character actor pool shrank. Those that achieved renown or were in demand included Charles Durning (*Dog Day Afternoon*, 1975), Ed Lauter (*Breakheart Pass*, 1976), John Vernon (*The Outlaw Josey Wales*, 1976), Robert Webber (*Private Benjamin*, 1980), Jack Warden (*So Fine*, 1981), Richard Libertini (*Best Friends*, 1982), Robert Loggia (*Big*, 1988), Denholm Elliott (*The Razor's Edge*, 1984), Christopher Lloyd in the *Back to the Future* series, Michael Madsen (*Money for Nothing*, 1993) and that ever sprightly crony of Laurence Olivier and Ralph Richardson, John Gielgud (*The Elephant Man*, 1980).

THE AFRICAN AMERICAN EXPERIENCE

The multitude of "blaxploitation" films was leavened with more and more serious depictions of black life. *Cooley High* (1975) was "a heartening comedy-drama . . . combines elements of tenderness and bawdiness with a good 'street' feel . . . no uptight sociological blaxploitation potboiler."[12] A decade later Steven Spielberg took a hiatus from epic adventure to direct *The Color Purple* (1985). Not only were fewer blaxploitation action flicks produced as the 90s approached (*Action Jackson*, 1988), but African Americans themselves took the helm. Spike Lee (*Do the Right Thing*, 1989) and John Singleton (*Boyz N the Hood*, 1991) were the most prominent black filmmakers. In front of the cameras, Denzel Washington was the supporting actor Academy Award winner for *Glory* (1989) and became a presence strong enough to play civil rights leader *Malcolm X* (1992). Morgan Freeman was of equal magnitude, whether accompanying Jessica Tandy in *Driving Miss Daisy* (1989), serving with Denzel Washington in *Glory*, or acting as Clint Eastwood's somewhat reluctant cohort in *Unforgiven* (1992).

On the distaff side, the Supremes lead singer Diana Ross was a smash in *Lady Sings the Blues* (1972) but *Mahogany* (1975) was panned and *The Wiz* (1978) was only a moderate hit. Who would have suspected that standup comedian Whoopi Goldberg would become number one? She surprised many with her portrayal of Celie in *The Color Purple*. A few forgettable films were redeemed by her supporting actress Academy Award performance in *Ghost*. She had a big comedy hit in 1992 with *Sister Act*.

· FROM FAR AFIELD

International success attended South Africa's *The Gods Must Be Crazy* (1984), from Jamie Uys, and Scotland's *Gregory's Girl* (1982), from director Bill Forsyth. The fame that Australia's Bruce Beresford achieved with *Breaker*

Morant (1980) gave him the opportunity in the United States to direct *Tender Mercies* (1983) and *Driving Miss Daisy* (1989). *Black Robe* (1991) was a Canadian-Australian coproduction he directed that was favorably compared with *Dances with Wolves*. English actor-turned-director Richard Attenborough made big, some said flabby, films like *Gandhi* (1982) and *Chaplin* (1992). Actor-director Kenneth Branagh achieved renown for *Henry V* (1989) and *Dead Again* (1991).

THE PAST, THE PRESENT

The National Film Preservation Act of 1988 aimed to preserve the significant American films. The Library of Congress compiled the first list of 25: *The Best Years of Our Lives, Casablanca, Citizen Kane, The Crowd, Dr. Strangelove: Or, How I Learned to Stop Worrying and Love the Bomb, The General, Gone with the Wind, The Grapes of Wrath, High Noon, Intolerance, The Learning Tree, The Maltese Falcon, Mr. Smith Goes to Washington, Modern Times, Nanook of the North, On the Waterfront, The Searchers, Singin' in the Rain, Snow White and the Seven Dwarfs, Some Like It Hot, Star Wars, Sunrise, Sunset Boulevard, Vertigo,* and *The Wizard of Oz.*

Although some suffered as well-rounded storytelling, there were some affecting films made between 1975 and 1993. For example: *One Flew Over the Cuckoo's Nest* (1975), *The Black Stallion* (1979), *Alien* (1979), *Raging Bull* (1980), *Nighthawks* (1981), *Tootsie* (1982), *Victor, Victoria* (1982), *The Right Stuff* (1983), *Amadeus* (1984), *The Karate Kid* (1984), *Ruthless People* (1986), *The Princess Bride* (1987), *Midnight Run* (1988), *Henry V* (1989), *The Adventures of Baron Munchausen* (1989), *Shirley Valentine* (1989), *GoodFellas* (1990), *True Colors* (1991), *The Last of the Mohicans* (1992), *Unforgiven* (1992). Nevertheless, it remains to be seen how many will be worth watching a decade from now, or how many might be designated significant by the Library of Congress.

Epilogue

In my judgment, the theater will never be replaced as the basic
medium for the public showing of current motion pictures.
—Samuel Goldwyn, "Is Hollywood Through?"

Theatrical movies may be a uniquely 20th century phenomenon.
Technology can make them obsolete. Big screen, high-resolution television
screens plus cable services that permit the viewer to dial up "any" film (making
even video stores dinosaurs) might keep audiences home. Most of the grand
movie palaces built in the 20s and 30s have disappeared—they have been
destroyed entirely, converted into parking lots or carved into minitheaters. Yet
new multiplex theaters are undergoing a boom and are more spacious than the
boxes of a few years past. Will enough people continue paying the price of
theatrical admission to ensure that expensive movies show the return necessary
to keep the industry viable? Or will theaters survive only as sites for birthday
parties and the showing of old films?[1]

It will be a shame if Japanese director Akira Kurosawa's words are allowed
to go unheeded because of economic necessity. At the Academy Award telecast
on March 26, 1990, he confessed he did not yet know the essense of cinema.
Perhaps screenwriter Garson Kanin's hopeful 1972 opinion is correct: "You can
make movies out of the dreams that are movies themselves.... But I think that
eventually we shall develop a breed of film-maker who will understand film
and what can be done with it."[2] Questions remain. Where will these movies
be shown? The method of display affects the viewer and the message. Is video
conducive only to small dreams?

Notes

PREFACE

    1. James Stephenson and Guy Phelps, *The Cinema as Art,* rev. ed. (London: Penguin, 1989), p. 222.
    2. Josef Von Sternberg to Alexander Walker in Kevin Brownlow, *The Parade's Gone By...* (New York: Ballantine, 1968), pp. 231–32.
    3. Alexander Walker, *The Shattered Silents: How the Talkies Came to Stay* (New York: William Morrow, 1978), p. viii.

1 THE SILENT ERA

    1. Background of a more primitive sort includes Javanese shadow play, illuminated silhouettes on sticks, magic lanterns, photography itself.
    2. See chapter 2 in Terry Ramsaye, *A Million and One Nights: A History of the Motion Picture through 1925* (reprint; New York: Touchstone, 1986).
    3. Kenneth Macgowan, *Behind the Screen: The History and Techniques of the Motion Picture* (New York: Delacorte Press, 1965), p. 51.
    4. Lewis Jacobs, *Th Rise of the American Film: A Critical History* (New York: Harcourt Brace and Company, 1939), p. 12.
    5. Robert C. Allen, "From Exhibition to Reception: Reflections on the Audience in Film History," *Screen,* Winter 1990, pp. 349–50.
    6. David Naylor, *Great American Movie Theaters* (Washington, DC: Preservation Press, 1987), p. 15.
    7. King Vidor, *A Tree Is a Tree* (reprint; Hollywood, CA: Samuel French, 1981), pp. 16–17.
    8. Allen, p. 352.
    9. Dalton Trumbo, "Stepchild of the Muses," *North American Review,* Dec. 1933, p. 56.
    10. Kevin Brownlow, *The Parade's Gone By...* (New York: Ballantine, 1968), p. 376.
    11. Macgowan, p. 137.
    12. Francis Marion, *Off with Their Heads! A Serio-Comic Tale of Hollywood* (New York: Macmillan, 1972), p. 4.
    13. Brownlow, p. 376.
    14. Neal Gabler, *An Empire of Their Own: How the Jews Invented Hollywood* (New York: Crown, 1988), p. 29.
    15. Brownlow, p. 30.
    16. Macgowan, p. 151.
    17. Vidor, p. 152.
    18. "Negroes Object to Film, Say *Birth of a Nation* Characterizes Race Improperly," *New York Times,* March 7, 1915, p. 13.

19. Kenneth S. Lynn, "The Torment of D. W. Griffith," *American Scholar,* Spring 1990, p. 259.

20. Tino Balio, *United Artists: The Company Built by the Stars* (Madison: University of Wisconsin Press, 1976), p. 46.

21. Ethan Mordden, *The Hollywood Studios: House Style in the Golden Age of the Movies* (New York: Fireside, 1988), p. 93.

22. On acting, Pickford said, "It is not my prerogative as an actress to teach them [the audience] anything. *They* will teach *me.* And that's how it should be, because I am a servant of the public. I have never forgotten that." Brownlow, p. 154.

23. Ben Hecht, *A Child of the Century* (New York: Signet, 1954), p. 435.

24. Elizabeth Kendall, *The Runaway Bride: Hollywood Romantic Comedy of the 1930s* (New York: Knopf, 1990), p. 151.

25. Kendall, p. 17.

26. James Agee, "Comedy's Greatest Era," in Daniel Talbot, ed. *Film: An Anthology* (Berkeley and Los Angeles: University of California Press, 1966), p. 137.

27. Brownlow, p. 131.

28. John Baxter, *Sixty Years of Hollywood* (South Brunswick, NJ, and New York: A. S. Barnes, 1973), p. 58.

29. Douglas Gomery, "If You've Seen One, You've Seen the Mall," in Mark Crispin Miller, *Seeing through Movies* (New York: Pantheon, 1990), p. 58.

30. Gomery, pp. 57–58.

31. Gomery, p. 59.

32. Gomery, p. 59.

2 THE COMING OF SOUND, 1927–1929

1. Harry M. Geduld, *The Birth of the Talkies* (Bloomington: Indiana University Press, 1975), p. 43.

2. Geduld, pp. 39–40.

3. Gilbert Seldes, "The Movies Commit Suicide," *Harpers,* Nov. 1928, p. 708.

4. Neal Gabler, *An Empire of Their Own: How the Jews Invented Hollywood* (New York: Crown, 1988), p. 138.

5. Gabler, p. 141.

6. Mordaunt Hall, *New York Times,* Oct. 7, 1927, p. 24.

7. Hall, p. 24.

8. Alexander Walker, *The Shattered Silents: How the Talkies Came to Stay* (New York: William Morrow, 1978), pp. 60–61.

9. Geduld, p. 253.

10. Geduld, p. 257.

11. Seldes, pp. 711–12.

12. Walker, p. 97.

13. Seldes, p. 709.

14. Walker, p. 46.

15. *New York Times,* July 9, 1928, p. 25.

16. King Vidor, *A Tree Is a Tree* (reprint; Hollywood, CA: Samuel French, 1981), p. 183.

17. Mordaunt Hall, *New York Times,* August 21, 1929, p. 33.

18. Walker, p. 125.

19. Walker, p. 205.

20. Kenneth Macgowan, *Behind the Screen: The History and Techniques of the Motion Picture* (New York: Delacorte Press, 1965), p. 478.

21. Walker, p. 197.

22. Ethan Mordden, *The Hollywood Studios: House Style in the Golden Age of the Movies* (New York: Fireside, 1988), pp. 93–94.

23. Walker, p. 170.

24. Vidor, p. 138.

25. Walker, p. 135.

26. Tino Balio, *United Artists: The Company Built by the Stars* (Madison: University of Wisconsin Press, 1976), pp. 83–84.

27. George Perry, *The Films of Alfred Hitchcock* (London: Studio Vista, 1965), p. 28.

28. Mordaunt Hall, *New York Times,* October 7, 1929, p. 22.

3 THE GOLDEN AGE, 1930–1939

1. John Baxter, *Hollywood in the Thirties* (New York: Paperback Library, 1968), p. 9.

2. "Bank Night," *Time,* Feb. 3, 1936, p. 57.

3. George Perry, *The Films of Alfred Hitchcock* (London: Studio Vista, 1965), p. 34.

4. Alexander Bakshy, "Concerning Dialogue," *Nation,* August 17, 1932, pp. 151–52.

5. Charles Helmetag, "Walter Hasenclever: A Playwright's Evolution as a Film Writer," *German Quarterly* 64.4 (1991): 458.

6. Fritz Lang in Charles Higham and Joel Greenberg, *The Celluloid Muse: Hollywood Directors Speak* (Chicago: Henry Regnery Company, 1969), pp. 108–9.

7. Jean Negulesco, *Things I Did and Things I Think I Did: A Hollywood Memoir* (New York: Simon and Schuster, 1984), pp. 89–90.

8. Negulesco, p. 96. In the 40s Negulesco had full directorial command on such items as *The Mask of Dimitrios, Deep Valley,* and *Johnny Belinda.* In the 50s he was entrusted by Fox with big CinemaScope productions like *How to Marry a Millionaire* and *Three Coins in the Fountain.*

9. Mordaunt Hall, *New York Times,* Jan. 6, 1933, p. 23.

10. George MacDonald Fraser, *The Hollywood History of the World: From "One Million Years B.C." to "Apocalypse Now"* (New York: Fawcett Columbine, 1988), p. 65.

11. *Time,* Nov. 21, 1938, p. 53.

12. Leonard J. Leff and Jerold L. Simmons, *The Dame in the Kimono: Hollywood, Censorship, and the Production Code from the 1920s to the 1960s* (New York: Anchor/Doubleday, 1990), pp. 45–46.

13. Gilbert Seldes, "S-e-x," in Daniel Talbot, ed., *Film: An Anthology* (Berkeley and Los Angeles: University of California Press, 1966), p. 177.

14. For full text see Gerald Gardner, *The Censorship Papers: Movie Censorship Letters from the Hays Office, 1934 to 1968* (New York: Dodd, Mead, 1987); Leff and Simmons; or Cobbett Steinberg, *Reel Facts: The Movie Book of Records* (New York: Vintage Books, 1980).

15. Leff and Simmons, p. 46.

16. Thomas Schatz, *The Genius of the System: Hollywood Filmmaking in the Studio Era* (New York: Pantheon, 1988), pp. 196–97.

17. See Leff and Simmons, p. 47; Steinberg, p. 427.

18. Steinberg, pp. 427–28.

19. "No Particular Taste," *Time,* Dec. 9, 1935, pp. 25–26.

20. Robin Wood, *Howard Hawks* (Garden City, NY: Doubleday, 1968), p. 68.

21. Andrew Bergman, *We're in the Money: Depression America and Its Films* (New York: Harper Colophon, 1971), pp. 132–33.

22. Ethan Mordden, *The Hollywood Studios: House Style in the Golden Age of the Movies* (New York: Fireside, 1988), pp. 182–83.

23. Neal Gabler, *An Empire of Their Own: How the Jews Invented Hollywood* (New York: Crown, 1988), p. 172.

24. This quintuple win of the "major" awards occurred only two more times: in *One Flew Over the Cuckoo's Nest* (1976) and *The Silence of the Lambs* (1991).

25. Elizabeth Kendall, *The Runaway Bride: Hollywood Romantic Comedies of the 1930s* (New York: Knopf, 1990), p. 54.

26. Schatz, pp. 192–96.

27. John Springer and Jack Hamilton, *They Had Faces Then: Super Stars, Stars, and Starlets of the 1930s* (Secaucus, NJ: Citadel, 1974), p. 94.

28. Richard Corliss, *Talking Pictures: Screenwriters in the American Cinema* (New York: Penguin, 1974), p. 146.

29. Ethan Mordden, *Medium Cool: The Movies of the 1960s* (New York: Knopf, 1990), p. 129.

30. Bergman, p. 133.

31. Springer and Hamilton, p. 168.

32. Kendall, pp. xv–xvi.

33. Mordden, *Hollywood Studios*, p. 112.

34. Baxter, pp. 29–30.

35. Bergman, pp. 59–60.

36. Mordaunt Hall, *New York Times*, Dec. 1, 1932, p. 25.

37. Fraser, pp. 69–70.

38. Fraser, p. 54.

39. Flynn and DeHavilland appeared later in *Four's a Crowd* (1938), *Dodge City* (1939), *The Private Lives of Elizabeth and Essex* (1939), *Santa Fe Trail* (1940), *They Died with Their Boots On* (1942), and separately in *Thank Your Lucky Stars* (1943).

40. Hal Wallis and Charles Higham, *Starmaker: The Autobiography of Hal Wallis* (New York: Macmillan, 1980), p. 193.

41. Carrie Rickey, "Mob Rule," *Philadelphia Inquirer*, Dec. 23, 1990, p. 14. Compare "The Western Is American History," in Jim Kitses, *Horizons West: Anthony Mann, Budd Boetticher, Sam Peckinpah. Studies of Authorship Within the Western* (Bloomington and London: Indiana University Press, 1969), p. 8.

42. Bergman, p. 13.

43. Lewis Milestone in Higham and Greenberg, p. 151.

44. Mordden, *Hollywood Studios*, p. 243.

45. Kingsley Canham, *The Hollywood Professionals: Michael Curtiz, Raoul Walsh, Henry Hathaway* (London: Tantivy Press, 1973), p. 29.

46. Mordden, *Hollywood Studios*, p. 232.

47. Bergman, p. 105.

48. King Vidor, *A Tree Is a Tree* (reprint; Hollywood, CA: Samuel French, 1981), p. 225.

49. Wallis and Higham, p. 56.

50. Andrew Sarris, *The American Cinema: Directors and Directions, 1929–1968* (New York: E. P. Dutton, 1968), p. 173.

51. Mordaunt Hall, *New York Times*, March 10, 1933, p. 19.

52. Kendall, p. 98.

53. Andre Sennwald, *New York Times*, Jan. 11, 1935, p. 29.

54. Robert Baral, "Jessie Matthews' Memoirs," *Variety*, Jan. 19, 1977, p. 36.

55. Fraser, p. 126.

56. Andre Bazin, *Orson Welles: A Critical View* (New York: Harper Colophon, 1978), p. 34.

57. Mordden, *Hollywood Studios*, p. 97.

58. Houston, Penelope, and Gillett, John, "Kanin Talking," *Sight and Sound*, Summer 1972, p. 135.

59. Norman Zierold, *The Moguls* (New York: Avon, 1969), p.32.

60. Mordden, *Medium Cool*, p. 50.

61. Mordaunt Hall, *New York Times*, March 15, 1930, p. 22.

62. Bergman, pp. 53–54.

63. J. T. V., *New York Times*, Oct. 3, 1932, p. 15.

64. Edward G. Robinson in 1963 interview quoted in David Shipman, *The Great Stars: The Golden Years* (New York: Crown, 1970), p. 465.

65. Mordden, *Hollywood Studios*, p. 153.

66. Shipman, p. 451.

67. Robin Cross, *The Big Book of B Movies, or How Low Was My Budget* (New York: St. Martin's Press, 1981), p. 6.

68. Leslie Halliwell, *Halliwell's Harvest* (New York: Charles Scribner's, 1986), p. 157.

69. Gavin Lambert, *GWTW: The Making of "Gone with the Wind"* (Boston: Little, Brown, 1973), pp. 84–85.

70. Letter from David O. Selznick to Ed Sullivan, Sept. 20, 1938, in Rudy Behlmer, ed., *Memo from David O. Selznick* (New York: Viking, 1972), p. 167.

71. Letter to Selznick's assistant and secretary of Selznick International Corporation, Daniel T. O'Shea, Nov. 21, 1938, in Behlmer, pp. 181–82.

72. Lambert, p. 56.

73. Letter to *New York Daily News* Hollywood columnist Ed Sullivan, Jan. 7, 1939, in Behlmer, p. 193.

74. Ben Hecht, *A Child of the Century* (New York: Signet, 1954), p. 456.

75. Frank S. Nugent, *New York Times*, Dec. 20, 1939, p. 31.

76. Surely the most used tune in cinema history is "Auld Lang Syne," heard this year most prominently here and in *Mr. Smith Goes to Washington*. To name a few of the innumerable films with the tune: *One More River* (1934), *Two in a Crowd* (1936), *Meet Me in St. Louis* (1944), *Buffalo Bill* (1944), *It's a Wonderful Life* (1946), *Room for One More* (1952), *Bundle of Joy* (1956), *Operation Petticoat* (1959), *Pocketful of Miracles* (1961), *The Interns* (1962), *Sleuth* (1972).

77. Frank S. Nugent, *New York Times*, Aug. 18, 1939, p. 16.

78. Frank S. Nugent, *New York Times*, April 21, 1939, p. 27.

4 THE WAR YEARS, 1940–1945

1. Hal Wallis and Charles Higham, *Starmaker: The Autobiography of Hal Wallis* (New York: Macmillan, 1980), p. 72. Kosleck also played Goebbels in *The Hitler Gang* (1944) and in 1962 in *Hitler!*

2. Curtis Bernhardt in Charles Higham and Joel Greenberg, *The Celluloid Muse: Hollywood Directors Speak* (Chicago: Henry Regnery Company, 1969), p. 45.

3. Leslie Halliwell, *Halliwell's Film Guide*, 7th ed. (New York: Harper and Row, 1989), p. 268.

4. *Times*, Jan. 3, 1943, p. 6.

5. Wallis and Higham, p. 95.

6. No Custer film is definitive. Often the soldier is a secondary character, e.g., James Millican in *Warpath* (1951). He is already dead in *7th Cavalry* (1956), while in *Little Big Horn* (1951) a troop of cavalry is unable to warn him. A Custer-like officer

leads his troops to disaster in *Fort Apache* (1948, with Henry Fonda) and *The Glory Guys* (1965, with Andrew Duggan). Robert Shaw's portrayal in *Custer of the West* (1967) is compromised by Spanish "location" shooting. Richard Mulligan makes him a self-important buffoon in *Little Big Man* (1970). One of the few films to pay attention to the surviving divisions of Custer's command is *Bugles in the Afternoon* (1952, Sheb Wooley as Custer).

7. Wallis and Higham, p. 106.

8. Vincente Minnelli in Higham and Greenberg, p. 175.

9. The other Hope-Crosby road films led to *Zanzibar* (1941), *Morocco* (1942), *Utopia* (1945), *Rio* (1948), *Bali* (1952), *Hong Kong* (1962).

10. "New Films in London," *Times*, Sept. 24, 1945, p. 24.

11. "Film and the Allies," *Times*, Sept. 25, 1945, p. 5.

12. "Objective, Burma! Suspended," *Times*, Sept. 26, 1945, p. 4.

13. James Agee, *Nation*, Feb. 24, 1945, p. 330.

14. Jacques Tourneur in Higham and Greenberg, p. 220.

15. Claude Chabrol, "Evolution of the Thriller," in Jim Hillier, ed., *Cahiers du Cinéma: The 1950s, Neo-Realism, Hollywood, New Wave* (Cambridge: Harvard University Press, 1985), p. 161.

16. Edward Dmytryk, *It's a Hell of a Life but Not a Bad Living* (New York: Times Books, 1978), p. 62.

17. Dmytryk, p. 59.

18. Ray Milland, *Wide-Eyed in Babylon: An Autobiography* (New York: William Morrow, 1974), p. 217.

19. John Ford in Peter Bogdanovich, *John Ford* (Berkeley: University of California Press, 1968), pp. 76–77.

20. Kingsley Canham, *The Hollywood Professionals: Michael Curtiz, Raoul Walsh, Henry Hathaway* (London: Tantivy Press, 1973), p. 33.

21. Canham, p. 97.

22. How often was the tune "Some Sunday Morning" used in the dance-hall sequences of Warner Bros. westerns?

23. Lewis Milestone in Higham and Greenberg, p. 162.

24. Other Tracy-Hepburn pairings: *Keeper of the Flame* (1942), *Without Love* (1945), *The Sea of Grass* (1947), *State of the Union* (1948), *Adam's Rib* (1949), *Pat and Mike* (1952), *Desk Set* (1957), *Guess Who's Coming to Dinner?* (1967).

25. George MacDonald Fraser, *The Hollywood History of the World: From "One Million Years B.C." to "Apocalypse Now"* (New York: Fawcett Columbine, 1988), pp. 242–43.

26. Beverly Linet, *Ladd: The Life, the Legend, the Legacy of Alan Ladd* (New York: Berkley, 1979), p. 90.

27. Gregory Peck to Ron Haver, "He's the Man," *American Film*, March 1989, p. 30.

28. "New Matinee Idol," *Life*, Nov. 13, 1944, p. 47.

29. "Court Rules for Actress," *New York Times*, Feb. 3, 1945, p. 16.

30. David Shipman, *The Great Stars: The Golden Years* (New York: Crown, 1970), p. 293.

31. "British Air Liner Lost/Mr. Leslie Howard a Passenger/Attacked by Enemy," *Times*, June 3, 1943, p. 4.

32. "Mr. Leslie Howard/Distinguished Film and Stage Actor," *Times*, June 4, 1943, p. 7.

33. *Nation*, April 26, 1941, p. 508.

34. Hermine Rich Isaacs, "*Citizen Kane* and One-Man Pictures in General," *Theatre Arts*, June 1941, p. 427.

35. François Truffaut in Andre Bazin, *Orson Welles: A Critical View* (New York: Harper Colophon, 1978), p. 7.

36. Gregg Toland, "The Motion Picture Cameraman," *Theatre Arts,* Sept. 1941, p. 652.

37. Truffaut in Bazin, p. 27.

38. Bazin, p. 76.

39. Roger Manvell, *New Cinema in the USA: The Feature Film Since 1946* (London: Studio Vista, 1968), p. 102.

40. Toland, p. 651.

41. Isaacs, p. 432.

42. Andrew Sarris, *The American Cinema: Directors and Directions, 1929–1968* (New York: E. P. Dutton, 1968), p. 117.

43. James Harwood, "U.S. Films Snubbing Bicentennial," *Variety,* July 9, 1975, p. 79.

44. Florabel Muir, "They Risk Their Neck for You," *Saturday Evening Post,* Sept. 15, 1945, p. 34.

45. Murray Schumach, *The Face on the Cutting Room Floor: The Story of Movie and Television Censorship* (New York: William Morrow, 1964), p. 61.

46. "Cleavage and the Code," *Time,* Aug. 5, 1946, p. 98.

5 APOGEE, 1946–1947

1. Thomas Schatz, *The Genius of the System: Hollywood Filmmaking in the Studio Era* (New York: Pantheon, 1988), p. 435.

2. A. D. Murphy, "1974 Looms as 28-Year Peak for B.O.," *Variety,* Dec. 18, 1974, p. 3.

3. "Gen. Bradley Lauds Film," *New York Times,* Dec. 11, 1946, p. 42.

4. James Agee, *Nation,* Dec. 14, 1946, p. 710.

5. William F. Nolan, *The Black Mask Boys: Masters in the Hard-Boiled School of Detective Fiction* (New York: Mysterious Press, 1985), p. 228.

6. Leslie Halliwell, *Filmgoer's Companion,* 6th ed. (New York: Hill and Wang, 1977), p. 419.

7. James Agee, *Time,* Sept. 15, 1947, p. 101.

8. James Agee, *Time,* Nov. 3, 1947, p. 100.

9. Philip T. Hartung, *Commonweal,* Feb. 6, 1948, p. 425.

10. François Truffaut in Andre Bazin, *Orson Welles: A Critical View* (New York: Harper Colophon, 1978), p. 20.

11. "Capra's *Christmas Carol*/The Stewart Touch," *Newsweek,* Dec. 30, 1946, p. 73.

12. Leslie Halliwell, *Halliwell's Harvest* (New York: Charles Scribner's, 1986), p. 170.

13. Gene Tierney and Mickey Herskowitz, *Self-Portrait: Gene Tierney* (New York: Wyden Books, 1978), p. 129.

14. Leslie Halliwell, *Halliwell's Film Guide,* 7th ed. (New York: Harper and Row, 1989), p. 948.

15. Benjamin Harrow, *Film and Radio Guide,* June 1946, p. 39.

16. Carolyn Harrow, *Film and Radio Guide,* June 1946, p. 39.

17. Lenore Vaughn-Eames, *Film and Radio Guide,* June 1946, p. 39.

18. Flora Rheta Schreiber, *Film and Radio Guide,* June 1946, p. 39.

19. Edward Dmytryk, *It's a Hell of a Life but Not a Bad Living* (New York: Times Books, 1978), pp. 89–90.

20. James Agee, *Nation,* Aug. 2, 1947, p. 129.

21. Carolyn Harrow, *Film and Radio Guide,* June 1946, pp. 38–39.

6 SEASONS OF CHANGE, 1948–1955

1. "A Blacklisting Document: The Annual Report of the Committee on Un-American Activities for the Year 1952," *Film Culture,* Summer-Fall 1970, pp. 77–78, plus ten-page Dec. 28, 1952, report.

2. Ethan Mordden, *The Hollywood Studios: House Style in the Golden Age of the Movies* (New York: Fireside, 1988), p. 368.

3. *United States v. Paramount Pictures,* 68 S.Ct. 915. Loew's, Columbia, United Artists, Universal, and American Theatres Association were also cited. *Supreme Court Reporter* 332–335 U.S. 68/October Term 1947. St. Paul, MN: West Publishing, 1948, pp. 915–941.

4. Neal Gabler, *An Empire of Their Own: How the Jews Invented Hollywood* (New York: Crown, 1988), p. 410.

5. *Supreme Court Reporter,* p. 917.

6. *Supreme Court Reporter,* p. 922.

7. Victor McLaglen, Broderick Crawford, Ernest Borgnine, and George Kennedy may at first seem to be unorthodox leading men, but all won best actor Academy Awards. It's a myth that only pretty boys made it big in American films. Contrariwise, except for "the great female grotesques" alluded to in Ian Cameron and Elisabeth Cameron's *Dames* (New York: Frederick A. Praeger, 1969, p. 21), many lovely women, from the radiant Elizabeth Taylor to the more unusual beauty of a Gloria Grahame, graced the silver screen until recent times, when anorexic or gaunt types have been favored and proposed as the ideal.

8. Axel Madsen, *Billy Wilder* (Bloomington and London: Indiana University Press, 1969), p. 143.

9. *Variety,* April 4, 1951.

10. Stal., *Variety,* Sept. 5, 1951.

11. The generally held and unquestioned view is that the best movie posters were produced in the silent era and the first decade or so of sound films. However, a strong case can be made that those posters, although their color and design were top-notch, were rather dull. After all, the audience was virtually captive, and the stars' names and likenesses were usually sufficient to bring in patrons. With the competition from television and other leisure time activities, movies souped up posters in the 50s, adding a pizzazz that makes, say, 1950 to the mid-70s a rather more interesting and entertaining era of poster art.

12. Frank Westmore and Muriel Davidson, *The Westmores of Hollywood* (Philadelphia and New York: J. B. Lippincott, 1976), pp. 194–95.

13. Richard Carlson in Westmore and Davidson, p. 195.

14. "Cinema: Newsreel," *Time,* Sept. 27, 1954, p. 98.

15. Arthur Knight, *Saturday Review,* Aug. 8, 1953, p. 26.

16. "From Here to Eternity," *Collier's,* Aug. 7, 1953, p. 28.

17. Mr. Harper, "Morality Play," *Harper's,* October 1953, p. 93.

18. Philip T. Hartung, *Commonweal,* Nov. 12, 1954, p. 168.

19. John McCarten, *New Yorker,* Oct. 16, 1954, p. 147.

20. Bosley Crowther, *New York Times,* Nov. 9, 1951, p. 22.

21. George Perry, *The Films of Alfred Hitchcock* (London: Studio Vista, 1965), p. 103.

22. Philip T. Hartung, *Commonweal,* Feb. 6, 1948, p. 424.

23. James Agee, *Nation,* Jan. 31, 1948, p. 136.

24. Hollis Alpert, *Saturday Review,* Oct. 3, 1953, p. 44.

25. "The New Pictures," *Time,* Sept. 28, 1953, p. 84.

26. François Truffaut, "A Full View," *Cahiers du Cinéma* 25 (July 1953), reprinted

in Jim Hillier, ed., *Cahiers du Cinéma: The 1950s, Neo-Realism, Hollywood, New Wave* (Cambridge: Harvard University Press, 1985), p. 274.

27. Jacques Rivette, "The Age of *metteurs en scene*," *Cahiers du Cinéma* 31 (January 1954), in Hillier, p. 277.

28. Eric Rohmer, "The Cardinal Virtues of CinemaScope," *Cahiers du Cinéma* (January 1954), in Hillier, pp. 281–82.

29. Robert Warshow, "The Westerner," in Daniel Talbot, ed., *Film: An Anthology* (Berkeley and Los Angeles: University of California Press, 1966), pp. 156–57.

30. Philip T. Hartung, *Commonweal*, April 17, 1953, p. 52.

31. *Time*, April 13, 1953, p. 104.

32. Pete Martin, "The Man Who Made the Hit Called *Shane*," *Saturday Evening Post*, Aug. 8, 1953, p. 53.

33. *Two Flags West* (1950), *Rocky Mountain* (1950), and *Major Dundee* (1965) were others in this western subgenre.

34. DuPre Jones, "The Merit of Flying Lead," *Films and Filming*, Jan. 1974, p. 34.

35. Andrew Bergman, *We're in the Money: Depression America and Its Films* (New York: Harper Colophon, 1971), p. 104.

36. Jim Kitses, *Horizons West: Anthony Mann, Budd Boetticher, Sam Peckinpah. Studies of Authorship Within the Western* (Bloomington and London: Indiana University Press, 1969), p. 29.

37. Philip T. Hartung, *Commonweal*, April 17, 1953, p. 52.

38. Janet Leigh, *There Really Was a Hollywood* (Garden City, NY: Doubleday, 1984), p. 159.

39. Leigh, p. 160.

40. Mordden, *Hollywood Studios*, pp. 162–63.

41. Mordden, *Hollywood Studios*, p. 169.

42. David Shipman, *The Great Stars: The International Years* (London: Angus and Robertson, 1972), p. 182.

43. Miles Kreuger, "Dubbers to the Stars, or Whose Was That Voice I Heard You Singing With?" *High Fidelity*, July 1972, p. 52.

44. John McCarten, *New Yorker*, July 22, 1950, p. 62.

45. Tony Thomas, *Music for the Movies* (South Brunswick, NJ, and New York: A. S. Barnes, 1973), p. 182.

46. John Russell Taylor, *Times*, Feb. 22, 1968, p. 13.

47. Elia Kazan, *A Life* (New York: Alfred A. Knopf, 1988), p. 538.

48. Kazan, p. 538.

49. Kazan, p. 538.

50. Ann Doran was born in Texas in 1913 and contributed to over 150 films and serials from 1934 to 1968: *Charlie Chan in London* (1934), *You Can't Take It with You* and *Blondie* (1938), *Meet John Doe* (1941), *So Proudly We Hail* (1943), *Them!* (1954), *It! The Terror from Beyond Space* (1958), *The Carpetbaggers* (1964).

51. Ethan Mordden, *Medium Cool: The Movies of the 1960s* (New York: Alfred A. Knopf, 1990), p. 30.

52. Axel Madsen, *Billy Wilder* (Bloomington and London: Indiana University Press, 1969), p. 91.

53. Other important 50s cinema wives included Barbara Rush in *Bigger Than Life* and *No Down Payment*, and Joanne Woodward in *No Down Payment*. Working women of the 40s had left the workforce to become these suburban housewives—some happy, others not.

54. Cobbett Steinberg, *Reel Facts: The Movie Book of Records*, rev. ed. (New York: Vintage Books, 1980), p. 68.

55. Myro., *Variety*, Aug. 22, 1951.

56. Michael Balcon, *Michael Balcon Presents* . . . *A Lifetime of Films* (London: Hutchinson and Company, 1969), p. 159.

57. Robert Hatch, *New Republic*, Sept. 26, 1949, p. 28.

58. *Commonweal*, Sept. 16, 1949, p. 560.

59. Donald Lyons, "Dances with Aldrich," *Film Comment*, March-April 1991, p. 72.

7 THE LAST GREAT DAYS OF MOVIEGOING, 1956–1974

1. George MacDonald Fraser, *The Hollywood History of the World: From "One Million Years B.C." to "Apocalypse Now"* (New York: Fawcett Columbine, 1988). Britishers like Boyd, who "wore Roman armour as though it belonged to him" (p. 28), and Hawkins were preferred for Roman roles. Jean Simmons had been in *Androcles and the Lion* and would be in *Spartacus*. Peter Ustinov was Nero and Leo Genn, Petronius in *Quo Vadis* with Deborah Kerr. Claude Rains starred with Vivien Leigh in *Caesar and Cleopatra*. Rex Harrison was Caesar in *Cleopatra*, while Richard Burton was Antony; he'd also been in *The Robe*. Stewart Granger was in *Salome*. James Mason, Greer Garson, Deborah Kerr, and John Gielgud were in *Julius Caesar*; Alec Guinness, Boyd, and Mason in *The Fall of the Roman Empire*. Two fatherly British character actors—Felix Aylmer and Finlay Currie—were fixtures in roadshow and nonroadshow spectaculars and adventure epics. Aylmer appeared in *Hamlet, Quo Vadis, Knights of the Round Table, Saint Joan,* and *Becket*. Currie was in *Treasure Island, Quo Vadis, Ivanhoe, Rob Roy, Ben-Hur, Kidnapped,* and *The Fall of the Roman Empire*.

2. Alex North, *Spartacus*, DECCA DL 79092, 1960.

3. Charlton Heston, *The Actor's Life: Journals, 1956–1976* (New York: E. P. Dutton, 1978), p. 131.

4. *Lawrence of Arabia* program (New York: Richard Davis and Company, 1962), p. 14.

5. Walter Wanger and Joe Hyams, *My Life with Cleopatra* (New York: Bantam, 1963), pp. 12–13.

6. More or less comprehensive treatments of the Egyptian queen were made by Claudette Colbert in *Cleopatra* (1934), Vivien Leigh in *Caesar and Cleopatra* (1945), and Rhonda Fleming in *Serpent of the Nile* (1953). Virginia Mayo played her in *The Story of Mankind* (1957).

7. *Variety*, Jan. 7, 1970, p. 25.

8. Jack Brodsky and Nathan Weiss, *The Cleopatra Papers: A Private Correspondence* (New York: Simon and Schuster, 1963), p. 116.

9. Brodsky and Weiss, p. 23.

10. Brodsky and Weiss, p. 82.

11. Hollis Alpert, *Saturday Review*, June 29, 1963, p. 20.

12. A. D. Murphy, "Still Powerful *Gone with the Wind*," *Variety*, Oct. 18, 1967, p. 6.

13. Joseph Morella, "Par's Big Roadshow Splash," *Variety*, June 25, 1969, p. 3.

14. In *Apache Drums* (1951), the tune was sung during a similar siege by Arthur Shields and citizens.

15. Bosley Crowther, *New York Times*, May 31, 1956, p. 21.

16. Robert Larkins, "Hollywood and the Indian," *Focus on Film*, March-April 1970, p. 51.

17. Richard Corliss, *Talking Pictures: Screenwriters in the American Cinema* (New York: Penguin, 1974), p. 331.

18. DuPre Jones, "The Merit of Flying Lead," *Films and Filming*, January 1974, p. 35.

19. Like actors who play private eye Philip Marlowe, no one seems capable of doing a bad job portraying Wyatt Earp or Doc Holliday. Some other Earp-Holliday combinations: *Frontier Marshall* (1939), with Randolph Scott and Cesar Romero; *My Darling Clementine* (1946), with Henry Fonda and Victor Mature; *Wichita* (1955), with Joel McCrea; *Hour of the Gun* (1967), with James Garner and Jason Robards, Jr.; *Doc* (1971), with Harris Yulin and Stacy Keach.

20. Comparison: Kirk Douglas and Burt Lancaster played opposite each other many times, from *I Walk Alone* to *Tough Guys*. Unless Lancaster had a cameo, as in *The List of Adrian Messenger,* Douglas got second billing. For some reason, Lancaster at first seems just one iota more important. Why? Lancaster did not get his Oscar till 1960. Compare their 50s careers: Douglas had 23 movies released between 1950 and 1959, Lancaster 19. A subjective rating gives Lancaster an average of 3.3 on a scale of 4. Douglas gets 3.1—because he had four films that were 2.0, i.e., fair. On the other hand, Douglas starred in excellent (four-star) films like *Ace in the Hole, Detective Story, The Bad and the Beautiful, 20,000 Leagues Under the Sea, Lust for Life, Paths of Glory,* and *The Vikings.* Lancaster's four-star films are *The Flame and the Arrow, Come Back, Little Sheba, From Here to Eternity, Vera Cruz,* and *The Rose Tattoo.* (This is subjective, remember.) In any case, Douglas needs reevaluation vis-à-vis Lancaster.

21. Edward Dmytryk, *It's a Hell of a Life but Not a Bad Living* (New York: Times Books, 1978), pp. 236–37.

22. Vernon Scott, "H'wood's New Queen Bee Has to Be Natalie Wood," *Philadelphia Daily News,* Jan. 31, 1963, p. 34.

23. Lawrence Cohn, "All-Time Film Rental Champs," *Variety,* Feb. 24, 1992, p. 148.

24. Pauline Kael, *New Yorker,* Feb. 19, 1972, p. 84.

25. Ethan Mordden, *Medium Cool: The Movies of the 1960s* (New York: Knopf, 1990), p. 162.

26. Sidney Pink, *So You Want to Make Movies: My Life as an Independent Film Producer* (Sarasota, FL: Pineapple Press, 1989), p. 53.

27. Bill Warren, *Keep Watching the Skies! American Science Fiction Movies of the Fifties,* vol. 2, *1958–1962* (Jefferson, NC: McFarland & Company, 1986), p. 22.

28. Warren, 2:75.

29. David Pirie, *A History of Horror: The English Gothic Cinema, 1946–1972* (New York: Avon, 1973), p. 47.

30. Pirie, pp. 50–51.

31. Leslie Halliwell, *Filmgoer's Companion,* 6th ed. (New York: Hill and Wang, 1977), p. 184.

32. Leslie Halliwell, *Halliwell's Harvest* (New York: Charles Scribner's, 1986), p. 176.

33. "Chi Critic Ebert Raps 'Living Dead' in *Reader's Digest,*" *Variety,* May 28, 1969, p.34. One year later Russ Meyer's *Beyond the Valley of the Dolls* appeared with a Roger Ebert script. The put-on violence—a Meyer trademark—remained disconcerting.

34. Janet Leigh, *There Really Was a Hollywood* (Garden City, NY: Doubleday, 1984), p. 255.

35. Leigh, p. 256.

36. Judith Crist, *New York,* Feb. 15, 1971.

37. "*Baby Doll,* Condemned in '56, Now R," *Variety,* Oct. 8, 1969, p. 13.

38. Philip T. Hartung, *Commonweal,* Jan. 17, 1958, p. 409.

39. Samuel Fuller in Eric Sherman and Martin Rubin, *The Director's Event: Inter-

views with Five American Filmmakers. Budd Boetticher, Peter Bogdanovich, Samuel Fuller, Arthur Penn, Abraham Polonsky (New York: New American Library, 1969), pp. 177–78.

40. Lem Dobbs, "Obsession: Forever Young" *[The Great Escape]*, *Sight and Sound*, June 1991, p. 31.

41. Axel Madsen, *Billy Wilder* (Bloomington and London: Indiana University Press, 1969) p. 109.

42. Lucien Ballard in Leonard Maltin, *Behind the Camera: The Cinematographer's Art* (New York: Signet, 1971), p. 175.

43. Budd Boetticher in Sherman and Rubin, pp. 66–67.

44. The pace at which television gobbled up old Hollywood product gave someone a brainstorm: make movies for television. Of course, these were not true movies. Under the curse of censorship more than were theatrical films, often made with commercial breaks in mind, featuring has-been and not-yet stars, produced on a fast schedule, frequently made as pilots for possible television series, they were nevertheless popular enough to make them a fixture. "World premiere" was a misnomer. As the years passed, many of these television movies would become lessons in the guise of entertainment. They raise intriguing questions: When is a television movie a miniseries, and vice versa? If a film is made for television but deemed too violent and released to a theater instead, is it really a movie? (See Don Siegel's *The Killers*, 1964.) *See How They Run* with John Forsythe and *The Hanged Man* with Robert Culp appeared on NBC in 1964, the first and second television movies.

45. Alexander Walker, *Sex in the Movies: The Celluloid Sacrifice* (Baltimore, MD: Penguin, 1966), pp. 198–99.

46. Murf., *Variety*, April 26, 1967, p. 6.

47. Alexander Walker, *Hollywood, England: The British Film Industry in the Sixties* (London: Harrap, 1974), p. 223.

48. *Variety*, May 20, 1970, p. 26.

49. Kingsley Amis, *Memoirs* (New York: Summit Books, 1991), pp. 198–99.

50. Murray Schumach, *The Face on the Cutting Room Floor: The Story of Movie and Television Censorship* (New York: William Morrow, 1964), p. 141.

51. Walker, *Hollywood, England*, p. 445.

52. Clive Donner, *Here We Go Round the Mulberry Bush*, soundtrack, 1968.

53. "Catholics Rap Sexier 'Mulberry' Print for U.S.; Nude Stuff Draws 'C' Tag," *Variety*, March 27, 1968, p. 20.

54. "Parents Forewarned Re 'Papillon' as Rough, Father's Plea Rejected," *Variety*, Dec. 11, 1974, p. 3.

55. "Connery, Who May Earn $6-Mil on 'Diamonds,' Wants No More 'Agent 007,'" *Variety*, July 19, 1972, p. 1.

56. Walker, *Hollywood, England*, p. 139.

57. Richard Corliss, *Talking Pictures: Screenwriters in the American Cinema* (New York: Penguin, 1974), p. 312.

58. Corliss, p. 313.

59. Bosley Crowther, *New York Times*, Aug. 14, 1967, p. 36.

60. Moira Walsh, *America*, Sept. 2, 1967, p. 227.

61. Wilfrid Sheed, *Esquire*, Nov. 1967, p. 32.

62. Nigel Andrews, "Sam Peckinpah: The Survivor and the Individual," *Sight and Sound*, Spring 1973, p. 69.

63. Murf., *Variety*, July 19, 1972, p. 14.

64. Joseph McBride, "The Most Powerful Movie Actor in the World: He'll Blow Your Head Clean Off," *Bijou: The Magazines of the Movies*, April 1977, p. 23.

65. Murf., *Variety*, July 24, 1974, p. 20.

66. Robe., *Variety*, April 3, 1968, p. 6.

67. Mordden, *Medium Cool*, p. 185.

68. Heston, p. 275.

69. Lucien Ballard in Maltin, p. 178.

70. Vincent Canby, *New York Times*, March 13, 1969, p. 50.

71. Maria Harriton, *Dance Magazine*, July 1969, p. 26.

72. "Trade Watches 'Charity' on Crix-Mix; Ditto Philip Roth on Screen Material," *Variety*, April 9, 1969, p. 32.

73. Jacob Brackman, *Esquire*, January 1970, p. 40. Notice the bossa nova gyrations the characters do around the house in this and other 60s films like *In Like Flint* and *Sex and the Single Girl*.

74. Land., *Variety*, May 14, 1969, p. 6.

75. Rick., *Variety*, Nov. 26, 1969, p. 14.

76. Rick., *Variety*, Oct. 8, 1969, p. 15.

77. For an alternate view of directors, see science fiction/fantasy writer Michael Moorcock in John Brosnan, *Future Tense: The Cinema of Science Fiction* (New York: St. Martin's Press, 1978, p. 287.) "He was the usual effete type in a leather jacket — they're all called Clive or Lindsay."

78. George Perry, *The Films of Alfred Hitchcock* (London: Studio Vista, 1965), p. 107.

79. Rui Nogueira, "James Mason Talks About His Career in the Cinema," *Focus on Film*, March-April 1970, p. 36.

80. "All-Time Boxoffice Champs," *Variety*, Jan. 7, 1970, p. 25.

81. Gordon Gow, *Films and Filming*, May 1972, pp. 51–52.

82. "WB, Parks Jr. No Talk on NAACP 'Super Fly' Swat," *Variety*, Aug. 23, 1972, p. 5.

83. *Variety*, Aug. 16, 1972, p. 15.

84. Murf., *Variety*, Aug. 16, 1972, p. 15.

85. Murf., *Variety*, Aug. 23, 1972, p. 6.

86. Jim Brown, *Out of Bounds* (New York: Zebra Books, 1989), p. 217.

87. Addison Verrill, "Road to *Dragon* and $10-Mil.," *Variety*, Sept. 19, 1973, p. 3.

88. Richard Davis, *Films and Filming*, Jan. 1971, p. 53.

89. "High Court's 'Carnal' Ruling Seen as Crucial for Cinema Freedom," *Variety*, June 26, 1974, pp. 1, 79.

90. "Think MPAA Moving to Regard Violence and Not Only Erotica," *Variety*, Nov. 20, 1974, p. 4.

91. A. D. Murphy, "1974 Looms as 28-Year Peak for B.O.," *Variety*, Dec. 18, 1974, pp. 3, 24.

92. Murf., *Variety*, Dec. 11, 1974, p. 16.

93. "Film Trade's Femme 'Shutout' Gets Spotlight Tonight (Wed.)," *Variety*, Oct. 9, 1974, p. 7.

8 GETTING SERIOUS—AND SILLY, 1975–1993

1. See Carol Clover, *Men, Women, and Chain Saws: Gender in the Modern Horror Film* (Princeton: Princeton University Press, 1992).

2. Alexander Walker, *The Shattered Silents: How the Talkies Came to Stay* (New York: William Morrow), p. 139.

3. Murf., *Variety*, May 25, 1977, p. 20.

4. Randy Pitman, *Library Journal*, Feb. 15, 1990, p. 228.

5. "Asked 'Why No Anti-Viet War Film?' Foreman Quips, 'Who'd Finance?'" *Variety*, May 28, 1969, p. 4.

6. Sege., *Variety*, March 3, 1976, p. 21.

7. Raymond Durgnat, *A Mirror for England: British Movies from Austerity to Affluence* (London: Faber and Faber, 1970), p. 57.

8. David Ansen, "How the West Was Lost," *Newsweek*, Nov. 19, 1990, p. 67.

9. Rick Marin, "Dressed to Kill," *Premiere*, March 1991, p. 20.

10. Larry Swindell, "They Had More Than Faces," *American Film*, Nov. 1976, p. 66.

11. Not to be confused with B *video* queens like Linnea Quigley, Brinke Stevens, and Michelle Bauer.

12. Murf., *Variety*, June 25, 1975, p. 23.

EPILOGUE

1. Ralph Vigoda, "Going on with the Show," *Philadelphia Inquirer*, December 20, 1990, p. 5-M.

2. Penelope Houston and John Gillett, "Kanin Talking: An Interview," *Sight and Sound*, Summer 1972, p. 139.

Glossary of Film Terms

For comprehensive treatment, see Ira Konigsberg, *The Complete Film Dictionary;* Virginia Oakey, *Dictionary of Film and Television Terms;* and Robert E. Carr and R. M. Hayes, *Wide Screen Movies: A History and Filmography.*

auteur   French word for *author* applied by French critics to directors whose films seem to demonstrate a personal style and worldview; popularized by American critic Andrew Sarris.

B movie   (low) budget films. Strictly speaking, B films have low budgets and consequently employ — presumably — lesser technicians and actors; *Detour* (1945) is considered the definitive B movie.

best boy   gaffer's assistant.

Big 8 Studios   Metro-Goldwyn-Mayer, Paramount, Warner Bros., Universal, 20th Century–Fox, Columbia, United Artists, and RKO.

blaxploitation   fast moving urban films of the early and mid–70s geared toward black audiences and typically focusing on cops, private eyes, dope pushers, and sometimes cowboys and monsters, e.g., *Soul Soldier* (1972), *Boss Nigger* (1975), *J.D.'s Revenge* (1976).

block booking   abolished method by which a studio forced exhibitors (theaters) to take a block of films, be they good, bad or indifferent.

Cahiers du Cinéma   high quality and very influential French film periodical.

character actor/actress   performer playing a type or even a stereotype, e.g., kindly father, rustler, gang member. Ruth Donnelly, Nestor Paiva, Helen Broderick, James Millican, Morris Ankrum, James Griffith are examples.

CinemaScope   wide-screen process introduced by 20th Century–Fox to commercial features in 1953 with *The Robe;* an anamorphic lens ("form anew") takes a scene slightly more than two and a half times as wide as high and squeezes it onto a 35mm negative; a similar lens on the projector swells the scene to the original width; mostly used for color features.

Cinerama   wide-screen process whereby three cameras film the movie and three projectors display it in a theater on a larger, curved screen; in earlier manifestations, two vertical lines could be discerned on the screen, e.g., *How the West Was Won* (1963).

cult movie   usually a low budget film of enough quality and/or eclectic subject matter that it finds a devoted audience and may, in fact, become a financial success, e.g., *Carnival of Souls* (1962), *Night of the Living Dead* (1968), *Harold and Maude* (1971); cult stars include Barbara Steele and Ingrid Pitt.

dailies   unedited day's film.

291

director's cut   implies the original version of a film from the director's point of view—
  before studio moguls mandate different editing. Many films on videotape have
  had scenes added. A problem: Presumably director Jacques Tourneur did not like
  inclusion of a visible demon in *Night of the Demon*. Does this mean the "director's
  cut" eliminates the monster? Ken Russell's *Whore* (1991) came in various formats—R, X, etc.—depending on the video store's policies.

dissolve   one shot fades out and next fades in. See Alfred Hitchcock's *Blackmail* and
  George Stevens' *Shane;* in the latter Jack Palance crosses the barroom via dissolve.

dolly shot / tracking shot   camera's shot taken from a moving platform, e.g., the ar-
  chery contest in *The Adventures of Robin Hood* (1938).

fade   out of a darkening screen a new shot appears.

film noir   French-originated term for Hollywood's "dark cinema," which may be said
  to have begun in 1941 with *The Maltese Falcon.*

foley artist   sound effects person.

frames per second   about 16 in silent movie cameras, 24 in sound.

front projection   a projector whose film or image is bounced off a semitransparent mirror onto a special screen behind the performers. The camera records through the
  mirror. See also **rear projection.**

gaffer   chief electrician.

genre films   oddly, when Hollywood felt that anyone could enjoy any film, studios
  targeted specific audiences with topic movies, e.g., gangster, western, musical,
  crime, melodrama, comedy.

Golden Globes   awards presented by the Hollywood Foreign Press Association, which
  was established in 1940 to cover the southern California entertainment industry.

grip   chief stagehand on a movie set.

lobby card   miniposters, usually 11″ × 13″, with one scene or artwork, displayed in a
  theater.

looping   putting sound to film in the studio.

Lubitsch touch   witty and sophisticated filmmaking taking its name from 30s director
  Ernst Lubitsch and sometimes applied to the work of Rouben Mamoulian and
  Preston Sturges.

major minors   small but respected studios like Republic that were capable of an occasional large-scale production.

matte   backdrop paintings designed to be indistinguishable from live scenes and very
  much used when on-location shooting was not feasible or fantastic elements were
  needed.

melodrama   stories giving plot and action emphasis over character.

method acting   based on the teachings of Russian director Konstantin Stanislavsky and
  promoted by the American Group Theatre and the Actor's Studio in New York,
  it posed a concept of internalization whereby the actor/actress became the
  character he/she was playing.

mise-en-scène   all elements composed in an individual frame of film.

montage   editing to facilitate more than mere narrative progression.

nickelodeon   early motion picture theaters where the price of admission was a nickel.

one-reeler   short films of approximately 11 minutes in length.

pan   scene shown by horizontal camera movement.

Panaglide   harness and strap rig allowing a cameraman to go where traditional
  methods prevent access.

Panavision   trade name for anamorphic lens which squeezes picture onto 35mm film and is later used to project film onto the screen. Sometimes superseded by Ultra-Panavision (a 65mm process with some anamorphic squeeze and special projection lenses to increase image size) and Super Panavision (nonanamorphic 70mm).

persistence of vision   eye maintains an image on the retina after that image has disappeared.

potboiler   lousy movie that may or may not have been designed as a second feature.

poverty row   small studios like Producers Releasing Corporation (PRC) and Monogram that specialized in low-budget films.

pressbook   glossy publication sent to theater owners to help them promote a film; contains star bios, photos (mostly black and white), and sample posters and gimmicks.

producer   a movie's administrator, from (ideally) the beginning to the end of production; Jerry Wald and Hal Wallis supervised innumerable productions during Hollywood's studio years.

programmer   film made to a low standard, e.g., a B western.

rear or back projection (process shot)   to avoid the expense of location filming, a projector projects an image or film onto a screen in front of which are the performers. See *Dangerous Mission* (1954), when Victor Mature and Piper Laurie cross a "lake" in a motorboat.

runaway production   motion pictures filmed outside Hollywood, often outside the United States, to take advantage of cheaper labor and material and to avoid taxes.

rushes   *see* dailies.

screwball comedy   Depression Era comedies where the female character's status was at least equal to the male's.

script "girl"   person who makes sure that costumes, furniture, etc., are the same when retakes are made or the crew returns to the same set.

second feature   a less than sterling film playing the back half of a double feature.

setup   the individual scene in the making of a film; many setups will take place each day as the camera is repositioned or the setting changes.

sleeper   a film of which no one expects much but which achieves audience success. See *Hitler's Children* (1943); cost to make is low, profit unexpectedly high.

splatter films   graphic horror—either psychological or supernatural—films in which much blood is spilled and most of the characters are killed in gruesome ways, e.g., *The Texas Chainsaw Massacre* (1974), *Friday the 13th* (1980).

split screen   two or more scenes shown concurrently on the screen, e.g., *Pillow Talk* (1959), *Bye Bye Birdie* (1963), and *The Thomas Crown Affair* (1968).

squib   explosive pellets of fake blood, e.g., *The Wild Bunch* (1969), or explosive charges representing bullets striking an object, e.g., logs in *The Plainsman* (1936).

states' rights   films sold to distributors on a state by state or specific metropolitan area basis.

stop action (or motion) photography   a painstaking technique for photographing miniature rubber models and sets so that they appear as large as or larger than life on the screen, e.g., *King Kong* (1933).

supporting actor/actress   performers with substantial parts but who are not the featured stars; some actors like Walter Brennan could move between supporting and character parts.

Technicolor   color process most familiar to cinemagoers that was invented by Herbert T. Kalmus and Daniel F. Comstock; originally two-color, e.g., *The Black Pirate* (1926).

Todd-AO   a 65mm photography process used for such 50s films as *Oklahoma! Around the World in 80 Days*, and *Raintree County*. Todd was Michael Todd; AO was the American Optical Company.

VistaVision Paramount's answer to Fox's CinemaScope was to photograph one image onto two frames of film, necessitating a higher and wider screen when projected.

wipe new scene pushes out prior one, signifying passage of place or time, e.g., *Alice Adams* (1935) and *Tom Jones* (1963).

Bibliography

ARTICLES

Albarino, Richard. "Roadshows: Glamour and Grief." *Variety*, April 12, 1967, pp. 7, 24.

Allen, Robert C. "From Exhibition to Reception: Reflections on the Audience in Film History." *Screen*, Winter 1990, 347–56.

"All-Time Boxoffice Champs." *Variety*, Jan. 7, 1970, p. 25.

Andrews, Nigel. "Sam Peckinpah: The Survivor and the Individual." *Sight and Sound*, Spring 1973, 69–74.

Ansen, David. "How the West Was Lost." *Newsweek*, Nov. 19, 1990, pp. 67–68.

Arneel, Gene. "Expect Film Biz to X-Out Its X." *Variety*, May 6, 1970, pp. 1, 92.

"Asked 'Why No Anti-Viet War Film?' Foreman Quips, 'Who'd Finance?'" *Variety*, May 28, 1969, p. 4.

"'Baby Doll,' Condemned in '56, Now R." *Variety*, Oct. 8, 1969, p. 13.

Baker, Lida Belt. "Henry Mancini: Making Film Score Magic." *Instrumentalist*, March 1987, 10–15.

Bakshy, Alexander. "Concerning Dialogue." *Nation*, Aug. 17, 1932, 151–52.

Baltake, Joe. "Don't Be Too Quick to Put the Knock on the 50s." *Philadelphia Daily News*, Sept. 8, 1972, p. 36.

————. "Movies Are Everything." *Philadelphia Daily News*, Feb. 22, 1974.

————. "Secret Confessions of a Movie Groupie." *Philadelphia Daily News*, April 20, 1973, p. 34.

————. "Women Deserve Better." *Philadelphia Daily News*, Feb. 15, 1974.

"Bank Night." *Time*, Feb. 3, 1936, pp. 57–58.

Baral, Robert. "Jessie Matthews' Memoirs." *Variety*, Jan. 19, 1977, p. 36.

Barra, Allen. "The Incredible Shrinking Epic." *American Film*, March 1989, 40–45, 60.

Basinger, Jeanine. "Our Towns: Small-Town America on the Screen." *Bijou: The Magazine of the Movies*, April 1977, 39–42, 59, 60.

————. "When Women Wept." *American Film*, Sept. 1977, 52–57.

Beaupre, Lee. "Black Capers Pace Sequels." *Variety*, Aug. 16, 1972, pp. 7, 30.

————. "Rodeo Themes in Out-Chute." *Variety*, Sept. 6, 1972, pp. 3, 26.

Bernstein, Elmer. "What Ever Happened to Great Movie Music?" *High Fidelity*, July 1972, pp. 55–58.

"Birthday of the Revolution." [CinemaScope] *Time*, Oct. 12, 1953, p. 110.

"A Blacklisting Document: The Annual Report of the Committee on Un-american Activities for the Year 1952." Introduction by Gordon Hitchens. *Film Culture*, Summer/Fall 1970, 77–78, plus 10-page Dec. 28, 1952, report.

Bodeen, DeWitt. "Lon Chaney: Man of a Thousand Faces." *Focus on Film*, May-Aug. 1970, pp. 21–39.

Bombeck, Erma. "Incredible Shrinking Theaters." *Sunday News Journal* (Wilmington, DE), Jan. 21, 1990, p. G3.
Brewin, Bob. "Hollywood Takes on Vietnam." *Video,* Oct. 1987, pp. 52–55, 112.
"British Way with Ratings; 'Violence' Worse Than 'Erotica.'" *Variety,* May 7, 1975, p. 260.
Brooke, Austin. "Hurry Sundown" [drive-ins]. *Joe Franklin's Nostalgia,* July 1990, pp. 26–37.
"Business File: Jerry Goldsmith Calls the Tune." *Films Illustrated,* Feb. 1976, p. 218.
Butler, Ivan. "Cinema 69–70." In Speed, F. Maurice, ed. *Film Review, 1970–1971.* London: W. H. Allen, 1970.
————. "Shakespeare on the Screen." In Speed, F. Maurice, ed. *Film Review, 1971–1972.* London: W. H. Allen, 1971.
————. "The Story of the Picture Palace." In Speed, F. Maurice, ed. *Film Review, 1968–1969.* London: W. H. Allen, 1968.
"Capra's *Christmas Carol* / The Stewart Touch." *Newsweek,* Dec. 30, 1946, pp. 72–73.
Castle, Robert. "Average Nobodies: The Dark Knights of *GoodFellas.*" *Film Ex,* Winter 1993, pp. 1–3.
"Catholics Rap Sexier 'Mulberry' Print for U.S.; Nude Stuff Draws 'C' Tag." *Variety,* March 27, 1968, p. 20.
"Charisma of Judy Garland Reflected in Global Press on Her Death at 47." *Variety,* June 25, 1969, p. 4.
"Chi Critic Ebert Raps 'Living Dead' in *Reader's Digest.*" *Variety,* May 28, 1969, p. 34.
"Cleavage and the Code" [Googie Withers, Patricia Roc, Margaret Lockwood]. *Time,* Aug. 5, 1946, p. 98.
Cohn, Lawrence, comp. "All-Time Film Rental Champs." *Variety,* Feb. 24, 1992, p. 125.
"Competition from London" [J. Arthur Rank]. *Time,* June 11, 1945, pp. 84–85.
"Connery, Who May Earn $6-Mil on 'Diamonds,' Wants No More 'Agent 007.'" *Variety,* July 19, 1972, pp. 1, 102.
Corliss, Richard. "Bond Keeps Up His Silver Streak." *Time,* Aug. 10, 1987, pp. 54–55.
————. "Calling Their Own Shots: Women Directors Are Starting to Make It in Hollywood." *Time,* March 24, 1986, pp. 82–83.
Cox, Meg. "To Tom Clancy, The Real Bad Guys Work in Hollywood." *Wall Street Journal,* Jan. 22, 1992, pp. 1, A6.
Delp, Laurel. "Mr. Monster" [Forrest J Ackerman]. *Us,* April 11, 1983.
Denby, David. "Everybody's All-American" [James Stewart]. *Premiere,* Feb. 1990, pp. 26–27.
Diehl, Digby. "Roger Corman: The Simenon of Cinema." *Show,* May 1976, pp. 27–30, 86–87.
————. "'What We Have Here Is a Failure to Communicate.' Strother Martin from *Cool Hand Luke* to Sudden Success in Nine Words." *Show,* July 9, 1970, pp. 21–23, 36.
Dobbs, Lem. "Obsession: Forever Young" *[The Great Escape]. Sight and Sound,* June 1991, p. 31.
Edelman, Rob. "John Garfield: Playing Out a Role." *Views and Reviews,* Fall 1974, pp. 37–44.
Ellison, Harlan. "Them or Us." *Show,* April 1970, 44–47.
"An End of 25-Year Film Decline?" *Variety,* May 10, 1972, p. 6.
Eyles, Allen. "Film Magazines: A Survey of Today's Situation." In Speed, F. Maurice, ed. *Film Review, 1971–1972* London: W. H. Allen, pp. 59–62.
Farber, Stephen. "Theresa Russell: Why Won't They Let Her Be a Good Girl?" *Cosmopolitan,* March 1992, p. 76.

"Film Trade's Femme 'Shutout' Gets Spotlight Tonight (Wed.)." *Variety,* Oct. 9, 1974, p. 7.

Fox, Julian. "A Man's World" [William Wellman]. *Films and Filming,* April 1973, pp. 33–40.

Francis, David. "The Film and Television." In Speed, F. Maurice, ed. *Film Review, 1970–1971.* London: W. H. Allen, 1970, pp. 33–35.

Frazier, Joel, and Hathorne, Harry. *"20,000 Leagues Under the Sea:* The Filming of Jules Verne's Classic Science Fiction Novel." *Cinefantastique,* May 1984, pp. 32–53.

Gammon, Roland. "Biblical Films: Many and Often." *Variety,* Sept. 10, 1969, p. 46.

Gehr, Richard. "Huston." *Video,* Sept. 1988, pp. 106–9.

————. "Stanley Kubrick's Disturbing Visions." *Video,* Dec. 1987, 71–73.

Gelman-Waxner, Libby. "Dance Crazed: If You Ask Me." *Premiere,* July 1990, 100–01.

"Gen. Bradley Lauds Film" *[The Best Years of Our Lives]. New York Times,* Dec. 11, 1946, p. 42.

Gold, Ronald. "Code Hits Pic Rating Ripoff." *Variety,* May 10, 1972, p. 3.

Goldwyn, Samuel. "Is Hollywood Through?" *Collier's,* Sept. 29, 1951, 18–19.

Gow, Gordon. "The Dancing Screen." In Speed, F. Maurice, ed. *Film Review 1972–1973.* South Brunswick, NJ, and New York: A. S. Barnes, 1972, pp. 69–75.

Green, Peter. "The Movies Make Hay with the Classic World." *Horizon,* May 1961, pp. 52–57.

Guerin, Ann. *"Gone with the Wind:* The History of a Major Motion Picture." *Show,* July 1972, pp. 33–37.

Guild, Hazel. "Europe GI's Losing Pix Admish Price Bargain with 100% Boost." *Variety,* Jan. 19, 1977, p. 47.

Gussow, Mel. "The Last Movie Tycoon" [Darryl F. Zanuck]. *New York,* Feb. 1, 1971, pp. 27–33.

"Hammer Ends Longtime Taboo — Mates Sex to Its *Crescendo* Horror Pic." *Variety,* May 6, 1970, pp. 1, 92.

Hanks, Stephen. *"The Jolson Story." Memories,* Oct. 1990, pp. 46–51.

Harwood, James. "Stallone Visualizes Himself as 'Rocky' Reaching Ages 40 and 50." *Variety,* April 6, 1977, p. 32.

————. "U.S. Films Snubbing Bicentennial." *Variety,* July 9, 1975, pp. 1, 79.

Haver, Ron. "He's the Man" [Gregory Peck]. *American Film,* March 1989, pp. 26–30, 52.

Helmetag, Charles. "Walter Hasenclever: A Playwright's Evolution as a Film Writer." *German Quarterly* 64.4 (1991): 452–63.

Hendrickson, Paul. "The Town West of Hollywood: In the Canyons of Moab, Utah, Where Cowboy Movies Came to Life." *Washington Post,* Aug. 14, 1990, pp, C1, C2.

"High Court's 'Carnal' Ruling Seen as Crucial for Cinema Freedom." *Variety,* June 26, 1974, pp. 1, 79.

Hooper, Laurence. "Coming Soon: A Movie Theater Near You!" *Philadelphia,* Sept. 1989, 100–03.

Hope, Warren. "Everyman in Uniform" *[Soldier in the Rain]. Film Ex,* Winter 1992, pp. 4–6.

Horn, John. "101 Woes at Disney's Film Division." *Sunday News Journal* (Wilmington, DE), Nov. 3, 1991, p. H2.

Horton, Robert. "Mann and Stewart: Two Rode Together." *Film Comment,* March–April 1990, pp. 40–44.

Houston, Penelope, and Gillett, John. "Kanin [Garson] Talking: An Interview." *Sight and Sound,* Summer 1972, pp. 134–39.

Hughes, Kathleen A. "Going for Broke: Hunt for Blockbusters Has Big Movie Studios in a Spending Frenzy." *Wall Street Journal,* May 3, 1990, pp. A1, A8.

Hunter, Stephen. "James Bond Smoothly Ages into Superstar Sean Connery." *Sunday News Journal* (Wilmington, DE), March 4, 1990, p. H2.

Hyde, Christina. *"Black Robe." Australian Expatriate* 3.1 (1992): 56–56. Includes "Biography: The Director — Australian Bruce Beresford."

"Invasion of the Body Snatchers: An Interview with Director Don Siegel." *Castle of Frankenstein* 6.1:28–35. Includes Peter Bogdanovich's *Movie* (no. 15) interview and a new one by Jim Meyer.

Isaacs, Hermine Rich. *"Citizen Kane* and One-Man Pictures in General." *Theatre Arts,* June 1941, pp. 427–29, 431–34.

Jaffe, Lance. "Video Valentine: 'Annie Hall' Redux." *Premiere,* March 1990, p. 108.

Jones, DuPre. "The Merit of Flying Lead." *Films and Filming,* Jan. 1974, pp. 31–36.

Kenney, Edward L. "Endangered Images: 202 Drive-In Among Last of a Breed." *Sunday News Journal* (Wilmington, DE), Aug. 19, 1990, pp. GI, G5.

Kerbel, Michael. "3-D or Not 3-D." *Film Comment,* Nov.-Dec. 1980), pp. 11–20.

Klemensen, Richard, ed. "Hammer's *Karnstein* Trilogy." *Little Shoppe of Horrors,* May 1984.

Knepper, Max. "Is Hollywood Growing Up? — I." *Forum,* June 1946, pp. 880–85.

———. "'Is Hollywood Growing Up? — II." *Forum,* July 1946, pp. 21–27.

Kreuger, Miles. "The Birth of the American Film Musical." *High Fidelity,* July 1972, pp. 42–48.

———. "Dubbers to the Stars, or Whose Was That Voice I Heard You Singing With?" *High Fidelity,* July 1972, pp. 49–54.

Landro, Laura. "Hot Streak: Warner Bros.' Success at Box Office Feeds Its Global Ambitions." *Wall Street Journal,* June 1, 1990, pp. 1, A6.

Landry, Robert J. "Black Pix: 'Menial' to 'Mean.'" *Variety,* Aug. 23, 1972, pp. 5, 22.

Larkins, Robert. "Hollywood and the Indian." *Focus on Film,* March-April 1970, pp. 44–53.

"LBJ Assistant Jack Valenti Named Film Industry 'Czar.'" *Independent Film Journal,* April 30, 1966, p. 7.

Leifert, Don. *"Cinemacabre* Interview: Henry Brandon." *Cinemacabre,* Summer 1984, pp. 19–29.

"Life Visits Nine Hopeful Starlets." *Life,* Feb. 18, 1946, pp. 123–26.

Lynn, Kenneth S. "The Torment of D. W. Griffith." *American Scholar,* Spring 1990, pp. 255–64.

Lyons, Donald. "Dances with Aldrich." *Film Comment,* March-April 1991, p. 72.

McBride, Joseph. "More Sharks, Other Killers, Due; 'Jaws' Quickens Monster Spree; Recall Fatal Frogs, Bugs, Bees." *Variety,* July 30, 1975, pp. 7, 32.

———. "The Most Powerful Movie Actor in the World: He'll Blow Your Head Clean Off" [Clint Eastwood]. *Bijou: The Magazine of the Movies,* April 1977, 19–23.

McCarthy, Todd. "John Ford and Monument Valley." *American Film,* May 1978, pp. 10–16.

Mariani, John. "The Missing American Hero." *New York,* Aug. 13, 1973, pp. 34–38.

Marin, Rick. "Dressed to Kill." *Premiere,* March 1991, p. 20.

Marshall, Lorne, and Miner, Nathan. "The Hell with Sub-Plots! A History of Anthology Films." *Bits N Pieces,* Summer 1990, pp. 3–16.

Martin, Pete. "The Man Who Made the Hit Called *Shane"* [George Stevens]. *Saturday Evening Post,* August 8, 1953, pp. 32–33.

Marton, Elise J. "Spellbinder: 30 Years Ago. A Psycho Runs Loose in Movie Theaters." *Memories,* June-July 1990, pp. 74–77.

Mathews, Jack, and Smith, Steven. "1939." *Los Angeles Times Calendar,* Jan. 1, 1989, pp. 4, 5, 25.

Milbank, Dana. "Ah, the Glamour, the Stars, the Films; It's . . . Pittsburgh?" *Wall Street Journal,* March 26, 1992, pp. A1, A4.

Morella, Joseph. "Par's Big Roadshow Splash." *Variety,* June 25, 1969, pp. 3, 28.

Mountjoy, John. "Where Have All the Organs Gone?" In Speed, F. Maurice, ed. *Film Review 1970–1971.* London: W. H. Allen, 1970, pp. 37–43.

"Movies Come Out of the Dog House." *Business Week,* Nov. 10, 1951, pp. 140–42.

Muir, Florabel. "They Risk Their Neck for You" [stuntwomen]. *Saturday Evening Post,* Sept. 15, 1945, pp. 26–27.

Murphy, A. D. "Adversary Exhibs, Who Invented 'Consent,' May Now Self-Finesse 'Product Split.'" *Variety,* Feb. 16, 1977, p. 13.

_____. "1974 Looms as 28-Year Peak for B.O." *Variety,* Dec. 18, 1974, pp. 3, 24.

_____. "Still Powerful *Gone with the Wind.*" *Variety,* Oct. 18, 1967, p. 6.

"The New Pictures. *Shane*" [with George Stevens profile]. *Time,* April 13, 1953, pp. 104, 106.

"New Zealand, Once a Haven for Daring Pix, Now Arts and Bands." *Variety,* July 30, 1975, p. 39.

Newsom, Ted. "The Ray Harryhausen Story, Part One: The Early Years, 1920–1958." *Cinefantastique,* December 1981, pp. 24–45.

"The 1980s: sex, lies, and celluloid." *Premiere,* November 1989, pp. 87–89.

Noble, Peter. "Black Power." In Speed, F. Maurice, ed. *Film Review, 1972–1973.* South Brunswick, NJ, and New York: A. S. Barnes, 1972, pp. 26–37.

Nogueira, Rui. "James Mason Talks About His Career in the Cinema." *Focus on Film,* March-April 1970, 18–43.

"No Particular Taste" [UK censorship]. *Time,* Dec. 9, 1935, pp. 25–26.

"One Hundred Years of Moviemaking." *Premiere,* Winter 1991.

"'Operation Rescue' for 1912–42 Films in Race Against Decaying Nitrate." *Variety,* Oct. 8, 1969, p. 29.

Owen, Nicolas. "The Art Cinema — Does It Exist?" In Speed, F. Maurice, ed. *Film Review 1970–1971.* London: W. H. ALlen, 1970, pp. 29–31.

"Parents Forewarned Re 'Papillon' as Rough, Father's Plea Rejected." *Variety,* Dec. 11, 1974, p. 3.

Pearson, Mike. "'Sound of Music' Marks 25th Year as Top Musical." *Daily Local News* (West Chester, PA), Sept. 13, 1990, p. C1.

Pignone, Raymond. "A Brief History of 3-D Horror Films." *Cinemacabre,* no. 4, p. 24–29.

Pitman, Jack. "British Film Biz's 'Messiah.'" *Variety,* Aug. 20, 1969, pp. 29, 32.

"Press Violent About Film's Violence; Prod Sam Peckinpah Following 'Bunch.'" *Variety,* July 2, 1969, p. 15.

Pryor, Thomas. "Hollywood and 'Runaway.'" *Variety,* April 26, 1967, p. 41.

Pye, Douglas. "Genre and Movies." *Movie,* Spring 1975, pp. 29–43.

Rebello, Stephen. "Behind the Curtain" [filming the *Psycho* shower sequence]. *Memories,* June-July 1990, pp. 78–79.

_____. "Selling Nightmares: Movie Poster Artists of the Fifties." *Cinefantastique,* March 1988, pp. 40–101.

Rickey, Carrie. "The Fade-Out of Old Movies." *Philadelphia Inquirer,* May 31, 1987, pp. 1-G, 12-G.

_____. "Mob Rule." *Inquirer,* Dec. 23, 1990, pp. 13–17.

Risser, John. "John Barrymore." *Old News,* 1991, pp. 10–12.

Ryan, Desmond, *Hollywood Reporter,* and *Los Angeles Times.* "The X Rating Goes
    to Court." *Philadelphia Inquirer,* June 3, 1990, p. 2-D.
Salt, Barry. "Film Style and Technology in the Forties." *Film Quarterly,* Fall 1977,
    pp. 46–57.
Sarris, Andrew. "After the *Graduate.*" *American Film,* July-Aug. 1978, pp. 32–37.
————. "James Stewart." *Film Comment,* March-April 1990, pp. 29–30.
————. "My Criticism, My Politics." *American Film,* Feb. 1978, pp. 50–54.
————. "Why Sports Movies Don't Work." *Film Comment,* Nov.-Dec. 1980,
    pp. 49–53.
Scoliard, Jennifer L. "'Reel' Women in Cinema History." *Dome* [Widener University,
    Chester, PA, re: speaker/filmmaker Ally Acker], March 20, 1992, p. 1, 4.
Scott, Vernon. "H'wood's New Queen Bee Has to Be Natalie Wood." *Philadelphia
    Daily News,* January 31, 1963, p. 34.
Sealfon, Peggy. "The Art of Film Posters." *US Air,* November 1985, pp. 38–48.
Segers, Frank. "Gallup: Check RE Likes. Theatre, and/or, Home." *Variety,* May 25,
    1977, pp. 13, 38.
Seldes, Gilbert. "The Movies Commit Suicide." *Harpers,* Nov. 1928, pp. 706–12.
————. "The Quicksands of the Movies." *Atlantic Monthly,* Oct. 1936, pp. 422–31.
Shaffer, Lawrence. "Some Notes on Film Acting." *Sight and Sound,* Spring 1973,
    103–6.
Sheehan, Henry. "Dark Worlds" [Don Siegel]. *Sight and Sound,* June 1991, pp. 28–30.
————. "The Fall and Rise of Spartacus." *Film Comment,* March-April 1991,
    pp. 57–58.
Shevey, Sandra. "A Critique of Women's Roles in U.S. and European Pics." *Variety,*
    May 8, 1974, p. 71.
Silverman, Syd. "U.S. Four-Walling: Boon or Threat?" *Variety,* May 8, 1974, pp. 3, 64.
————. "*Variety* Chart Summary for 1974." *Variety,* May 7, 1975, p. 133.
Slide, Anthony. "The Feminine Angle—Women Film Directors." In Speed, F.
    Maurice, ed. *Film Review 1978–1979.* London: W. H. Allen, 1978, pp. 94–105.
Soter, Tom. "Comedy on the Rocks: Screwball Films Mix One Part Romance with a
    Dash of Action and a Jigger of Wit." *Video,* Nov. 1988, pp. 69–71.
Speed, F. Maurice. "Ealing and the Late Sir Michael Balcon." In *Film Review,
    1978–1979.* London: W. H. Allen, 1978, pp. 106–8.
————. "The Stuntmen." In *Film Review, 1972–1973.* South Brunswick, NJ, and
    New York: A. S. Barnes, 1972, pp. 43–50.
Spotnitz, Frank. "Stick It in Your Ear" [sound effects]. *American Film,* Oct. 1989,
    pp. 40–45.
Sragow, Michael. "*The Wild Bunch.*" *Film Society Review,* Nov. 1969, pp. 31–37.
Steiner, Fred. "Bernard Herrmann: An Unauthorized Biographical Sketch." *Film Music
    Collection,* Summer 1975, pp. 4–9.
Stephenson, Ralph. "Posters and Credits." In Speed, F. Maurice, ed. *Film Review,
    1971–1972.* London: W. H. Allen, 1971, 30–34.
"*Sunset Boulevard:* Hollywood Tale That Gloria Swanson Makes Great." *Newsweek,*
    June 26, 1950, pp. 82–84.
"'Super Fly' Goes Through N.Y. Roof on Black Trade." *Variety,* Aug. 9, 1972, p. 5.
Swindell, Larry. "They Had More Than Faces." *American Film,* Nov. 1976, pp. 64–69.
Tarbox, Aubrey. "Western Cycle Rolls Again." *Variety,* June 25, 1969, pp. 5, 20.
"Think MPAA Moving to Regard Violence and Not Only Erotica." *Variety,* Nov. 20,
    1974, p. 4.
Thomas, Bob. "Salaries Soar for Top Film Stars." *News-Journal* (Wilmington, DE),
    May 8, 1986, p. D4.

Thomson, David. "Better Best Westerns." *Film Comment,* March-April 1990, pp. 5–13.

Toland, Gregg. "The Motion Picture Cameraman." *Theatre Arts,* Sept. 1941, pp. 647–54.

"Trade Watches 'Charity' on Crix-Mix; Ditto Philip Roth as Screen Material." *Variety,* April 9, 1969, p. 32.

Trumbo, Dalton. "Stepchild of the Muses." *North American Review,* Dec. 1933, pp. 559–66.

Verrill, Addison. "Road to *Dragon* and $10-Mil." *Variety,* Sept. 19, 1973, pp. 3, 16.

Vertlieb, Steve. "The *Star Wars* Trilogy: A Glimpse of the Eternal." *Cinemacabre,* Summer 1984, pp. 4–8.

Vigoda, Ralph. "Going on with the Show." *Philadelphia Inquirer,* Dec. 20, 1990, pp. 4-M, 5-M.

Vizzard, Jack. "Beware Wishful Idea of Rising Crest, Then Ebbing Pornography Flood." *Variety,* April 29, 1970, p. 16.

Watkins, Roger. "'Express' May Be Turning Point in British Film Biz Fate: Cohen." *Variety,* Dec. 25, 1974, p. 21.

"WB, Parks Jr. No Talk on NAACP 'Super Fly' Swat." *Variety,* Aug. 23, 1972, p. 5.

Wells, Graham. "Glorious Swansong, 40 Years Ago: *Sunset Boulevard* Dazzles Expectant Crowds." *Memories,* Aug./Sept. 1990, pp. 42–47.

Zimmerman, Paul D. "Kubrick's Brilliant Vision." *Newsweek,* Jan. 3, 1972, pp. 26–31.

BOOKS AND MONOGRAPHS

Amis, Kingsley. *Memoirs.* New York: Summit, 1991.

Balcon, Michael. *Michael Balcon Presents . . . A Lifetime of Films.* London: Hutchinson, 1969.

Balio, Tino. *United Artists: The Company Built by the Stars.* Madison: University of Wisconsin Press, 1976.

Baxter, John. *Hollywood in the Thirties.* New York: Paperback Library, 1968.

_____. *Sixty Years of Hollywood.* South Brunswick, NJ, and New York: A. S. Barnes, 1973.

Bazin, Andre. *Orson Welles: A Critical View.* New York: Harper Colophon, 1978.

Behlmer, Rudy, ed. *Memo from David O. Selznick.* New York: Viking, 1972.

Bergan, Ronald. *The United Artists Story.* New York: Crown, 1986.

Bergman, Andrew. *We're in the Money: Depression America and Its Films.* New York: Harper Colophon, 1971.

Blum, Daniel. *A New Pictorial History of the Talkies.* New York: G. P. Putnam's Sons, 1968.

_____. *A Pictorial History of the Silent Screen.* New York: Grosset and Dunlap, 1953.

_____, and Willis, John. *Screen World.* New York: Crown, annually since 1949.

Bogdanovich, Peter. *Allan Dwan: The Last Pioneer.* New York: Praeger, 1971.

_____. *Fritz Lang in America.* New York: Praeger, 1967.

_____. *John Ford.* Berkeley: University of California Press, 1968.

_____. *Pieces of Time: Peter Bogdanovich on the Movies.* New York: Arbor House, 1973.

Bordwell, David, Staiger, Janet, and Thompson, Kristin. *The Classical Hollywood Cinema: Film Style and Mode of Production to 1960.* New York: Columbia University Press, 1985.

Breakwell, Ian, and Hammond, Paul, eds. *Seeing in the Dark: A Compendium of Cinemagoing.* London: Serpent's Tail, 1990.

Brode, Douglas. *The Films of the Fifties*. Secaucus, NJ: Citadel, 1976.
_____. *The Films of the Sixties*. Secaucus, NJ: Citadel, 1980.
Brodsky, Jack, and Weiss, Nathan. *The Cleopatra Papers: A Private Correspondence*. New York: Simon and Schuster, 1963.
Brosnan, John. *Future Tense: The Cinema of Science Fiction*. New York: St. Martin's, 1978.
_____. *The Horror People*. New York: St. Martin's, 1976.
_____. *Movie Magic: The Story of Special Effects in the Cinema*. New York: St. Martin's, 1974.
Brown, Geoff, and Kardish, Laurence. *Michael Balcon: The Pursuit of British Cinema*. New York: Museum of Modern Art, 1984.
Brown, Jim. *Out of Bounds*. New York: Zebra Books, 1989.
Brownlow, Kevin. *The Parade's Gone By.* ... New York: Ballantine, 1968.
Butler, Ivan. *Horror in the Cinema*. New York: Paperback Library, 1971.
Cameron, Ian, and Cameron, Elisabeth. *Dames*. New York: Frederick A. Praeger, 1969.
_____. *The Heavies*. New York: Frederick A. Praeger, 1967.
Canham, Kingsley. *The Hollywood Professionals: Michael Curtiz, Raoul Walsh, Henry Hathaway*. London: Tantivy, 1973.
Capra, Frank. *The Name Above the Title: An Autobiography*. New York: Macmillan, 1971.
Clover, Carol J. *Men, Women, and Chain Saws: Gender in the Modern Horror Film*. Princeton: Princeton University Press, 1992.
Collins, Joan. *Past Imperfect: An Autobiography*. New York: Simon and Schuster, 1984.
Corliss, Richard. *Talking Pictures: Screenwriters in the American Cinema*. New York: Penguin, 1974.
Croce, Arlene. *The Fred Astaire and Ginger Rogers Book*. New York: E. P. Dutton, 1972.
Cross, Robin. *The Big Book of B Movies, or How Low Was My Budget*. New York: St. Martin's, 1981.
Custen, George F. *Bio/Pics: How Hollywood Constructed Public History*. New Brunswick, NJ: Rutgers University Press, 1992.
Davis, Brian. *The Thriller: The Suspense Film from 1946*. London: Studio Vista, 1973.
Dmytryk, Edward. *It's a Hell of a Life but Not a Bad Living*. New York: Times Books, 1978.
Durgnat, Raymond. *A Mirror for England: British Movies from Austerity to Affluence*. London: Faber and Faber, 1970.
Eames, John Douglas. *The MGM Story: The Complete History of Fifty Roaring Years*. London: Octopus, 1975.
_____. *The Paramount Story*. New York: Crown, 1985.
Eyles, Allen. *John Wayne and the Movies*. South Brunswick, NJ, and New York: A. S. Barnes, 1976.
_____, Adkinson, Robert, and Fry, Nicholas, eds. *The House of Horror: The Complete Story of Hammer Films*. 2d ed. London: Lorrimer, 1981.
Fenin, George N., and Everson, William K. *The Western: From Silents to the Seventies*. Rev. ed. New York: Grossman, 1973.
Finler, Joel. *The Hollywood Story*. New York: Crown, 1988.
Fordin, Hugh. *The World of Entertainment! Hollywood's Greatest Musicals*. Garden City, NY: Doubleday, 1975.
Franklin, Joe. *Classics of the Silent Screen: A Pictorial Treasury*. New York: Citadel, 1959.

Fraser, George MacDonald. *The Hollywood History of the World: From "One Million Years B.C." to "Apocalypse Now."* New York: Fawcett Columbine, 1988.

Froug, William. *The New Screenwriter Looks at the New Screenwriter.* Beverly Hills, CA: Silman-James, 1991.

Gabler, Neal. *An Empire of Their Own: How the Jews Invented Hollywood.* New York: Crown, 1988.

Gardner, Gerald. *The Censorship Papers: Movie Censorship Letters from the Hays Office, 1934 to 1968.* New York: Dodd, Mead, 1987.

Garfield, Brian. *Western Films: A Complete Guide.* New York: Rawson, 1982.

Geduld, Harry M. *The Birth of the Talkies: From Edison to Jolson.* Bloomington: Indiana University Press, 1975.

Gifford, Denis. *Science Fiction Film.* London: Studio Vista, 1971.

Goldman, Frederick. *Highlights in the American Musical Films, 1933–1958.* Philadelphia, PA: Division of Education, Philadelphia Museum of Art, 1970.

Goldner, Orville, and Turner, George E. *The Making of "King Kong": The Story Behind a Film Classic.* South Brunswick, NJ, and New York: A. S. Barnes, 1975.

Gow, Gordon. *Hollywood in the Fifties.* New York: A. S. Barnes, 1971.

Grey, Rudolph. *Nightmare of Ecstasy: The Life and Art of Edward D. Wood, Jr.* Los Angeles: Feral House, 1992.

Grodin, Charles. *It Would Be So Nice If You Weren't Here: My Journey Through Show Business.* New York: William Morrow, 1989.

Halliwell, Leslie. *Filmgoer's Companion.* 6th ed. New York: Hill and Wang, 1977.

————. *Halliwell's Film Guide.* 7th ed. New York: Harper and Row, 1989.

————. *Halliwell's Harvest.* New York: Charles Scribner's, 1986.

Harryhausen, Ray. *Film Fantasy Scrapbook.* 3d ed. San Diego and New York: A. S. Barnes, 1981.

Hawkins, Jack. *Anything for a Quiet Life.* New York: Stein and Day, 1973.

Hecht, Ben. *A Child of the Century.* New York: Signet, 1954.

Heston, Charlton. *The Actor's Life: Journals, 1956–1976.* Edited by Hollis Alpert. New York: E. P. Dutton, 1978.

Higham, Charles, and Greenberg, Joel. *The Celluloid Muse: Hollywood Directors Speak.* Chicago: Henry Regnery, 1969.

————. *Hollywood in the Forties.* London: A. Zwemmer, 1968.

Hillier, Jim, ed. *Cahiers du Cinéma: The 1950s, Neo-Realism, Hollywood, New Wave.* Cambridge: Harvard University Press, 1985.

Hirschhorn, Clive. *The Columbia Story.* New York: Crown, 1989.

————. *The Universal Story.* New York: Crown, 1983.

————. *The Warner Bros. Story.* New York: Crown, 1979.

Jacobs, Lewis. *The Rise of the American Film: A Critical History.* New York: Harcourt, Brace and Company, 1939.

Jewell, Richard B., and Harbin, Vernon. *The RKO Story.* New York: Arlington House, 1982.

Johnson, William, ed. *Focus on the Science Fiction Film.* Englewood Cliffs, NJ: Prentice-Hall, 1972.

Katz, Ephraim. *The Film Encyclopedia.* New York: Thomas Y. Crowell, 1979.

Kazan, Elia. *A Life.* New York: Knopf, 1988.

Kendall, Elizabeth. *The Runaway Bride: Hollywood Romantic Comedy of the 1930s.* New York: Knopf, 1990.

King, Stephen. *Danse Macabre.* New York: Berkley, 1983.

Kitses, Jim. *Horizons West: Anthony Mann, Budd Boetticher, Sam Peckinpah. Studies of Authorship Within the Western.* Bloomington and London: Indiana University Press, 1969.

Lambert, Gavin. *GWTW: The Making of "Gone with the Wind."* Boston: Little, Brown, 1973.

Leff, Leonard J., and Simmons, Jerold L. *The Dame in the Kimono: Hollywood, Censorship, and the Production Code from the 1920s to the 1960s.* New York: Anchor/Doubleday, 1990.

Leigh, Janet. *There Really Was a Hollywood.* Garden City, NY: Doubleday, 1984.

Linet, Beverly. *Ladd: The Life, the Legend, the Legacy of Alan Ladd.* New York: Berkley, 1979.

McFarlane, Brian. *Australian Cinema.* New York: Columbia University Press, 1987.

McGee, Mark Thomas. *Fast and Furious: The Story of American International Pictures.* Jefferson, NC: McFarland, 1984.

Macgowan, Kenneth. *Behind the Screen: The History and Techniques of the Motion Picture.* New York: Delacorte, 1965.

Madsen, Axel. *Billy Wilder.* Bloomington and London: Indiana University Press, 1969.

Maltin, Leonard. *Behind the Camera: The Cinematographer's Art.* New York: Signet, 1971.

_____. *Movie Comedy Teams.* New York: Signet, 1970.

Manvell, Roger. *New Cinema in Britain.* London: Studio Vista, 1969.

_____. *New Cinema in the USA: The Feature Film Since 1946.* London: Studio Vista, 1968.

Marion, Frances. *Off with Their Heads! A Serio-Comic Tale of Hollywood.* New York: Macmillan, 1972.

Mayersberg, Paul. *Hollywood: The Haunted House.* New York: Ballentine, 1967.

Meyers, Richard. *For One Week Only: The World of Exploitation Films.* Piscataway, NJ: New Century Publishers, 1983.

Michael, Paul, ed. *The American Movies Reference Book: The Sound Era.* Englewood Cliffs, NJ: Prentice-Hall, 1969.

Milland, Ray. *Wide-Eyed in Babylon: An Autobiography.* New York: William Morrow, 1974.

Miller, Mark Crispin, ed. *Seeing Through Movies.* New York: Pantheon, 1990.

Mordden, Ethan. *The Hollywood Studios: House Style in the Golden Age of the Movies.* New York: Fireside, 1988.

_____. *Medium Cool: The Movies of the 1960s.* New York: Knopf, 1990.

_____. *Movie Star: A Look at the Women Who Made Hollywood.* New York: St. Martin's, 1983.

Morella, Joe, Epstein, Edward Z., and Griggs, John. *The Films of World War II.* Secaucus, NJ: Citadel, 1973.

Naylor, David. *Great American Movie Theaters.* Washington, DC: Preservation Press, 1987.

Negulesco, Jean. *Things I Did and Things I Think I Did: A Hollywood Memoir.* New York: Simon and Schuster, 1984.

Nolan, William F. *The Black Mask Boys: Masters in the Hard-Boiled School of Detective Fiction.* New York: Mysterious Press, 1985.

Parish, James Robert. *The Fox Girls.* New Rochelle, NY: Arlington House, 1970.

_____. *The Great Combat Pictures: Twentieth-Century Warfare on the Screen.* Metuchen, NJ: Scarecrow, 1990.

_____. *The Paramount Pretties.* Secaucus, NJ: Castle, 1972.

_____. *Prison Pictures from Hollywood.* Jefferson, NC: McFarland, 1991.

_____. *The Tough Guys.* Carlstadt, NJ: Rainbow, 1976.

_____, and Stanke, Don E. *The Glamour Girls.* New Rochelle, NY: Arlington House, 1975.

_____, and _____. *The Swashbucklers.* Carlstadt, NJ: Rainbow, 1976.

Perry, George. *The Films of Alfred Hitchcock.* London: Studio Vista, 1965.

Pickard, Roy. *The Hollywood Story.* Secaucus, NJ: Chartwell, 1986.

Pink, Sidney. *So You Want to Make Movies: My Life as an Independent Film Producer.* Sarasota, FL: Pineapple, 1989.

Pirie, David. *A History of Horror: The English Gothic Cinema, 1946–1972.* New York: Avon, 1973.

Powdermaker, Hortense. *Hollywood: The Dream Factory.* New York: Little, Brown, 1950.

Quinlan, David. *British Sound Films: The Studio Years, 1928–1959.* Totowa, NJ: Barnes and Noble, 1984.

Ramsaye, Terry. *A Million and One Nights: A History of the Motion Picture Through 1925.* Reprint. New York: Touchstone, 1986.

Robertson, Patrick. *Guinness Film Facts and Feats.* London: Guinness Superlatives, 1985.

Rovin, Jeff. *From the Land Beyond Beyond: The Films of Willis O'Brien and Ray Harryhausen.* New York: Berkley, 1977.

Sackett, Susan. *The "Hollywood Reporter" Book of Box Office Hits.* New York: Billboard, 1990.

Saleh, Dennis. *Science Fiction Gold: Film Classics of the 50s.* New York: Comma/McGraw-Hill, 1979.

Samuels, Charles Thomas. *Encountering Directors.* New York: G. P. Putnam's Sons, 1972.

Sarris, Andrew. *The American Cinema: Directors and Directions, 1929–1968.* New York: E. P. Dutton, 1968.

Schatz, Thomas. *The Genius of the System: Hollywood Filmmaking in the Studio Era.* New York: Pantheon, 1988.

Scherle, Victor, and Levy, William Turner. *The Films of Frank Capra.* Secaucus, NJ: Citadel, 1977.

Schickel, Richard. *The Stars.* New York: Dial, 1962.

Schumach, Murray. *The Face on the Cutting Room Floor: The Story of Movie and Television Censorship.* New York: William Morrow, 1964.

Sellar, Maurice. *Best of British: A Celebration of Rank Film Classics.* London: Sphere, 1987.

Sennett, Ted. *Warner Bros. Presents.* New Rochelle, NY: Arlington House, 1971.

Shadoian, Jack. *Dreams and Dead Ends: The American Gangster/Crime Film.* Cambridge: MIT Press, 1977.

Shepherd, Jean. *In God We Trust, All Others Pay Cash.* Garden City, NY: Doubleday, 1966.

Sherman, Eric, and Rubin, Martin. *The Director's Event: Interviews with Five American Filmmakers. Budd Boetticher, Peter Bogdanovich, Samuel Fuller, Arthur Penn, Abraham Polonsky.* New York: New American Library, 1969.

Shipman, David. *The Great Stars: The Golden Years.* New York: Crown, 1970.

_____. *The Great Stars: The International Years.* London: Angus and Robertson, 1972.

Spada, James. *Peter Lawford: The Man Who Kept the Secrets.* New York: Bantam, 1991.

Springer, John. *Forgotten Films to Remember: And a Brief History of Fifty Years of the American Talking Picture.* Secaucus, NJ: Citadel, 1980.

Springer, John, and Hamilton, Jack. *They Had Faces Then: Super Stars, Stars and Starlets of the 1930s*. Secaucus, NJ: Citadel, 1974.

Steinberg, Cobbett. *Reel Facts: The Movie Book of Records*. Rev. ed. New York: Vintage, 1980.

Stephenson, James, and Phelps, Guy. *The Cinema as Art*. Rev. ed. London: Penguin, 1989.

Strode, Woody, and Young, Sam. *Goal Dust: An Autobiography*. Lanham, MD: Madison Books, 1990.

Talbot, Daniel, ed. *Film: An Anthology*. Berkeley and Los Angeles: University of California Press, 1966.

Thomas, Tony. *The Great Adventure Films*. Secaucus, NJ: Citadel, 1976.

_____. *Music for the Movies*. South Brunswick, NJ, and New York: A. S. Barnes, 1973.

_____, and Solomon, Aubrey. *The Films of 20th Century-Fox: A Pictorial History*. Secaucus, NJ: Citadel, 1979.

Tierney, Gene, and Herskowitz, Mickey. *Self-Portrait: Gene Tierney*. New York: Wyden, 1978.

Vance, Malcolm. *The Movie Ad Book*. Minneapolis, MN: Control Data, 1981.

Vermilye, Jerry. *The Films of the Thirties*. Secaucus, NJ: Citadel, 1982.

Vidor, King. *A Tree Is a Tree*. Reprint. Hollywood, CA: Samuel French, 1981.

Walker, Alexander. *Hollywood, England: The British Film Industry in the Sixties*. London: Harrap, 1974.

_____. *Sex in the Movies: The Celluloid Sacrifice*. Baltimore, MD: Penguin, 1966.

_____. *The Shattered Silents: How the Talkies Came to Stay*. New York: William Morrow, 1978.

Wallis, Hal, and Higham, Charles. *Starmaker: The Autobiography of Hal Wallis*. New York: Macmillan, 1980.

Wanger, Walter, and Hyams, Joe. *My Life with Cleopatra*. New York: Bantam, 1963.

Warren, Bill. *Keep Watching the Skies! American Science Fiction Movies of the Fifties*. Vol. 1, *1950–1957;* Vol. 2, *1958–1962*. Jefferson, NC: McFarland, 1982 and 1986.

Weldon, Michael, et al. *The Psychotronic Encyclopedia of Film*. New York: Ballantine, 1983.

Westmore, Frank, and Davidson, Muriel. *The Westmores of Hollywood*. Philadelphia and New York: J. B. Lippincott, 1976.

Wood, Robin. *Howard Hawks*. Garden City, NY: Doubleday, 1968.

Wright, Basil. *The Long View*. New York: Knopf, 1974.

York, Michael. *Accidentally on Purpose: An Autobiography*. New York: Simon and Schuster, 1991.

Zierold, Norman. *The Moguls*. New York: Avon, 1969.

Index